The Taking of the Bastille

JACQUES GODECHOT

*Doyen de la Faculté des Lettres
et Sciences humaines de Toulouse*

The Taking of the Bastille
July 14th, 1789

translated by
Jean Stewart

Preface by
Charles Tilly

CHARLES SCRIBNER'S SONS

NEW YORK

Printed in Great Britain
Library of Congress Catalog Card Number 69-17044

Preface

The great revolutionary day of July 14th, 1789, began and ended appropriately. In the morning militant crowds formed at the Invalides and at the Bastille. In the evening, King Louis capitulated to the people of Paris by ordering the withdrawal of the troops with which he had been ringing the city. In between, the Bastille fell. The notorious fortress fell to a thousand-odd ordinary Parisians stiffened by sixty-odd renegade troops.

Within days, the fortress was torn down, stone by stone; within months, the regime was dismantled, privilege by privilege. The seizure of the Bastille served notice that the people of Paris were ready to act. The popular revolution had begun.

The news spread fast. 'The Bastille', declared Michelet, 'was known and detested by the whole world. Bastille and tyranny were, in every language, synonymous terms. Every nation, at the news of its destruction, believed it had recovered its liberty.'

Jacques Godechot's account of the Bastille's fall has a spiritual affinity with Michelet's, although in method, style, detail and even in argument the two differ sharply. The twelve decades between Michelet's *History of the French Revolution* and Godechot's *Taking of the Bastille* have brought forth a sober, documented, academic form of historical writing, as well as a shift of explanations away from conscious political intentions toward presumably deeper economic and social changes. Godechot's treatment of the Revolution expresses the modern French historical style very well. For Michelet's poetic fancy and political apostrophe Godechot substitutes a cool, judicious examination of the sources.

The affinity with Michelet nonetheless remains in two chief themes of the book: first, the powerful independent role of the

v

Preface

Parisian people in the early revolution; second, the location of the Parisian and French revolutions within a much larger European movement. Godechot has transformed both themes. Michelet took the Parisian people to represent all Frenchmen, and saw Paris as the fountainhead of a great European transformation. Godechot treats the Parisian people as a very special class of Frenchmen, and sees the French Revolution as the greatest act of a drama already well begun by 1789.

The idea of an autonomous 'popular revolution' led by the ordinary inhabitants of Paris has been a fixture of French historical writing for some years now. George Lefebvre installed it in the official histories; later scholars like Albert Soboul, Richard Cobb and George Rudé have reinforced and adapted it in a number of important ways. The idea of a larger 'Revolution of the West', on the other hand, has a less certain official standing, and a more personal connection with Jacques Godechot. He and R. R. Palmer have vigorously argued the connections among the American, Dutch, Genevan and French revolutions, as well as the contemporaneous revolutionary movement elsewhere in the West. The thesis has been slow to gain general acceptance, perhaps in part because it diminishes the convenient, satisfying uniqueness of the French Revolution and in part because it is hard to reconcile with the explanation of revolution in terms of the internal development of each individual country.

If these two chief themes do not quite contradict each other, their simultaneous use introduces a considerable tension into Godechot's analysis. For to assert both that the Parisian people made their own revolution and that the revolution as a whole grew out of a movement arising throughout the West, he must also show that the neighborhood politics of the capital had their own special links with the 'slow, deep, international movement . . . growing from the demographic and economic upheaval, the rise of the bourgeoisie, and the spread of "enlightened" ideas.' Hence a book of which at least two-thirds deals with the background of the revolutionary movement and at most a hundred pages deal with the events of Paris in July 1789. Godechot sets out the events in careful, critical detail. But he fixes his eye on the connection between those events and the great changes occurring in France and the West at the end of the eighteenth century.

That longer view, paradoxically, helps us see the actors in the

Preface

events more clearly. Since World War II, some of the most illuminating work on the French Revolution has begun with questions, often drawn from the Marxist tradition, concerning the connection between changes in the class structure of France and the origins and development of the Revolution; these studies have commonly ended with lovingly detailed enumerations and analyses of the ordinary, everyday participants in the Revolution. As Godechot's discussion of the Bastille's besiegers indicates, the new research has ruled out some common conceptions of the revolutionary.

The revolutionary savage, for example, has virtually disappeared. Gone is the noble savage portrayed by D. H. Lawrence:

When the skies are going to fall, fall they will
In a great chute and rush of débâcle downwards.
Oh and I wish the high and super-gothic heavens would come
    down now,
The heavens above, that we yearn to and aspire to.

Gone, too, the ignoble savage James Madison identified:

an unhappy species of the population . . . who, during the calm of regular government, are sunk below the level of men; but who, in the tempestuous scenes of civil violence, may emerge into the human character, and give a superiority of strength to any part with which they may associate themselves.

The workaday revolutionary who showed up at the Bastille and during the other great Parisian *journées* turns out to have been a civilized man.

If the civil twentieth-century reader finds the civility of the eighteenth-century rioter difficult to appreciate, it is no doubt because a great dividing line separates the reader from the rioter. That line represents the final victory of the nation-state (and its conception of national citizenship, with attendant obligations of taxes, voting and military service) over the autonomies of communities, provinces, creeds and kinship groups. Although in recent years a communal theme has reappeared in the protests and programs of students and other young people, westerners of the last three generations or more have generally been able to take that victory of the nation-state for granted. Most of modern western politics has had to do with how the state apparatus should be controlled and employed, not with its right to conscript, tax, police and impose political duties. The contest was still open in western countries (except perhaps for England) during the eighteenth century. The French Revolution itself provided a model of nation-building.

The builders of western nations imposed the state by force. Those people whose livelihoods depended on the integrity of the smaller units which the nation-builders strove to break open and blend resisted the nation-builders forcibly. That resistance appeared most clearly in the three most common forms of collective violence under the old regime: the antitax rebellion, the anticonscription uprising, and the food riot. (As we shall see later, the unlikely food riot qualifies because instead of simply acting out starvation it usually grew out of the conflicting demands of the local community and the regional or national capital.)

While the resistance to conscription dragged on for two centuries, it rarely reached a large scale; the exceptions, like the great Vendée rebellion of 1793, came when the issue of conscription merged with other political grievances. By its nature, the food riot generally had no more than a local scope; sometimes (as in the *Guerre des Farines* of 1775, which Godechot describes), however, a great many localities flared up at the same moment. Tax rebellions could more easily assume huge proportions because they ordinarily developed from the attempts of state officials to impose new exactions on large populations or whole regions more or less simultaneously.

The seventeenth century was the time of taxes; the eighteenth century, the time of bread. The shapers of the nation had first to assure the revenues of the state. Then they had to build a national market and secure a food supply for their cities. The first problem came to a head during the seventeenth century. Many scholars see the great turbulence of the seventeenth century as a symptom of the economic crisis which beset much of western Europe during the century. Marxist scholars, in particular, tend to interpret the innumerable revolts as the birth pangs of a bourgeois society. They may be right. But the great rebellions of the seventeenth century actually took the form of furious opposition to the claims of the central state—especially its demands for taxes. By the end of the century, the French kings and their minions had hammered out

Preface

the state's right to impose regular taxes. From that point on, the struggle concerned who would pay, and how.

The eighteenth century saw fewer large insurrections. On a smaller scale, nevertheless, the incessant war against the tax collector continued. Moreover, the debate over the food supply grew grimmer, pitting merchants, city councils, rudimentary police forces and apologists of free trade against both the little people of the big cities and the little people of the countryside. As food grew more abundant, so did food riots.

Godechot attaches great importance to hunger and misery as conditions which moved ordinary people to protest. For that reason, he devotes an important part of the book to the ways in which eighteenth-century Paris was fed and policed. (It is more than coincidence that the early French uses of the word 'police' had to do with the maintenance of an orderly trade in grain; for centuries, the control of disorder and the control of the urban food supply were virtually indistinguishable problems.) The city had an enormous, impatient appetite. In times of shortage, it raged.

We should understand, however, the meaning of 'shortage'. Richard Cobb, who has written most lucidly on the technics and politics of the Parisian food supply, makes the essential point:

Toward the end of the eighteenth century and during the Revolution, the problem of food supply was essentially a problem of distribution, of transportation rather than of production. Bad harvests were rarely universal, and food shortages, which no longer had that character of catastrophic famine which was theirs at the beginning of the eighteenth century, became less pronounced under Louis XVI. The problem was not the production of grain, but its shipment.[1]

The difficulty of shipment still meant that *local* famines could occur. Furthermore, most Frenchmen had retained the old conviction that the 'authorities' of any particular locality bore the responsibility of assuring its food supply before meeting the needs of anyone else. This combination of circumstances presented a marvellous dilemma to the authorities of big cities, especially of Paris:

[1] Richard Cobb, 'Le ravitaillement des villes sous la Terreur: La question des arrivages,' *Terreur et subsistances*, Clavreuil, Paris, 1965, p. 211.

ix

accept the shortage and face the indignant rebellion of the city's population

or

requisition in the provinces, and incite smaller rebellions everywhere else.

The city's population being close at hand and dangerous of reputation, the authorities usually took the second course. As a consequence, the chief breeding grounds for food riots during the eighteenth century (and, for that matter, during the first half of the nineteenth century) were the hinterlands of France's great cities.

We should not interpret too literally the 'hunger' in Godechot's beautifully-titled chapter 'Between Hope, Hunger and Fear.' For that chapter actually describes people obsessed with right and justice, issues which in our abundant times we find hard to associate with the price of bread. In the eighteenth century those issues touched ordinary men quite directly, through the way 'the authorities' chose to deal with the threat of dearth. And they often took justice into their own hands, violently.

Not that they were violent men, and we are peaceful ones. Quite likely today's average western man, equipped with lethal machinery and warmaking organizations, kills and wounds more in his lifetime than his eighteenth-century counterpart did. Leaving war aside, the amount of violence has changed less than its form and meaning. For most eighteenth-century violence flowed out of local conflicts or out of resistance to the demand of the central power. Nowadays organized bids for power and for change on a large scale much more regularly produce violence. The revolutions of the late eighteenth century brought something new, because in their course collective violence by ordinary people became a serious means of bidding for some control over the operation of the state itself.

Frenchmen already lived a fairly rich political life at the local level before the Revolution. But for almost everyone direct participation in *national* politics was a novelty. With the provincial assemblies of 1787 and the preliminary assemblies for the Estates-General of 1789, a national political mobilization on an unprecedented scale began. Frenchmen could participate in national politics by voting, by holding office, by joining clubs, by attending meetings and rallies, by adopting politically stylish modes of speech and dress, by reading or hearing the pamphlets and papers which began to appear everywhere, or simply by arguing over the evening glass of wine. The early Revolution brought a frenzy of participation.

Frenchmen could also demonstrate, could also riot. Collective violence was already a normal form of relationship to the state; no surprise that it should continue. Continuing in the midst of a vast political mobilization, however, violence became a means of political change instead of simply a way of resisting it. There's the innovation: the Frenchman of 1789 demonstrated, rioted and occasionally killed, to be sure; but in doing so he extended his everyday, peaceful political activity. He was angry, certainly; but he was angry about the way the authorities and the privileged were treating him and his fellows. And political participation by riot did, in fact, often accomplish his objectives.

The workaday revolutionary also turns out to have been far from the drifter or desperado we have often thought him to be: these *vainqueurs de la Bastille* and their counterparts in the other popular outbursts of the early Revolution came from the settled world of shopkeepers and artisans. It was precisely this integration into a world whose members talked politics, aired their grievances, named their enemies and began to work out political programs which drew them into collective action, both violent and non-violent. At the beginning of his analysis, Godechot stresses the distinction between 'political' and 'economic' incentives to mass action. So long as that distinction remains firm, one can easily imagine two separate groups of participants in collective violence: the doctrinaires and the miserables. But by the end, Godechot demonstrates, perhaps despite himself, the intimate interdependence of political and economic incentives. In the process, it becomes clearer and clearer that economic hardship most reliably incited mass protest when to the eyes of ordinary people, it produced or revealed injustice, and that the people readiest to strike against revealed injustice were not the miserables, but the men who felt most strongly the connection between their own fates and the ways other men wielded power. They were the political men.

The taking of the Bastille illustrates the way political men faced with injustice take justice into their own hands. This may seem a highfalutin phrase for a large crowd's breaking into an old fortress

containing 120 soldiers, 4 accused counterfeiters, 1 wayward noble
and 2 lunatics. Three things about the event justify our attaching
exceptional importance to it: the symbolic significance of the
Bastille as an expression of arbitrary power; the rapid impact of
the Parisian rising on the city's governing council of electors, on
the National Assembly, on the king and, indeed, on all of France;
the justice-fulfilling actions of the crowd itself.

Even outside of France, the Bastille represented the worst
features of royal absolutism. William Blake, writing in 1791,
evoked its meaning:

For the Commons convene in the Hall of the Nation. France
shakes! And the heavens of France
Perplex'd vibrate round each careful countenance! Darkness of old
times around them
Utters loud despair, shadowing Paris; her grey towers groan, and
the Bastille trembles.
In its terrible towers the Governor stood, in dark fogs list'ning
the horror;
A thousand his soldiers, old veterans of France, breathing red
clouds of power and dominion.
Sudden seiz'd with howlings, despair, and black night, he stalk'd
like a lion from tower
To tower; his howlings were heard in the Louvre; from court to
court restless he dragg'd
His strong limbs; from court to court curs'd the fierce torment
unquell'd,
Howling and giving the dark command; in his soul stood the
purple plague,
Tugging his iron manacles, and piercing through the seven towers
dark and sickly,
Panting over the prisoners like a wolf gorg'd. . . .

And then, inevitably, Blake musters the Bastille's supposed
inmates: the Man in the Iron Mask, the unbowed dissenter, the
woman who 'refus'd to be whore to the Minister'. Regardless of
the truth of these traditions, the Bastille stood for the abuse of
power, and its subjugation stood for the rise of popular sovereignty.
Some symbolic acts say unmistakably to actors and to spectators
that they have made a decisive break with the past. The seizure of
the Bastille was such an act.

It was more than symbolic. The attack on the Bastille precipitated, or at least revealed, the separation of a significant part of the army from the regime, its sympathy with the people of Paris. The unreliability of the army sapped whatever plans Louis XVI had for reasserting his authority, and led him to what was widely considered to be his first acknowledgment of popular power: his trip to the Assembly on the 15th, and his trip to Paris on the 17th. Observers inside and outside France had, at last, reason to believe a genuine revolution was occurring. Later, Wordsworth looked back to the times

> In which the meagre, stale, forbidding ways
> Of custom, law, and statute, took at once
> The attraction of a country in romance!
> When Reason seemed the most to assert her rights,
> When most intent on making of herself,
> A prime enchantress—to assist the work,
> Which then was going forward in her name!
> Not favoured spots alone, but the whole Earth
> The beauty wore of promise. . . .

Thus Paris became capital of what Godechot calls the Revolution of the West.

Finally, the taking of the Bastille had the imprint of natural justice. The hanging of the Bastille's governor and the dragging of his body through the streets at a horse's tail (which members of the crowd proposed) and his decapitation, followed by display of the severed head (which they actually performed) were gruesome solemn means the royal justice of the old regime had once employed in the punishment of traitors. And the Parisian crowd had condemned de Launey as a traitor to the people. Lynch law and frontier justice have such bad odor today that it is hard for us to appreciate the forceful metaphor 'taking justice in your own hands'. To eighteenth-century Europeans, justice was almost tangible; one could seize it from incompetent or unworthy authorities. Babeuf, in the phrase Godechot quotes, saw clearly what was going on: 'I can understand the people taking the law into its own hands, and I commend such rough justice when it is satisfied by the destruction of the guilty, but how can it fail today to be cruel?'

By our lights, the revolutionary crowd was often cruel and often unjust. Looking back at the Bastille, we may well find the popular belief in de Launey's treason wrongheaded. We may begin to wonder how such a series of misperceptions and missteps could amount to a great revolutionary action. The virtue of Jacques Godechot's analysis, with its careful sketching of the eighteenth-century context, of the revolutionary milieu and of the meaning of the Bastille itself, is to help us see how enormous, how revolutionary, was this first great movement of the Parisian people toward power over the nation as a whole.

CHARLES TILLY,
Department of Sociology
University of Toronto

Contents

Contents

Contents

Illustrations

Plates

xix

Illustrations

Illustrations

Figures

Plan and Maps

Chronology

1773: 16th December
Boston 'Tea Party'

1775: 19th April
Victory of American 'patriots' over British troops at Lexington

April–May
Île-de-France: 'Flour War' (*Guerre des Farines*)

1780: 2nd–9th June
Gordon Riots in London

1782: 8th April–2nd July
Democratic rising in Geneva
Holland: Van der Capellen tot den Pol calls his compatriots to arms against the statdhouder

1785: 19th December
Riot at Utrecht

1786: 28th May
Riot at Amsterdam

1787: 22nd February
Versailles: opening of the Assembly of Notables

25th May
Failure and closing of the Assembly of Notables. Its request for the convocation of the Estates-General

1787: 24th July
The Paris Parlement refuses to register the financial edicts and demands the convocation of the Estates-General

13th August
The Paris Parlement exiled to Troyes

28th September
Return of the Parlement to Paris. Demonstrations in its honour, which degenerate into riots

12th November
Paris: fresh violent demonstrations in the streets

1788: 3rd May
The Paris Parlement invokes the 'fundamental laws' of the kingdom

8th May
Decree depriving the French Parlements of their chief prerogatives

10th May
Riots at Rennes

7th June
Riots at Besançon
Riots at Grenoble: the *journée des Tuiles*

19th June
Riots at Pau

8th August
Convocation of the Estates-General for 1st May, 1789

28th–30th August
Demonstrations in Paris, faubourg Saint-Antoine, on the occasion of Brienne's resignation

23rd September
Paris: demonstrations and riots on the occasion of the Parlement's return to Paris

December
Versailles: second Assembly of Notables

Chronology

1788: 27th December
'Result of Council' ordering 'double representation' of the Third Estate in the Estates-General, but not deciding the manner of voting

1789: 24th January
Electoral regulations for the elections to the Estates-General

26th–27th January
Riot at Nantes

February–April
Throughout France: elections to the Estates-General, and drafting of the *cahiers de doléances*

23rd March
Riot at Marseilles. Creation of a 'citizen militia'

30th March–3rd April
Riot at Besançon

15th April
Riot at Montlhéry

20th April
Peasant rising in the Gap region

27th–28th April
Paris: Réveillon riots

4th–6th May
Riot at Limoux

5th May
Versailles: opening of the Estates-General

23rd–27th May
Conciliatory conference between the three Orders

28th May
Riot in the market place at Rouen

9th June
Admission of failure of conciliatory conference

9th–10th June
Granaries plundered at Châteaulin

13th June
Versailles: three *curés* join the Assembly of the Tiers

1789: 17th June

Versailles: the Assembly of the Tiers proclaims itself *National Assembly*

20th June

Versailles: Tennis Court Oath (*Serment du Jeu de Paume*)

23rd June

Séance royale at the Estates-General

26th June

Versailles: first marching orders to the troops concentrated by the King around Versailles and Paris

28th June

The *gardes-françaises* begin to mutiny in Paris

8th July

Versailles: the National Assembly protests against the concentration of troops around Paris

5th–9th July

Paris: demonstrations in the Palais-Royal

11th July, Saturday

Louis XVI dismisses Necker

12th July, Sunday

Paris: 9 *a.m.* The news of Necker's dismissal reaches the city

About midday. Camille Desmoulins speaks in the Palais-Royal. First demonstrations in the streets of Paris

5 *p.m.* The Royal-Allemand regiment charges on the crowd in the Tuileries

10 *p.m.* The Swiss regiments reach the Champs-Elysées, then withdraw

13th July, Monday

Paris: 1 *a.m.* 40 of the 54 *barrières* giving access to Paris set on fire

6 *a.m.* Plundering of the monastery of Saint-Lazare

8 *a.m.* Meeting of the Assembly of Electors of Paris at the Hôtel de Ville. They form a 'permanent committee' and a 'civic militia' (*milice bourgeoise*)

1789: 13th July, Monday

>> 8 *a.m.* Plundering of the armoury at the *Garde-Meuble*

>> 5 *p.m.* Delegation from the Electors of Paris sent to the Invalides to demand arms

> 14th July, Tuesday

> The price of corn reaches its highest point for a century

> Paris: 10 *a.m.* Invasion of Les Invalides

>> 10.30 *a.m.* First deputation to the Bastille (the Electors of Paris)

>> 11.30 *a.m.* Second deputation to the Bastille (Thuriot and Ethis de Corny)

>> 1.30 *p.m.* The defenders of the Bastille open fire on the assailants

>> 2 *p.m.* Third deputation to the Bastille (Delavigne, the abbé Fauchet)

>> 3 *p.m.* Fourth deputation to the Bastille (Ethis de Corny)

>> 3.30 *p.m.* A detachment of *gardes-françaises* with cannon, led by Hulin, arrives at the Bastille

>> 5 *p.m.* The Bastille surrenders

>> 6 *p.m.* Massacre of de Launey, Governor of the Bastille

> Versailles:

>> 6 *p.m.* Louis XVI orders the troops to evacuate Paris

> 15th July, Wednesday

> Paris: 2 *a.m.* The deputy Dupont de Nemours reports this order to the Hôtel de Ville in Paris

> Versailles:

>> 10 *a.m.* Louis XVI goes to the National Assembly

> Paris: 2 *p.m.* Deputation from the National Assembly to the Hôtel de Ville

> 16th July, Thursday

> Versailles:

>> 9 *a.m.* The National Assembly demands the dismissal of the new Cabinet and the recall of Necker

1789: 16th July, Thursday

> 9 *a.m.* The King presides over a Council which takes decisive measures: dismissal of new Cabinet, recall of Necker, withdrawal of troops concentrated around Paris

Paris: 5 *p.m.* Troops start withdrawal

17th July, Friday

> Louis XVI goes to the Hôtel de Ville in Paris, confirming by his presence the victory of the Revolution, and fastens the tricolour cockade to his hat

Abbreviations

Arch. nat.: *Archives nationales*
Bibl. nat.: *Bibliothèque nationale*
A.H.R.F.: *Annales historiques de la Révolution française*
R.H.: *Revue historique*
R.H.M.C.: *Revue d'histoire moderne et contemporaine*

Introduction

The fall of the Bastille was by no means unheralded. For twenty years previously, the cities and country districts of the whole Western world had been the scene of repeated uprisings, of which that which took place on July 14th, 1789, was far from being the most violent. Was it in Paris that forty-six dwellings were set on fire, that seven prisons were attacked or burnt down and all their prisoners set free, that the principal Bank was threatened, and that more than 200 persons were killed and 300 injured? No, it was in London, in 1780, during riots which lasted from the 2nd to the 9th of June. Was it in Paris that the patriots gained control of the Government and the municipal authority, and had all the 'aristocrats' arrested, imprisoned or kept under surveillance? No, it was in Geneva, in 1782, and the disturbances lasted from April 8th to July 1st. Was it in Paris that barricades were set up in the streets, that the patriots demonstrated in arms, defeated the Governmental forces and obliged the head of the Government, or his representative, to take flight? No, it was in Boston, in 1775: in Utrecht, Amsterdam and The Hague in 1783. As for rural disturbances, they were rife in North America, in England, in Ireland, in the United Provinces, and in Belgium between 1770 and 1789. But the almost unique character of the *journée* of the Fourteenth of July 1789 lay in its epilogue. The capture of the Bastille brought about the capitulation of the King before the insurgent population and, less than one month later, the fall of the *ancien régime*, that is to say of the feudal regime which had prevailed in France for almost a thousand years. True, in America, the Boston rising had analogous consequences, but these were only achieved at the cost of ten years of war, with the help of several

Introduction

great European powers. The Fourteenth of July 1789 thus confronts us with two problems: were France's disturbances of the same nature, and did they spring from the same source as those that were agitating other Western countries during the same period? Why was it that, except in the United States, the riots which broke out in foreign capitals, notably in London, did not entail the collapse of the old regime or the capitulation of the royal or aristocratic power before the insurgent masses?

These are the two essential problems which we shall endeavour to solve in this book.

I

Social Peace and Unrest in the Western World during the Eighteenth Century

The fall of the Bastille has frequently been described as a bolt from the blue. Up till July 14th, 1789, it is implied, things had been peaceful inside and outside France, men lived happily in the best of all possible worlds and a handful of fanatics provoked an uprising which took all Frenchmen by surprise. 'Why, it's a revolt,' Louis XVI is said to have exclaimed in astonishment on the morning of July 15th, to which the Duc de Liancourt replied: 'No, Sire, it is a revolution.' These remarks ensured credence for the legend that the Governor of the Bastille was taken unawares by events and surrendered the fortress without having been able to organize its defence.

The facts are quite different. The taking of the Bastille, which made manifest to the entire world a revolution that had begun in France over two years before and had been latent throughout the Western world for the previous twenty, must be seen in its context, an atmosphere of social unease, of insurgency, of violent uprisings. It became significant because it confirmed the failure of the King's efforts to resist the revolutionary movement, and also because the fortress had come to be considered as a symbol of arbitrary power and identified with absolute monarchy.

The history of the Western world, when we consider it from a certain distance, is seen to consist of alternate periods of social disorder and stability. The sixteenth century witnessed great popular risings under the cloak of religious strife. This was the period of discoveries and of religious reforms, closely interconnected.

The exploration of unknown worlds disturbed men's minds and was partly responsible for the challenging of the truths laid down by the Catholic religion. Meanwhile the influx into Europe of the gold and silver extracted from American mines entailed a rise in prices and emphasized social inequalities. Already in 1524 a great peasant revolt had begun in South Germany and in Austria. The insurgents stormed and captured cities (Ulm, Freiburg-im-Breisgau, Bamberg; Wissembourg and Saverne in Alsace). Sometimes artisans and city workers joined forces with the peasantry. Mainz had to negotiate on an equal footing with the rebels; Trier and Frankfurt were threatened. Gradually a leader emerged, Thomas Münzer. But Luther disowned the insurgents, who claimed to be fighting in the name of religion. In 1525, in his 'Peaceful exhortation concerning the twelve articles of the Swabian peasantry', he forbade the rebels to use force and justified servitude 'in the flesh'; the essential thing, for him, was the safeguarding of 'spiritual freedom'. The peasants, deserted by those whom they considered their leaders, gave battle at Frankenhausen on May 15th, 1525, and at Saverne on May 17th. Luther, writing to denounce 'the peasant gangs of robbers and murderers', inveighed against the insurgents and congratulated the nobles who defeated them: 'Now is the time of the sword, the time of anger . . . Deliver us then, kind lords, save us, succour us, exterminate; let him who has the power take action . . .' The revolt came to an end in Germany, but it was soon to reach France. The wars of religion on more than one occasion took the form of social unrest, with the peasants rising against their lords in the countryside, the poor against the rich in the towns. The movement assumed a revolutionary character in Paris at the time of the Catholic League, notably in 1588 and 1589. On May 12th, 1588, Henri III occupied Paris with his royal troops, assisted by the bourgeois militia, which had remained loyal to him; the citizens rose immediately in one district after another; barricades were set up in the streets. The royal troops were checked and forced to capitulate; the king took flight. The Parisians had won a great victory over the monarchy. In January 1589 the municipal authorities of Paris and the Parlement decided to cease administering justice in the name of the King; and on August 1st of the same year Henri III was assassinated. Henri IV had great difficulty in securing recognition of his right to succeed, and had to pay for the recovery of Paris by abjuring his religion and waging war on Spain and the German princes, who were allied to the Catholic League. Even so, the legitimacy of Henri IV was not universally recognized, as was proved by his assassination in 1610. The death of Henri IV and the minority of Louis XIII provoked the revival of disturbances and religious strife throughout France; the Thirty Years' War, which ravaged Central Europe from 1618 onwards, was as much a civil and religious war as a conflict between foreign powers. In Great Britain, between 1640 and 1648, the struggle assumed a revolutionary aspect, and a social significance. Not only were Catholics and Protestants at war in England, Ireland and Scotland, but the poor attacked the rich; the Roundheads drew support from among humble artisans, tailors, coopers, brewers' apprentices, carters and cobblers. Charles I, suspected of intriguing with the Catholics, was arrested, judged, condemned to death and executed. Following on the murders of Henri III and Henri IV, this was the third 'regicide' in Western Europe within sixty years. At the very moment when Charles mounted the scaffold, there were signs of impending revolt in France, especially in Paris. The attempts of Henri IV, Louis XIII and Richelieu to establish absolutism in France resulted, after the death of the latter king and his minister, in violent demonstrations from all those whose powers were liable to be reduced, members of the Parlement, nobles, and those who held official posts in law and finance. This revolt, again, undoubtedly forms part of a movement that spread throughout the West, overstepping national boundaries to a remarkable extent. It may have been provoked by climatic changes and the economic depression resulting from these between the years 1619 and 1660: the revolt in Bohemia (1619), agrarian troubles in France (the *Nu-pieds* rising in Normandy, 1639–40), the Fronde in Paris and in the provinces (1643–1653), the 'split' in the Iberian peninsula (1640), the English Revolution (1641–1649). These rifts, as Pierre Chaunu has rightly pointed out,[1] 'inevitably accompany the reversal of the major trend of activities and of prices' which had been an upward one since the beginning of the sixteenth century. 'Western Europe', he continues, 'was paying with a long succession of disturbances for its precocious adherence to a world economy constructed round certain Atlantic poles of domination.' And he

---

[1] *A travers la Normandie des XVIIe et XVIIIe siècles* (Cahier des Annales de Normandie, no. 3), introduction by Pierre Chaunu, Caen, 1963, p. 11.

contests Porshnev's hypothesis[1] that these disturbances are purely 'national', for the Marxist historiographer, paradoxically enough, confines himself to a framework which is scarcely valid for the *ancien régime*, and seems deliberately to ignore continental and semi-continental phenomena. During these disturbances, at all events, on August 16th, 1648, the barricades went up in the streets of Paris again, the revolt being precipitated by the arrest of one of the most popular Councillors in the Parlement, Broussel. The citizens' militia, summoned to re-establish order, shouted: 'Vive Broussel!' He was set free, but the barricades stayed up until after his triumphant return to Paris on August 28th. The little king—Louis XIV, then aged ten—and the queen mother had to fly from Paris, like Henri III sixty years earlier, and took refuge at St-Germain-en-Laye. Civil war spread throughout France; Bordeaux rose up in arms, and Paris was to remain insurgent until October 1652. Then followed a period of calm. However closely we study the history of Central and Western Europe or their American dependencies, we observe no more social upheavals comparable to those we have enumerated, before the 1770s. Mention should doubtless be made of the so-called 'second English revolution' of 1688-89, but this is characterized essentially by the replacement of James II by William of Orange on the English throne, and by the consolidation of the chief results of the earlier revolution, that of 1640-48: namely the confirmation of Parliamentary prerogatives, the admission of the Protestant bourgeoisie to most public positions, and the increasing participation of the nobility, without loss of prestige, in trade and industry.

Thus a period of disorders lasting about 135 years was succeeded in Western and Central Europe and in their American dependencies by almost 110 years of social peace: of social peace only, for wars between States were very numerous during this period. But unlike those of the preceding epoch, they did not take on the character of civil strife. In France at any rate, if the end of Louis XIV's reign witnessed a certain number of uprisings, particularly that of the Protestant *camisards* in the Cévennes, and some local riots provoked by acute food shortage, the years 1710-1775 were undisturbed by any notable upheaval. We must therefore ask ourselves, before embarking on a study of the most

[1] Boris F. Porshnev, *Les soulèvements populaires en France de 1623 à 1648*, Paris, 1963 (French translation of the original Russian).

4

significant insurrection of modern times, why certain periods were more favourable than others to popular uprisings, and why the last thirty years of the eighteenth century were, throughout the Western world, years of revolution.

1. The growth of a revolutionary mentality

It is a commonplace to say that when a nation is contented it feels no wish to rebel or struggle against anyone whatsoever. The hardships of life, fear, and anxiety about the future are the prime causes among the masses of latent discontent and a predisposition to revolt. Now, among the chief sources of anxiety are certain economic and social phenomena of a very general nature, which cannot be circumscribed within those State frontiers which, particularly under the *ancien régime*, are wholly artificial. For instance, an extended rise in prices, when it is not followed by a rise in wages; this entails a slow and continuous decline in the standard of living. Or again, any rapid increase of population, what is known as 'demographic pressure', when it is not accompanied by a corresponding increase in employment. Now this is precisely what occurred in the whole of Central and Western Europe between 1730 and 1770. After a long period (1660–1730) when prices fell, about 1730 they rose; this resulted from the arrival in Europe of gold from Brazilian mines and silver from other parts of America. Prices rose almost continuously from 1730 to 1770, but the progress of wages was far slower. The disproportion between wages and prices grew: in other words, the standard of living declined. This disproportion became particularly noticeable after 1770, especially since after that date, as a result of a succession of poor harvests, the price of foodstuffs in Western Europe and notably in France soared to dizzy heights while wages remained static.

Parallel to the rise of prices we notice throughout Europe a rapid growth of population. Between 1715 and 1789 it increased by as much as 100% in certain countries, England for instance, and 60% in France. Here, the maximum population level, 18 million inhabitants, which had possibly been reached in the fourteenth century and certainly in the sixteenth, was exceeded for the first time, and the figure of 26 million was reached in about 1789. At first this increase in the number of inhabitants was welcomed, since the soil needed men to till it and expanding industry needed workers. The population-growth was primarily due, no doubt, to the transformation of agriculture, the increased areas under cultivation thanks to the reclaiming of land, and the slow but continuous substitution of biennial for triennial rotation of crops, the development of industrial cultivations bringing money into the hands of the peasantry (vines, flax, hemp, dyestuff plants), the introduction and widespread cultivation of new plants, mostly imported from America: maize, potatoes, tobacco, beans, pumpkins. To begin with, and until 1770 or thereabouts, increased agricultural production, which was originally responsible for the demographic rise, was easily able to keep pace with the demands of the new generations. From 1770 onwards, however, the increase in the population combined with a succession of bad harvests made it difficult to feed the masses. It also became difficult to find them work. The rise in prices obliged consumers to spend most of their available money on foodstuffs; industry, particularly the textile industry, suffered thereby. Unemployment increased in agriculture as well as in industry. These are general phenomena, to be met with on a greater or lesser scale throughout the Western world. One proof of the anxiety aroused by the growth of the population from 1770 onwards is the increasing number of demographic studies, such as those of Moheau in France or Malthus in Great Britain.

Anxiety about the future, uneasiness, and discontent contribute to the creation of a revolutionary mentality. Moreover, the uneasy masses need to find reasons for their distress. Of course, they scarcely suspect that economic contingencies, demographic evolution, and social disequilibrium are the underlying causes of their difficulties. Even those who were best informed, at the time, about political and social problems were rarely aware of the basic causes of social discontent. These men explained to the masses the grounds for their unrest in terms that were easier for them to understand. In the sixteenth century, religious problems were put in the foreground: the corruption of the Catholic church or the heresies of the Reformers. From the mid-eighteenth century onwards, political thinkers, those who were known as the *philosophes*, attacked the political regime; they were perhaps inaccurate from a juridical point of view in describing it as 'feudal', but it was nevertheless a regime based on inequality and privilege, on the dominance of the nobility and clergy, and on an irrational traditional system of law and justice. And the ideas of

6

the *philosophes*, propagated through thousands of books, pamphlets, newspapers, Masonic lodges, and discussion groups of every sort, finally penetrated into the smallest villages. The regime was indicted and its reform demanded, with ever-increasing vigour, from the seventies onward.

However, there is a considerable gap between a widespread discontent and spirit of protest and the development of an aggressive state of mind. Revolutionary demonstrations are not, in fact, organized by 'crowds' but by 'gatherings'. Georges Lefebvre has introduced this distinction into the analysis of revolutionary action. He defines the crowd as an aggregate of individuals brought together by chance in some particular place, without any precise purpose and without organization. The crowd represents a disintegration of the usual social groups, it includes people who do not normally live together, artisans who have deserted their workshops, bourgeois who have left their shops or their offices, peasants who have come in from their fields. It is rare for a crowd, even if its members share the same anxieties and preoccupations, to proceed to concerted action.[1]

Between the simplest form of crowd, as for instance the strollers along the Boulevard on a Sunday, and gatherings formed with a political end in view, there exist what Georges Lefebvre calls 'semi-voluntary aggregates'. The term implies crowds assembled for some specific purpose, among whom news and slogans can be rapidly passed round, thus giving rise to gatherings with revolutionary objectives: for instance the crowds that forgather at fairs and markets, form queues outside shops, pour out of church, watch sporting events or entertainments, and of course those that are summoned together for electoral purposes. These semi-voluntary aggregates are the easiest to transform into revolutionary gatherings, and it has been observed that uprisings most frequently take place on Sundays or market days.

But in addition to the gatherings that result from such semi-voluntary aggregates, there may exist others deliberately organized by clubs and societies, public or secret associations.

Within these crowds and gatherings, news is generally transmitted by word of mouth. In the last third of the eighteenth century, education was still sparse, and not much reading went on. Only a minority studied the newspapers, and it was the

[1] Georges Lefebvre, 'Foules révolutionnaires', *A.H.R.F.*, 1934, pp. 1–26.

members of this minority who communicated, by their talk, the news they had read or learned. This information would be exaggerated or minimised according to the mentality of the crowd, and its traditions, which date back several centuries. As a general rule the information was soon distorted and its distortion was liable to involve quite unforeseeable consequences.

But as well as conversation, which was the most usual means of communicating news, certain men—the leaders—might try to act upon the crowd by more efficacious methods of propaganda, including songs, pictures and drawings, and images of wax or wood, stone or bronze.

Nevertheless the crowd, or more precisely the semi-voluntary aggregate and the gathering, only breaks loose when it has been shown, in a highly simplified form, the essential pattern of its anxieties and apprehensions. Fear would seem to be the most powerful means of action on crowds, particularly fear of famine. So when they are shown a scapegoat whom they can blame for their sufferings, they are liable to take mass action against some individual, some building or institution. On the other hand, the recognition of some man as their 'saviour', who can do away with their misery or dispel their fear, is equally liable to result in demonstrations. Thus anxiety, fear, suspicion of those 'responsible', and the unhesitating trust placed in some particular leader are the principal motives that provoke gatherings and are capable of transforming them into revolutionary uprisings, which may display astonishing audacity and an aggressive spirit far beyond the reach of their individual members. The revolutionary aggregate does in fact exercise upon each of its members a powerful compulsion from which they can scarcely escape. Within a revolutionary gathering, the sense of individual responsibility seems to dissolve. Each of the members of the group feels himself lost in the mass and, thinking that he will never be recognized, he commits actions of which he would be incapable in isolation, and if later he should be called to account for these he will be astonished. Within the revolutionary gathering, violence spreads like a contagion, individuals strike because they see others striking. The gathering may display an effectiveness that specialists in the maintenance of law and order could hardly have imagined. And in case of success, its members are conscious of their solidarity, and tend to form amongst themselves permanent associations to safeguard the results they have gained. Thus a revolutionary gathering of casual origin may lead to organized revolution.

2. Early revolutionary upheavals: insurrection in America (1773–1783)

It was in the English colonies of North America that, towards 1770, the unrest originated which was to spread throughout the Western world. On the surface, there is no relation between this colonial uprising against the parent state and the European revolutions which were to come. But only on the surface. Here too the underlying causes of the movement were demographic pressure and the rise of prices. It may seem absurd to talk of demographic pressure in connection with England's thirteen American colonies, which at that time numbered scarcely one million inhabitants. But these inhabitants were for the most part farmers, whose number increased rapidly, both through immigration from Europe and through their very high birth rate. These farmers needed new lands, fertile and easy to cultivate. Now the English colonies were confined to poor lands between the Atlantic and the Appalachians. Their inhabitants could only find the lands they coveted in the regions won from France between 1756 and 1763. War had been waged, and won by them, to obtain these lands. Now as soon as the war was over a law of October 7th, 1763, forbade the English colonists to settle in these newly-annexed territories. The British government, on the one hand, was not anxious to antagonize its new Canadian subjects, and on the other intended to reserve these lands for future immigrants from Britain. The law of October 7th, 1763, intensified demographic pressure in the older colonies. On the other hand, prices had increased; not only, as throughout the West, as a result of the general trend, but also as a result of the new indirect taxes imposed by the British government, without previous consultation with the colonies, on certain products sold in these territories: molasses, paper, glass, lead, tea, etc. Discontent was naturally focused against the regime. The colonies claimed the right to be consulted on all matters that concerned them. They were not slow to demand administrative autonomy, and then independence. But the British rule to which they were subject was at the same time the 'old régime', the 'feudal system', although in a far milder form than in Europe; in certain States, such as New York, there still existed fiefs and feudal rights; the citizens clamoured for their abolition.

The first revolutionary gatherings took place in Boston, which was then the chief trading port of England's American colonies. The almost prohibitive duty on molasses, exported from the French West Indies by Boston traders to be re-exported into Europe, threatened to ruin the trade. The Stamp Act, and then the tax on tea, aggravated American discontent. Resistance groups, pervaded with a revolutionary mentality, were formed: the 'Sons of Liberty'. These won the adherence of merchants who had been injured by the new taxes, and of small farmers hungry for land. The Sons of Liberty organized resistance; increasingly numerous clashes took place in the streets of Boston between the Americans and the British customs officers and soldiers. Economic and social problems formed the background, but it was in the name of liberty, of independence, of all the ideals that the *philosophes* had been proclaiming for the past twenty years, that men were fighting. The English soldiers, the redcoats, having been bombarded with snowballs on March 5th, 1770, finally opened fire; three civilians were killed. This was the 'Boston massacre', a significant event. For the first time in sixty years (since the war of the *camisards*) civil strife had broken out in the Western world. The British Government, alarmed, made some concessions, abolished certain taxes, but maintained the duty on tea. This provided the pretext for fresh demonstrations. The Sons of Liberty were now asking for more than the abolition of the hateful taxes; one of their leaders, Samuel Adams, spoke of independence. Groups of the Sons of Liberty grew and multiplied; 'correspondence committees' were formed in every town; they succeeded in organizing a general boycott of tea. Then, as the revolutionary mentality grew stronger, the 'Boston Tea Party' took place on December 16th, 1773. Sons of Liberty in the dress and war-paint of Mohawk Indians boarded three vessels of the East India Company and flung overboard 342 cases of tea. We know who these bogus Indians were: carpenters, masons, blacksmiths, barbers from Boston, and farmers from the surrounding countryside. They were victims of the economic crisis, but they rose in the name of Liberty. The British Parliament, this time, was indignant; it voted 'laws of coercion'; the port of Boston was closed until the cost of the tea thrown into the sea should be paid back to the East India Company, and certain elected officials and jurymen were replaced by agents nominated by the British Government. This exacerbated the American patriots. The English General Gage, commanding the Boston contingent, had an American wife and understood the colonists' point of view, but he was obliged to obey and enforce the 'coercive laws'. Informed that American 'patriots' had collected gunpowder and military equipment in the village of Concord, 20 miles north-west of Boston, he sent troops on April 18th, 1775, to take possession of this depot and arrest two of the 'patriot' leaders, Samuel Adams and John Hancock. On the morning of April 19th, while they were passing through the village of Lexington, the redcoats were greeted with musket shots. After a moment's hesitation they opened fire in return, and eight patriots were killed; civil war had begun. The English troops succeeded in getting through Lexington; but at Concord they met with fresh resistance. They were unable either to capture the arms depot or to arrest the patriot leaders; they were forced to turn back, and make their way to Boston under fire from the patriots. The British column lost 247 of its 2,500 men; almost one-tenth. Even though the actual figures seem inconsiderable, such casualties inflicted by armed peasants and artisans were significant. The failure of the English soldiers' mission, their retreat and the losses they suffered amounted to a real defeat. For the first time since the great civil and religious wars of the first half of the seventeenth century, a corps of regular soldiers had been defeated by armed revolutionaries. This was a significant event, as the Americans did not fail to recognize. A 'continental' congress, held at Philadelphia, summoned American colonists to arms and formed militias under the command of George Washington, who had distinguished himself, from 1755 to 1763, in the war against France. But the 'battle' of Lexington had repercussions far beyond the limits of America. It marks the beginning of the great revolutionary movements which were to disturb the Western world. It was the first great victory of the people in arms against the forces of 'tyranny'. The Boston rising inaugurated civil war. Three years later this civil war had become a general conflict, as a result of the alliance of France, then of Spain and the United Provinces with the young United States. And in 1783 the war ended with the victory of this coalition and the recognition of the independence of the United States.

3. The 'Guerre des Farines' (May 1775)

At the very moment when the country people of New England were joining battle with the redcoats, the peasants of the regions around Paris were attacking the constabulary. The causes, here, seem to have been essentially economic. The harvest of the year 1774 had been a bad one, and the price of wheat in France shows a rise in 1775 (see graph no. 1) which is noticeably sharper in the countryside (at Avallon for instance, see graph no. 2) than in Paris (see graph no. 3). Prices, however, were generally lower in 1775 than in 1771 and 1773 (see graphs 1, 2, 3). It is true that three successive crises, coming so close together, exhausted the available funds of both agricultural and urban workers, increased distress and exasperated the masses. But economic difficulties were complicated by a political problem. Louis XVI, when he came to the throne in 1774, entrusted the important office of Controller-General of Finance to Turgot, a *philosophe*. Turgot applied certain of the new ideas and decreed free trade in grain and flour within the kingdom, in an edict which the Paris Parlement was forced to register on December 19th, 1774. Free trade in grain inevitably entailed a further rise in prices, since those who possessed stocks naturally tended to sell them dear in the more poorly-provided regions. Thus at Rozoy-en-Brie the price of a *setier* of wheat rose from 25 livres in January 1775 to over 30 livres in April, a rise of one-fifth; in Paris, a four-pound loaf rose from 11 sous in September 1774 to 14 sous on May 3rd, 1775, an increase of more than a third. This rise provoked riots in the markets of the Ile-de-France, of Brie, Orléanais, Normandy, Picardy and Champagne; these riots became known as the *guerre des farines* or 'Flour War'.[1]

Chronologically, the first rising occurred on the market-place of Dijon on April 18th, 1775. The mob attacked a miller named Carré, who was accused of hoarding. He was able to save his skin by climbing on to the roof of a lawyer's house, but his own home was plundered and his flour, condemned as adulterated, was thrown into the water. Next day, April 19th, the army was brought in, but there were no clashes between soldiers and demonstrators; in Burgundy the riot had no sequel. Others, however, were to develop in the neighbourhood of Paris and even within the capital itself.

[1] Edgar Faure, *La Disgrâce de Turgot*, Paris, 1961.

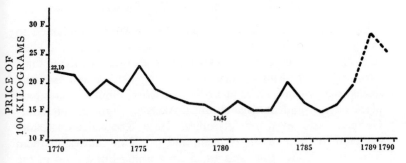

Fig. 1. Price of corn in France, 1770–1790

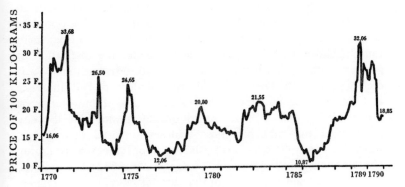

Fig. 2. Price of corn at Avallon, 1770–1790

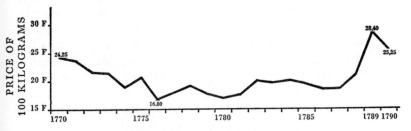

Fig. 3. Price of corn in Paris, 1770–1790

On April 27th, at Beaumont-sur-Oise, porters complained to the town clerk that certain bakers 'refused to sell bread'. Then they arrested a corn merchant who was charging 32 livres for a *setier* of wheat. Finally they invaded the market and formally settled the price of wheat at 12 livres a *setier*. Similar scenes took place on subsequent days at the markets of Pontoise, of Saint-Germain and even of Versailles. Here 8,000 demonstrators gathered in front of the château, and the King addressed them from the balcony; they still asked for nothing but a drop in the price of wheat. The Prince de Poix, governor of Versailles, fixed the price of wheat at the level demanded by the demonstrators, who then dispersed. Fourteen years later, things were to be very different; in 1775 the great economic and political crisis which was to sweep away the *ancien régime* had barely begun.

On May 3rd, Paris—where a four-pound loaf had risen to fourteen sous—witnessed scenes of plunder as the populace attempted to control prices. The bookseller Hardy describes them thus:[1] 'The mob, which had collected under the instigation of gangs of ruffians and bandits who were said to have entered Paris chiefly through the Porte Saint-Martin, the Porte de la Conférence and the Porte de Vaugirard, ran riot at the Halles and plundered the bakers' shops. Unrest spread quickly throughout the city centre and the suburbs; most tradesmen closed their shops, warned by people who were rushing about the streets urging citizens to take this precaution. The mob attempted to ransack the Corn Market and tear open all the sacks of flour; but fortunately they were unable to achieve their object; they made up for it by visiting all the markets and forcing the bakers to hand over their bread, as well as private individuals who happened to have some in store and whose doors were broken down if they showed the slightest reluctance to open them. Having looted the markets, the same mob now set about forcing open bakers' shops in one district after another, attacking the doors with poles, sticks and even iron tongs, if any resistance was put up.' Actually, the police enquiry showed that the plundering of bakeries in various districts and in the Halles had gone on practically simultaneously. The bakers, under threat of death, gave way. Thus Chappe, a baker in the rue Beauregard, was forced to 'throw his bread down from the first floor to individuals who had collected in the street, for fear of

[1] Hardy, *Mes loisirs*, Paris, 1764–1789, 8 vols., vol. III, p. 58.

having his shop broken into.' The bakers in the districts of Saint-Marcel and Saint-Victor—working-class neighbourhoods on the left bank—reckoned that they had had more than 20,000 pounds of bread taken from them, for which they had been paid little if anything.

The watch—that is to say the police—did not intervene until the evening, and arrested a few looters. There was no clash between the crowd and the forces of order. Three days later (May 6th) the movement reached its climax on the market place of Meaux. The crowd plundered two hundred sacks of grain with cries of 'Twelve livres for wheat, eight for rye-wheat!' Bakeries and private houses were attacked. The dragoons, who were responsible for restoring order, intervened only half-heartedly.

Subsequently, however, the violence of the uprisings died down, although we still hear of unrest at Dreux, Vernon, Montdidier, Chauny, La Fère, Noyon, Soissons and Joigny.

The Controller-General, Turgot, did not yield to the rioters. He blamed the Prince de Poix for having fixed the price of grain at Versailles. He persisted in maintaining the freedom of trade and of prices. To prevent further rioting he set up two armies, one under Biron to keep watch over Paris, the other to maintain order in the Île-de-France, and he organized a vigorous repression. More than 400 people had been arrested during the disturbances; 162 of these were prosecuted; two looters were condemned to death on May 11th and hanged in the place de Grève that same day, at three o'clock in the afternoon. One of the victims was only sixteen. A third who had been condemned to death was reprieved through the intervention of the comte d'Artois, in whose service he was.

A study of the occupations of those demonstrators who were prosecuted reveals that the great majority of them belonged to the working-class; nail-smiths, ragmen, cobblers, carpenters, market-porters, harness-makers, quarrymen, navvies and a number who are described as workless and even homeless. The insurgents of 1789 were to be drawn from the same social stratum, but so were those who took part in the Boston rising and in the London riots. Out of the 162 persons indicted, only two are described as 'masters', a locksmith and a cobbler, but in these crafts there was practically no social distinction between master and journeyman. However, several clerics had been arrested, notably the abbé Saurin, author of *Reflections of a Citizen on the Corn Trade*—strongly hostile to free trade—and seven parish priests accused of making no attempt to stop the looting.

The scale of the riots, the fact that their target was a Minister who was also a *philosophe*, the first that France had ever had, surprised many people. The *philosophes* refused to believe that the people, whose welfare they desired, had thus misinterpreted Turgot's intentions. They suspected a plot organized either by the nobility, who hated the Minister, or by the clergy, opponents of enlightenment, or else by the Jesuits, whose order had been suppressed in 1764 and who were supposed to be seeking revenge. This was the opinion of Voltaire, of Miromesnil, Minister of Justice, of the bookseller Hardy and many others. The same theory has been put forward by many historians, such as Henri Carré,[1] Marcel Rouff, Leon Say,[2] Schelle, and Bernard Faÿ.

The most recent studies draw a different conclusion. G. Rudé,[3] Edgar Faure[4] V. S. Lublinski,[5] see these riots as a spontaneous uprising provoked by the price of wheat and bread. Turgot's adversaries exploited the disturbances in order to justify their political and economic attitude and persuaded the weak king, Louis XVI, to disgrace the Controller-General.

In fact, the risings of 1775 are primarily a consequence of the three bad harvests of 1770, 1772 and 1774, occurring at the precise moment when demographic pressure had begun to make itself felt. The free trade in grain introduced by Turgot probably contributed little to the rise in prices, but it had a psychological significance: crowds prefer to blame one man, rather than meteorological contingencies, for their misfortunes. The same underlying causes played a part in France as in America in 1775: rising prices, a swollen population with no hope of seeing any quick end to its distress. But in America, for several years previously, economic discontent had been strengthened by political demands, formulated by the bourgeoisie. In France, the enlightened middle class was on the side of Turgot, the reforming Minister, from whom it

[1] In the *Histoire de France* edited by E. Lavisse, vol. IX, 1, p. 32.

[2] Léon Say, *Turgot*, Paris, 1887.

[3] G. Rudé, 'La taxation populaire de mai 1775 à Paris et dans la région parisienne' (*A.H.R.F.*, 1956, pp. 139–179).

[4] *Op. cit.*

[5] V. S. Lublinski, 'New data on the disturbances of May 1775 in Paris' (in Russian), *Voprosi Istorii*, 1955, n. 11; 'Voltaire et la guerre des Farines' (*A.H.R.F.*, 1959, pp. 127–145). See also Furio Diaz, *Filosofia e politica nel Settecento francese*, Turin, Einaudi, 1962.

August 25th, 1788. The recall of Necker

Bibl. Nat., Print Room, Vinck Collection, 1354

August 28th, 1788. Brienne's effigy burnt by the people

Bibl. Nat., Print Room

expected great things. It therefore supported the authorities, and completely failed to understand these bread riots, believing like the bookseller Hardy that they were the work of 'bandits and brigands'. Moreover the forces of order played a rather passive part in the affair, and there was no fighting as at Lexington. In other words, the French crowds had as yet no revolutionary mentality or organization comparable to those of the American crowds.

The fact remains, none the less, that the 'Flour War' was, as Edgar Faure has said, 'an event rich in historical and sociological significance', a link connecting the risings of a hungry populace, so frequent under the *ancien régime* (to be precise, up till 1715) 'with the political movements of the revolutionary period . . . According to the angle from which we view it, we may consider it either as a concluding episode or as a precursory episode, but to some extent it possesses the characteristics of both.' We shall interpret it chiefly as a precursory episode, but to the same extent as the contemporary risings in Boston or those of London, Geneva and Holland, which we shall now proceed to examine.

4. The Gordon Riots in London (June 2nd–9th, 1780)

Five years after the *Guerre des Farines*, the greatest city of the Western world was literally set ablaze by a violent revolutionary movement. The 'Gordon Riots', whose underlying causes were the same as those of the risings in Boston and the Île-de-France, namely economic crisis and demographic pressure, brought into action a similar social stratum (artisans, small shopkeepers, unemployed workers) but with totally different aims. In contradistinction to the tendency towards liberty and tolerance which marked the European enlightenment, their object was to oppose the equality of political rights for English Catholics. They were more violent than the risings in Boston and Paris and yet, unlike these, they failed. We shall examine the reasons why. But let us first study the facts.[1]

For seven days London was at the mercy of the rioters and, during the night of June 7th, 1780, the whole of the City and the

[1] On the Gordon riots, see: J. P. de Castro, *The Gordon Riots*, Oxford, 1926; G. Rudé, 'I Tumulti di Gordon' in *Movimento operaio*, 1955, pp. 833–855, and 'The Gordon Riots' in *Transactions of the Royal Historical Society*, 1956, 5th series, VI, pp. 93–114.

districts south of the Thames were ablaze. Ten times as many houses were destroyed in London during the riots of 1780 as in Paris during the whole of the Revolution. Sébastien Mercier writes in his *Tableaux de Paris* that the 'havoc and horror' that spread throughout London under the instigation of Lord George Gordon would have been 'inconceivable in a town boasting as efficient a police force as Paris', but Sébastien Mercier had later to lower his tone since, during the French Revolution, if there were fewer buildings destroyed in Paris the demonstrations were far more effective and the bloodshed was greater. The Gordon riots broke out at the moment when the American war was at its height. England's American colonies had been in open rebellion since 1773; they had proclaimed their independence in 1776; since 1778 they had enjoyed the support of European allies, and England had little by little been losing ground. She had suffered serious defeats, particularly at Saratoga in October 1777; an English army had been forced to capitulate in the open field before the insurgents. Whereas in the previous wars of the eighteenth century, the war of the Spanish Succession and the Seven Years War, England had won an almost unbroken series of victories, she had now suffered defeat on land and had won no victories at sea. At home, disturbances had broken out in Ireland. The volunteers who had been assembled to guard against a possible French landing—and this constituted a real threat—took advantage of their armed state to demand reforms in the administration of Ireland. The Dublin Parliament wanted to enjoy the same rights as the British Parliament, to which it was in theory subordinate. The Irish Catholics, who had at first been excluded from the volunteer force because they were not considered reliable, had to be enlisted for lack of sufficient Protestants. They took advantage of this situation to press, not indeed for complete civil and political equality as yet, but for the abolition of the 'Test Bill' in Ireland.

In England itself, the House of Commons displayed violent opposition to George III's Government, which tended towards ever-increasing absolutism. A motion was passed that 'The power of the Crown has increased, is increasing, and ought to be diminished.' As a result of the Volunteers' demands, the Government sought to conciliate the Irish Catholics by various concessions, and abolished the Test Bill which debarred them from holding public office. The British Protestants were alarmed

18

at this decision, which reminded them of the policies of James I and James II. An atmosphere of disquiet reigned in London in 1780. It explains the Gordon riots. The most obvious, the clearest cause of these riots is the relative tolerance shown towards English Catholics by the British Parliament, from 1778 onwards. In 1778, in fact, a member of Parliament, Sir George Saville, had proposed a bill granting certain slight concessions to English Catholics provided they took an oath of loyalty to the King and renounced the jurisdiction of the Pope in civil lawsuits. A law of William III's reign, the time of the second English revolution (1688), forbidding Catholics to keep schools on penalty of life imprisonment and depriving them of the right to inherit or acquire land, was revoked.

Saville's bill was unanimously passed by both Chambers and was approved by the King on June 3rd, 1778. This law was valid for England and Wales; a similar law was put forward for Scotland during the next Parliamentary session. It was a very anodyne law, since it was far from granting equality to English Catholics and still debarred them from holding public office. In spite of this, and although the law had been passed unanimously, many members of the Church of England displayed considerable uneasiness. There was strong resentment among the Scottish Presbyterians, who formed a committee for the defence of Protestant interests and the repeal of the Saville law. On February 2nd, 1779, rioting broke out in Edinburgh and Glasgow; two Catholic chapels were destroyed, and Catholic homes and shops were looted. The disturbances did not subside until it was announced that the law would not be applied in Scotland. The more fanatical English Protestants formed an association to secure the revocation of the Catholic Relief Act (the Saville law); and in November 1779 Lord George Gordon became president of this association. Lord George Gordon was the son of a Catholic father and a Protestant mother, and his aunt, the Duchess of Perth, was also a Catholic. However, he had been brought up as a member of the Church of England and was known to be a fanatical Protestant. His election as president of the Protestant Defence Committee for the repeal of the Catholic Relief Act was the signal for the Scottish disturbances to spread to England. Gordon summoned the members of the Association to a mass meeting in St George's Fields, Southwark, at ten o'clock on the morning of June 2nd, to demonstrate and sign a petition to be presented to Parliament demanding the repeal of the Catholic Relief Act. Gordon had declared that if there were fewer than 20,000 demonstrators he would resign as president of the Association. On Friday June 2nd, 1780, at the appointed hour, the mass meeting took place. The size of the crowd exceeded Gordon's highest hopes. Over 60,000 people were present, wearing the blue cockade and carrying the blue banners of the Association. The demonstrators were invited to sign a petition; it was delivered, bearing 40,000 signatures, to the House of Commons. The London police force, which was a small one, was soon overwhelmed. The demonstrators converged on Parliament by different routes, all shouting: 'No Popery! Repeal, repeal!'. Meeting various members of both Houses on their way to the session, they abused and even assaulted some of these, forcing them to take refuge in nearby houses or to seek police protection. They hurled insults at Lord North, the Prime Minister, and at Burke, who was later to be champion of the counter-revolution, but who as the son of a former Irish Catholic was known to be personally sympathetic to Catholicism. At a packed meeting of the House of Commons, it was decided by 192 votes to 7 to postpone the debate on the petition to the following Tuesday, four days later. Thus the great majority of members were clearly opposed to the petition and in favour of retaining the law. The demonstrators, massed in front of the Houses of Parliament, were soon informed of this decision, which infuriated them. Still shouting, they scattered through the streets of London and began to attack Catholic chapels. There were no Catholic churches in London at this time, for they had been forbidden by religious laws since the beginning of the seventeenth century. But the ambassadors of Catholic powers had been allowed to set up their own chapels, and these were attended by English Catholics. The number of Catholics in England was small, but it included members of the highest aristocracy, who worshipped in these chapels. The first to be attacked by the rioters was that of the Ambassador of Piedmont and Sardinia, which they burned to the ground. This chapel stood in Duke Street, one of the busiest streets in London's fashionable quarter. During the tumult that ensued fourteen people were arrested by the police, five of them being sent to prison. Then the demonstrators moved on to the chapel of the Bavarian Ambassador, which was ransacked but not destroyed. In the evening they gathered in the streets again and threatened the house of a Frenchman named Jacques Malo, a native of Cambrai who had long been settled in London. He promptly sent to the Lord Mayor to ask for military protection. This was refused him, which shows that the city authorities were in sympathy with the demonstrations and hostile to the Catholic Relief Act. None the less Malo's attitude, and his approach to the Lord Mayor, made an impression on the mob and it dispersed for the time being, although, as we shall see, it was subsequently to return to Malo's house. Two days later, on June 4th, a Sunday and therefore a holiday, there were fresh gatherings and demonstrations. A Catholic chapel was burnt down in Moorfields; so were several of the neighbouring houses, which were not the homes of Catholics. On Monday June 5th, although this was not a holiday, the demonstrators still filled the streets, and this time they directed their hostility against the two magistrates responsible for arresting and prosecuting the incendiaries of the Sardinian ambassador's chapel. Sir George Saville, the sponsor of the Catholic Relief Act, was also threatened. This time the city authorities sent troops to protect his house. The demonstrators then turned their attention to an Irish chapel in the same district, Virginia Street, which they destroyed, together with several neighbouring houses. In Spitalfields a certain number of houses owned or inhabited by English or Irish Catholics were burnt down during the afternoon of the same day, June 5th. Parliament met next day, Tuesday, as had been decided, to examine the petition. The demonstrators, who were aware of this, gathered in front of the Houses of Parliament, shouting and hurling abuse unremittingly at the members. Lord Sandwich, First Lord of the Admiralty, was violently assaulted. The House of Commons then announced that it would not hold its debate under threat from the mob, and adjourned its sitting till the following Thursday. As the demonstrators persisted in surrounding the Houses of Parliament, the authorities had to summon a regiment of cavalry to charge and disperse the rioters; these then attacked and burned down the house of Judge Hyde, who had brought in the troops. Then the mob proceeded to set fire to a police station in Covent Garden; at eight that evening they gathered in front of the Old Bailey, a new prison which had only been in use for a few months. They attacked it, destroyed the keeper's dwelling and set the prisoners free. Then they moved on to other prisons, where, in order to save their homes, the warders released the prisoners. The mob also attacked the home of Lord

Mansfield, who was known for his liberal and tolerant views; they burned down his house with its library, which contained many rare books and precious manuscripts. The fire brigade was called in to put out the blaze, but the rioters slashed the hoses and put the pumps out of action. Then they proceeded to the homes of other noblemen suspected of holding liberal or tolerant opinions; they threatened Lord North's house, that of the Lord Chancellor, and that of the Archbishop of York, suspected of liberalism. Several more Catholic chapels were destroyed. A number of houses, in order to avoid being attacked, put out the blue flag of the Association. Wednesday June 7th was the sixth day of the rising, and marked its climax; it has remained famous in British history as Black Wednesday. Many more houses were destroyed: not only the homes of noblemen, liberals and Catholics, but also of a number of Protestants. Particularly savage attacks were launched against the homes of a Catholic brewer named Cox, of one Judge Wilmot who was presumably suspected of having tried to repress the riots, and of a leading police officer, as well as against those of Judge Hyde and the French trader Jacques Malo which, as we have seen, had already been attacked but not destroyed. Among the buildings burnt down must be mentioned the Langdale distillery, the owner of which was a Catholic; the fire spread to the alcohol in the vats, so that the whole neighbourhood was soon a mass of flames. It is impossible to say exactly how many people died in the course of this vast conflagration: perhaps a hundred men, women and children. Then a number of other prisons, hitherto unscathed, were assailed: the great jail in Fleet Street, the King's Bench prison, the New Gaol, the Surrey House of Correction, the debtors' prison in the Marshalsea. Blackfriars Bridge was also attacked; this was a toll bridge, and the toll-keepers' houses were destroyed. A total of 36 gigantic fires raged simultaneously throughout London, and Horace Walpole, in his letters, vividly describes their fury.[1] The Bank of England itself was threatened, but this time the City merchants proceeded in a body to its defence and repulsed the rioters. We can see what a pitch the London riots had reached by Wednesday, June 7th, 1780. There is no comparable scene to be found through the whole history of the French Revolution, either in Paris or in the provinces. Emotions had reached their peak, and during the night of June

[1] Horace Walpole, *Letters*, VII, 392.

7th–8th the authorities rallied. The Court of Common Council, one of the most important law courts in London, summoned all the inhabitants of the City 'to unite under the direction of sheriffs for the defence of their property' and of order. The 'London Military Association', a voluntary organization, assembled at six in the morning and mobilized its members to resist fresh onslaughts on private property or public buildings. The rioters who tried to attack the Bank of England once more were driven off. Meanwhile, however, other fires were started during the morning of June 8th, particularly in Southwark and other London suburbs, while on the other hand the voluntary police force set up by the Military Association arrested in the street a number of individuals who were extorting money from passers-by, ostensibly in aid of the movement for the repeal of the Saville Law. Nevertheless during the morning of June 8th a change could be felt in the atmosphere, as opposition to the rioters, from the great majority of Londoners, began to take an organized form. Resistance groups were set up in different districts. Finally the Government itself took action, and on Friday morning, June 9th, Lord George Gordon was arrested and taken to the Tower. By Saturday June 10th, the riots were over. What was the final balance-sheet? No complete list was ever drawn up of those who lost their lives by fire or in street fighting. But what we do know is the number and the profession of persons arrested and condemned. 450 were arrested; out of these 160 appeared either before a special court or before the Surrey assize-court. Out of these 160, 62 were condemned to death, and 25 were hanged, including four women and one sixteen-year-old boy. The others had their sentences commuted to varying terms of imprisonment. Twelve more received prison sentences of from one month to five years, and the rest of the accused were declared not guilty and released. Gordon himself was accused of high treason and, being a Lord, was summoned before the King's Bench on February 5th, 1781. He was defended by Thomas Erskine, a barrister who was to win great fame during the revolutionary period for his defence of all the English liberals, those who were to be known, with questionable accuracy, as the English Jacobins. Apart from this, it was asserted that 210 people were killed by the police or by the soldiers, and that 75 died from injuries in hospital; 173 recovered from their injuries. The Government paid compensation to all those who had suffered losses, 110 persons receiving indemnity amounting to a total of £70,000; 32 of these were compensated for the total loss of their property. Thus at least 32 private houses had been completely destroyed, in addition to the total or partial destruction of public buildings such as the Old Bailey and Newgate prisons.

It is reckoned that the Treasury spent at least £30,000 on the rebuilding of these. The bare facts thus imply that these riots were far more violent than those we have so far studied, whether in America or in France, and even than those European disturbances which we shall subsequently study. Public opinion was taken by surprise and completely bewildered. The Left Wing Whig opposition declared that the Government had allowed the disturbances to develop so that when the time came they might bring in the army, impose martial law and assume a sort of dictatorial power. This opinion was shared by certain Frenchmen at the time, such as the bookseller Hardy. It is undeniable that the riots proved useful to Lord North's government, which was very shaky and, in consequence of the serious setbacks suffered during the American war, seemed about to fall. Its position was undoubtedly strengthened by the energy it displayed in repressing the riots, and it remained in power for two years longer. We should not conclude from this that it had any deliberate intention of provoking disturbances in order to repress them, display its strength and stay in power. In fact, if we study the list of houses destroyed or looted, we find that as many belonged to members of the Opposition as to members of the Government. Burke, for instance, was at this time a member of the Whig opposition; he remained a Whig until 1790. Saville, the sponsor of the Catholic Relief Act, was also a Whig, as were Rockingham and Dunning. Among Government supporters whose houses were attacked were the Archbishops of York and Canterbury, the Prime Minister, Lord North, and the First Lord of the Admiralty, Lord Sandwich. The accusations we have reported are thus unconvincing. It is inconceivable that a Government should provoke a riot whose first consequence was the destruction of its own members' homes, merely in order to prove its strength by repressing this riot. So Machiavellian a plot seems improbable. The Government moreover itself accused the extremist opposition, then known as 'radical'; the radicals formed the extreme left wing of the Whigs. In particular, it indicted Wilkes, whose famous battle for the liberty of the Press, ten years earlier, had called forth huge and violent demonstrations at the time. And yet, during the Gordon riots, Wilkes had led the volunteers who undertook to put down the rising. This indictment of the radicals thus seems as unfounded as the rumours current in London and Paris about the Government's own responsibility. The story was also put about that French and American agents had secretly made their way into England and bribed the rioters; this is a familiar charge, and during the French Revolution we shall find 'the agents of Pitt and Coburg' being continually blamed for provoking discontent in France. The French Catholics have also been blamed; this again is a familiar charge. We must not forget that during the Seven Years' War, in 1760–61, in the Toulouse region, although Catholics and Protestants had been at peace for some thirty years, there was a revival of anti-Protestant activity as a result of the war between France and the Protestant powers, England and Prussia. A notable feature of this persecution was the condemnation at Toulouse of the Grenier brothers, Pastor Rochette, and Calas.[1] The English anti-Catholic movement of 1780 was the result of the war being waged by Great Britain against the Catholic powers, France and Spain, and thus offers a parallel to the earlier anti-Protestant movement in France. We must not conclude therefrom that the English Catholics were encouraged by French agents, any more than we can assume that the Protestants of the Languedoc were influenced by British or Prussian agents. The responsibility of Lord George Gordon is unquestionable. There is no doubt that the troubles started with the formation of the Protestant Association and his appointment as its President. But their scale was unexpected; and the King's Bench, in acquitting Gordon, recognized that he was not solely responsible for them. The rioters soon got beyond his control. When he appealed to English Protestants to sign a petition to be presented to the House of Commons, he certainly did not intend to burn down fifty houses and cause the death of five or six hundred people. Again, and for the same reason, the King's Bench forbore to prosecute Lord Fisher, the General Secretary of the Association, recognizing that the scale of the demonstrations went far beyond the intentions of the two leaders. Thus none of the existing explanations of the Gordon riots will stand up to analysis, and in order to discover the underlying causes of these riots, we need to

[1] D. Bien, *The Calas Affair*, Princeton, 1962.

study the social origins of the demonstrators; unfortunately we have no information about those people who were killed or injured, which would have been welcome. Our analysis can only take into account those who appeared in court, because their civil status and professions are known. And even so, whereas 162 persons were tried, we know the professions of only 110 of them. But these include one pharmacist, twenty-two small shopkeepers or independent craftsmen, one hangman, four soldiers and six sailors. Then we find 76 wage-earners or workmen, forming 70% of the total; amongst them 36 journeymen or apprentices, twenty wage-earning women and thirteen domestic servants. There are no unemployed persons, or practically none. Most of these wage-earners lived in furnished lodgings; they did not belong to the poorest class of worker. The proletariat—and in any case the word means little in the eighteenth century—is really not represented among those brought to trial. This analysis of the social origins of the rioters allows us to define our hypotheses about the underlying cause of the disturbances. Walpole, in the letters quoted above, points out that the fire-raisers attacked chiefly prisons and the houses of the rich, and concludes that their basic motives were not religious ones. He writes: 'The Pope need not be alarmed: the rioters thought much more of plundering those of their own communion, than his holiness's flock.' In other words, the demonstrators' hostility was directed against wealthy Anglicans rather than against Catholics. Certain historians have concluded that the riots began by having a purely religious motivation, until June 6th, but that from then onwards they assumed the very different character of social insurrection. It was from that date that the demonstrators began to attack the homes of the rich and even, as we have seen, the Bank of England. One curious point is that less than half the victims were of the Catholic persuasion. In one parish, St Andrew's, out of 26 houses attacked only 5 belonged to Catholics. But it seems hardly likely that a movement which was at first directed against the Catholic Church should suddenly, and for no clear reason, become anti-capitalist, directed against the rich. In any case, a statistical survey of the number of houses attacked in each district shows this to be in inverse ratio to the number of Catholics living there. The higher the Catholic population, the fewer houses were attacked. For instance, in the parish that contained most Catholics (1,581), that of St George in the

East, only two houses were attacked; in that of St John (1,364 Catholics), not a single house; seven houses in that of St Giles in the Fields (1,223 Catholics); in Piccadilly (987 Catholics) two houses; and a single one in St George's (860 Catholics). On the other hand, twenty-six houses were attacked in St Andrew's parish, where there were only 443 Catholics; eight in St Luke's (188 Catholics), three in St Leonard's (536 Catholics). The number of houses attacked is thus clearly unrelated to the number of Catholics in the district, but it is just as certainly related to the wealth of the inhabitants. The rioters' main targets were the homes of rich noblemen, prominent tradespeople or manufacturers. Out of the 136 people who were granted compensation for the total or partial loss of property during the riots, only four were wage-earners and 132 'independent workers', who might be described as capitalists. Thus, among the underlying causes of the Gordon riots, we must no doubt include the anti-Catholic feeling which was traditional in England and had been revived by the war against two Catholic powers, France and Spain, as well as by the Saville Law and the few concessions made to the Irish Catholics. There was also anti-Irish feeling, which had always been keen in England and was intensified by the fact that most of the Catholics living in London were Irishmen. But these feelings, which were certainly real, should not disguise from us the existence of other far deeper causes, and of a whole social background. The wish to settle accounts with the wealthy, to seize this opportunity of revenge on London's high and mighty, is shown by the attacks on the Bank of England and the toll-gates of Blackfriars Bridge. One rioter, to whom the judge pointed out that the owner of the house he had been attacking was a Protestant, made this characteristic reply: 'Protestant or not, nobody needs more than ten thousand pounds a year.' The Gordon riots were thus far more than anti-Catholic or anti-Parliamentary risings, they were a violent and almost spontaneous manifestation of that hostility between those who have little (not those who have nothing) and those who have plenty. The attack on the jails was the expression of a wish for social justice; that on the debtors' prison, in particular, can only be explained as a desire to set free those who were victims of their creditors, in other words of the rich, of the capitalists. True, men demonstrated in favour of the Protestant religion, but even more in favour of the poor and against the rich. Moreover by June 6th the Government had become aware of the danger of this demonstration, which was assuming a revolutionary tone. They were afraid lest it should spread to the countryside, where many small farmers had been dispossessed of their lands and reduced to the status of labourers. A general uprising of these labourers against the big landed proprietors might have turned into a 'peasants' revolt' more terrible, no doubt, than the *grande peur* in France nine years later. The Government therefore favoured the rapid formation of bourgeois militias responsible for keeping guard over the capital and the surrounding countryside. Peace was soon restored, moreover, showing that the hostility between rich and poor had failed to develop. It was a spontaneous movement with no ideological basis, unlike what was to occur in other countries, particularly in France. The London rising, which at first enjoyed the support of the bourgeoisie, so long as it had a religious content, was quickly dropped by these middle class citizens as soon as it threatened their property. Hence the difference in character between the riots of Wednesday, June 6th, and those of the following day. Overnight, the London bourgeoisie had realized that the movement which Gordon had instigated threatened them far more than it threatened the Catholic church. And this accounts for the sudden drop in tension, the swift cessation of a movement which had been on a larger scale, more important and more violent than all other revolutionary risings of the time, in the various countries affected by the Revolution. The *milice bourgeoise* or citizens' militia created during these disturbances was rapidly disbanded, under pressure from the army, which apprehended rivalry from this sort of national guard. We shall notice a similar attitude in Holland and in France during the following years.

Londoners were subjected to an emergency tax to enable the Government to pay compensation to the victims. By 1783 all indemnities had been paid; the same year witnessed the end of the American war and the recognition of the United States by Great Britain.

It is time to sum up: in spite of their pretext—a petition against a law favourable to the Catholics—these riots display features which are common to most of the risings of the end of the eighteenth century, a hostility of the poor towards the rich, an urgent desire for greater social justice. If they did not result in any change in England's political regime, nor even in the fall of the Tory

Government, it was due to the sudden change of heart of the London middle class, who, having sympathized with the rioters and then connived at their activities, turned against them when they realized that their property was in jeopardy. It is due, too, to the strange character of the leader of the revolt, Lord George Gordon. He was neither a demagogue nor a profound political thinker, but an unreliable eccentric; he was later to become a supporter of the French Revolution, and to be imprisoned for his opinions. He died in 1793, having become a convert to Judaism while in prison.

5. Revolt in Geneva (1782)

The social and economic origins of the Genevan rebellion of 1782 are far easier to discern than those of the Gordon riots, although it has not been as minutely studied as the latter or as the *guerre des farines*.[1] In Geneva in the eighteenth century the population was divided into four quite distinct groups: the patricians, who alone sat on the Councils that governed the Republic; the *bourgeois* or 'representatives', who enjoyed the right of citizenship and formed part of the General Council, but did not sit on Governmental councils; the 'natives', descendants of the émigrés who had come to Geneva within the past two hundred years, and the 'inhabitants' or foreigners. The two latter categories included the poorer sections of the community, who had no political rights. According to most scholars, Rousseau's *Contrat Social* had been written with the unavowed intention of criticizing this state of affairs; in any case its publication in 1762 provoked unrest, followed in 1765 by a rising of the 'natives' against the patricians. The *bourgeois* sided with the patricians, and after three years of struggle the 'natives' obtained only the minimum of concessions, through the compromise of March 9th, 1768: each year five families of 'natives' were to be promoted into the bourgeoisie. The conflict subsided, but was not settled. The economic difficulties of the years 1770–1790, common to all the West, revived it. The *bourgeois*, affected by the slump, deserted the patrician cause. At the General Council they decided, through the 'beneficent edict' of February 10th, 1781,

[1] On the disturbances in Geneva, see E. Chapuisat, *La Prise d'Armes de 1782 à Genève*, Geneva, 1932; and Patrick O'Mara, *Geneva in the Eighteenth Century: A socio-economic study of the Bourgeois City during its Golden Age*, University of California thesis, 1956. A copy of the typescript is in the Bibliothèque de Genève.

that the 'natives' should be granted equality of civil status and incorporated into the bourgeoisie, from the third generation. But the Syndics—the patricians who ruled the Republic—refused to implement the edict, and the Attorney-General Du Roveray, who had supported it, was exiled. The conflict between *bourgeois* and 'natives' on the one hand, and patricians on the other, became bitterer. On April 7th, 1782, the First Syndic of Geneva announced that the principal council of the Republican Government, that of the 'two hundred', would henceforward cease to recognize the decisions of the General Council and would not carry out the 'beneficent edict' because it had been imposed by force.

It was this decision that provoked revolution.

Next day, Monday, April 8th, the leaders of the 'natives' met at the house of the lawyer Grenus. They included, in particular, Marat (brother of the future Friend of the People), Flournoy, Chauvet, Du Roveray and Clavière (later, in 1792, Minister of Finance in France). They decided to take action. The 'natives' assembled in the streets, armed, and with considerable encouragement from the *bourgeois*. That evening bonfires were lit, but, in the Cornavin district, a clash occurred between the military and the rioters. A captain and a syndic were wounded, while the 'natives' suffered heavier casualties: fifteen injured, one fatally. Then the 'natives' made an armed attack on the Hôtel de Ville, where some fifteen patrician Councillors were surrounded and taken hostage. Other patricians were put under house arrest, under surveillance by armed 'natives'.

Next day, Tuesday, April 9th, the revolutionaries were masters of the city. They reorganized the Government Councils so as to exclude their opponents, and established a militia of armed 'natives'. In forty-eight hours, and with relatively small losses, an economically under-privileged section of the population had seized power, which it was to share henceforward with the bourgeoisie. The patricians, who were only a small minority, could not hope, unaided, to regain control of the State. They therefore had recourse to a strategy which was to be repeated during all subsequent revolutions: the appeal to foreign aid. A certain number of patricians, who had escaped arrest during the night of April 8th–9th, hurriedly sought help from Geneva's traditional allies, Berne, Zürich, France, and Piedmont-Sardinia.

The conflict between 'natives' and patricians thus moved on to the international plane. Its revolutionary aspect alarmed the powers, great and small. Frederick II, the 'philosopher-king', expressed his fear of the Genevan uprising. The patricians of Berne and Zürich had no sympathy for the 'natives' of Geneva, and decided 'not to recognize a government set up by an armed faction'. At Versailles the French Government, which was helping the no less revolutionary American insurgents, hesitated. But the French representative in Geneva, Castelnau, left the city as soon as revolution had triumphed there, returned to Versailles, spread alarm there and appealed for armed intervention in favour of the patricians. Vergennes, the French Foreign Minister, who had intervened in America not for the sake of upholding a revolution but in order to weaken England, was very ready to yield to persuasion. He had already written to the King of Sardinia's Minister at Versailles, on January 6th, 1782, that the Genevans were dangerous in so far as they drew inspiration from Rousseau's theory that 'sovereignty lies with the people, who alone can give it or take it away.' The attitude of the Sardinian Government was less clear-cut. Their Minister wrote: 'It is not in our interest to allow a strictly aristocratic government, or one enjoying supreme power, to be set up in Geneva.' He added, however: 'The government which we must eliminate is that of an unrestrained and tumultuous democracy.' The King of Sardinia was afraid lest Geneva, which bordered on his own province of Savoy, should fall completely under the sway of France. But he was equally apprehensive of the democratic contagion affecting his States. These conflicting aims, together with the slow pace of communications, account for the six weeks' delay before the final formation of the coalition. A treaty between France and Sardinia was signed on June 6th; France was to send 6,000 men and Sardinia 4,000 against the Genevan revolutionaries. The cantons of Berne and Zürich, for their part, promised to send a first instalment of 2,000 men, with 4,000 more as reinforcements.

Meanwhile the Genevan democrats, aware of these hostile intentions, were preparing to defend their city and their revolution. Volunteers hurried to repair the ramparts, which had been restored in 1720 according to Vauban's plans but had been badly kept up since then. On Sunday April 28th, more than 500 people were working at the fortifications. The revolutionaries' faith in the justice of their cause was fostered and strengthened by many clubs, which had been set up on the English or American pattern, in various districts: there was the *cercle de l'Egalité* with Clavière and Du Roveray, that of *La Cloche*, that of the *Bons Ragoûts*, etc. The British Government, anxious to prevent France from achieving further success, offered to mediate, but in vain. On May 13th the canton of Berne sent an ultimatum to the Genevans: they must immediately lay off the 213 Bernese serving in the tiny Genevan army of 618 men, release the hostages, and keep the gates of the city permanently open. The ultimatum was rejected. The Genevans hurriedly completed their preparations. A *Comité de Sûreté* was formed to direct the resistance. It proclaimed that the Genevans were determined to 'live and die free'. It called all able-bodied men to arms and ordered the arrest or surveillance of those patricians who were still at liberty, notably the celebrated de Saussure.

By June 28th, French and Sardinian troops stood before the walls of Geneva. Their generals, Jaucourt and La Marmora, called on the citizens to release the patricians and banish twenty-one revolutionary leaders (including Grenus, Clavière, Francis d'Ivernois and Du Roveray), failing which the city would be taken by storm.

The General Council met and decided that in spite of the work done on the fortifications the city would be unable to resist. The hostages were set free and the revolutionary leaders went into exile. On July 2nd the city was occupied by French, Sardinian and Bernese troops. It is ironical to note that among the French regiments taking part in the repression there was one which had just been helping the American insurgents to win their freedom! In France, Madame Roland exclaimed: 'Virtue and liberty find refuge only in the hearts of a handful of honourable men, a fig for the rest and for all the thrones in the world!'

On November 4th, 1782, an 'edict of pacification', nicknamed 'the black code' by Genevan democrats, not only restored the old regime but made it more oppressive by reducing the powers of the General Council and increasing those of the Council of Two Hundred. Clubs and discussion groups were shut down, the militia suppressed, the carrying of firearms forbidden, and the Republican army was henceforward always to be under the command of a foreign colonel. Thus, for the first time in the history

August 29th, 1788. Burning of the guard-house on the Pont Neuf

Bibl. Nat., Print Room, Vinck Collection, 1354

December 27th, 1788. Double representation granted
to the Third Estate

Bibl. Nat., Print Room

Riot at Rennes, on the Place du Parlement de Bretagne,
January 27th, 1789

Rennes Museum

of late eighteenth-century revolutionary movements, a victorious popular rising was suppressed by foreign intervention. It was a dangerous precedent, of which all Europe took note as Genevan exiles, settling in many countries, described in books or articles the triumph and fall of their city's democratic movement.

6. The disturbances in Holland (1783–1787)

The democratic uprising in Geneva had scarcely ended, with the triumph of reaction, when a revolutionary movement characterized by urban riots developed in the United Provinces of the Netherlands. Here again we have a conflict between social groups and a demand for a more liberal policy, but things are somewhat more complex than in America or in Geneva. The basic causes for the uprising are to be found in the policy of the stadthouder—practically a sovereign—William V of Orange, and the influence of the American revolution.

The stadthouder, in theory the elected head of the United Provinces, had in fact for the past 150 years been chosen from the same family, and William V would have liked to be crowned king. He was encouraged in this ambition by his family, his mother, an English princess, and his wife, a Prussian princess. But he longed for more than a mere title. He wished to strengthen the powers of the throne and lessen those of the estates-general and the provincial government, as well as of the municipal authorities. He had shown his hostility towards enlightenment by banning Rousseau's *Contrat Social* in 1762.

The stadthouder's ambitions were resisted by the 'regents', members of the estates-general and municipal corporations who sought to maintain the traditional organization that guaranteed their powers, and by the 'patriots', who came from the ranks of the liberal nobility and bourgeoisie; these 'patriots' furthermore were anxious to provide a more democratic organization for provinces and cities by depriving the 'regents' of their monopoly of power. It must be observed, however, that the stadthouder enjoyed the support of the old-established nobility, the patricians of the hinterland, the Jewish population whose traditional protector he was, and the proletariat of the seaboard regions, Holland and Zeeland.[1]

[1] See de Peyster, *Les Troubles de Hollande à la veille de la Révolution française*, Paris, 1905; P. Geyl, *De Patriottenbeweging*, Amsterdam, 1947.

The patriots, being more zealous and enthusiastic, formed the active wing of the Revolution. Their leader was Van der Capellen tot de Pol, who had in 1782 issued a call to arms to the Dutch nation.[1] The patriots included such men as Van der Kemp, Luzac, Paulus, Vreede, Daverhoult, Daendels, Schimmelpenninck, who were all to play an important part in the revolutionary movement during the next twenty years. They had been inspired by the American example (many Dutchmen still had relatives among the inhabitants of New York, formerly New Amsterdam). But here again the economic crisis played a significant role. The war between the United Provinces and England dealt a serious blow to Dutch trade and interrupted business relations with London. Now these were important, for 40% of the British debt was in Dutch hands. Many Dutch ships were captured by British cruisers. Holland, the most 'patriotic' of the Provinces, was also the one where trade was keenest. After three years of crisis and political debate, the Provincial Government of Holland withdrew from William V his title of stadthouder and Captain-General of Holland; and the era of violence began.

At Utrecht, on December 19th, 1785, the city bourgeois held a vast protest meeting because the stadthouder had refused to ratify a regulation 'democratizing' the election of Regents. This demonstration failed to move William V. However, another held on March 20th, 1786, at which the bourgeois were armed and organized in militias, forced him to yield. But the old Regents refused to admit to their Council those new members who had been elected from among the patriots. The latter rose, put the city in a state of siege, dug trenches, cut down trees and finally won the day.

Nine months later, similar risings took place in Amsterdam and at Zwolle, in the province of Over-Yssel. In Zeeland opinions were more divided. The stadthouder had staunch support from the numerous fishermen, who were mostly traditional upholders of the House of Orange. Fierce rioting broke out, notably at Goes. Both parties sought foreign aid. The Orangists were supported by Prussia and above all by England. The British ambassador, Harris, the future Lord Malmesbury, lavished subsidies on the stadthouder's partisans.[2] Louis XVI's representative at The Hague,

---

[1] Translated into French by the author in *La Pensée révolutionnaire*, Paris, 1964, pp. 51–59.

[2] A. Cobban, *Ambassadors and secret agents*, London, 1954.

Rayneval, assisted the patriots but, owing to the French financial crisis, the funds at his disposal were scanty. Furthermore, now that the American war was over the French Government was reluctant to support rebels, and had already showed by its intervention in Geneva in 1782 that it was ready to oppose them if the occasion arose.

It was in these circumstances that the trial of strength between the patriots and the stadthouder began, in May 1787. William V refused to recognize the new Regents' Councils of Amsterdam and Rotterdam, composed solely of patriots to the exclusion of the representatives of the former oligarchy. He also declared that he would not accept his dismissal as Commander of the Hague and Captain-General of Holland.

At the news of the manifesto in which William V announced these decisions, a general uprising took place in Amsterdam, the most populous city in the United Provinces. The homes of Orangists were attacked and plundered. On May 28th one of the Orangists was killed and thrown into the canal. Next day their headquarters was destroyed. Orangist sailors met patriots in a pitched battle on the Ij bridge, and there were several deaths. On May 30th the patriots sacked the district inhabited by fishermen and sailors, who were reputed to be Orangists, and took forty of them prisoner. Orangist families left Amsterdam hurriedly. At Utrecht, the militia commanded by Daverhoult (who was subsequently elected deputy in France and even became President of the *Assemblée Législative*) repulsed the regular troops dispatched by the stadthouder. The patriots seemed to be winning the day.

But the stadthouder, who had left his residence in The Hague, followed the example of the Genevan patricians and summoned foreigners to his aid. He asked England and Prussia to reinstate him in his former powers. The King of Prussia sent an army into the United Provinces by way of its eastern frontiers, while the British fleet cruised along its coasts. The patriots hoped that France would come to their aid: but the French Government was paralysed by the financial crisis, and was moreover increasingly reluctant to support revolutionaries, who constituted an equal threat to itself. France therefore refused all support. The bourgeois militia, being badly trained, collapsed before the Prussian army. The patriots fled. Over 40,000 of them crossed the frontier and made their way towards the Austrian Netherlands (now Belgium) and France.[1] Like the Genevan refugees, these Dutchmen brought with them into France a revolutionary spirit. They tended, however, to belong to a less privileged social class than the Genevans. Thus at Saint-Omer and Gravelines 1025 Dutch families received help at the end of February 1788. These included 15 'regents' or gentlefolk, 230 tradesmen and functionaries, who may be classed as bourgeois, but as against these we find 8 gardeners, 23 farm workers, 383 'masters' of various crafts (some of whom were probably bourgeois) and 619 artisans or workmen, totalling over 1,000 members of the working class. These statistics prove that the Dutch 'patriots' belonged, for the most part, to the middle or lower classes.

The Dutch revolution thus affected people belonging to the same social categories as the American rebels, the French bread-rioters, the insurgents of London and Geneva. The background of all these uprisings is the same: economic difficulties and demographic pressure. Sometimes their ideologies differed. In France, in 1775, there was no apparent political aim. In London, in 1780, the movement was directed against the Catholic Church and against the Parliament. But in America, in Geneva, in Holland, people were fighting for more liberty, for greater equality, for a more democratic regime; they demanded more social justice. We cannot disregard these struggles, nor the upheavals that took place between 1775 and 1789 in the great capitals of the Western world —Boston, London, Geneva, Amsterdam—if we wish to understand fully the basic causes and the significance of the Parisian rising on July 14th, 1789.

[1] This surprisingly large figure is quoted by several sources. See M. T. Colenbrander, *De Patriottentijd*, 3 vols. The Hague, 1897–1899; and de Peyster, *op. cit.*, pp. 332–338.

II

Social Inequalities in France at the End of the Eighteenth Century

We have dwelt at some length on the revolts that occurred in foreign capitals from 1775 onwards in order to show more clearly that the Parisian rising of July 14th, 1789 was no isolated incident. But to understand its causes more fully we require some knowledge, however superficial, of the social structure of France at the end of the eighteenth century.

At this period France was essentially a rural country. Out of its 26 million inhabitants less than 2 million lived in towns; thus 92% of the population was rural. Paris, the capital city, is generally reckoned to have had about 600,000 inhabitants, but no other town had more than 100,000, and in only four—Marseilles, Lyons, Bordeaux and Nantes—did the population exceed 60,000.

1. The social structure of rural France

Although the revolt of July 14th was an urban and indeed a specifically Parisian rising, it is indispensable to say a few words about the social structure of the country districts, for, as we have seen, rural riots preceded those in Paris, and the disturbances that spread through the countryside after July 14th and that were known as the *grande peur* completed the work of the Parisian revolution. How can one imagine, in any case, that in a country where 92% of the population were peasants a great social, economic and political revolution could have taken place without the participation of the rural masses?

During the past fifty years the social structure of rural France has been the object of a number of studies;[1] although there are noticeable differences between one region and another, we are now in a position to offer a valid picture of this structure.

In this brief review we must distinguish two elements. On the one hand, the legal system under which the peasants lived; on the other, the division of wealth, that is to say, in fact, of land ownership.

The legal system in France at the end of the eighteenth century was the feudal system; this is particularly noticeable in rural areas. True, this definition is often contested by historians who are medieval specialists, since eighteenth-century feudalism is very different from the 'classic' feudalism of the thirteenth century. None the less people at the time did describe as feudal the system under which they were governed; the decrees of August 4th (1789) abolished 'the feudal regime', and the chief committee set up by the Constituent Assembly to carry out these decrees assumed the title of *Comité des droits féodaux* (committee on feudal rights).

What did this feudal regime consist of, and how far was it responsible for social inequalities? The soil of France was divided, with a few exceptions, into a large number of fiefs. Each fief belonged to one or several lords. Often a village would coincide with a fief and be governed by a lord. It generally happened, from the Middle Ages onward, that the lord divided his fief into two parts, one of which, his *réserve*, he exploited directly, the other over which he exercised the right of *eminent domain* and left to his vassals to exploit, on condition of paying seignorial dues, the number and total amount of which varied widely from one fief to another. The peasant, legally speaking, was merely a tenant, but since he had exploited his land from time immemorial, selling and

---

[1] See, in particular: G. Lefebvre, *Les paysans du Nord pendant la Révolution française*, Paris, 1924, 2nd edition, Bari, 1959; Id., 'Les Paysans et la Révolution française' (*A.H.R.F.* 1933, pp. 97–128); M. Chamboux, *La Répartition de la propriété foncière et de l'exploitation dans la Creuse à la fin de l'Ancien Régime*, Paris, 1955; J. Dupaquier, *La Propriété et l'exploitation foncière dans le Gâtinais septentrional*, Paris, 1956; A. Soboul, *Les Campagnes montpelliéraines à la fin de l'Ancien Régime*, Paris, 1958; R. Laurent, *Les Vignerons de la Côte d'Or au XIXe siècle*, Paris, 1958; P. Bois, *Les Paysans de l'Ouest*, Paris, 1960; P. Goubert, *Beauvais et le Beauvaisis de 1600 à 1730*, Paris, 1961; P. de Saint-Jacob, *Les Paysans de la Bourgogne du Nord au dernier siècle de l'Ancien Régime*, Paris, 1961; P. Rascol, *Les Paysans de l'Albigeois à la fin de l'Ancien Régime*, Aurillac, 1961; Plaisse, *La Baronnie du Neubourg*, Paris, 1962.

buying or handing it down as he chose (unless he were a serf, or subject to *mainmorte*) he considered it as his own property. There were by now in France only some million and a half '*mainmortables*', scattered over Franche-Comté, Berry and the Bourbonnais. Since 1770 a powerful current of opinion had condemned serfdom, and in 1779 Louis XVI abolished *mainmorte* throughout the royal domain. But it still persisted on various lords' estates, particularly those of the clergy, although it affected only a minority of the peasantry.

Whether serfs or not, all peasants were subject to the feudal regime and paid seignorial dues. These varied widely, as we have seen, from one manor to another, depending on their category. The lord was entitled to personal rights, monopolies and real dues. Personal rights undoubtedly provided the lord with certain advantages; the *corvée* (forced labour) owed him by the peasants ensured him a free supply of workers; but in France the *corvées* were of slight importance, and the lord's personal rights served chiefly to stress his superiority over his vassals. Thus he had a special seat in church, the right to put a weathercock on the tower of his chateau, and so forth. Monopolies, hunting rights, rights of jurisdiction, *banalités* (control over the communal mill or bakehouse), were transitional between the personal, or honorary, rights and the real dues. The latter have to be subdivided into several categories: annual dues, paid in cash or in kind, and casual dues. When paid in cash, the annual dues were generally not burdensome, because they had been fixed at some earlier period and, as a result of the devaluation of money, their value had continuously decreased. On the other hand the dues in kind, generally known as *champarts*, had lost none of their weight. The scale of the *champarts* varied greatly from one fief to another, as did that of the *cens* or money dues. As for the casual, or exceptional, dues, these were a heavy burden. They consisted generally of taxes on transfer of property, of *lods et ventes* payable in case of sale or transfer of the land through indirect inheritance.

Tithes were usually associated with feudal dues, although they did not, strictly speaking, form part of these. A tithe, or tenth, of every harvest went to subsidize the Church and the many institutions (hospitals, universities, colleges and schools) under its administration. Although they were oftener one-twelfth or one-fifteenth than one-tenth of the gross harvest, these tithes were a crushing burden. They were associated with the feudal regime, on the one hand because the considerable role played by the clergy in society seemed essentially to belong to that system, and on the other because many tithes had been bought back or 'enfeoffed' by laymen, often nobles, and simply added to the list of seignorial dues.

It might seem surprising that the French peasantry should suddenly, at the end of the eighteenth century, have displayed their resentment of the seignorial dues and the tithes which they had been paying for hundreds of years. But this outbreak of bitter feeling can easily be explained. Until the end of the seventeenth century, in addition to these dues the peasants only paid one tax to the State, the *taille*, from which nobility and clergy were exempt. But the increased expenses of the State, especially the need to meet the cost of the long wars of the late seventeenth and the eighteenth century, forced Louis XIV and Louis XV to impose fresh taxes, the *capitation* (poll-tax), the tenths and twentieths which laid a heavy burden on the peasantry. State taxes and seignorial dues seemed incompatible; since the State had now undertaken to run the principal public services, it seemed unnecessary to go on paying seignorial dues and tithes.

We must also take into account a phenomenon that historians call the 'feudal reaction'. From about 1750 onward, secular and ecclesiastical lords, who themselves had some difficulty in living on their incomes, as a result of the depreciation of money and the rise in prices, revised their *terriers* (charters), that is to say the lists of their seignorial rights and dues. The 'feudists', legal specialists entrusted with this operation, strove to discover rights fallen into abeyance, and to which the prescription would not yet apply; they assiduously sought to recover these rights, often going to law about them. The costs of these lawsuits ruined the *communes*; to cover them, they had to resort to heavy borrowings, the final weight of which fell on the peasantry. On the eve of the Revolution there was scarcely a *commune* in France that was not at law with its lord on the subject of seignorial rights. The 'feudal reaction' exasperated the peasants and led them to clamour loudly for 'the abolition of feudalism'.

Finally, we must not underestimate the influence of the Enlightenment. True, many peasants were illiterate, and among those who knew how to read very few were familiar with the ideas of Montesquieu, Voltaire and Rousseau. But their lawyers knew these. Moreover many middle-class men, members of *'sociétés de pensée'* (Masonic lodges, agricultural associations, provincial academies) were owners of real estate, had to pay seignorial dues and tithes and demanded their abolition, which had already been decreed in 1771 in the neighbouring kingdom of Piedmont-Sardinia. Thus, from 1770 onward, the rural masses in France were pervaded by a violent spirit of revolt against the 'feudal regime', and certain priests, noticing this spirit, unhesitatingly described it as 'republican'.[1]

Meanwhile the division of land, which was a matter of economics rather than of jurisdiction, proved a further source of discontent to the mass of the peasantry.

As regards the ownership of the soil (and here we shall consider tenure by *roturiers*, commoners, as real ownership) the land of France may be said to have consisted of three main categories: communal or manorial estates, those of the privileged classes (nobility and clergy), and those of commoners. The division of land between these three categories varied widely in different regions. In certain *communes*, the manorial property (particularly forests) or the communal property (forests and pastures) might be very extensive; in others, ecclesiastical property predominated. Everywhere, the nobility owned a considerable share of the land. To give an average for the whole of France would mean little. It seems likely that, in 1789, the nobility and the clergy owned 30 to 40% of the land. Generally speaking, the Church owned more land in the North than in the South. In certain Northern communes, more than half the land might belong to the Abbey; in certain Southern villages, Church property was infinitesimal.

What did not belong to the manor, the communes or the privileged classes was divided between the bourgeoisie and the peasants. It is still very hard, even today, to assess the share of bourgeois landowners, because it is hard to define a bourgeois. A landowner who lived in town and did not cultivate the land himself was obviously a bourgeois, but there was also a rural middle-class which, though living in the village (lawyers, tradesmen, the

[1] See two characteristic texts, published by the author in *A.H.R.F.* 1951, pp. 85–86, and 1956, pp. 299–300.

wealthier artisans), did not directly cultivate its own property. Finally, among the peasants themselves, the land was very unequally divided, a small number (two million perhaps) having properties of some size, at any rate large enough to live off, with their families, these being known as *laboureurs* or farmers, while the mass of the peasantry had only a cottage with a garden plot attached.

In order to define the rural regime, we must examine not only the way the land was owned but the way it was cultivated.

Throughout the whole of France, at the end of the eighteenth century, property was parcelled out to a considerable extent, which facilitated indirect exploitation. For in fact the Church, the nobility, the bourgeoisie and even certain rich peasants leased out their land, either to tenant-farmers (in the North) or to *métayers*, share-croppers (in the South). Thus many of these peasants who owned nothing but a cottage and a garden plot were tenant-farmers or share-croppers. None the less, at the end of the eighteenth century the majority of French peasants had not got enough land to live off. These landless peasants depended on their arms for their subsistence and hence were known as *brassiers*; they worked as farm labourers. The landlords, farmers or share-croppers, employed them at busy seasons, but in winter their situation was a precarious one, and they had to practise some subsidiary trade in order to live: spinning or weaving at home, small-scale carpentry or ironwork. When unfavourable weather conditions brought a bad harvest they would not be needed, and then came unemployment, with all its attendant distresses.

Now, from about 1770 onwards, two species of phenomena increased the hardship of the labourers' condition, and even that of small farmers and share-croppers, that is to say of the great majority of the French peasantry. On the one hand, demographic pressure: from 1730 onwards, the population of France, which hitherto had been relatively stable (a high deathrate making up for an invariably high birthrate) increased. In the countryside, from 1730 to 1789, it went up by 50 or 80% and sometimes even doubled. What was to be done with all these newcomers? 'The number of our children drives us to despair, we cannot feed or clothe them . . .' wrote the peasants of La Caune, in the *bailliage* of Châlons. Now, just when new jobs ought to have been created in rural areas in order to help the poorer peasants to live, conditions were becoming even harder for them.[1]

Landlords and big farmers tended to extend their estates, cultivating them more effectively so as to increase their yield. In 1789, the *cahiers de doléances*[2] of Northern France complain unceasingly about the formation of large farms by the merging of several small or middle-sized ones. Wouldbe farmers could find no land to lease, and its scarcity meant a considerable rise in rent and consequent shrinking of the farmers' income, while the increase in taxation and seignorial dues and the growing number of mouths to feed imposed even heavier burdens on them.

The *brassiers*, or labourers, had one resource left them in their destitution. They might own one or two head of cattle and put them to graze on common land, or even on the whole of the land after harvest, by virtue of the rights of free grazing. Now during the second half of the eighteenth century these rights were in process of disappearing in France. Under the influence of agronomists and physiocrats, and in order to increase the yield of the soil, the Government proceeded to divide up the common land, as had been done in England. In one province after another, in Béarn and in Lorraine for instance, partition was authorized and the enclosure of allotments permitted. When the common land was divided the lord took one-third for himself, by virtue of the *droit de triage*; the rest was shared out among the villagers, generally in proportion to their wealth. Thus the poor peasants received only a minimal share, which they were forced to sell, together with the cow or the goats that had grazed on the common land, and their destitution increased. The right of free grazing was threatened by the spread of enclosures, and its disappearance affected the poor peasants as disastrously as the partition of common land had done. Thus the number of rural unemployed rose sharply during the latter part of

[1] On demographic problems, see: M. Reinhard and A. Armengaud, *Histoire générale de la population mondiale*, Paris, 1961; Christiane Pinède-Toujas, 'La population du Quercy à la fin du XVIIIe siècle', in *Actes du LXXXIIe Congrès national des Sociétés savantes*, Bordeaux, 1957, pp. 51–103; E. Gautier and L. Henry, *La Population de Crulai, paroisse normande*, Paris, 1958; M. Reinhard, *Contributions à l'histoire démographique de la Révolution française*, Gap, 1962; P. Chaunu, *A travers la Normandie des XVIIe et XVIIIe siècles*, Caen, 1963; J. Godechot and S. Moncassin, *Démographie et subsistances en Languedoc au XVIIIe siècle*, Paris, 1965; P. Valmary, *Familles paysannes en Bas-Quercy au XVIIIe siècle*, Paris, 1965.

[2] Memorials or petitions of grievances.

the eighteenth century. Finding no work in their own parishes, they took to the forests, where some burned charcoal or reclaimed land clandestinely, others formed bands of vagrants, homeless wanderers, armed beggars who terrified the inhabitants of lonely farms and turned readily to banditry and looting. Other workless peasants made for the towns, where they swelled the population, particularly the floating section of it.

2. The social structure of French towns, and of Paris, at the end of the eighteenth century

The social structure of the population of French towns in the eighteenth century has received far less attention than that of rural areas.[1] These towns, Paris in particular, were often densely populated; the analysis of parish registers, fiscal documents and lawyers' minutes, making possible a census of the population and its distribution between various socio-economic categories, involves such long and tedious labours that it has discouraged research. On the other hand, scrutiny by districts yields only partial and unreliable results. M. Ernest Labrousse has devised a new method of investigation, which makes it possible to arrive quickly at a rough but adequate idea of the social structure of a town in the eighteenth century. A study of marriage contracts over a year or a number of years enables one, in fact, to classify the couples married according to their different social and professional categories. These couples provide an epitome of the social structure of the town. If the result obtained is to be statistically acceptable, it is essential to recover an adequate proportion of contracts, or summaries of them in the *régistres de l'insinuation*, the parish registers of the old regime. Now the proportion of contracts signed, or of those that have survived, varies widely in different towns. In the South of France, where marriage contracts followed the dowry system (whereby a wife retained ownership of her dowry), all marriages, even among the lowest order, involved a contract. The question of their survival is thus merely a matter of archives; when the legal files have been kept, the contracts can all be found; where the contracts are missing, the parish registers, if

---

[1] See for instance L. Fracard, *La Fin de l'Ancien Régime à Niort*, Paris, 1957; Daniel Ligou, *Montauban à la fin de l'Ancien Régime et aux débuts de la Révolution (1787–1794)*, Paris, 1958; G. Lefebvre, *Études orléanaises*, vol. I, Paris, 1962.

these have been preserved, serve the purpose. In the North of France, on the contrary, where other matrimonial systems were the rule, not every young couple signed a contract; generally the poorer ones avoided this costly and apparently useless formality. Thus we cannot obtain as accurate a social cross-section in the North as in the South, since the poorer classes escape our analysis.

This method of studying social structures has so far only been applied to a small number of towns.[1] Since in Toulouse a very large proportion of marriage contracts has been recovered (94% for 1785, or 345 contracts for a total of 367 marriages) we shall attempt a rapid analysis of the social structure of Toulouse at the close of the *ancien régime*. This will enable us to obtain some idea of the structure of society in a large French city on the eve of the Revolution, when its population numbered some 50 to 60 thousand.

An investigation of the marriage portions of the newly-wed of 1785 shows that the five couples belonging to the nobility, who represent only one sixty-fifth of that year's weddings, possessed altogether some 86,050 livres, that is to say one quarter of the total amount inscribed in the contracts for that year. It is thus immediately apparent that the feudal regime weighed heavily on the towns, in spite of the absence of seignorial dues and tithes. Among these young couples—and presumably the same holds good for the aggregate of society—one sixty-fifth of the urban population owned a quarter of the total wealth. In a study of the aggregate, the share of the privileged classes would undoubtedly be even greater, since it would include the property of the clergy.

The upper bourgeoisie, consisting of legal and merchant families, accounts for 42 contracts, an eighth of the total. But this eighth represents half the sum total of the marriage portions (167,560 livres). Thus the nobility and the upper bourgeoisie, which formed only a small minority of the population, enjoyed three-quarters of its wealth. The 290 other contracts, representing nine-tenths of the population, only add up to a quarter of the total wealth involved (62,549 livres). We see then that the socio-economic structure of Toulouse might be illustrated by a pyramid,

[1] Mlle Petit, 'Mariages et contrats de mariage à Agen, en 1785 et 1786', in *Annales du Midi*, 1960, pp. 215–229; A. Daumard and F. Furet, *Structures et relations sociales à Paris au XVIIIe siècle*, Paris, 1961; J. Godechot and S. Moncassin, 'Les structures sociales de Toulouse en 1749 et en 1785', in *A.H.R.F.*, 1965.

broad at the base and very narrow at the apex. Yet a closer study enables us to distinguish nuances within this whole. Among these 290 contracts, 205 were concluded by members of the lower middle-class or artisans, who represent two-thirds of the newly-wed, not entirely deprived of means since the total of their marriage portions amounts to 50,030 livres. On the other hand, 85 contracts signed by servants, agricultural labourers or unskilled workers shows a total of only 3,519 livres. And yet these 85 contracts form one quarter of the whole. We may therefore assume that a quarter of the population was very poor, and this assumption is confirmed by an enquiry ordered in 1790 by the Constituent Assembly's Commission on Mendicancy, which disclosed that a quarter of the population of Toulouse were paupers.[1] Thus the social structure of that city reveals a considerable contrast between an almost poverty-stricken mass and a small minority of very wealthy members of the privileged classes and the bourgeoisie.

A closer examination of this social classification shows, however, that the different social and professional classes were not so sharply divided as one might think. If certain tradesmen or master craftsmen enjoyed marriage portions of as much as 10,000 livres, two journeymen received dowries of the same order.

When we attempt to break down the population of Toulouse into its different social and professional categories, on the basis of the marriage contracts of 1785, we reach the following results: drapers and clothiers form 12% of the total,[2] building trades 10%, servants 10%, small wage-earners and day-labourers 10%, trades connected with foodstuffs 7%, small Government functionaries 6%, then lawyers, professions connected with transport, doctors and apothecaries, jewellers and goldsmiths.

A study of the parents' professions shows that we are not dealing with a rigid society composed of closed castes. Except in the aristocracy, where plebeian origin is rare, although perhaps concealed, we observe that among the men who married in 1785 about one-third had fathers of different professions from their own, and usually of an economically inferior social and professional group. Thus 32% of the members of the upper bourgeoisie were

[1] C. Bloch and Tuétey, *Les Procès-verbaux et rapports du comité de mendicité de la Constituante (1790–1791)*, Paris, 1911.

[2] G. Marinière, 'Les marchands d'étoffe de Toulouse à la fin du XVIIIe siècle', in *Annales du Midi*, 1958, pp. 251–308.

the sons of small tradesmen, or even master-barbers, market-gardeners or masons. In the case of journeymen, one out of two practised a different trade from his father. As for domestic servants, two-thirds of them were sons of peasants.

The social group from which they took their wives is also characteristic. 80% of the nobility married into the nobility, 63% of the bourgeoisie married girls of the same class. But 35% of the tradesmen married the daughters of artisans and peasants. Only 6% of the sons of petty bourgeois parents married above them, but in 25% of cases their wives came from a lower economic class. A few journeymen, a few small craftsmen married middle-class girls. One-third of domestic servants married into their own class.

We may conclude by saying that there was a vast gulf between the tiny number of those who were privileged by rank and fortune, and the mass of the population. But this gulf was not impassable. There was a slow but steady upward trend in society; too slow, probably, at the close of the eighteenth century, to alleviate the growing social tensions of urban life.

In another respect, the study of the social structure of Toulouse shows how closely the population of the city was still linked to that of the neighbouring countryside. An examination shows that in Toulouse, as in most other French towns in the eighteenth century, deaths exceeded births. The town could only increase or maintain its population by the influx of immigrants from the countryside. And in fact, the recorded birth-places of almost all domestic servants, of many small wage-earners, journeymen and even master-craftsmen, were in the villages of the Languedoc.

It is possible to gain a rough idea of the social structure of Paris, thanks to the researches undertaken by Mlle Daumard and M. Furet for the year 1749.[1] True, the date is somewhat remote from the revolutionary period; forty years earlier than the fall of the Bastille. But an analogous enquiry about Toulouse, for the same year,[2] shows that there was relatively little variation in the social structure between the two dates: marriage portions, and hence, presumably, fortunes, had increased by and large, but the differences between the social groups were of the same order.

However, the chief reason why the Parisian investigation is less informative than that which was carried out in Toulouse is that

[1] A. Daumard and F. Furet, *op. cit.*
[2] J. Godechot and S. Moncassin, *op. cit.*

many young couples in Paris signed no contract. In fact, for the year 1749, only 2,597 contracts have been found for a total of 4,263 marriages: 60%. A study of these immediately shows us that it was the poorer couples that signed no contract. Thus this investigation, unlike that made in Toulouse, does not allow us to study a cross-section of the whole population.

What strikes one on analysing the social structure of the population of Paris is, primarily, the presence of certain very wealthy families. Whereas in Toulouse no marriage portion exceeded 100,000 livres, in Paris 2% of marriage settlements mention still higher figures, some even reaching a million livres. Great fortunes, which were scarce in Toulouse, were plentiful in Paris. Thus, in Toulouse only 10% of marriage settlements mention sums higher than 5,000 livres, as opposed to 31% in Paris. But we must not forget that we do not know the doubtless meagre fortune of 40% of the newly married couples, which would bring the proportion of well-to-do people down to about 20% of the total population of Paris. 44% of the settlements refer to dowries of between 1,000 and 5,000 livres, the remaining couples owning less than a thousand each.

Thus in Paris we find a contrast between a fairly large number of very rich families and a great mass of poor ones, with some moderately well-off people in between. How do the various social classes and professional groups fit in with this economic classification? The largest fortunes belong exclusively to the nobility, who have all the marriage portions exceeding 200,000 livres. But among those owning between 50 and 200 thousand we find nobles, merchants, 'officers' both civil and military, lawyers, doctors. Only fifty-six commoners (out of 4,263 couples) are included in this category: 19 'officers', 11 persons of private means, 8 lawyers, 7 'masters' or tradesmen, 5 wholesale merchants, 3 army officers, 1 doctor, 1 Government functionary, 1 artisan.

Settlements of between 2,000 and 50,000 livres involve chiefly tradesmen, wholesale and retail, or journeymen; few nobles. Below 2,000 livres we find predominantly artisans, domestic servants or casual labourers (*gagne-deniers*). But, it must be stressed, 40% of the couples marrying in Paris made no contract, and among these we should doubtless find the vast majority of the journeymen, apprentices, unskilled labourers and domestic servants. Thus the contrast is even more violent than in provincial towns between

May 4th, 1789. Ceremonial dress of the Deputies of the three Orders at the Estates General

Bibl. Nat., Print Room, Vinck Collection, 1449

May 5th, 1789. Procession of the Estates General

Bibl. Nat., Print Room, Vinck Collection, 1426

an extremely rich minority, composed chiefly of nobles, and the impoverished mass of the people.

The marriage contracts, furthermore, enable us to form some idea of the proportion of the population belonging to the various professions. Domestic servants form the largest section (16%), then come textile workers (15%), next day-labourers, casual labourers and unskilled workers (13·6%), those employed in food trades (11%), 'idle persons' (11%—a significantly large figure in the capital city), building workers (10%), persons in Government service (8·4%), jewellers and goldsmiths (4%), professions connected with the arts and culture (3%) or with transport (2%) or the law (1·7%), doctors and apothecaries (1·5%). If we knew the professions of those who signed no contract, undoubtedly the proportions of 'idle persons', casual labourers and domestic servants would be far higher. Thus the population of Paris included, at the close of the eighteenth century, a great number of inhabitants who might be expected to take part in uprisings.

The study of the professions of the parents of these newly married couples enables us to see, in the case of Paris as in that of Toulouse, how far society was 'open' or, on the contrary, made up of exclusive castes. The group of civilian 'officers' belonging to the nobility, consisting chiefly of members of the Supreme Courts, had strong hereditary bonds, since 86% of the fathers practised the same profession as their sons. Of Army officers who were noblemen, only 60% were practising their father's profession, but 28% were sons of noblemen of no profession, and only 12% sons of civilian 'officers' (whether noble or not). Thus the nobility tended to form a caste. They intermarried for the most part, although not exclusively. On the other hand, the other socio-professional groups were to a large extent open. For instance only 35% of civilian 'officers' who were commoners belonged to their father's profession, 13% being sons of tradesmen and 22% sons of master craftsmen. Those in the King's service were in only 21% of cases sons of Government employees like themselves. On the other hand in the tradesmen's group and in that of master-craftsmen a hereditary profession was far more common (50% and 62% respectively). The general trend was towards climbing upward in the social scale. Domestic servants, in 44% of cases, and journeymen in 10% of cases, were sons of agricultural labourers; members of the liberal professions were descended from master-craftsmen and tradesmen (28%), from civilian 'officers' (10%) and from bourgeois without other qualifications (10%). Rather more than a third (36%) of these members were following in their father's footsteps. Marriages increased this upward trend in the social scale. Nineteen per cent of domestic servants and 13% of casual labourers married the daughters of master-craftsmen or trades-men, 15% of Government employees married the daughters of civilian 'officers', 32% of journeymen married the daughters of masters. Only the nobility formed a relatively closed group (yet 37% of nobles of no profession married the daughters of bourgeois).

The links between town and country, which we have mentioned in the case of Toulouse, were equally close in Paris. 87% of Parisian servants were born in the provinces, as were 74% of casual labourers, 71% of wholesale tradesmen, 69% of bourgeois and 76% of army officers of noble birth. The proportion of country-born persons was low only in the case of master-craftsmen or tradesmen (36%), or commoners of no profession (25%) and of nobles of no profession (35%). Thus provincial happenings must have had profound repercussions in the minds of Parisians.

A study of those people who were called as witnesses to marriage contracts allows us to complete our knowledge of the relations between various socio-professional groups. It is noticeable that only among the nobility and in the category of master-craftsmen and tradesmen were witnesses chosen from within the group itself. Bourgeois often served as witnesses to the marriages of servants, casual labourers and artisans. We must add, finally, that the population of France at the end of the eighteenth century, in the towns as well as in the country, was a young population, for the birth rate was very high, while the death rate had not yet begun to drop. Almost half the population of France was under twenty years of age in 1789.

The following points emerge as significant from this analysis: first, the great wealth of the nobility—for, whatever may be argued, it was the nobility which, by virtue of its riches and its privileges, towered above all other classes. But also the wealth of a section of the bourgeoisie. In spite of the relatively small number of middle-class families, it would seem that in France the bour-geoisie was proportionately more numerous than in any other Western country except England. It had acquired considerable wealth during the eighteenth century, and played a large part in the rise of industry and commerce: France's foreign trade had increased from 215 million livres in 1716 to 725 million in 1776, and to 1753 million in 1787. These bourgeois acquired education at the same time as wealth, witness the numerous schools that we find towards the end of the *ancien régime* in quite unimportant small towns, many of which, after the Revolution, failed to restore even the humblest sort of secondary school. The bourgeoisie, although rich and well educated, were debarred from holding office in the Government or the administration, and this ban operated increasingly as time went on. Most of the Parlements, which had been open to commoners throughout the seventeenth century, drew their members solely from the aristocracy during the eighteenth. Ministers, bishops, intendants were exclusively noblemen from 1715 onwards. The enactments of Sartine and Saint-Germain in 1775 and 1776 restricted advancement in the army and navy to the nobility. Thus, paradoxically, the more numerous, the wealthier and better educated the French bourgeoisie became, the scarcer became the number of governmental and administrative posts to which they could aspire. Now the bourgeois considered access to such posts as the crowning of their sons' careers. No doubt they could attain it by acquiring noble rank, and there were various means of doing this, for instance by the purchase of an office conferring nobility. But this was a lengthy, costly and often vexatious business. Things were different in Great Britain where, ever since the Revolutions of 1640 and 1688, the bourgeois had had ready access to important Government posts, and again in the Dutch or Belgian Netherlands, where the bourgeois had control of the administration.

A further difference between the situation in France and that in Britain and the United Provinces was that the middle class kept up its close connection with the peasant class from which it frequently sprang. Many bourgeois lived in small country towns, and there was in fact a sort of rural bourgeoisie. If the interests of the bourgeois might seem identical with those of the aristocracy in any attempted opposition to the Government, they were obviously incompatible where the aristocracy sought to maintain its privileges. Indeed, the bourgeoisie might well make common cause with the peasantry against the feudal system from which the nobility derived its privileges. Now the feudal regime, despite what may have been argued to the contrary, was still strongly entrenched in France at the end of the eighteenth century, whereas only traces of it still lingered in England, Holland and Belgium and in most of Northern Italy. Of course feudalism in France was very different from what it had been in the thirteenth century, or what it still was in central or eastern Europe. Nevertheless it laid heavy burdens on the peasantry; detailed descriptions by many eighteenth century specialists in feudal law bear witness to its active existence, and it constituted a barrier which prevented the bourgeoisie from attaining the posts they coveted.

The result was a general discontent among the bourgeoisie, directed against the 'feudal' régime which appeared responsible for the opposition between a tiny minority of privileged or very wealthy persons (these two categories tending to be identified) and a young, dynamic society frustrated in its upward trend by the presence, at the top, of an exclusive caste; while an enduring and deep-rooted association between towns and country districts (although with occasional conflicts) resulted in the rapid repercussion throughout the countryside of all urban happenings, and vice versa. All these conditions help to explain the events of the spring and summer of 1789.

III

Paris in 1789

In 1789 Paris had, as we have said, about 600,000 inhabitants; the census of 1792 gives a figure of 635,504, and that of 1795 626,582. But these returns are unreliable. There was a large floating population in Paris which it is not easy to assess. Perhaps we should increase the previous estimate and reckon the population of Paris at 650,000. This figure represents one-fortieth of that of France, a far smaller proportion than at present, when the urban area of Paris with its ten million inhabitants includes almost one-fifth of the inhabitants of France. None the less Paris was, in respect of population, far the largest city in France and the second largest in Europe, next to London, which even then numbered over a million inhabitants.

1. The walls and districts of Paris

The bounds of Paris were much narrower than today and, since 1785, had been clearly marked.[1] At this time, indeed, the tax-farmers responsible for collecting the toll from persons entering Paris had had a ten-foot wall built around the city, which was of no military value but which made their task easier, since access to Paris was possible only through one or other of the fifty-four gates in the wall. The erection of this wall annoyed the Parisians considerably, since it entailed a rise in the price of essential goods,

[1] General studies of Paris in 1789: A. Babeau, *Paris en 1789*, and H. Monin, *Paris en 1789*, Paris, 1889; A. Demangeon, *Paris, la ville et la banlieue*, Paris, 1933. On the population of Paris see: Necker, *De l'administration des finances de la France*, 3 vols., Paris, 1784; *Statistique générale de la France*, vol. III, Paris, 1837; P. Meuriot, *Un recensement de l'an II*, Paris, 1918; L. Cahen, 'La population parisienne au milieu du XVIIIe siècle', in *La Revue de Paris*, 1919, pp. 146–170.

which all had to pay toll benefiting the exchequer by between 28 and 30 million livres a year.

> *Le mur murant Paris*
> *Rend Paris murmurant*
> The wall walling in Paris
> Makes Paris grumble

as a wit commented. But Paris did not merely grumble. The unpopularity of the wall rebounded on the Finance Minister, Calonne, who had authorized its construction, and the Parisians' dislike of it, reflected in the *cahiers* of 1789, was to take a violent form, as we shall see, in July of that year.

The 'tax-farmers' wall' ran concentrically with the old city walls, traces of which were still more or less visible: that of Charles V, built in the fourteenth century, the chief fortress of which was the Bastille, and the toll-bar set up by Louis XIII on the site of the present *grands boulevards*. The 'tax-farmers' wall' thus took in many districts hitherto considered as forming part of the suburbs or outskirts of the city, such as the faubourgs of Saint-Victor, Saint-Marcel, Saint-Jacques and Saint-Germain on the left bank, and the villages of Chaillot and Passy on the right bank. The faubourgs of Saint-Antoine, Saint-Martin and Saint-Denis on the Right Bank, however, were not included.

The extended area comprised within this new wall bears witness to the growth and rapid renovation of Paris during the eighteenth century. True, the old town still subsisted in the Île de la Cité and the neighbouring districts bordering the Seine. But it was in process of transformation. The houses that cluttered up the bridges were pulled down. Louis XV wanted to rebuild all this ancient core of Paris, but he met with opposition from the clergy, who owned numerous monastic buildings there. The wealthy districts of the old town were still situated in this neighbourhood. True, the Marais, the centre of Parisian life under Henri IV and Louis XIII, was already being deserted by certain rich families, who were moving further West. But the Saint-Sulpice district remained one of the wealthiest in Paris. The investigation of marriage contracts for the year 1749 reveals that more than half the dowries of over 50,000 livres belonged to the inhabitants of this district. On the other hand, the population of Sainte-Marguerite and the Halles was less exclusive. Of course, there was far less distinction between 'working-class' and 'wealthy' districts in eighteenth-century Paris, as was to be the case in the nineteenth century. The various social groups of the population lived one above the other rather than in juxtaposition. In the houses of that time, the ground floor would be taken up by shops, the first (or 'best') floor inhabited by some nobleman or rich bourgeois, the second by tradesmen or artisans, the third by workmen—journeymen or apprentices. Servants, casual labourers, and country folk newly come to town to look for work would live on the fourth floor. However, in some streets the houses consisted entirely of *'chambres garnies'*, furnished rooms let for four sous a night to unmarried journeymen or apprentices: for instance the rue de la Mortellerie, the rue des Jardins and the rue Galande, close by the Hôtel de Ville. Certain districts, however, were the apanage of particular corporations. Carpenters, cabinet-makers, in general all those concerned with making furniture lived in the faubourg Saint-Antoine; tanners, cobblers, leather-workers and upholsterers in the faubourg Saint-Marcel (or Saint-Marceau); butchers, bakers, fishwives around the Halles; unskilled workers and newcomers to Paris in the northern faubourgs of Saint-Martin and Saint-Denis.

From 1750 onwards the rich tended to settle in new, or at least renovated districts, such as that around the Théâtre-Français (the present Odéon) built in 1789 on the site of the Hôtel de Condé, close to the Luxembourg.

But it was the new districts on the Right Bank that attracted all those whom fortune had favoured. According to Sebastien Mercier, over 10,000 houses were built there between 1760 and 1783, and some of them with astonishing speed: the Opéra in seventy-five days, the château de Bagatelle in six weeks.[1] In the Champs-Elysées region, the comte d'Artois, the King's brother, had several new streets built: the rue de Berry, the rue d'Angoulême, the rue du Colisée and the rue Milet. In the quartier Saint-Honoré, the rue d'Astorg was begun in 1789, and the banker Laborde was granted letters-patent for the construction of the rue de Provence, the rue d'Artois, the rue Taitbout and the rue Houssaye. In all these new districts the bourgeoisie owned most of the property. Jaurès was struck by this, and commented: 'Except for certain great families, the nobility itself was the bourgeoisie's

[1] Sébastien Mercier, *Tableau de Paris*, 12 vols., Amsterdam, 1783.

tenant. On the eve of 1789 the Parisian bourgeoisie was the supreme property-owning, producing and consuming power.'[1]

Thus, in the Paris of 1789, in spite of the generally stratified grouping of social classes, a distinction had begun to arise between the 'smart districts' of the West and the 'working-class districts' in the North and East. The meeting-point of these very different populations occurred roughly in the centre of the new Paris, the Palais-Royal.

2. The Palais-Royal

The Palais-Royal was thus called because Richelieu, who had built it, left it at his death to the King, Louis XIII. Louis XIV inherited it, but passed it on as an apanage to his younger brother the duc d'Orléans. Thus it became the property of this branch of the royal family, which was traditionally in opposition. Until 1780 it was a palace behind which lay a fine garden open only to members of the aristocracy. Frénilly describes it thus: 'The Palace stood on the western side of a vast garden, and on the other three sides stood rows of houses which their position rendered priceless. Straight paths, ornamental pools and flowerbeds divided it, and on the southern side there rose that splendid avenue of chestnuts that is unequalled throughout France for its age, its breadth, and that splendid vault through which the sun could not pierce. At its further end stood the orangery. This vast gallery of verdure had been, ever since the days of Anne of Austria, the meeting-place for the social élite of Paris, from whatever district . . . It was a parade of luxury, of festal gaiety and formality. Feathers and diamonds, embroidered coats and red heels prevailed; anyone in humble bourgeois dress, a "caterpillar", would not have dared appear there. The café de Foy and the café du Caveau, which alone have survived revolutions, made colossal fortunes there. In short the Palais-Royal was the heart and soul, the centre and core of the Parisian aristocracy.'[2]

In 1780 the duc d'Orléans, Louis-Philippe, nicknamed The Fat, retired with his mistress Mme de Montesson to his house in the Chaussée d'Antin and left the Palais-Royal to his son, the duc de Chartres, the future Philippe-Egalité. The latter, closely associated with the big business men and financiers who had

[1] J. Jaurès, *Histoire socialiste de la Révolution française*, Paris, 1904.
[2] Frénilly, *Mémoires*, Paris, 1908.

undertaken to transform Paris, decided to make the Palais-Royal into a meeting-place for all Parisians, not merely for the aristocracy —for bourgeois and the working-class, as well as for noblemen. Frénilly regrets this transformation: 'The leafy salon', he writes, 'turned into a market-place, red heels gave way to shops, swords to tape-measures, and the reign of democracy began in the city of Paris.'

In fact the duc de Chartres made the Palais-Royal into what was then known as a *palais marchand*, a 'trading palace'. He lined it with galleries imitating those of the Piazza San Marco in Venice, and under these galleries were set up dress shops, jewellers, book-sellers, printsellers, cafés, literary salons and clubs. Needless to say the two cafés that were already established there, the Café de Foy and the Caveau, enjoyed renewed prosperity. However, lack of money prevented the building of a fourth gallery on the north side, and this was replaced by a wooden gallery which became known as the *camp des Tartares*. An amphitheatre was added in 1787. The Palais-Royal, being the private property of the duc d'Orléans, was a privileged area into which the police might not penetrate (as also were the Luxembourg, property of the comte de Provence, and the Temple, which belonged to the comte d'Artois). This special circumstance, together with the charm of the place, the ingenuity of its layout, the variety of shops, cafés and entertain-ments, the opportunities for pleasure and culture, the proximity of the Bourse (then in the Hôtel de Nevers, the present Bibliothèque Nationale), and finally fashion, attracted to the Palais-Royal, from 1780 onwards, a vast crowd of Parisians of every class. Women of rank, of fashion, or of easy virtue flocked under the arcades and thronged before the shop-windows. Here they could show off the latest fashion in dress or hair-style, here they could find ephemeral or even enduring romance. The cafés were never empty. Besides those who came there to rest after walking through galleries and gardens there might be seen a certain number of journalists—a small number as yet, for the Press was subject to strict censorship, which however was tending to relax. The first French daily paper, the *Journal de Paris*, had been founded in 1777, three years before the opening of the Palais-Royal; the second, the *Journal général de la France*, appeared in 1785. The columnists who dealt with Parisian life collected most of their news items at the Palais-Royal. Besides the journalists, there were the *feuillistes* or gossip-mongers.

Since the Press at that time was scarcely developed, a number of important persons both in France and in other countries had little trust in the newspapers, or at least considered them inadequately informed. They subscribed to manuscript news-sheets which informed them, or professed to inform them, about the most intimate secrets of the Court and the town. Most of the time these secrets were merely rumours picked up under the arcades or in the cafés of the Palais-Royal by the authors of these 'secret correspondences'. However, as a meeting-place for these journalists and gossip-mongers the Palais-Royal soon became the centre of rumours and information, the place to which people flocked from all over Paris to get the latest news.

The information they acquired there was undoubtedly somewhat biassed. Indeed the duc d'Orléans, Grand Master of a Masonic Lodge, had opened up the Palais-Royal to the most advanced and liberal cultural societies of the day. Here were the headquarters of the Club Olympique, a Masonic organization, and an 'adoptive lodge' that welcomed women who were sympathetic towards freemasonry.

Here, too, were held the meetings of the Musée, where the most famous scholars of the day gave lectures on literary and scientific subjects. Its rival, the Salon des Arts, was also established in the Palais-Royal.

Those for whom such serious matters as political and philosophical discussion held no attraction could listen to concerts, or even dance, either at the Club Olympique or in some neighbouring hall. And at a time when gaming was a widespread passion, clubs or gambling dens were available in every café for those who hoped to make rapid fortunes without working for them. The money so quickly won might be even more easily lost, not only round a gaming-table but as a result of the many thefts committed within the precincts of the Palais-Royal; since the police were forbidden entry there, it had become the haunt of pickpockets, swindlers, card-sharpers and thieves of every kind. The proximity of the Bourse had resulted in the establishment, on the steps that led into the rue Vivienne, of a kind of annex filled with a hustling crowd of money-changers and speculators.

As the political, economic and social crisis intensified, the Palais-Royal seemed to crystallize all the political activities of Paris. From 1787 onwards it became a permanent centre of agitation. Arthur Young, the famous English traveller who left such a fascinating description of France on the eve of the Revolution,[1] did not fail to visit the Palais-Royal in 1789 to get the latest news. After going there on June 9th he wrote: 'The business going forward at present in the pamphlet shops of Paris is incredible. I went to the Palais-Royal to see what new things were published, and to procure a catalogue of all. Every hour produces something new. Thirteen came out today, sixteen yesterday, and ninety-two last week. We think sometimes that Debrett's or Stockdale's shops at London are crowded, but they are mere deserts, compared to Desein's [Desenne's], and some others here, in which one can scarcely squeeze from the door to the counter . . . But the coffee-houses in the Palais-Royal present yet more singular and astonishing spectacles; they are not only crowded within, but other expectant crowds are at the doors and windows, listening *à gorge déployée* to certain orators, who from chairs or tables harangue each his little audience; the eagerness with which they are heard, and the thunder of applause they receive for every sentiment of more than common hardiness or violence against the present government, cannot easily be imagined. I am all amazement at the ministry permitting such nests and hotbeds of sedition and revolt. . . .'

On June 24th the crowd was denser than ever at the Palais-Royal; ten thousand people, according to Arthur Young. On the night of the 26th a great fête attracted a throng of spectators; 'The spectacle the Palais-Royal presented this night, till eleven o'clock, and, as we afterwards heard, almost till morning, is curious. The crowd was prodigious, and fireworks of all sorts were played off, and all the building was illuminated; these were said to be rejoicings on account of the duc d'Orléans and the nobility joining the commons [i.e. the Third Estate, during the meetings of the Etats-Généraux at Versailles, as we shall see later]; but united with the excessive freedom, and even licentiousness, of the orators, who harangue the people.' The bookseller Hardy, who witnessed the same scene, describes it thus: 'Wild displays of fireworks, squibs and illuminations are still taking place in the gardens and even under the galleries of the Palais-Royal, in spite of heavy rain.' He mentions that owing to the huge throng that evening

---

[1] Arthur Young, *Travels in France during the years 1787, 1788, 1789*, Dublin 1793; ed. C. Maxwell, Cambridge, 1929.

pickpockets stole 'a great quantity of watches, purses and handker-chiefs.'

But at the Palais-Royal the Café de Foy had become the centre of political discussions. Rivarol writes: 'The gatherings at the Café de Foy were like another Assembly of the Commons which, by the liveliness of its debates, the unendingness of its sessions and the number of its members surpassed that of Versailles.'[1] Camille Desmoulins adds a picturesque note: 'At the Palais-Royal those who have stentorian voices take it in turn, every night, to climb up on to a table, around which people crowd to hear them read. They read out the most forceful statements on current affairs. The silence is only broken by applause at the most daring places. Then the patriots shout Encore!'[2]

3. Working classes and dangerous classes in Paris in 1789

The Palais-Royal was a rendezvous for news-bearers, agitators and ringleaders. But it was not here that they could enlist the masses needed to carry out great political demonstrations, capable of shaking or even overthrowing the régime. These masses were to be composed—as an analysis of the rioters' professions will show—of humble artisans, small shopkeepers and particularly wage-earners, clerks, shop assistants, journeymen and apprentices.[3] They belonged, no doubt, to that 40% of the population of Paris which, having signed no marriage contracts, eluded the analysis which we attempted in the previous chapter, but also to a section of those whom it covered. Indeed, out of a population of 600,000 inhabitants Paris included, in 1789, a well-off class (the nobility and clergy, the upper and middle bourgeoisie) forming, as we have seen, about 20% of the total: 120,000 individuals, comprising about 5,000 nobles, 10,000 members of the clergy and 105,000 bourgeois. The mass of the future '*sans-culottes*' and their families thus numbered over 500,000 persons.[4] Strictly speaking there was as yet no working-class 'proletariat', in the Marxist sense of the

[1] Rivarol, *Journal politique et national*, July 14th, 1789.

[2] Camille Desmoulins, *Lettres à son père*, ed. E. Despois, Paris, 1865, II, p. 65.

[3] G. Rudé, *The Crowd in the French Revolution*, Oxford, 1959; E. Tarlé, *La classe operaia nella rivoluzione francese*, 2 vols., Rome, 1961.

[4] On this subject see F. Braesch, 'Essai de statistique de la population ouvrière de Paris vers 1791', in *La Révolution française*, 1912, pp. 289–321; Id. *La Commune de 10 août*, Paris, 1911; A. Soboul, *Les sans-culottes parisiens en l'an II*, Paris, 1958.

word, for the industrial revolution had barely begun and there was, in Paris, no real large-scale industry which would form a focus for working-class communities.

One of the largest factories was that of Réveillon, which made printed wallpapers. Situated in the rue de Montreuil, in the faubourg Saint-Antoine, it employed 350 workers. Not far off was the Santerre brewery, with a staff of about a hundred. The Paris Water Company, in the suburb of Chaillot, was of the same order; it was directed by Constantin Périer, whose grandfather Claude owned the château of Vizelle, in Dauphiné, where one of the most important incidents of the eve of the Revolution was to take place. In the faubourgs of Saint-Martin and Saint-Denis there were a few spinning mills or cloth mills employing altogether some 800 hands. In the Gobelins district stood the famous royal tapestry factory set up there by Colbert in 1662. It employed quite a large number of workers, many being of Flemish or Dutch origin.

Apart from these few factories, small workshops were the rule in Paris, with a few journeymen and apprentices working together under a master-craftsman. Considerable traces of the medieval distribution of guilds in streets and districts still lingered at the end of the eighteenth century; clockmakers, jewellers and goldsmiths were grouped together on the quai de l'Horloge, the quai des Orfèvres, the place Dauphine, and under the newly built arcades of the Palais-Royal; carpenters, joiners, cabinet-makers in the faubourg Saint-Antoine; tanners, cobblers and shoemakers in the faubourgs Saint-Marcel, Saint-Victor and Saint-Jacques. They had been installed there by Colbert, who had expelled them from the embankment of the Île de la Cité because of the unpleasant smells exuding from their workshops. They were reputed to be aggressive. Sébastien Mercier wrote of them: 'These fellows drink for a week on end, they are more vicious, more quarrelsome and more inclined to mutiny than those of other districts.' Shop assistants and commercial employees lived in the rue des Lombards, the rue Saint-Denis and the rue des Gravilliers. South of this district stood the markets, the Halles, with their fishwives—the '*dames de la Halle*'—who were never slow to join in street disturbances.

The densest working-class concentrations were thus assembled around the Halles, in the Northern faubourgs (Saint-Martin and Saint-Denis), and in the Eastern ones (Saint-Antoine. Saint-

Marcel and Saint-Victor). Out of the 500,000 workers and employees of Paris in 1789, about two-thirds, or over 300,000, were wage-earners. In 1792—and things can scarcely have changed much in three years—wage-earners formed the great majority of the seven 'sections' of central Paris (Beaubourg, Gravilliers, Ponceau, Mauconseil, Bonne-Nouvelle, Poissonnière, Saint-Denis), half of the four other sections covering the Halles district (Louvre, Oratoire, Innocents, Lombards) but only one-third of the sections formed by the faubourgs Saint-Antoine and Saint-Denis, which were inhabited chiefly by small independent employers. Many wage-earners were seasonal workers who came to Paris from the country to practise some trade during the winter, and then went home to work in the fields. The Savoyards, for instance, were chimney-sweeps, the Limousins and Auvergnats building workers, dwelling chiefly in furnished rooms in the rue Mouffetard and the Cité, while peasants from Picardy provided a sizeable contingent to the guild of tough market-porters, the *'forts de la Halle'*.

What was the condition of the working-class in Paris in 1789? It is difficult to assess, and it would be rash to generalize. We must distinguish between the master, who was a small contractor working on his own account with the help of journeymen and apprentices, and the master-craftsman, who although employing journeymen and apprentices was himself paid by a contractor to carry out some particular job: thus master masons worked on behalf of building contractors. A journeyman would be paid wages but often received his board, at any rate his midday meal, and sometimes his lodgings. The apprentice, on the contrary, received nothing, and indeed his parents had to pay the cost of his apprenticeship.

A worker's wages varied greatly from one trade to another. An unskilled labourer earned 20 to 30 sous a day in 1789, a mason 40 sous, while a joiner or locksmith could make up to 50 sous. This did not amount to much when, as we know, a four-pound loaf—considered indispensable for a worker's daily consumption—cost in normal times eight or nine sous, but in time of crisis soon rose to twelve or fifteen and even, as we have seen, twenty sous, or half the daily wages of an average worker. Now bread generally accounted for 50% of a worker's expenses, vegetables, fats and wine for 16%, clothing 15% and lighting 1%. He would furthermore have to provide food and lodging for his family.

Faced with the constant rise in prices, from about 1730 onwards, Parisian workers had striven to secure an increase in wages. Yet, whereas prices had risen on an average by 62% between 1730 and 1789, nominal wages had only risen by 22%. To secure an increase, workers had frequently resorted to strikes, to what was then known as *coalition*, 'combination'. Thus, in 1724, the stocking-weavers had come out on strike to try and prevent a fall in wages; the leaders were arrested. In 1737 there was a strike of weavers to protest against a new regulation. In 1749, the hatters struck, despite a decree by the Parlement of Paris. In 1776, the book-binders struck for a reduction of the working day to 14 hours! In 1785, the building workers struck in protest against a proposed cut in wages; several hundreds of them presented their complaints to the Lieutenant of Police, Lenoir; others even went to try and find the King, who was believed to be at the Château de Brunoy, to beg him to intervene in their favour. The Parlement of Paris finally declared itself in sympathy with their complaints, and wages were not cut. In 1786, the carpenters and joiners struck, and so did the street-porters; in June 1789, the hatters went on strike again.

In spite of such activities, the rise in wages had been inadequate. Many Parisian workers were destitute. The poorest districts were the faubourgs on the Left Bank, and the faubourg Saint-Antoine. In 1790, the Commune of Paris (i.e. the municipal authorities) decided to distribute the sum of 64,000 livres among the poor of the city. Now the districts which received the largest shares were the faubourgs Saint-Jacques and Saint-Marcel (7,000 livres), the Val-de-Grâce district (5,300 livres), that of the Enfants-Trouvés in the faubourg Saint-Antoine (4,800 livres) and that of the church of Sainte-Marguerite in the same faubourg (4,800 livres). Many of these destitute persons were unemployed workers. The number of these increased rapidly during periods of economic depression, for the rural unemployed poured into the cities, particularly Paris, in the hope of finding work there or, failing this, some well organized system of public assistance, which was completely lacking in rural areas. In 1789, 14,000 destitute persons were laid up in the hospitals of Paris. According to La Fayette, there were at this period over 30,000 workless persons and '*gens sans aveu*', vagrants. Attempts were made to provide occupation for these in '*ateliers de charité*', charity workshops, which were set up in times of crisis.

This horde of wretchedly poor workers and workless persons were obviously liable to suffer from the least rise in the price of bread. At the end of the eighteenth century, as during the first half of the nineteenth, the working class of Paris could readily be transformed into a dangerous or subversive class. As soon as the price of bread rose the Parisian populace laid the blame not on the shortage of wheat or on the weather conditions which had caused it, but on farmers, millers such as the Lelau family who worked the Grands Moulins at Corbeil, and corn merchants such as the famous Malisset, who was accused of having concluded a 'famine pact' with the Government; as well as bakers, and *'accapareurs'* (hoarders) of every description. The Government thus had to keep careful watch over the provisioning of Paris and had laid down strict regulations for the baking trade.

4. The provision of bread for Paris

The provision of bread for Paris had for a long time been a major problem for the royal administration: Paris needed at least a million loaves a day, that is to say two pounds per head. And the system by which the capital was stocked with grain, flour and bread had been organized in minute detail.[1]

The grain trade, here as throughout France, was strictly regulated. Around Paris a zone ten leagues wide had been marked out, where all grain not needed for local consumption was allocated to satisfy the requirements of the city, and was sent there either directly by the producer or through the intermediary of merchants.

The latter were of three sorts: cornchandlers, 'petty cornchandlers', and the large companies supplying grain. The cornchandlers could only purchase outside the ten-league zone and, within this, only at the markets of Brie-Comte-Robert, Limours, Mennecy, and Corbeil. Any attempt to buy up in advance of the harvest, to go direct to the farmer or to lay in stocks was strictly forbidden. Some of these dealers were provided with a special letter from the city authorities, constituting them *marchands pour*

---

[1] See Léon Cahen, 'La question du pain, à Paris, à la fin du XVIIIe siècle', in *Cahiers de la Révolution*, vol. I, 1934, pp. 51–76; R. C. Cobb, 'Les disettes de l'an II et de l'an III dans le district de Melun et la vallée de la basse Seine', in *Mémoires de la fédération des sociétés historiques et archéologiques de Paris et de l'Île-de-France'*, vol. III, 1954, pp. 227–233; G. Lefebvre, *Études orléanaises*, 1962, vol. I, pp. 231–265: 'Les marchés, le commerce des grains et la boulangerie.'

June 20th, 1789. The oath in the Tennis Court

Bibl. Nat., Print Room, Vinck Collection, 1458

End of May 1789. An abuse that must be suppressed

Bibl. Nat., Print Room, Vinck Collection, 2784

June 13th, 1789. Your hands, gentlemen; I knew you'd
be on our side

colour print. Bibl. Nat., Print Room, Vinck Collection, 2018

June 23rd, 1789.
Monsieur Bailly's fine
speech

Bibl. Nat., Print Room

la provision de Paris. Their sole concern was to supply Paris with grain, but they were liable to severe penalties should they infringe this order, provide inferior grain, and so forth. On the other hand they might be rewarded for zealous service, particularly during times of crisis.

Cornchandlers from the outskirts of Paris also purchased supplies for the city beyond the ten-league zone. They stored this grain in granaries in towns on the perimeter: Chartres, Corbeil, Nemours. Moreover, this stockpiling allowed them to speculate.

The 'petty cornchandlers' practised similar operations, but on a much smaller scale.

As for the large companies, they were responsible for bringing into the Parisian region corn from the French provinces and particularly from abroad. The most important of them were the Malisset company (accused of the famous 'famine pact') and those of Mabille, Doumerc and Thélusson. These companies bought wheat for Paris in Burgundy, the Ardennes and Hainault. When harvests were really bad they brought it from the districts of Lyonnais, Velay, Nivernais, Champagne, Lorraine and Franche-Comté. Abroad, during periods of bad harvest, France bought wheat in North Africa and imported it by way of Marseilles, or in Holland and Poland, when it came in through Le Havre.

The wheat thus bought was taken to mills in the neighbourhood of Paris; there were over 4,000 of these, 3,000 water mills in the valleys of the Seine, the Oise, the Marne and the Loing, and 1,000 windmills on the plains of Beauce, Brie, Valois and Vexin. The most famous of these windmills overlooked Paris from the top of the Butte Montmartre.

The flour that came into Paris was checked at the customs posts, the *barrières*, and apart from that which was intended for private individuals making their own bread, was all taken to the Halles by special porters known as *plumets*.

At the Halles the flour was measured yet again in special measures and transferred to new sacks. Unfortunately the measuring-vessels were often dirty, so that the flour became contaminated and was quickly spoiled. After years of discussion, the bakers of Paris managed to ensure that the flour should no longer be measured but that the sacks in which it came should merely be weighed. 'Royal scales' were specially constructed. Nevertheless there were many protests as a result of this change.

At the end of the eighteenth century, all the flour stored at the Halles was bought by the bakers of Paris. These, subjected to strict regulations, were divided into three categories: the bakers of the city, those of the faubourgs, and itinerant bakers. The city bakers numbered two to three hundred. They were privileged to bake rolls, fine wheaten bread and bread for special orders. They had a stall in the bread-market at the Halles, or else kept shops in central streets, particularly the rue au Maire, the rue Béthizy, the rue Coquillière, the rue du Bouloi, the rue Beaubourg, the rue Saint-Denis, and a few streets on the Left Bank. This distribution of bakeries meant that certain districts were left without any. The city bakers were on the whole rather poor. Their equipment was mediocre and often old-fashioned. Each of them was allotted only a small quantity of flour, 4 *muids* a week, enabling them to bake 200 to 250 pounds of bread a day. They could only serve about a hundred customers each, and in the event of shortage their shops were soon emptied. They had failed to adapt to the demographic growth of Paris.

The bakers of the faubourgs numbered some three hundred; they included the privileged bakers of the faubourg Saint-Antoine and those who supplied the Court. They were in frequent conflict with the city bakers, whose privileges they contested, and yet their economic and social characteristics were very similar. Both the city bakeries and those of the faubourgs were small-scale undertakings, inadequate to supply the demands of a population of 600,000. They lacked capital; they were often obliged to sell their bread on credit and then had difficulty in recovering their debts. Thus they were forced to borrow money themselves; one baker named Gérard was said to have owed up to 20,000 livres. They frequently went bankrupt.

To cope with the considerable requirements of Paris the number of itinerant bakers, formerly very limited, had greatly increased, and there were now over 1,000 of them, each of whom produced far more bread than the bakers of the city or faubourgs. They got their supplies of flour from markets on the outskirts, and sold more bread than their Parisian colleagues. Bakers were particularly numerous at Limours, at Versailles and above all at Gonesse (there were over a hundred in this village) whose white bread was highly appreciated by Parisians.

These itinerant bakers came into Paris to sell their bread at various markets. The bread-market at the Halles was the most important, being frequented by over a hundred vendors, and its display served as an index of plenty or penury to the people of Paris: if it was well stocked, they felt reassured; if bread was scarce, they were afraid of famine. So the state of the Halles bread-market was one of the most important pieces of information among those received each day by the Lieutenant of Police. But there were other bread-markets: those of Saint-Germain (with more than 70 vendors), of Les Augustins, of Saint-Michel, of Maubert (with 125 vendors), of La Cité (an inferior market which was rapidly being deserted), of the Carrousel, the Boucheries, the Palais-Royal, Saint-Paul, the Cimetière Saint-Jean (frequented chiefly by bakers from Gonesse) and that of the Marais, which was perhaps the best appointed.

The sale of bread was, needless to say, strictly regulated. There were three categories of bread: white bread, which was sold not by weight but by the loaf, and practically reserved for the wealthy; brownish-white bread; and brown bread. The two latter categories could only be sold by weight. They formed the staple diet of the people; and the police kept a close watch on their quality. Nevertheless complaints about the quality and weight of bread were very frequent.

The regulations forbade all tradesmen who brought bread to the markets to take it away again after closing time. As there were no shops where it might be kept, the vendors had to lower their prices; this was the moment eagerly awaited by poor customers, but if such forced price-reduction occurred frequently, the baker was in danger of ruin. When bread was dear, bakers were reluctant to send their bread to the Paris markets for fear of either being forced to sell it cheap at the end of the day, or having their stalls plundered. For in fact when queues formed at the doors of bakers' shops in time of famine, discontent soon engendered violence, as had already happened during the *Guerre des Farines* in 1775. But every year, the period of the 'gap' between the exhaustion of last year's stocks and the broaching of the new harvest was a critical one. The price of bread went up fast and disturbances were liable to ensue. The end of the eighteenth century was a time of particular unrest, for, under the influence of economists, of whom Turgot was one of the most notable, the Government tended to relax its regulations and allow free competition, which resulted in a rise in prices, whereas the masses demanded State intervention and price control.

It would seem then that by 1789 the danger-points of Paris were, on the one hand, the Palais-Royal, the information-centre and haunt of agitators, and on the other hand the markets, particularly the Halles, where there was always a risk that, in case of food-shortage, there might form the nucleus of a gathering which would swell into a city-wide uprising. The Government and those who feared disturbances saw no reason for alarm, however: had not Paris the best police system in the world? When in 1780 news came of the Gordon riots in London, the respectable citizens of Paris were soon reassured: London was not policed like Paris, such disorders could never, so they said, have arisen in the French capital. How, then, was the Paris police organized?

IV

The Maintenance of Order in Paris at the End of the Eighteenth Century

The organization of the Paris police had begun in the reign of Louis XIV and had gradually developed until, by the eighteenth century, it had become an important administration with a relatively large force at its disposal for the maintenance of law and order.[1]

1. The Lieutenant of Police and his administration

In the seventeenth century, and ever since the medieval period, the police force of Paris had been under the control of a *prévôt* who was also responsible for administering justice. In fact, this latter function was exercised by his deputies: the *lieutenant civil*, who passed summary judgment, in his own home, in many civil or contentious lawsuits, and the *lieutenant criminel*, who judged minor offences. These lieutenants had been so fully occupied by their juridical functions that they inevitably neglected the problems of policing Paris.

In 1667, therefore, Louis XIV had created the office of *Lieutenant du prévôt pour la partie de la police*. This post was to be suppressed in 1790, but revived in 1800 under the title of *Préfet de police*; and the Prefect's functions have endured, with certain modifications, until the present day.

This Lieutenant of Police had to assume responsibility for security, for action in case of fire or flood, for public hygiene, for supplying Paris with food and forage, for itinerant traders, for

[1] On the police of Paris, see M. de Sars, *Le Noir, lieutenant de police* (1783–1803), Paris, 1948; H. de Montbas, *La Police parisienne sous Louis XVI*, Paris, 1949.

inns and lodging-houses, for public meetings and demonstrations, for corporations of trades and industries, for buildings threatening to collapse, for soldiers on leave, for the upkeep and administration of prisons, for tax-collecting within the bounds of his jurisdiction. Sébastien Mercier wrote in his *Tableaux de Paris*: 'The Lieutenant of Police has become an important Minister, although he does not bear that title. His secret influence is prodigious . . .' His powers were constantly extended throughout the eighteenth century and particularly from 1774 onward, under Louis XIV. They came to include judicial functions: every Thursday the Lieutenant of Police sat in judgment at the Châtelet, in a police-court, without assistants. He was also entitled to judge certain criminal cases, concurrently with the *lieutenant criminel*. He was furthermore endowed with unofficial jurisdiction over matters concerning wills, the affixing and breaking of seals, etc.

From 1740 onwards the Lieutenant of Police had set up *bureaux* to carry out these various duties. By 1789 there were seven of them. The *bureau de cabinet* received and answered letters, addresses, complaints and reports. It also sent out *lettres de cachet*, which we shall discuss more fully at the end of this chapter, and it supervised the prisons in which were detained the persons arrested by virtue of these letters.

The *bureau de sûreté* comprised three inspectors who, turn about, were freely at the disposal of the public to listen to complaints and undertake enquiries and investigations. These two *bureaux* functioned from the Châtelet, the headquarters of the Lieutenant of Police.

The *bureau de ravitaillement* for Paris employed six officials. It was responsible not only for the capital's food supplies but also for refuse-collecting and street cleaning and, more generally, for the upkeep of public thoroughfares. It was also concerned with 'general information', the reports of the city guard, military matters, the supervision of fairs and entertainments, pedlars and hawkers, 'new converts' (in other words, Protestants) and requests from innkeepers for dispensation from Lenten fasts.

The *bureau des prisons et maisons de force* was concerned with all places of confinement except the State jails (the Bastille and the Château de Vincennes). It was also responsible for surveillance of the Jewish population and for control of public lotteries. Three officials worked here.

The *bureau des arts et manufactures*, with a staff of eight, had jurisdiction over trade corporations, manufactures, commerce, the Bourse, foreign exchange, licences to import and export, and the suppression of smuggling.

A special *bureau* was in charge of wet-nurses; this was a highly important matter at a time when all children of the nobility and bourgeoisie, and even many working-class infants, were put out to nurse. It has been reckoned that on the eve of the Revolution not one child out of thirty was breast-fed by its mother, despite Jean-Jacques Rousseau's propaganda in favour of mother's milk. Peasant women had to be recruited as wet-nurses, and arrangements made to bring them into Paris to collect the babies, or else to send the babies out to the country.

A seventh *bureau* was in charge of disputed claims.

A total of twenty-seven officials worked in these *bureaux*, having at their disposal a central card-index which enabled them to trace readily anybody wanted by the police.

In 1774 Lieutenant Sartine was appointed to the *Ministère de la Marine* by Louis XVI, and his functions were taken over by Le Noir, who held this post until 1785 and was then succeeded by Thiroux de Crosne. Le Noir opposed Turgot's policy of free trade in grain, and was forced to resign his post, which however he resumed after Turgot's fall in 1776. He thus played a vital part in the maintenance of law and order in Paris during the years immediately preceding the Revolution.

2. Police control of the streets, of public safety and of the press

One important function of the Lieutenant of Police was, as we have seen, the cleansing and upkeep of public thoroughfares; this was an essential factor in the maintenance of order, since the health of the city and the control of epidemics depended on it to some extent. Now it was no small matter to maintain cleanliness in a city of 600,000 inhabitants, lacking any proper sewage or hygienic installations. Le Noir tried to improve things as far as possible. He perfected the street-cleaning system, had the cesspools emptied regularly, and set up sewage farms around Paris. He also established knackers' yards with 'veterinary pits'. He ordered constant watering of the streets. To avoid food poisoning he forbade the use of copper milk pans, and leaden counters in wine shops.

Le Noir also improved the city's hygiene by closing down cemeteries, particularly the 'charnel-house' of Les Innocents, close to the Halles. Henceforward cemeteries were confined to the outskirts of Paris.

To decrease the number of deaths by drowning, Le Noir instituted a service of rescue work, with medals for life-saving.

It was he, too, who reorganized the Paris fire brigade. Before his time, monks of the mendicant orders—Carmelites and Franciscans—had been responsible for fire-fighting. Henceforward a body of sixty volunteer firemen or *garde-pompes* took over the duty, in collaboration with the police and the army.

A pawn office, modelled on the many that existed in Italy, was opened by Le Noir on December 7th, 1777. By lending money on security at reasonable rates, it provided relief to people who were in temporary straits, and thus helped to combat usury.

Other measures taken by Le Noir contributed more directly to the maintenance of order: he had the streets numbered, enabling the police to locate houses more speedily, and above all he improved street lighting, which greatly facilitated their nocturnal duties.[1] It was Le Noir's predecessor, Sartine, who had set up the first oil-burning street-lamps, instead of the lanterns containing candles which had cast so dim a light in the streets of Paris ever since the time of Louis XIV. These oil-lamps were hung on ropes, and were let down to be lit; we know to what macabre use these '*lanternes*' were to be put during the Revolution. But Le Noir's great innovation was his decision to light the street-lamps every night; hitherto they had never been lit when the moon was shining. The road from Paris to Versailles was also illuminated at all seasons.

> *Sur le chemin qui conduit à la Cour*
> *On établit maint et maint réverbère.*
> *De plus en plus, de jour en jour,*
> *Je vois avec plaisir que mon pays s'éclaire.*

(On the road that leads to the Court many street-lamps are now being set up. I watch with pleasure, every day, the growing enlightenment of my country.)

Thus, conditions for the maintenance of public safety had unquestionably improved during the reign of Louis XVI. Among

[1] General Herlaut, *L'Éclairage de Paris à l'époque révolutionnaire*, Paris, 1932.

72

the essential functions of the police were the repression of the illicit carrying of weapons, the dispersal of prohibited meetings, the supervision of lodging-houses and the control of secondhand dealers.

The laws controlling the carrying of arms were old and complex. It was forbidden, under the severest penalties, 'to go about the city, either by day or by night, with forbidden weapons such as pistols, daggers, bayonets and others of the same sort', that is to say, short and easily concealed weapons. On the other hand, dress swords were regarded as a part of certain costumes, and were allowed. The police, moreover, were subject to the same regulations and, as in England today, were not permitted to carry arms of the prohibited sort. Officers wore a straight sword, and lower ranks a sabre.

Prohibited meetings were of widely varying sorts. In theory, any gathering for the purpose of games of chance was illicit. But the police tolerated these. Certain meetings of trade guilds, even if their object was only to organize processions, might be forbidden. And of course the police were bound to disperse any 'seditious' gathering; this adjective could be freely interpreted. It was generally the Lieutenant of Police who decided whether or not to give the order to break up a meeting on the public thoroughfare. But, as we saw in the preceding chapter, there were in Paris certain privileged places, the Temple, the Luxembourg, and the Palais-Royal, to which the police had no right of entry.

It was essential, for police purposes, to control newcomers to the capital. Lodging-house keepers and landlords were in theory subjected to strict regulations. In order to exercise their profession, they must first be provided with a permit, after which they had to keep a register of each guest's arrival and departure, mentioning the length of each one's stay, and must immediately report any 'suspect' to the police. These *logeurs* were divided into three categories: hotel-keepers, whose establishments were relatively expensive and available only to 'persons of quality'; those who kept inns or lodging-houses; finally the *logeurs à la nuit*, who came under special supervision because they put up homeless persons, vagrants and the unemployed. The police made frequent raids on such doss-houses.

The object of supervising second-hand dealers was to trace stolen property. Pedlars or itinerant vendors, who were very numerous in Paris in 1789—over 1,400—were obliged to produce a permit and to keep an account of all their transactions. Some of them complied with the order, others deceived the police, or bought its connivance by turning informer.

The *ancien régime* did not only keep watch over the actions of the people of Paris, it tried to control their thoughts too. The press, by which must be understood the printing and book trades, was subject to a number of strict regulations, but like many regulations these had lost their effectiveness, because the individuals and organizations responsible for applying them were very numerous and often in rivalry. Control over the printing and sale of books was, in fact, exercised by three separate authorities: firstly, by the *Chambre royale et syndicale* of printers and booksellers, the corporate body in which all members of the trade were associated, and which was responsible for seeing that everything that was printed and sold conformed to the regulations; secondly, by the directors of the book trade, who were responsible not to the Lieutenant of Police but to the Minister of Justice; and thirdly by inspectors of books, who were subordinate to the Lieutenant of Police. There were thus in existence three different organizations which did not always agree amongst themselves. Control was exercised in three ways:

(1) Through the censorship, to which every published work was subject. We shall study this in further detail later on. The censorship was exercised partly by the directors of the book trade (and thus by the Minister of Justice) and partly by the inspectors of books (and thus by the Lieutenant of Police).

(2) Through control of publication: by making sure that every book put on sale was provided with the indispensable preliminary permit, or else by the royal privilege which ranked above this and guaranteed the work against prosecution.

(3) Through control of sales, aimed at making sure that only authorized booksellers could, in fact, sell books, and of circulation, particularly by pedlars, which required special authorization. Peddling of books was widespread under the *ancien régime*, and indeed right through the nineteenth century, and even, for certain publications, until our own day. In fact, the multiplicity of controls and of organizations responsible for enforcing these only facilitated fraud and evasion. Moreover, the controlling authorities were not very conscientious. True, they confiscated such books as

had infringed the regulations, either by lacking the necessary permit or by not having been submitted to the censor. They were supposed to burn such books. But in the eighteenth century, a book confiscated for one reason or another enjoyed enormous publicity, out of all proportion to its intrinsic merits, and consequently was worth a great deal of money, merely because it had been confiscated. The controllers therefore took good care not to burn the books they confiscated. They would burn one or two copies, which they displayed to the public, the rest of the bonfire being made up of old papers of no value. As for the books, they stored these in their homes or cellars and sold them under the counter for three, four or even ten times their value. Thus a certain d'Hémery, a book trade inspector, carried on this profitable traffic for over thirty years, from 1741 to 1773; it was only then that he was discovered and dismissed from his post for 'trading in forbidden books'. Not content with selling confiscated books at a high price, he had even provided his clients with librarians selected from among booksellers who had lost their jobs for infringing the regulations!

The directors of the book trade paid particular attention to books printed abroad, for, in order to dodge the French censorship, many writers had their books printed out of the country, or even if they had them printed in France they had Amsterdam, Geneva or Kehl inscribed on the frontispiece. Voltaire's works were published in this way. The 'Kehl edition' was in fact never printed in Kehl. Books printed abroad for circulation in France were only allowed in at ten points of entry. If they did not come in through these specific entrances, they were considered as banned books, liable to confiscation. Import duties were imposed on them, in order to raise the selling price artificially and thus make distribution more difficult; these were not abolished until 1775. Three successive visas were required, moreover, before a book could enter France. Actually, most books printed abroad evaded these controls and came into France by all sorts of ways. One of those most frequently used was simply the diplomatic bag. But books were also smuggled into the country by members of the aristocracy returning in their coaches from a visit abroad. Thus they circulated quite freely in France. In 1750 Malesherbes was appointed General Director of the book trade and the press. Now Malesherbes was a *philosophe*, a friend of the great writers of his day, and he turned a blind eye on these subterfuges and illicit trading methods. Only when complaints about some work were actually brought before the parlement would Malesherbes consent to intervene. In 1763 the Lieutenant of Police, Sartine, decided that Malesherbes was really too lenient.[1] He replaced him by Le Camus de Neville. But France was already flooded with banned books printed either at home or abroad, and Le Camus could do nothing. Malesherbes, moreover, was to become Minister on the accession of Louis XVI, in 1774, when his influence was felt once more. The censorship, which was under the control of the Director of the Book Trade, was in the hands of a board of royal censors which had been set up in 1624. On the eve of the Revolution, in 1780, there were 128 censors, chosen and appointed by the Minister of Justice. They were usually members of either the Académie française, the Académie des Inscriptions et Belles-lettres, or some provincial academy. When the manuscript of a work was finished, the author had to submit it for censorship, but he knew which censor had been appointed to read his book, and he would then get in touch with him. Author and censor generally came to some agreement; the censor might ask the author to suppress a certain passage, but this was a recommendation, not an order. Usually the censor would try to reach a friendly agreement about the suppression of the passage he considered dangerous for some reason; if, however, the author did not accept the alterations suggested by the censor, he had the right to appeal, to repudiate his censor and ask for a different one. Moreover, he was free to refuse to make any change, since the censor's advice was not an order. In that case the censor would send a report to the Lieutenant of Police, who would settle the matter, and might well decide to leave the author's text untouched. But if the book appeared against the advice of the censor, confirmed by the Lieutenant of Police, it was liable to be confiscated.

Even when it had slipped through the censor's net, a book could only be printed if it was provided with a permit issued by the police. The censors, indeed, merely expressed an opinion, and only the police could grant permission. Now there were four sorts of permit: the *ordre du roi*, which obviously was not merely a permit but an order to print a work, and was granted to those works which the Government was anxious to disseminate; the

[1] See P. Grosclaude, *Malesherbes, témoin et interprète de son temps*, Paris, 1961.

privilège ordinaire, granted for varying lengths of time, and for a consideration, to a printer, and intended to protect the book from piracy; the *permission du sceau*, granted by the Chancellor, and for which he was personally responsible; finally the *permission tacite*, the one most frequently granted. The Lieutenant of Police might allow books to circulate which had been printed without permit and without the censor's visa; but these books were liable to confiscation at any moment.

Most of the works that appeared between 1750 and 1789 were published by 'tacit permission'. In theory, they should only have been circulated privately, but in fact they were sold quite openly. This almost official infringement of the regulations encouraged the printing and circulation of books which were really clandestine, that is to say lacking any sort of authorization. Even when a book had been 'suppressed' by the royal *Conseil d'État* and 'condemned to the flames' by the Parlement, it went on circulating, with the enhanced value of a rarity. In fact, only a small number of copies were actually burnt; the others, as we have pointed out, were either seized by the controllers, who sold them to their own advantage, or else they were stored away in the cellars of the Bastille, and sometimes allowed to drift back, a few at a time, into clandestine circulation. The regulations governing the printing and book trades in France at the end of the eighteenth century undoubtedly imposed a certain constraint upon writers, and many great works were condemned, including Voltaire's *Siècle de Louis XIV*, Helvétius' *De l'Esprit*, Rousseau's *Émile*, Holbach's *Système de la Nature*. But these regulations did not really impede the circulation of works attacking the régime, nor of licentious and pornographic booklets. Some authors, indeed, were arrested, and the prison sentences served by Voltaire, Diderot and Morellet have remained famous. Mirabeau and de Sade were also imprisoned, but not for offences under the Press laws. These arrests provided the *philosophes* with a martyr's halo, but did not protect the Government. Most of those who attacked it took refuge abroad, in England, Holland, Switzerland, or just over the border, Voltaire for instance settling at Ferney.

The regulation of periodical publications was more effective, for it restricted the number of newspapers published in France and above all prevented them from criticizing the régime or the Government. In 1789 only four political newspapers were as yet published in Paris, the *Gazette,* founded in 1631 by Renaudot, the *Mercure,* which dated from 1672, the *Journal de Paris,* the first French daily, founded in 1777, and the *Journal général de la France,* another daily first published in 1785. In the provinces there appeared about sixty papers, mostly weeklies.[1] But there were plenty of French newspapers printed abroad, in England or in Holland, notably the famous *Gazette de Leyde,* or in Belgium, such as the *Journal encyclopédique* edited by Rousseau de Toulouse, or Lebrun-Tondu's *Journal général de l'Europe.* These papers were freely available to French readers and reminded them daily that the régime under which they lived was an anachronistic one, out of keeping with eighteenth century enlightenment. The censorship of the press was tiresome and embarrassing, but it discredited the régime without really protecting it.

Censorship of the stage might have been more effective, but in Paris the censors were indulgent and allowed quite violent satire against the Government to get by. The performances of Beaumarchais' *Barbier de Seville* and *Mariage de Figaro* are a case in point.

A similar slackness was shown in the censorship of drawings, engravings and pictures; never had a greater number of licentious engravings been sold than during the second half of the eighteenth century. As for political caricatures, these had begun to prove an increasingly popular genre.

3. The police force of Paris

The Lieutenant of Police had at his disposal a varied and, for those days, a relatively large body of men to carry out his orders and enforce the laws and regulations. There were some 1,500 in all: 48 *commissaires de police,* or *commissaires du Châtelet,* 20 inspectors with their assistants, 150 watchmen (*archers du guet*), 3 companies of the Paris Guard comprising some 1,000 men, and 300 or 400 police officers (*exempts*).

Let us consider the functions of these various forces.

The *commissaires du Châtelet* were officers, holding their posts by right of purchase and for life; they could only relinquish their function by selling the post. There was no promotion in their career. They were *officiers de robe longue,* 'long-gowned' legal

---

[1] On the provincial press, see the excellent study by René Girard, *Le Journal de Marseille,* Paris, 1964.

officials who rarely left their offices and then with pomp and ceremony, whereas on the contrary the *officiers de robe courte* were constantly on the move. The forty-eight *commissaires* were scattered throughout Paris, two or three in each district or *quartier*, one of whom bore the title of *commissaire principal*. Apart from problems concerning his own district, each *commissaire* was in charge of certain general matters concerning the whole of Paris. Thus one *commissaire* was responsible for food supplies, particularly in connection with the Halles, another supervised the cattle market, a third the horse market, a fourth the forage and poultry markets; one dealt with the Bourse, another with the theatres, another with the interrogation of State prisoners, another with *lettres de cachet*, while another kept the register of the deaths of Protestants, who had no civil status before 1787. The *commissaires* were responsible for 'ensuring that decrees were carried out, seeing to the maintenance of order and everything concerning the public welfare, and informing the magistrate' (i.e. the Lieutenant of Police) 'of such abuses and disorders as require his personal attention.' The *commissaires* enjoyed four prerogatives: they were entitled to arrest persons on the public thoroughfare or in their own homes, or to undertake the preliminary examination if the arrest had been made by one of their assistants; they could pass the first sentence for minor offences; they could institute preliminary investigations after the offence had been established and the witnesses heard; and finally, by virtue of a special and formal order of the King, they could search private premises, affix seals to property distrained upon, and so forth.

According to the report drawn up in 1776 for the Emperor Joseph II by Commissaire Lemaire, the part played by these *commissaires* was highly effective. 'The prompt and summary justice which they render unremittingly and gratis must be considered one of the chief causes for *the good order and the remarkable tranquillity* which reign in Paris. It ensures fair dealing in the necessities of life. It provides great relief for the working classes, and thus for the poorest inhabitants of the city. They depend upon it for the payment of their wages, and they are unacquainted with any other judges or with the arguments and quarrels that are liable to arise between them on this subject. They know that these *commissaires* are readily accessible and will listen with the greatest attention to their grievances, and so they are eager to visit them. This is what controls or moderates, on most occasions, the irresponsible behaviour to which such uneducated people are prone. It prevents frequent acts of violence on their part, with the unfortunate consequences that might ensue. Finally, *it keeps them unconsciously in that habit of subordination and obedience, which is so necessary from the point of view of authority.* It is by means of this constant intercourse between *commissaires* and citizens that the former are informed of any irregularities or abuses that may develop, and that the magistrate, through the knowledge they bring him in all cases where he must attend to the matter personally, is always in a position to provide a prompt remedy.' Thus the *commissaires de police* were considered as the most perfect agents for maintaining law and order in Paris at the end of the eighteenth century.

As well as these *commissaires* there were, on the eve of the Revolution, twenty inspectors, one for each district, attached to the chief *commissaire* of the district. Their functions were similar to those of the *commissaires*, but they could be given special powers to act in certain cases. They were, for instance, responsible for what we might describe today as general information: they had to listen, watch, and make reports. They had to keep an eye on everything that happened, and immediately inform the *commissaire* of any crime, offence or irregularity that came to their notice. They had, in particular, to check all rumours that they heard, all true or false reports, the gossip in the market-place or in the queues outside the bakers' shops, and so forth; and they had to track down and identify the authors of such rumours. They had the right to make arrests, by virtue of warrants issued by the legal authorities. They provided escorts for foreign rulers and princes who came to visit the King or to stay in the capital. These inspectors were required to show detective abilities and, as a contemporary put it, 'make false allegations in order to find out the truth'. As well as its regular *commissaires* and inspectors, the police employed certain auxiliaries who were officially called 'observers', but popularly known as *mouches*, whence the modern term *mouchard*. There were a great many of these narks, who had no official function but kept in touch with the police and sent in reports at regular or irregular intervals. By the end of the eighteenth century the spy system had reached a point of perfection that aroused general admiration, and it was about this, above all, that

June 28th, 1789. Long live the King, long live our Country,
we too belong to the Third Estate

Bibl. Nat., Print Room

Evening of June 30th, 1789, at the Palais-Royal

Bibl. Nat., Print Room, Vinck Collection, 1492

Joseph II had asked for details in 1776. The *mouches* or informers had a bad reputation with the public, but it was very difficult to identify them, for they were drawn from all strata of society. They might help out the police for a limited period or even in a single case, but they were not employed permanently, nor paid regularly; they were rewarded, for each piece of information, on a widely varying scale: they might get 20 or 30 livres for valuable information, and thus make as much as 150 livres a month, or else they might merely be paid with a good meal or a trifling present. The lowest category of informers, the *basses mouches*, were responsible for shadowing suspects in the streets and getting them arrested when possible. They were paid three livres a day, and when they secured the arrest of some individual who had been wanted for a long time and had committed a notable crime or a serious offence, they might receive a bonus of up to 80 livres. Needless to say these *mouches* were themselves suspects, usually people who had been in trouble with the police. This age-old system was common throughout the eighteenth century. The police won over suspected persons by promising them immunity in return for their help. It was Lieutenant Sartine who had perfected the system. He had divided spies into four categories: society people (among them Mirabeau); the 'gazetteers' or petty journalists, who were usually down and out and of no fixed income; prostitutes; and what are now called *les gens du milieu*, the underworld. Police methods, in the eighteenth century, depended largely on the use of these spies. There was also the *cabinet noir*, the secret investigation of correspondence; but this was not a function of the police, depending directly on the Controller-General of Finance, who combined the functions performed nowadays by the Minister of the Interior and several other Ministers. The *cabinet noir* was in certain cases in direct contact with the King. Its officials opened and read letters addressed to persons suspect for one reason or another, and sometimes also the correspondence of ambassadors or ministers; any information likely to interest the Paris police was passed on to it.

Of the remaining active police forces, the *compagnie du guet* (the watch) was the oldest, being of medieval origin; since 1368, when it was formed, it had consisted of 50 'archers'—the term had been maintained, although bows and arrows were no longer used—20 on horse and 30 on foot. Its chief was the *chevalier du guet de Paris*, who had since 1667 been subordinate to the Lieutenant of Police. In 1771 Sartine reorganized this company entirely. Its numbers were increased to 150: 39 archers on horse and 100 on foot, together with 7 non-commissioned officers and 4 officers. The watch functioned as a guard of honour for royal persons or ambassadors, for magistrates, for the Parlement when it changed its venue or at solemn sessions; it also provided guards at the Châtelet, and warders for criminals or prisoners under trial at various courts, and helped to keep order at public executions. Members of the *guet*, like *commissaires* and inspectors, were entitled to arrest and imprison suspects; but it was too small a body to exercise this right effectively in case of public disturbances. In practice, it was not used for policing the streets. For this purpose Sartine had instituted the Paris guard in the same year, 1771, as he had increased the *guet*. The guard was on a much larger scale; it comprised three companies of varying size, one of 268 infantrymen, another of 516 infantrymen, and a third of 225 'masters' or cavalrymen: a total of 889 guards, with officers and non-commissioned officers, amounting to some thousand men. This body was also under the direct command of the *chevalier du guet*, and, above him, of the Lieutenant of Police. The two companies of infantry differed in size for the following reason: the smaller company, that of 268 men, was specifically responsible for guarding the walls and gates of Paris, and could only be diverted from this function by an express order from the King. The larger body of 516 men was divided amongst the different districts (*quartiers*) of Paris, into units consisting of 12 men on permanent duty at certain stations, including three non-commissioned officers, commanded by a sergeant. Six of these men had to patrol the streets of the district and the other six remain at their station. The patrol was relieved every two hours. As for the mounted company, it was detailed for night duties, being divided into brigades of five men who had to ride through the streets of Paris by night and stop for a few minutes at every cross-roads. There was thus a total of 120 men on duty in the streets by day, and 180 by night, not counting those in the police stations or at the gates. This was very few for a population of 600,000. However, until 1787 this force had appeared adequate, and the watch and the guard together had been found to ensure order quite satisfactorily. They had to keep particular watch over gaming-houses, taverns, dens and brothels. They had also to give the alarm in case of fire, and rouse the Paris fire brigade; disperse any sort of gathering, pick up drunkards, vagrants and prowlers, and bring them to the station. With these police forces must be included the *exempts*. These formed a 'short-coated' company (*compagnie de robe courte*) as opposed to the long-gowned *commissaires*. They were responsible for arresting criminals wanted by the law, not only in Paris but throughout France and even abroad. Thus the *exempt* of Bruguières arrested Mirabeau on a charge of abducting Sophie de Monnier, the daughter of a magistrate; the arrest took place in Franche-Comté. These police officers were also entrusted with missions abroad; they could, with the consent of the countries concerned, arrest refugees. The abbé Prévost, whose novels had brought him into trouble with the authorities, was hunted through England and Holland, and barely managed to escape from the *exempts* who were pursuing him.

Besides these regular forces for keeping order, there were reserves. Obviously 1,500 men were not enough to police Paris in case of serious uprisings. The reserve forces which could be called upon included, in the first instance, the body of *arbalétriers* (crossbowmen), *arquebusiers* and fusiliers commanded by a colonel and appointed by the King, on the recommendation of the *prévôt des marchands* of Paris.

These were amateur soldiers recruited from the civil population and serving chiefly for purposes of show. They wore a fine uniform, practised shooting from time to time and formed a guard of honour when the King came to Paris, or a foreign prince paid a visit, or when the Parlement changed its venue, or for some solemn occasion such as a Te Deum at Notre-Dame. Actually they could seldom be depended on in case of an uprising, for they were just as liable to join in it as to repress it. And in fact they formed the nucleus of the *Garde Nationale* of Paris when it was created during the night of July 12th–13th 1789, as we shall presently see.

The police could also call upon the *maréchaussée*, the equivalent of today's *gendarmerie* or constabulary. Its forces throughout the kingdom were very scanty, and it is indeed surprising that it managed to maintain order with such inadequate manpower in a country that was practically as extensive as France is today, and where communications were so slow that distances seemed much greater; it took a week to get from Paris to Toulouse. In view of these difficulties, the only *maréchaussée* that could be used in case of disturbances in the capital was that of the Parisian region. This consisted, first, of the *maréchaussée* of the Île-de-France, a mere 52 men, of whom 17 were garrisoned in Paris. The *maréchaussée* of the Paris district comprised 140 men, all stationed outside Paris; the *maréchaussée de la connétablie*—an ancient judiciary division that had survived although the office of *connétable* had disappeared in 1627—consisted only of 58 men, a small contingent. The *maréchaussée de la prévôté de l'hôtel du roi* (at Versailles) was used during Court ceremonies. The *maréchaussée de la prévôté des monnaies* was 82 strong; although it was stationed in Paris, it was little use during disturbances. The *garde des gouverneurs de Paris* comprised 53 cavalrymen and was equally useless. The total strength of the *maréchaussée* of the Parisian region amounted to 411 men, but it was difficult to summon them to Paris, since any disturbances in the capital might be expected to spread throughout the environs, and the local constabulary must therefore be kept on duty there. The third reserve force, after the *arbalétriers* and the *maréchaussée*, was the regiment of *gardes-françaises*, which dated from 1563. This was a corps 3,600 strong, stationed in Paris; it consisted of professional soldiers who had generally served a long time in other units. It has sometimes been described as a collection of pimps and hired assassins. This is untrue. But many of the *gardes-françaises* were married men, who, although they took part in exercises, parades and manœuvres, practised other professions privately to increase their earnings; they were cobblers, tailors, upholsterers, etc. and thus lived in close association with the ordinary people of Paris, sharing their thoughts, fears and aspirations. This body of men had always hitherto given satisfaction to the Government, but in view of its symbiosis with the population of Paris it was hardly to be relied on in case of serious disturbances. Nonetheless the monarchy did not suspect the loyalty of the *gardes-françaises*, and as we shall see, in a rising that took place in Paris on April 26th, 1789, they acted with vigour; things were to be otherwise in July. The Government could also call upon the Swiss guards. There were a number of Swiss regiments in France; they were not all based in Paris on the eve of the Revolution, but there was one regiment at Versailles. It could easily get to Paris on foot, and could thus be made use of. Normally the Swiss guards, like the

84

gardes-françaises, shared responsibility for keeping order with the police and the constabulary; they were on duty during official ceremonies held in theatres, but they could equally well be employed to repress riots or fight natural disasters such as fire and flood. Finally, among the troops stationed in Paris, there were companies of musketeers, the 'black musketeers' in barracks in the faubourg Saint-Antoine, who were drawn from the lesser aristocracy and were devoted to the throne, and the 'grey musketeers' in the faubourg Saint-Germain, whose social origin and whose numbers were much the same. The Lieutenant of Police could also in case of riots requisition the troops stationed at Versailles. It took the infantry four or five hours to come from Versailles to Paris; the cavalry could get there in three. Besides the Swiss, these troops included the *gardes du corps* or lifeguardsmen, who were not really soldiers. Many of them were former officers, enjoying a sort of retirement at Versailles; they were not in daily training, and were quite unfitted for keeping order. The *chevau-légers* or light cavalry were a show company like the musketeers, largely drawn from the nobility; the *gendarmes de la garde du roi* were also a show body of horsemen, few in number. These, then, were the troops which could be called upon at four or five hours' notice: 1,500 members of the police force, immediately available, 300 members of the *gendarmerie* providing an immediate reserve, and 5,000 that could be brought to Paris within a space of one to five hours: a total of some 6,800 men to keep order in a city of 600,000 inhabitants, which seems inadequate. It is thus not surprising that these troops were rapidly swamped by the demonstrators when the riots developed seriously. Further reinforcements might perhaps have been found, but this would have meant bringing in troops garrisoned in the provinces. The nearest garrisons were those of the North: Roubaix, Lille, Arras, Rheims and Amiens; it took four days to bring infantry from these towns. Those in the north-east were even more remote: Nancy, Metz and Strasbourg, ten days to a fortnight's march away. And meanwhile, if the frontiers were to be left undefended, relations with neighbouring countries had to be satisfactory; and the provinces themselves must enjoy a state of calm. However, as we have seen, during the *guerre des farines* in 1775, the Government had collected an 'army' under Biron to restore order in the Paris region.

The police force of Paris were well paid for those days, as a pledge for their loyalty. The budget for 1789 included a sum of 97,500 livres for the central administration of the police, almost half of this (38,500 livres) being the salary of the Lieutenant of Police, which was a very high salary for those days. The *commissaires* between them were allotted 104,000 livres, the inspectors 210,000, the censors in charge of the press 15,750 livres. But the highest sum went to the *guet* and the Paris guard, 1,142,276 livres, plus 4,350 livres bonus and 10,000 for officers' salaries. The total budget for the Paris police amounted to 1,583,876 livres. To this we must add the cost of the other services, such as the fire brigade, lighting, street-cleaning, say just under a million. Thus the greater part of the budget went to pay the armed forces of the police: the secret funds, which have been much exaggerated, only amounted to some 20,000 livres.

The budget for the police was not high in relation to that of the country as a whole. This partly explains the feeble part played by the police in the repression of uprisings. True, the Paris police was perfectly well organized as long as nothing serious or abnormal was taking place; but in time of trouble it proved inadequate. This inadequacy resulted from the lack of financial support provided by the monarchy; and this, in turn, can be explained by the state of France's finances in the closing days of the *ancien régime*, that considerable deficit which necessitated the meeting of the Assembly of Notables in 1787 and of the Estates-General in 1789.

4. The prisons of Paris: the Bastille

The monarchy could scarcely have resorted to that method of forestalling disturbances which Marshal Lyautey was later to recommend: a show of force, in order not to have to use force. It chose, rather, to display executions as a deterrent; these took place on the place de Grève, in the very heart of Paris: death by hanging, breaking on the wheel or even quartering, as in the case of Damien, who had wounded Louis XV with a penknife. There were also a number of prisons with sinister reputations: Bicêtre, La Force, Charenton or Saint-Lazare; jails for thieves and criminals, such as the Conciergerie, La Tournelle, the Grand Châtelet and the Petit Châtelet, debtors' prisons such as Fort l'Evêque, and finally State prisons, of which there were three in France, the château of Pierre-Encise near Lyons, the fortress of Vincennes, and the Bastille in Paris.

By the end of the eighteenth century the Bastille had become more than a prison; it was a symbol for all that was obsolete and feudal about the *ancien régime*, and above all for its arbitrary power.[1]

The word *bastille*, or *bastide*, meant a fortress in medieval times. In fact the Bastille had been built by Charles V as early as 1370 to guard the entry into Paris through the porte Saint-Antoine. It played its part in the fifteenth and sixteenth centuries and even during the Fronde. But by the beginning of Louis XIV's reign its military value was being called in question. The poet Claude Le Petit (who was burnt on the place de Grève on September 1st, 1662, for writing licentious verse) had asked:

> *A quoi sert ce vieux mur dans l'eau,*
> *Est-ce un aqueduc, un caveau,*
> *Est-ce un reservoir de grenouilles?*

(What's the use of this old wall in a ditch? Is it an aqueduct, a cellar or a frog pond?)

And the answer came:

> *C'est la Bastille, ce me semble,*
> *C'est elle-meme par ma foy,*
> *Ventre bleu, voila bien de quoi*
> *Faire que tout le monde tremble!*

(It's the Bastille, I do believe; it is indeed, I declare! Zounds, that's enough to make everybody shake with fear!)

He ended by defining its role:

> *. . . De ce château sans garnison*
> *Il tâche à servir de prison,*
> *S'il ne sert pas de forteresse.*

(. . . this unmanned castle, which is no use as a fortress, but tries to be a prison!)

The Bastille was a rectangular building consisting of eight round towers, joined by plain walls a hundred feet high. These towers

[1] On the Bastille, see Fernand Bournai, *La Bastille* (series called L'Histoire générale de Paris), Paris, 1893; F. Funck-Brentano, 'La Bastille d'après ses archives' (*Revue historique*, vol. XLII, 1890, pp. 38–73 and 278–316); Id., *Légendes et archives de la Bastille*, Paris, 1898.

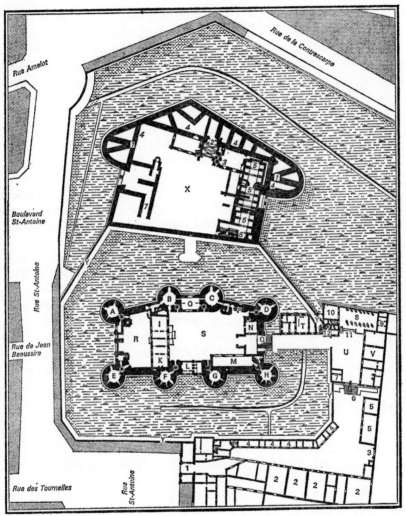

(a) PLAN OF THE BASTILLE, with the constructions discovered during the demolition of the bastion

each had a name: the Tour du Coin, de la Chapelle, du Puits, de la Bertaudière, de la Bazinière, du Trésor, de la Comté, de la Liberté. The latter was thus named because it contained those prisoners who were free to walk about the courtyards of the prison. Entry to the Bastille was restricted to a single carriage gateway with a wicket-gate for pedestrians. These gates were protected by two drawbridges over the deep wide moat that surrounded the fortress. This moat was sometimes full of water from the Seine, but in 1789 it was dry.

The fortress formed a quadrilateral with two courtyards separated by a building which connected the Tour de la Chapelle with the Tour de la Liberté. The first court, as one entered the castle, was called the Grande Cour or Cour de l'Horloge, because of a huge clock on the building between the two towers. This clock was supported by sculptured groups of figures representing prisoners in chains. The second court was known as the Cour du Puits (the Well).

To get into the Bastille one had to skirt the West and South walls and cross two courtyards surrounded by outbuildings. The first was known by the characteristic name of Cour du Passage, or Cour des Casernes (the Barracks). It was entered by a doorway on the site of the present no. 5, rue Saint-Antoine. On the fortress side of this courtyard stood a series of shops let out by the Governor of the Bastille for his own profit, and on the opposite side stood the barracks of the pensioners on guard over the castle. The Cour du Passage was open all day. At its further end, on the south side of the castle, a new doorway in the Doric style opened on to a second courtyard, called the Cour du Gouvernement. In front of this doorway was a moat five or six metres wide, crossed by two drawbridges, one for carriages and the other for pedestrians. This fortification, which connected the Cour du Passage with the Cour du Gouvernement, was called *l'avancée*, the advance-post. Along one side of the Cour du Gouvernement, facing the walls of the Bastille, stood the Governor's residence. This courtyard was connected with the interior of the fortress by means of the double gate, protected by drawbridges, which has already been mentioned. To the east of the fortress, a 'bastion' which had been turned into a kitchen garden defended the castle on the faubourg Saint-Antoine side.

For a long time the Bastille was only used as a military citadel and not as a prison. Important persons visiting Paris stayed there. The governorship of the Bastille was an honourable appointment, conferred on members of the aristocracy such as Leclerc du Tremblay, brother of Richelieu's *éminence grise* Father Joseph.

It was Richelieu who made the Bastille into a 'State prison', that is to say one where people were confined who had committed a crime or an offence not punishable under common law, and who had been arrested by means of *lettres de cachet*, arbitrary orders given by the King. In Richelieu's day as many as 55 prisoners were detained in the Bastille. These included men suspected of plotting against the Minister, three monks and two priests described as '*extravagant*', eccentric, probably some sort of heretic unless indeed they were mentally deranged, three forgers, one noble whose death sentence had been commuted to life imprisonment, some twenty other noblemen accused or convicted of various crimes, a few officers detained for disciplinary offences, and finally some foreigners, important prisoners of war or spies.

Under Louis XIV the Government began sending to the Bastille journalists or gazetteers who had written or published lampoons against his policy, duellists caught *in flagrante delicto* and, from 1685 onwards, Protestants and even Jansenists. Here, too, were sent individuals involved in the great 'scandals' of the time, the *affaire des poisons*, cases of witchcraft and forgery. It was at this period that orders were first given to maintain secrecy about the names and ranks of prisoners. The Bastille began to be surrounded by mystery. Legends arose. The Bastille seemed all the more redoubtable in that it had become a mysterious prison in which people were shut up without knowing why, and from which they were released—sometimes—without knowing how.

The Government of Louis XV used the Bastille in the same way, imprisoning there Jansenists, pamphleteers, writers, conspirators (under the Regency, the members of Cellamare's plot), but also, on occasion, those charged with offences or crimes under common law whose cases were being investigated by the Châtelet.

Under Louis XVI, the administration of the Bastille was more like that of the other prisons, except that the treatment of prisoners was better there. The Minister Breteuil gave orders that the *lettre de cachet* must bear some indication of the probable length of detention. During the reign of Louis XVI, from 1774 to 1789, 240 individuals were incarcerated in the Bastille, an average of 16 a

year. Now the Bastille could hold 42 prisoners in separate detention; it was thus never full. The number of prisoners detained
varied widely: there were 10 in September 1782, 7 in April 1783,
27 in May 1783, 9 in February 1789 and 7 when the Bastille fell
on July 14th, 1789.

Of these seven, four were forgers, arrested on warrants from the
Châtelet, who might equally well have been imprisoned in some
other jail: Jean La Corrège, Jean Béchade, Bernard Laroche,
known as Beausablon, and Jean-Antoine Pujade. All four were
accused of having forged bills of exchange which had been accepted
by the banking firm of Tourton-Ravel. Two other prisoners were
indubitably deranged: De Witt or De Whyte, an Irishman born in
Dublin, who took himself for Julius Caesar, St Louis or even God;
he had been accused of spying; and Tavernier, who had been
imprisoned in the Bastille since 1759, charged with complicity in
Damien's attempt on the life of Louis XV. Finally, the Comte de
Solages had been incarcerated by means of a *lettre de cachet*
obtained at the request of his family in 1765; he was suspected of
murder.

Life in the Bastille prison was easier than in other jails.
Originally, it was the custom for a prisoner detained there to bring
in his own furniture and servants and provide his own meals. If he
was poor, he was allowed a certain sum for his subsistence. In the
eighteenth century the administration of the Bastille was brought
into line with that of other prisons. The inmates were no longer
allowed money, and their food was provided by prison kitchens,
but the sum allotted for each one's board varied according to his
rank from 6 to 36 livres. The food was said to be good and plentiful.
The rooms were furnished by the State, but prisoners were allowed
to improve their surroundings with their personal belongings. By
the end of the eighteenth century, certain rooms had been turned
into cells with bars over the windows and locks on the doors. There
were also some very damp underground dungeons, but these had
not been used since 1776. The rooms high up in the towers, under
the domed roofs, were also particularly uncomfortable, being very
cold in winter and very hot in summer; refractory prisoners were
detained here.

As we have pointed out, the legends about the Bastille sprang
from the characteristic secrecy with which, since the end of the
seventeenth century, imprisonment had taken place there.

Prisoners were brought to the castle in a coach with drawn blinds, and the soldiers on guard had to face the walls. Jailers might have no sort of conversation with the prisoners, who were forbidden to write their names either on the walls, or on plates, or on the margins of their books. A sick prisoner could only be referred to by his doctor by the number of the floor and the name of the tower where he was incarcerated.

Any prisoner newly confined to the Bastille by *lettre de cachet*, that is to say by the King's arbitrary command, was supposed to be examined within twenty-four hours, but this principle was very loosely applied. Sometimes, if the man arrested was an important personage, he might be invited to lunch with the Governor immediately on his arrival. But he might equally well be kept waiting in the castle for two or three weeks before appearing in front of a *Commissaire du Châtelet* or, sometimes, before the Lieutenant of Police in person. In every case, a report on the prisoner was made by the Lieutenant of Police, in view of which the King might send another *lettre de cachet* ordering release or *non-lieu* (i.e. no grounds for prosecution). During the reign of Louis XVI 38 *non-lieux* were ordered out of a total of 240 prisoners, rather under one-sixth. Thus, although it was increasingly seldom used, the *lettre de cachet* remained a very arbitrary method. It is true that Napoleon I and even more recent régimes in France resorted in certain cases to administrative internments which were just as arbitrary; nonetheless, the *lettre de cachet* had come to symbolize, by the end of the eighteenth century, the arbitrary character of the 'feudal' régime. The fact that any prisoner unjustly incarcerated could secure compensation alters nothing.

Contrary to legend, prisoners in the Bastille were fairly well treated. They were not subjected to judicial torture except in cases provided for by law, that is to say neither more nor less than in other prisons; moreover torture was abolished by decree in 1780 and 1788. As has been said, the dungeons were not used after 1776; and from that date, too, prisoners were no longer in chains. On Malesherbes' orders in 1775, prisoners were given leave to read and write; however, the letters they wrote or received had to be read by the authorities. They might also work, provided they were not in possession of tools that would enable them to escape.

Those prisoners who were entitled to the 'freedom of the yard' might walk about there, play bowls, and chat with the officers of the garrison. Certain prisoners even had the right to go into town, on condition they undertook to return to the Bastille at night.

When the *lettre de cachet* ordering a prisoner's release was received, the officials of the Bastille returned his belongings to him; he had to sign a statement of release and promise to reveal nothing of what he had seen in the Castle. Sometimes other commitments were required of him which, if not fulfilled, would expose him to a second arrest.

The Bastille was not a pleasant place, but neither was it the horrible medieval jail that has so often been pictured. It was a prison in which 'enlightened' authorities had improved the prisoner's lot. But what contributed to maintaining and even enhancing its evil fame was the long series of individuals who had been detained there for no reason or, worse still, to prevent them from expressing themselves freely.

In the seventeenth century, one of the first famous prisoners was the 'man in the iron mask'—which was actually a velvet mask worn to conceal his identity. Legends have been rife about this much-discussed figure, who was confined in the Bastille from 1698 till 1703 and it seems clear today that he was an agent of the Duke of Mantua's named Mattioli, who was also in the service of Louis XIV and betrayed him.

In the eighteenth century, it was the arbitrary arrest of writers that gave the Bastille its sinister reputation. Voltaire, then aged twenty-two, was imprisoned there from May 17th, 1717, to April 14th, 1718, because of some scurrilous Latin verse he had written against the Regent and his daughter, the duchesse de Berry. He was back again for twelve days in April 1726, following a quarrel with the chevalier de Rohan-Chabot after he had dared to make fun of this nobleman, who had him beaten up and arrested. Later, Voltaire was to contribute in no small measure to the odium attached to the Bastille.

The abbé Morellet, one of the leaders of the *philosophes'* party, was sent there on June 11th, 1760, for publishing a virulent attack on the writer Charles Palissot, who was hostile to their movement, and on other members of the 'devout sect', notably Mme de Rebecq, who was to die of tuberculosis a few days later. Morellet was arrested on orders from Malesherbes, although the latter had often shown himself friendly to the *philosophes*. During his six weeks' detention in the Bastille Morellet wrote a *Treatise on the Freedom of the Press*.

Marmontel was imprisoned as the result of a complaint from the duc d'Aumont, for having read, in Mme Geoffrin's *salon*, a satire against this highborn nobleman. He remained in the Bastille for eleven days and on leaving declared that the food had been excellent. It was not in the Bastille but in the castle of Vincennes that Diderot was incarcerated. But did people make any clear distinction between these two fortresses, both of which were used to house State prisoners who had dared to express their opinions too freely? Diderot was arrested on July 14th, 1749, because of his *Lettres sur les aveugles à l'usage de ceux qui voient*. He was kept in jail for three months, and was able to go on correcting the proofs of the *Encyclopédie* and to correspond with his friends. It was in the Château de Vincennes, too, that the marquis de Mirabeau, the 'friend of mankind', was imprisoned for ten days because of his *Theory of Taxation*; his son, the comte de Mirabeau, was there in his turn from 1777 to 1781; he was accused of having abducted a minor, Sophie de Monnier. The imprisonment of these well-known writers had damned all State prisons in the eyes of the *philosophes*. But the general public learned to hate the Bastille by reading the works of two celebrated prisoners, Linguet and Latude.

Linguet, a lawyer and journalist, had been struck off the lawyers' register for libel in 1774, then imprisoned in the Bastille for two years, from 1780 to 1782. During this time he wrote his *Mémoires sur la Bastille*, which he published immediately on his release. The work excited great interest. Linguet depicted the Bastille in the darkest colours, in spite of the comparatively comfortable conditions that prevailed there, the plentiful and varied diet provided.

One remark made Linguet's memoirs famous. On the day of his arrival he was visited by the hairdresser.

'To whom have I the honour of speaking?'

'Monsieur, I'm the barber of the Bastille.'

'*Hé, que ne la rasez-vous*? Why don't you raze it to the ground?'

Linguet, needless to say, took refuge from fresh prosecution by settling in Belgium. He sided with the 'patriots' there in 1787 and returned to France in 1791. But his outspokenness caused him to be arrested once again, in 1793, this time by order of the *Comité de Salut Public*; he was condemned to death by the revolutionary

95

tribunal and executed in 1794. This tragic end to his story showed that the first republican government punished subversive opinions even more vigorously and harshly than did Louis XVI. But in 1794 it was a matter of victory or death for the Republic; in 1780, the *ancien régime* had not seemed as gravely threatened.

The writings of Latude did even more, possibly, than the memoirs of Linguet to spread and perpetuate the legend of the Bastille. Latude was born on March 23rd, 1725, at Montagnac, near Pézenas, in what is now the department of Hérault. He was the illegitimate son of a maidservant named Danry, and it was under that name that he enlisted in the army as a surgeon's assistant. He took part in the war of the Austrian Succession and when this was over, in 1748, he came to Paris. In order to better his position he devised a complicated intrigue, as a result of which he was accused of trying to poison Mme de Pompadour. He was therefore arrested and shut up in the Bastille on May 1st, 1749, then transferred to Vincennes on the following July 18th. He escaped on June 15th, 1750, but was caught and brought back to the Bastille, where he was kept in a cell until the end of 1751. He was eventually transferred to a room again, where with his companion, one d'Allègre, he made meticulous plans for an escape. This took place during the night of February 25th, 1756, by means of a rope ladder which the pair had contrived to make. They reached Belgium and then Holland, but were pursued thither by *exempts*, arrested with the consent of the Governor of the United Provinces on June 1st, 1756, and brought back to the Bastille. Latude was once again confined to a cell and this time was kept there for forty months, until September 1st, 1759, in spite of many protests.

After the death of the marquise de Pompadour (1764), Latude was transferred to the castle of Vincennes. He than assumed the name under which he was to remain famous. He claimed to be the son of Henri Vissec de La Tude, an officer in the King's army who had died at Sedan on January 31st, 1761. Latude thought that such a connection would gain more weight for the many petitions with which he ceaselessly assailed the Government. Since these failed to produce any results, Latude escaped for the third time. He was caught again, and wrote fresh statements and even pamphlets against the Ministers. On account of these pamphlets he was thought to be mad, and was transferred to the lunatic asylum at

July 7th, 1789. Bravery of the *gardes-françaises*

Bibl. Nat., Print Room, Vinck Collection, 1494

July 8th, 1789. A misfortune at the Palais-Royal

Bibl. Nat., Print Room

July 12th, 1789. The busts of the Duke of Orléans and
Necker being carried to the Place Louis XV

Bibl. Nat., Print Room, Vinck Collection, 1508

Charenton on September 27th, 1775. He was released at last on June 5th, 1777. But by July 16th of that same year he had already been arrested again, this time for fraud, and incarcerated at Bicêtre. His thirty years' imprisonment, his unsuccessful attempts to escape, and his misfortunes had finally come to the notice of the *philosophes* and even of the members of the French Academy. The latter now intervened in his favour, and he was finally released on March 24th, 1784. He was now famous. 'Enlightened' people and philanthropists gave him money; he was received by Jefferson, then United States ambassador in France. From the earliest days of the Revolution he figured as a hero, the most illustrious victim of that Bastille which had just been captured. He penned an 'Address to the French Nation', and his portrait was exhibited at the Salon of 1789. In 1799 he published his *Mémoires*, which had a tremendous success; they ran into 20 editions, and were translated into several foreign languages. A free copy was sent to the central administration of every department. It is in these *Mémoires* that we shall find the origin of all the widespread legends about the Bastille.

Latude had been granted a pension of 400 livres on his release. It was raised to 2,400 livres by the *Assemblée législative*. Latude published several pamphlets under the Republic, and eventually became a supporter of the Empire. He died at the age of eighty, on January 1st, 1805.

By 1789 the people of Paris had come to feel a violent hatred for the Bastille, fostered by the memoirs of Linguet and the tale of Latude's sufferings. They longed to have it destroyed. The Government itself was influenced by the current of opinion and wondered whether, for economy's sake, it might not be as well to close down the Bastille, which was expensive to run. The prison governor received a salary of 60,000 livres a year, a vast sum for those days; in addition to which there were the salaries of jailers, doctors, surgeons, apothecaries, almoners, the pay of the garrison, food and clothing for prisoners, and the upkeep of the building.

All this expense, for the sake of guarding a dozen prisoners and preserving an old fortress which could hardly contribute to the maintenance of law and order in a capital of 600,000 inhabitants, appeared excessive. The money spent on keeping up the Bastille would have been better employed on strengthening the Paris police force. So Necker, during his brief period as Minister, considered not only closing down the prison but even demolishing it. As early as 1784, an architect, Corbet, had prepared the plan for a public square to be laid out on the site of the Bastille, and in the centre of which there was to stand a statue of Louis XVI on a pedestal made by melting down the chains and padlocks of the Bastille. On June 8th, 1789, the architect Davy de Chavigné submitted to the Royal Academy of Architecture a proposal for a monument to be erected on the ruins of the Bastille in honour of Louis XVI, the liberator. The famous sculptor Houdon wrote to Chavigné: 'I am very anxious this project should be carried out. The idea of raising a monument to liberty on the very place where bondage has reigned hitherto seems to me a noble thought and one well calculated to inspire a man of genius.' A contractor named Palloy had already offered his services to pull down the building. Thus the destruction of the Bastille was 'in the air', even before it was attacked.

Ten years before the fall of the Bastille, it had lost its power as a deterrent, and the Government was aware of this. It was now merely an object of hatred and anger for the Parisians, for, as Servan wrote in his *Apologie de la Bastille*, it represented 'any place hermetically closed and carefully guarded, into which any persons, irrespective of rank, age or sex, may go without knowing why, stay without knowing how long, until they may perhaps get out without knowing how.' And the people of Paris wanted no more Bastilles, any more than they wanted the 'feudal' régime to linger on. Was the feeble Paris police force capable of preventing them from carrying out their plan? It might have been, had it felt the Government and the authorities behind it. But from 1787 to 1789, on many occasions, the authorities blamed the police for attempting to carry out their duties. In 1789, therefore, conscious of no longer enjoying the confidence of the Government, they were to act feebly and irresolutely. Thus the police force which was held to be the best in the world was soon to allow the insurgent Parisians to gain control of the capital.

V

The Development of the Revolutionary Spirit in France from 1787 to 1789

It has often been asserted that the fall of the Bastille on July 14th, 1789, marked the beginning of the Revolution in France. This is not strictly true. The Fourteenth of July marks, primarily, the end of something: of the *ancien régime*, of 'feudalism'. As for the Revolution, this had begun twenty years earlier in Western countries, and warning signs of it had been felt in France, as we have said, as early as 1775, when the *guerre des Farines* took place. But it was the meeting of the Assembly of Notables at Versailles in 1787 that brought France into the cycle of popular demonstrations and Governmental repression, of reforms undertaken in haste and often as hastily abandoned, in a word into the Revolutionary era.[1]

1. The first Assembly of Notables (1787)

After the fall of Turgot, which followed the *guerre des Farines* in 1776, after the subsequent fall of a few ephemeral ministers and the eventual fall of Necker in 1783, Calonne had been appointed Finance Minister.[2] He was expected to resolve the terrible contradiction that confronted all Western states at the end of the eighteenth century: to meet the constantly increasing expenditure indispensable to the functioning of a modern administration, without destroying the fiscal privileges enjoyed by the wealthiest orders, the nobility and clergy. For three years Calonne strove, as Necker had done, to evade the problem and cope with financial

---

[1] On this subject in general, consult Jean Egret, *La Pré-révolution française*, Paris, 1962; and the duc de Castries, *Le Testament de la monarchie : l'agonie de la royauté*, Paris, 1959.
[2] R. Lacour-Gayet, *Calonne*, Paris, 1963.

difficulties by means of borrowing. But by the end of 1786 the Government's credit was exhausted. The Controller-General of Finance had to choose between bankruptcy and a thorough reform of the fiscal system. But such a reform could not fail to provoke resistance from the 'established bodies' which supported the aristocracy, first and foremost the *parlements* which had been suppressed under Louis XV, by Maupeou and the abbé Terray, but rashly restored by Louis XVI on his accession. Calonne was reluctant to return to Maupeou's policy and suppress the *parlements* once more; such a *coup d'État* might have provoked the aristocracy to immediate revolt. He preferred to skirt the difficulty by submitting his plan of reform to an assembly of privileged persons who, being hand-picked, might be expected to prove docile. Such gatherings of eminent persons had on several occasions been summoned by French kings, for instance by François I in 1527, by Henri II in 1558, by Louis XIII in 1627. Louis XVI agreed. He also gave his approval to the plan that Calonne intended to present to the Assembly of Notables. This projected a thorough reform of the fiscal system, which was to result in the equality of all citizens under taxation. The most oppressive of all direct taxes, the *vingtième*, was to be suppressed and replaced by a land tax, already suggested by Turgot and Necker, and which, being proportional to the value of landed property, could be paid in kind. The *taille* was to be lightened, the *corvée royale* commuted, internal customs barriers abolished, and a great number of taxes diminished. Calonne also revived Necker's project of provincial assemblies elected by landowners, without distinction of 'orders', who would be responsible for assessing direct taxes. Calonne, finally, struck a first blow at the feudal nobility and the clergy by proposing to redeem, or buy back, seignorial dues collected by the Church. The sum thus raised would pay off the clergy's debt. The 144 members of the Assembly of Notables had been chosen by the Government; they comprised 7 princes of the blood royal, 37 magistrates, 14 prelates, 36 great lords, 12 Intendants and State councillors, 12 deputies from the *pays d'État* (i.e. provinces where the États met regularly) and 26 delegates from towns.

The Assembly was summoned to Versailles on January 19th, 1787. Public opinion was immediately hostile, assuming that the aim of the Assembly was to levy fresh taxes rather than to institute reforms. Satirical prints, caricatures and pamphlets against the Notables proliferated. Consequently, even those who were most favourably inclined towards the Government sided with its opponents for fear of unpopularity. The few allies of Calonne included Lamoignon, of the Parlement of Paris, who in any case was not supported by his colleagues, and the comte d'Artois, who had long been the official patron and friend of the Controller-General. Among Calonne's chief opponents were the Archbishop of Toulouse, Loménie de Brienne, who hoped to take his place, the Archbishop of Narbonne, Dillon, who was called upon to preside over the Assembly, the Maréchal de Beauvau, Necker's friend, La Fayette, leader of the 'liberal' faction, d'Aligre, First President of the Paris Parlement, and Nicolai, First President of the *Chambre des Comptes* (the Audit Office).

The opening of the Assembly[1] was delayed until February 22nd, owing to Calonne's illness and then to the death of Vergennes, the Foreign Minister. Thus the Notables who had foregathered at Versailles were kept waiting for three weeks, during which they were able to organize concerted action against the Government. The Assembly was divided into seven *bureaux* (panels) each of which had to study a project of reform, and its conclusions were to be presented on March 26th.

Of all Calonne's various projects, only the one dealing with the creation of provincial assemblies was agreed to; and even so, considerable alterations were demanded, in order to ensure the preponderance of the privileged orders, the division of seats between the three orders was to be maintained, except that the number of representatives of the Third Estate was to be doubled; and the President must be a noble or a prelate. On the other hand the projects for fiscal reform met with unanimous opposition.

[1] On the Assembly of Notables, see P. Renouvin, *L'Assemblée des notables de 1787, la conférence du 2 mars*, Paris, 1921; Id., *Les Assemblées provinciales*, Paris, 1920; A. Goodwin, 'Calonne, the Assembly of French Notables of 1787 and the origins of the "révolte nobiliaire"', in the *English Historical Review*, 1946, nos. 240 and 241, pp. 202–234 and 329–377; W. J. Pugh, 'Calonne's New Deal', in *The Journal of Modern History*, 1939, pp. 289–312; F. Nussbaum and W. S. Pugh, 'Finance et politique dans les dernières années de l'Ancien Régime' (*Commission d'histoire économique de la Révolution française*, 1939, *Assemblée générale*, vol. II, Paris, 1945, pp. 485–498); J. Egret, 'La Fayette dans la première assemblée des notables' (*A.H.R.F.*, 1952, pp. 1–31); L. Gottschalk, *La Fayette between the American and the French Revolution*, Chicago, 1950; M. P. Chevallier had edited the *Journal de l'Assemblée des notables de 1787, par le comte de Brienne et Étienne-Charles de Loménie de Brienne, archévêque de Toulouse*, Paris, 1960.

Loménie de Brienne denounced the land tax as being unjust, since it would affect the gross and not the rateable produce of the land; La Fayette demanded the publication of an exact statement of the national budget, prior to any reform. Almost unanimously the Notables asked for these projects to be submitted to the Parlements. The sale of the feudal dues belonging to the clergy was declared to be an infringement of property.

Calonne endeavoured to reach a compromise with the Assembly, so as to avoid a rupture. Discussions on a limited scale took place on March 1st and 2nd; Calonne's inconsistencies in his statement of the financial situation did not improve his position. On March 9th the Assembly declared that it accepted the creation of provincial assemblies, with certain alterations. It consented to the reduction of the *taille* and the suppression of the *corvée royale*. But it unanimously rejected the land tax, which had been the keystone of Calonne's project. Nevertheless he refused to admit defeat. He drew up other projects of reform, and passed them round among the Notables, who took advantage of this to formulate further criticisms affecting the entire administration. La Fayette demanded that the King should 'formally recognize certain constitutional principles'. The Assembly renewed its demand for an accurate statement of accounts. Calonne asked the King to dissolve the Assembly. But the comte de Provence, Brienne and other Notables, with the help of the Queen, brought influence to bear on Louis XVI, who on April 8th dismissed Calonne. After a brief interlude performed by Bouvard de Fourqueux, Brienne became 'Principal Minister'.

Brienne was known for the administrative gifts he had shown in his diocese of Toulouse, for his expertise as a bibliophile, for his hostile attitude towards monks[1] and his blatant indifference in matters of religion. However he was soon forced, as Calonne had been, to submit to the urgent needs of the financial situation. He therefore presented a new project, which dropped the proposed Provincial Assemblies and the redemption of Church property, but retained the land tax, although with certain modifications; various other accessory reforms were also suggested. The notables declared that they lacked the necessary powers to approve a land tax, that only the authentic representatives of the Nation could

[1] P. Chevallier, *Loménie de Brienne et la réforme de l'ordre monastique*, Paris, 2 vols., 1960.

pass such a bill. La Fayette, on May 21st, demanded 'the convocation of a truly national assembly', and, when asked by the comte d'Artois what he meant, he replied: 'The Estates-General of the kingdom.' A cautious silence greeted these words, but the great idea had now been launched. Henceforward it seemed likely that the crisis would only be solved by the convocation of the Estates-General. Louis XVI, unable to make up his mind, dismissed the Notables on May 25th, 1787.

The meeting of this Assembly marks the real beginning of the Revolution in France. It made manifest to all the attitude of the aristocracy, more violently hostile than ever to any strengthening of the power of the throne because it sought above all to maintain its fiscal privileges. It thus marks the beginning of that revolt of the nobles which resulted from this reaction. It spotlighted the financial crisis which, for the past twelve years, had undermined the Government. It showed that the problem of financial recovery was linked to the reform of the State and, basically, to an alteration of the regime. But it made it clear that the deficit belonged to the national treasury and that the conditions attached to the means of discharging the debt would constitute formidable weapons in the hands of those who knew how to use them.

2. The Nobles' Revolt

After the dissolution of the Assembly of Notables, the alternative before the Government was the same that had confronted Calonne six months earlier, bankruptcy or the reform of the State; but this reform would now have to be carried out by force, and, as in 1771, if the privileged persons who constituted 'intermediary bodies' were not to have their own way, they must be compelled to accept reforms.

Brienne asked the Parlement of Paris to register the draft bills that had been set before the Assembly of Notables. The Parlement raised no objection with regard to the liberation of the corn trade within the kingdom and the free export of grain in normal years, it accepted the replacement of the *corvée royale* by money loans, but like the notables it refused to register the land tax and the increased stamp duty (July 6th–9th, 1787). It declared itself incompetent to approve taxes the duration of which had not been fixed, and demanded the convocation of the Estates-General (July 24th). Brienne decided to resort to force and on July 30th announced a *lit de justice*, a special solemn session. The Parlement retorted: 'Only the nation, represented by the Estates-General, has the right to grant the King subsidies the need for which is clearly shown.' The *lit de justice* took place at Versailles on August 6th, but the very next day the Parlement declared the registration 'null and illegal'. On August 13th, after a speech from Councillor d'Eprémesnil, it asserted by 80 votes to 40 that the fiscal decrees were 'contrary to the rights of the nation', and began legal proceedings against Calonne, who left for England, thus becoming the first French émigré.

Brienne was reluctant to repeat Maupeou's *coup*. He hoped to intimidate the Parlements; in fact, he merely demonstrated to all classes of the nation the extreme weakness of the Government. He confined himself therefore to exiling the Parlement to Troyes. But immediately on their arrival in this town the councillors proclaimed that 'only the Estates-General could probe and cure the wounds of the State and impose taxes.' Simultaneously, in Paris, the *Cour des aides* (the body concerned with assessing subsidies) and the *Chambre des comptes* (the Audit Office) withdrew the approval they had originally given to Brienne's bills. In the provinces, all the supreme courts declared their opposition. This aristocratic revolt was supported by street riots. In Paris the home of Chénon, *commissaire* of police, was looted. A campaign of pamphlets, frequently very scurrilous, was launched against the Government, and did not spare the King and Queen. Lamoignon, Minister of Justice, was for taking strong measures; Brienne, shaken by the resistance he had met with, favoured concessions. Louis XVI listened to Brienne.

The Government therefore withdrew the edicts for stamp duty and land tax and confined itself to asking for a temporary increase in the *vingtième*. The Parlement accepted this and returned in triumph to Paris, amid public rejoicings which lasted three days and degenerated into anti-government riots.

According to Hardy, the bookseller, anti-royalist tracts had begun to circulate from August onwards,[1] and the Government, expecting trouble, had brought in 500 of the *gardes de Paris* to protect the Palais de Justice, supported by the regiment of *gardes-françaises*. Despite this, on September 28th, the day of the Parlement's return, an excited crowd of young people, consisting of

---

[1] S. P. Hardy, *Mes loisirs*, MS in the Bibliothèque nationale, vol. VIII, p. 178.

clerks, lawyers, apprentices, journeymen, and employees of the luxury trades in the place Dauphine, gathered on the Pont-Neuf and in the adjacent streets and attacked the police and the troops with squibs, fireworks and stones. The soldiers were obliged to open fire. One sergeant in the *gardes-françaises* was heard to shout: '*Foutez-moi du plomb dans les fesses de cette canaille.*' (Get some lead into the bastards' backsides!) The soldiers fired into the air and nobody was wounded, though one lawyer had his cloak pierced by a stray bullet. Five youths were detained and taken, in spite of abuse and stone-throwing from the crowd, before the Commissaire, Ferrand, in the rue des Lombards, who cross-examined them. Four prisoners (two building-trade apprentices and two goldsmiths' journeymen) were consigned to the prison of La Force. The fifth, a master tailor, was set at liberty. All of them lived in the neighbourhood of the Palais de Justice, or else in the Latin quarter.

For a whole week, nevertheless, disorder reigned in the streets. Squibs and rockets were let off in front of the Palais de Justice; pamphlets against Calonne and his friends were freely distributed,[1] and the comtesse de Polignac was hanged in effigy. Finally on October 3rd the Parlement issued a decree forbidding further demonstrations, or the letting-off of squibs and fireworks in the vicinity of the Palais. However, on November 12th a fresh demonstration took place, and 600 members of the police force had to be called in to break it up. Those involved in demonstrations seem to have been chiefly middle-class citizens, together with the journeymen and apprentices of the districts near the Palais and, above all, the members of the legal profession.[2] The harvest of 1787 had been a good one, the price of bread was normal, and so the faubourgs of Paris were unaffected.

The Parlement meanwhile was over-elated by the demonstrations which had been made in its honour and which it interpreted as a token of its popularity. It disavowed the efforts of the police to maintain order, and blamed those who had given orders to fire on the crowd. Henceforward the police proved reluctant to intervene, for fear of the magistrates' disapproval.

[1] R. W. Greenlaw, 'Pamphlet Literature in France during the Period of the Aristocratic Revolt', in the *Journal of Modern History*, 1957, pp. 349–354.
[2] G. Rudé, *The Crowd in the French Revolution*, Oxford, 1959; Id., 'The Outbreak of the French Revolution', in *Past and Present*, Nov. 1955, pp. 28–42.

Furthermore, while the mob was strenuously acclaiming the members of the Parlement 'fathers of their country', 'defenders of the people', the feeble reaction of the forces of order convinced it that it had gained control of the streets. The common people were to remember this during later demonstrations and to 'go out into the streets' without hesitation, even after the Parlement had lost its popularity. For after all, their demonstrations were still to be against the Government and in the name of 'the Nation', just as in those hectic days of September and October 1787.

Eventually the Parlement, conscious that it had the people of Paris behind it, refused to vote any new taxes, merely agreeing to a slight increase in the *taille*. Brienne was thus obliged, like Calonne, to resort to a system of loans, which moreover the Parlement opposed likewise. So that Brienne soon found himself faced with the following alternatives: either State bankruptcy—or a fresh *coup de force* against the Parlements—or else the convocation of the Estates-General. Brienne negotiated secretly with d'Éprémesnil, one of the ringleaders of the Parlement. It was agreed that the Parlement should consent to loans up to 420 million livres, spread out over five years (1787 to 1792) but on the other hand Brienne promised to convoke the Estates-General for 1792. These decisions, however, had to be registered.

The Parlement, assembled in a 'royal session'—intermediate between an ordinary session and a *lit de justice*—on November 19th 1787, expressed fresh and serious criticisms of the Government's financial policy. D'Éprémesnil asked for the meeting of the Estates-General to be brought forward to 1789. This the King promised, without specifying any date, and he ordered the Parlement to register the edict sanctioning a fresh loan. 'It's illegal!' exclaimed the duc d'Orléans. 'I don't care,' replied Louis XVI, and then added: 'Yes it's legal, since it's my will!' The King left the meeting and the duc d'Orléans was carried in triumph. Next day the King ordered his exile and had two councillors arrested. For the next six months, the Government and the Parlements were engaged in a minor war which intensified the financial crisis, showed up the weakness of the State even more clearly and caused the unrest in the Parlement to spread to the nobility and the bourgeoisie of the whole of France. When the Parlement of Paris raised fresh objections, the King replied quite justifiably, on April 17th, that if he gave way 'the monarchy would become nothing but an aristocracy of magistrates, as contrary to the true interests of the nation as to those of his own sovereignty.' He had clearly discerned the object of the Parlement: to place the State under the exclusive direction of the aristocratic bodies. But in order to retain popular support for its aims, the Parlement continued to pose as defender of the 'rights of the Nation', as it asserted once again in its proclamation of the 'fundamental laws of the kingdom' on May 3rd, 1788: this declared that the right to vote subsidies belonged solely to the Estates-General; that Frenchmen could not be arbitrarily arrested nor detained; that the privileges hallowed by law and tradition were inviolable. Since it seemed impossible to overcome the opposition of the Parlements, the only solution was to imitate Maupeou and suppress them. It would have been wiser not to reinstate them in 1774, or else to proceed to abolish them in the spring of 1787. By May 1788 it was too late, since there had been a clear demonstration both of the Government's weakness and of the strength of its various opponents. At this date, an act of force against the Parlements could only unleash the Revolution that had been brewing for the past year.

Having had the supposed ringleaders, Councillors d'Eprémesnil and Montsabert, arrested in somewhat dramatic circumstances, the King summoned a *lit de justice* at Versailles on May 8th, where he compelled the Parlement to register six edicts which deprived the Parlements of most of their functions and transferred these to forty-seven newly created judicial bodies called *grands bailliages*. A plenary court, a sort of permanent Assembly of Notables, was instituted to register the edicts; it was expected to prove subservient. Criminal procedure was reformed: judicial torture, which had already been much reduced by the decree of 1780, was entirely abolished. A very serious blow was dealt to 'feudalism' by the curtailing of the private jurisdiction of the nobility; henceforward, in civil lawsuits, a case could be deferred at the request of one of the contending parties and taken before a royal justice. However, contrary to the measures taken by Maupeou in 1771, the sale of judicial posts was retained.

After these decrees had been read, the King declared: 'You have now heard my wishes. The more moderate these are, the more resolutely they will be executed.' The firmness of his tone contrasted only too strongly with his timidity in practice. The edicts of May 8th displeased both the aristocrats whom they affected directly and the bourgeoisie, who found them inadequate, since they allowed the sale of functions to continue. In fact they satisfied nobody, but brought about an alliance between various opposing factions, and spread and intensified revolutionary tendencies.

The Parlement endeavoured, without complete success, to prevent the establishment of the *grands bailliages*. But they succeeded in arousing disturbances in the larger towns, which were all the more serious because the harvest of 1788, as we shall see later, was one of the worst of that century, the price of commodities was rising at a dizzy speed, while unemployment, in this rapidly expanding population, was assuming catastrophic proportions. Agitators found it easy to collect the raw material for a revolt: building or textile workers, shop assistants, even farm labourers come to town in quest of some problematical job. All were young; the average age of the 1788 rioters was 23.

In Paris, demonstrations succeeded one another in the streets. Lamoignon was burnt in effigy on the place de Grève. At Toulouse the *grand bailliage* was invaded by rioters, the judges were booed and barely managed to hold three sessions. At Pau, spurred on by their Parlement and anxious about their bad harvest, the peasants from the surrounding countryside occupied the town on June 19th, broke down the gates of the Palais de Justice, besieged the Intendant and the Governor in their own homes, and forcibly reinstated the Parlement, which declared Béarn 'alien to France, although subject to the same King'.

In Brittany the nobility united closely with the Parlement, for its interests were threatened by the suppression of 2,500 seignorial tribunals. On May 10th a riot broke out at Rennes. The Intendant, Bertrand de Molleville—later to become Minister of the Navy under the Legislative Assembly—and the *commandant* of the province, the comte de Thiard, who were hostile to the edicts, were half-hearted in their attempts to repress this riot, but this did not prevent them from being wounded by the demonstrators. Tumult reigned in the streets of Rennes until May 31st, when the *commandant* of Brittany was forced to order the *parlementaires* into exile. Demonstrations broke out with renewed violence and Bertrand de Molleville finally fled from Rennes on July 9th. On June 13th and 14th the nobles of Brittany met at Saint-Brieuc, and on June 19th and 20th at Vannes. Twelve members had already been nominated to present at Versailles the protests of the Breton aristocracy against the edicts of May 8th and the repression of the Rennes riots. The King refused to receive the delegates, and had them arrested and confined to the Bastille; this was the largest contingent of prisoners to enter the fortress before July 14th. Twelve new deputies set out for Versailles, but were stopped at Houdan and had to turn back. Finally on July 30th Louis XVI consented to receive 18 Breton delegates of all three orders. But this gesture did not allay discontent. The Breton nobles, following the example of the American insurgents, formed 'correspondence committees'. A central committee was set up at Rennes to 'co-ordinate resistance'. The Third Estate, however, was divided between partisans of the Parlement and of the King. Only two towns, Saint-Brieuc and Saint-Malo, adhered wholeheartedly to the aristocrats' movements and added their deputies to a new delegation of the nobility. This 'great deputation', in which the nobility was still preponderant, reached Paris on August 21st, but was not received by the King till ten days later, after the fall of Brienne.[1]

In Franche-Comté, the Parlement of Besançon, composed of elderly, authoritarian and redoubtable councillors, had constantly refused to register most of the royal edicts. A special session, a *lit de justice*, was held at which it was compelled to register not only the edicts of May 8th but also that of August 1779, which abolished *mainmorte* in the royal domain. For nine years, in fact, the Parlement had objected to this edict, because many of its councillors owned land under the *mainmorte* system and were afraid that the ban might be extended to private property. But the aristocracy of Franche-Comté organized resistance and demanded the restoration of the old provincial Estates.[2] In Dauphiné the nobility were resentful not only of Lamoignon's edicts but also of the creation of provincial assemblies; they demanded, as in Franche-Comté, the restoration of the provincial Estates suppressed in 1628. After the forcible registration of the edicts, on May 10th, the magistrates of Dauphiné protested violently, declaring that if these edicts were maintained 'Dauphiné would consider itself as completely released from loyalty towards

[1] J. Egret, 'Les origines de la révolution en Bretagne' (*R.H.*, 1955, pp. 189–215).
[2] Id., 'Le révolution aristocratique en Franche-Comté' (*R.H.M.C.*, 1954, pp. 245–271).

its sovereign.' On June 7th, they were ordered into exile. This provoked the popular rising known as the *journée des Tuiles*. The people of Grenoble, including some of the very poorest, those workless peasants who crowded in from the destitute countryside, climbed on to the roofs and hurled tiles at the soldiers who were forcibly escorting the *parlementaires* out of the town. The home of the *commandant* of the province was ransacked, and there was one fatal casualty. The *commandant* capitulated and, in order to pacify the rioters, announced that he would no longer attempt to carry out the King's order and that the Parlement was reinstated. On June 14th the aristocracy and bourgeoisie of Grenoble invited the three orders of the province of Dauphiné to assemble, elect deputies and send them to Grenoble. When this meeting took place on July 21st, Mounier and Barnave were seen to play a leading role. As the King forbade them to assemble at Grenoble the deputies moved to Vizille, to the country house of one of the richest and most powerful men in Dauphiné, Claude Périer.

On its own authority, the Vizille assembly decreed the restoration of the Provincial Estates of Dauphiné, and convoked their meeting for the beginning of September; they were to consist of an equal number of deputies from each of the privileged orders and from the Third Estate. It also demanded double representation of the Third Estate at the forthcoming Estates-General, recommended the privileged orders to abandon their fiscal privileges and advocated the admission of commoners to all functions. This programme had already gone well beyond that of the aristocracy, yet we must notice that the Vizille assembly demanded neither equality of rights, nor the suppression of the orders, nor the abolition of the feudal regime. The bourgeoisie remained united with the nobility against authority, but neither class gave much thought as yet to the claims of the common people.[1]

The aristocratic revolt nevertheless led gradually to the formation of a 'party' which entitled itself 'patriotic' or 'national'. This party, which to begin with supported the Parlements in their struggle against the Government, soon broke away from them. It was composed of *philosophes* such as Condorcet, of lawyers such as Target, Bergasse, Lacretelle, Danton, Barnave, Mounier, of magistrates—Hérault de Séchelles, Fréteau, Servan—of journalists

[1] Id., *Le Parlement du Dauphiné et les affaires publiques dans la seconde moitié du XVIIIe siècle*, Grenoble, 2 vols., 1942.

—Brissot, Volney—and of a few liberal nobles—La Fayette, Mirabeau, La Rochefoucauld. It demanded the immediate convocation of the Estates-General, profound structural reforms, a written constitution. This party very soon replaced the Parlements in the forefront of the movement. The police, disconcerted by constantly changing instructions, ceased to act. The officer class, being mostly aristocrats, made common cause with their order. The army intervened only half-heartedly, both at Rennes and at Grenoble. Even the *intendants*, who resented being deprived of part of their functions by the provincial assemblies, put up no resistance.

The Government, now supported only by a handful of paid pamphleteers, was forced to capitulate. Brienne, in a decree of the State Council of July 5th, 1788, announced the convocation of the Estates-General for the near future, without specifying a date. At the same time the King requested 'all well-informed persons . . . to send reports having a bearing on the forthcoming convocation.' It was an indirect concession of freedom to the press.

On August 8th the Estates-General were summoned for May 1st, 1789. But this measure could not fill the coffers of the State. For lack of funds, all payments were suspended for six weeks. Brienne's policy had failed, and he resigned on August 24th.

Necker was recalled to the Ministry, with the title of Director-General of Finance, then of 'Principal Minister'. His return to power aroused fresh demonstrations in the streets, like those which had greeted the return of the Parlements the year before. But this time the demonstrators had an additional motive: anxiety at the rise of prices, following the disastrous harvest which had just been brought in. On August 16th a four-pound loaf cost nine sous, next day nine and a half, ten on August 29th, ten and a half on September 2nd and eleven on the 7th, an increase of 50% on the normal price. People naïvely hoped that Necker was going to check this rise.

As soon as Brienne's resignation became known there was a renewed outbreak of squibs and fireworks, to which the police failed to react. In the faubourg Saint-Antoine, crowds gathered. On August 28th the workers and the *'menu peuple des marchés'*, the common people from the market-places, joined the demonstrators from the faubourgs. The occupants of carriages crossing the Pont Neuf were forced to shout: 'Down with Lamoignon!' According to Hardy, the bookseller, when 'the populace of the faubourg Saint-Antoine and that of the faubourg Saint-Marcel came to swell the crowd of local riff-raff, confusion only grew greater.'[1] On August 29th, the guards' posts on the Pont Neuf were looted and burnt to the ground. The Government once again appealed to Maréchal de Biron, the 'peace-making hero' of May 1775. Guards and soldiers were ordered to disperse the crowds by force. During the night of August 29th–30th, the guards of Paris fired on 600 demonstrators who had gathered in the place de Grève, and seven or eight persons were killed.[2] Calm was restored in Paris for a couple of weeks. But Lamoignon, who was responsible for the edicts of May 8th, handed in his resignation on September 14th.

This news provoked fresh demonstrations, which assumed an increasingly revolutionary character. There were shouts of '*Vive Henri IV!*' on the place de Grève, where yet again Lamoignon was burnt in effigy; a more serious matter was the attempt to set fire to his house, and the attack on that of the commandant of the Paris guard, Chevalier Dubois, in the rue Saint-Martin. The troops fired on the assailants, who were approaching along the rue Meslai. According to Hardy, fifty people were killed and twenty-five arrested;[3] according to the police, there were only eight injured and eighteen arrested. In any case, it was highly disturbing.

A declaration by the King on September 23rd reinstated the Parlements in all the functions and prerogatives they had enjoyed before May 8th. The return of the Parlement to Paris was the occasion for further demonstrations. The crowd yelled: '*Vive Henri IV! Vive le Parlement! Au diable les tristes à pattes!*'[4] In the rue de la Harpe there was a clash between demonstrators and *gardes-françaises* in which many people were injured. The Chevalier Dubois, conscious of his inability to maintain order, resigned his post; he was rewarded with a bonus of 10,000 livres and the post of Lieutenant of the fortress of Péronne. The Lieutenant of Police and the Commandant of Paris were summoned before the Parlement for having attempted to suppress the demonstrations in favour of the 'fathers of the people'. It was only on an express order from the Government that Brienne and

[1] S. P. Hardy, *op. cit.*, vol. VIII, pp. 61–62.
[2] Arch. nat., X, I*b* 8989.
[3] S. P. Hardy, *op. cit.*, vol. VIII, p. 80.
[4] 'A common, unflattering term for the cavalry.' (G. Rudé).

July 12th, 1789. The *gardes-françaises* repulsing a detachment
of the Royal-Allemand regiment

Bibl. Nat., Print Room, Vinck Collection, 1522

July 12th, 1789. The *Conférence* customs post set on fire

Bibl. Nat., Print Room

July 12th, 1789. The people closing the Opéra

Bibl. Nat., Print Room. V'nel Coll. tôme 8444

Lamoignon were not prosecuted. Faced with such a situation, one can imagine the heartsearchings of the police; must they go on obeying, and thus run the risk of incurring censure and even prosecution in the near future?

As for the instigators of the demonstrations, who were so ready to rush out into the street and tackle the Parisian police force without a moment's hesitation, who were they? We cannot of course be certain, but George Rudé has examined the problem by noting the professions of those killed, injured and arrested.[1] The fifty professions mentioned include 24 journeymen, apprentices, small farmers, *'gagne-deniers'* (casual workers), 10 master-craftsmen, 16 small tradesmen or shopkeepers. In so far as a survey based on such a small sample can be of value, it suggests that half these demonstrators were unemployed or unskilled workers, that is to say belonging to the poorest section of the community, and half small artisans or self-employed tradesmen. This is roughly the social composition of the mob of Parisian *sans-culottes* of the Year II.[2] The districts in which these individuals lived shows the starting-point of the demonstrations: the rue de l'Oratoire, the rue Mauconseil, rue des Innocents, rue des Lombards, rue des Gravilliers, all central districts—or again the rue des Quatre-Nations, rue Sainte-Geneviève, rue des Thermes-de-Julien, rue de l'Observatoire, that is to say the faubourg Saint-Germain or the Latin quarter. Is it pure coincidence that none of those whose names have survived lived in the faubourg Saint-Antoine or the faubourg Saint-Marceau? There are only two joiners among them, as opposed to 11 workers from the clothing trade, 4 from the food trades, 8 building workers and 5 metal workers: employers and apprentices in equal proportions. Undoubtedly the section of the Parisian population that rose on this occasion was identical with that which was to take part in the memorable *journées* of the next few years.

3. The convocation of the Estates-General
Necker was welcomed as a saviour, and even the Queen, who detested him, received him with a good grace. His most urgent mission was to avoid bankruptcy. Thanks to his popularity and the public's confidence in his financial gifts, he was able to set new

---

[1] G. Rudé, *op. cit.*
[2] A. Soboul, *Les Sans-culottes parisiens en l'an II*, Paris, 1958.

loans on foot. He himself lent 2 million livres to the State out of his private fortune. To persuade the reassembled Parlements to register these loans, Necker made concessions to them, restoring their right of remonstrance, at any rate until the forthcoming meeting of the Estates-General. Brienne had announced the convocation of the Estates for May 1st, 1789. There was no question of going back on this decision, for the loans and other financial expedients to which Necker might resort to enable the State to survive without bankruptcy would not serve much beyond that date. But it was indispensable to state clearly the conditions under which the Estates were to meet, since they had last been convoked in 1614. Which Frenchmen would have the right to vote? Which were to be the electoral constituencies? How would voting within the Estates take place? These questions shattered the apparent unanimity which seemed to have united all adversaries of the regime behind the Parlements. The aristocracy hoped that the Estates-General would defend and maintain their privileges as the Parlements had done, but this would only be possible if the privileged classes were in the majority, that is to say if the Estates were convoked 'according to the forms of 1614' with an equal number of deputies for each Order, and if voting took place *par ordre*. On the contrary, the bourgeoisie and the wealthier, and therefore most enlightened, section of the peasantry wanted the forthcoming Assembly to abolish the 'feudal' regime and its privileges, to construct the rational State which the philosophes had been describing for the past forty years and which was being realized in America, and to allow wealthy and educated commoners the share to which they felt themselves entitled in the government of the Nation. For this it was indispensable that the unprivileged class should be in a majority in the Estates, that is to say that the deputies of the Third Estate should be twice as numerous as those of each of the privileged Orders, as the Vizille Assembly had demanded, and that voting should be *par tête*.

The 'national' or 'patriot' party therefore closed its ranks. Following the example of America, the United Provinces and Belgium, the patriots met in groups such as had been forming for the last fifty years, Masonic lodges, reading-rooms, agricultural and economic societies, or simply in cafés; furthermore, like the American insurgents or the Breton nobility, they formed 'correspondence committees' to defend their ideas, to set out and even to impose their programme. Taking advantage of the decree of July 5th they flooded France with their propaganda; over 2,500 pamphlets were published, and the first revolutionary periodicals, such as Volney's *Sentinelle du peuple*, began to appear. Necker, who was responsible for summoning the Estates-General, had thus to come to a decision about the number of deputies from each order, and even about the way they should vote once the Assembly was constituted. Anxious to retain the support both of the patriots and of the Parlements, he endeavoured to evade this heavy responsibility by passing it on to the Assembly of Notables, which had been revived and summoned for November 6th, 1788.

The second Assembly of Notables differed from that which met in February 1787 in that it consisted of 152 members instead of 144, 40 of these sitting for the first time.[1] The Assembly received a list of 25 questions to be decided, all relating to the composition, convocation and election of the Estates-General. Six panels were formed, which studied these questions for a month and presented their answers on December 11th; the Assembly was dissolved the following day. The notables had split up into two camps; the majority, centred around the *parlementaires*, declared in favour of maintaining the 'forms of 1614'. But a minority, led by the comte de Provence, brother of the King, resentful of the nobles' revolt and avid for popularity, demanded 'double representation for the Third Estate.' An even larger majority opposed the vote *par tête*, and even those that were favourable to this insisted that it must previously have been approved by the majority of the deputies of each order. During these deliberations, press campaigns were proceeding apace. The 'national' party pressed, with increasing violence, its demands for double representation of the Third Estate and the vote *par tête*; the pamphlets of Target, and Sieyès' *Essai sur les Privilèges* were published at this time. Many municipal bodies petitioned Paris in favour of 'double representation'. Disturbed by this campaign, the princes of the blood royal presented to Louis XVI, on December 12th, a petition which amounted to a manifesto from the aristocracy, belatedly aware of the dangers that menaced it, and which it had itself unleashed: 'The State is in peril . . . the very principles of government are

[1] J. Egret, 'La deuxième assemblée des notables' (*A.H.R.F.*, 1949, pp. 193–228).

threatened by revolution; soon the rights of property will be attacked, the inequality of fortunes will be presented as a subject for reform; already the suppression of feudal rights has been proposed ... Can your Majesty consent to the sacrifice and humiliation of your brave, ancient and deserving nobility?' And the princes suggested a compromise: the privileged orders would accept fiscal equality if the Third Estate gave up its request for double representation.

Necker, too, was considering a compromise. But the pressure of public opinion, the fall of prices on the Bourse, and a somewhat reluctant decree of the Paris Parlement persuaded him to decide in favour of double representation, which was readily accepted by the King and Queen, who resented the nobles' revolt. The *Result of the Council of December 27th*, 1788, announced that the Third Estate was to have double representation and that the number of deputies would be proportionate both to the population and to the assessment of each electoral constituency. The Third Estate was to be able to choose its deputies from other orders. As regards the vote, it pointed out that voting *par ordre* was laid down by the rules, but that each of the Orders could take a decision on this matter when the Estates-General met. This meant confronting that Assembly at its very first meeting with a burning question, and one of capital importance.

The Assembly of Notables had instructed a Commission of the State Council, consisting of four councillors (two of them being former 'notables' and one a *maître des reqûetes*), under the chairmanship of Barentin, Minister of Justice, to settle the details of the procedure of convocation. Their conclusions were set forth in the *Règlement électoral* (Electoral Statutes) of January 24th, 1789. These statutes first laid down the electoral constituencies: these were to be the *bailliages* (in the North) and the *sénéchaussées* (in the South), old judiciary divisions dating from the thirteenth century. These divisions, however, were of varying extent. There were some *bailliages* whose area was very small; these were known as *bailliages secondaires* and their delegates met at the headquarters of the principal *bailliage* to elect deputies to the Estates-General. Paris formed a single constituency.

The statutes fixed the conditions of suffrage and of eligibility. A voter must have attained the age of twenty-five, 'the usual majority in the kingdom'; however, each order had its own special provisions. As regards the clergy, all clerks in holy orders had the right to vote. But only parish priests, bishops and archbishops could sit in person in the electoral assemblies; regular canons, monastic orders (except the mendicant orders) only sent their representatives. The assemblies of the clergy, meeting at the chief town in the *bailliage*, elected their deputies to the Estates; the clergy's elections were thus made in some cases by direct, in others by indirect, suffrage.

All hereditary nobles were electors, even if they possessed neither fief nor property. Women and minors could be represented, but a proxy could not represent more than two persons. The assembly of the nobility also met at the chief town of the *bailliage*; in its case suffrage was direct, with a very few exceptions.

As regards the Third Estate, things were far more complex. An elector must not only be over twenty-five, he must be inscribed on the roll of tax-payers, which excluded vagrants and beggars but not servants. In the villages, the inhabitants met in primary assemblies; in the towns, the trade guilds also formed primary assemblies, and in the larger towns people who did not belong to a guild met in the various wards. The delegates elected by these assemblies forgathered at the chief town of the *bailliage* with the village delegates, in a ratio of two for every hundred households ('*feux*') to form the electoral assembly of the Third Estate, which elected the deputies. All electors were eligible as deputies. Thus for the Third Estate, suffrage was two degrees removed in the case of villages, three in the case of towns; in the case of the secondary *bailliages*, there was even a further degree, since their assemblies sent a quarter of their members to the chief town of the principal *bailliage*.

The Statutes specified that all members of the nobility possessing fiefs, and all members of the clergy, would receive a personal summons to appear at the assembly of their respective orders, while nobles without fiefs and members of the Third Estate would be informed by public notices. The Statutes also indicated how the presidents of the assemblies were to be chosen. The clergy would appoint the member highest in the hierarchy, the nobles' president was to be elected; as for the assemblies of the Third Estate, they would be presided over by the *bailli* or the *sénéschal*.

The Statutes prohibited multiple votes for the Third Estate. Each elector had to vote in the locality of his 'principal domicile'.

A noble, on the other hand, could sit in the Assemblies of all *bailliages* in which he owned a fief.

Voting was open in assemblies of rural parishes or trade guilds. In the assemblies of *bailliages*, however, deputies must be elected by secret ballot. An absolute majority was required in the first two rounds; in the third, a bare majority was enough. A man might be elected in his absence, but in that case a substitute must also be elected in case of his refusal.

Each assembly had to draw up a *cahier* setting forth the complaints of the electors. A '*cahier général*' presented the synthesis of the complaints of the whole constituency.

We see, then, that the electoral statutes went into great detail. They settled the country's electoral procedure for a long time to come, indeed in many instances up to our own day. But the rules they laid down would fail to secure for the Third Estate any of the advantages it sought if, when the Estates met, the deputies were to vote *par ordre* and not *par tête*. The need to settle this fundamental question made the choice of each order's deputies even more important. The publication of the *Règlement* of January 24th, the novelty of the procedure it set in motion, the conflict of ideas aroused by the drawing up of the *cahiers*, the general anxiety in face of the uncertainty about conditions of voting within the Assembly, all this provoked, from February onwards, a feverish excitement among the electorate of France.

VI

Electoral Excitement

Georges Lefebvre, the great historian of the Revolution, liked to assert that had the Estates-General not been convoked for 1789, the Revolution would not have broken out in France that year. Probably not; but it is doubtful whether it could have been indefinitely avoided, since, as we have seen, there were only three solutions to the financial problem facing France at this time. First, State bankruptcy, more or less palliated perhaps by an issue of paper money inadequately backed by property; considering the state of public opinion at the time, this would have brought about a revolution. Second, far-reaching reforms carried out by an energetic Government. It is doubtful whether reforms involving serious infringement of the privileges of the two higher Orders of the State could have been carried out without violent opposition from the latter, and this in turn would have developed into revolution, as happened in Belgium at the same period. Finally, recourse to the Estates-General. The novelty of this procedure, which had become unfamiliar through disuse and indeed almost forgotten, the extent of the franchise, since almost every Frenchman over twenty-five was required to express his opinion, the immensity of the interests at stake, could not fail to provoke violent excitement. But this unrest, though political in its origin, was strengthened and increased by the haunting dread of scarcity, indeed of famine. The elections of 1789 coincided, in fact, with one of the sharpest economic crises of the whole eighteenth century.

1. The economic crisis of 1789
The basic cause of this crisis was the disastrous harvest of 1788,

which caused a catastrophic rise in the price of corn and consequently of bread. Its accessory causes were the slow but continuous collapse of the wine trade, and the first difficulties encountered by French industry as a result of the trade treaty concluded with England in 1786, known as the Eden Treaty, which considerably lowered the tariff rates on products manufactured in Great Britain.[1]

The bad harvest of 1788 was a consequence of the disastrous weather conditions of that year. A prolonged drought had already made it clear, by the end of the Spring, that the harvest was likely to be a poor one. But a terrible storm which ravaged all the region around Paris, the best cornfields in France, on July 13th, 1788, transformed the prospect of a mediocre harvest into the certainty of a very bad one. We have seen that the price of grain had already begun to rise by mid-August, which was an exceptional phenomenon, and that in Paris, by mid-September, the price of bread was 50% above the normal rate. The accompanying graphs will show, better than any lengthy explanation, the considerable rise in the price of cereals and bread.[2] For ease of understanding, the quantities have been converted into metric quintals and the prices into francs (germinal). Graph no. 4 shows the evolution of the price of grain in the market of a small town in Champagne, Sézanne, between 1789 and 1793. Sézanne, in a rich corn-growing region, reflects the immediate result of the fluctuations in the harvest. Following a mediocre harvest in 1783, the price of wheat had risen in 1784 to 31·60F per quintal, but the excellent harvest of 1785 had brought it down to 16 francs in 1786. Since that year, on the contrary, there had been a constant rise, reaching its maximum, 46 francs, in July 1789. Graph no. 5 represents the price of corn at Avallon, a small town situated in a more fortunate region than Sézanne. The curve here is almost the same as for Sézanne, except that the prices at Avallon are lower than at Sézanne. But we recognize on this graph the crisis of 1784, the drop in prices of 1786

---

[1] On the economic crisis of 1789, see E. Labrousse, *Esquisse du mouvement des prix et des revenus en France au XVIIIe siècle*, Paris, 1933; Id., *La Crise de l'économie française à la fin de l'Ancien Régime et au début de la Révolution*, Paris, 1944 (important studies of the crisis in general, and in particular of the crisis in the wine trade).

[2] On the rise in the price of grain and bread, see E. Blin, 'Le prix du blé à Avallon, de 1756 a 1790', in *Commission d'histoire économique de la Révolution, Assemblée générale de 1939*, vol. II, Paris, 1945, pp. 11–25.

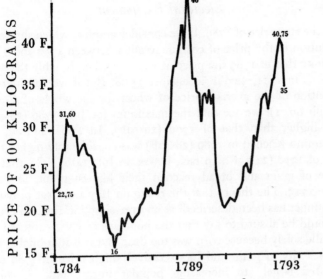

Fig. 4. Price of wheat at Sézanne, 1784–1793

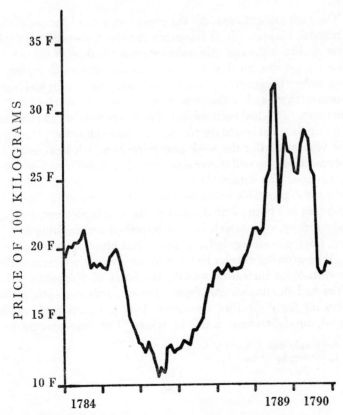

Fig. 5. Price of corn at Avallon, 1784–1790

and the steep rise of 1789. If we consider graph 2, which shows the evolution in the price of corn at Avallon between 1770 and 1790, we note that in 1789 the price of wheat reached roughly the same level as in 1771, 32·06F as against 33·68. But if we consider the evolution of the average price of wheat for the whole of France (graph no. 1)[1] we see that the maximum for July 1789 (28·40F) was higher than that of 1770 (22·10F). In Paris, indeed, the maximum reached in 1789 (28·40F) was considerably higher than that of 1770 (24·25F). In fact, it was on July 14th, 1789, that the price of grain and bread reached their highest point, in Paris, since 1715. The theory that the rising on July 14th was provoked by hunger has been described[2] as an over-simplification. Of course it would be absurd to say that the populace of Paris captured the Bastille solely because corn was too dear, but it is indubitable that the scarcity of grain and its excessively high price in 1789 contributed largely to increasing popular unrest and, all things considered, to provoking the Parisian rising of July 11th to 14th.

The high price of bread hit the poorer sections of the population —manual workers, casual labourers and the like—with particular severity. But at the same time the catastrophic drop in the price of wine ruined the small vine-growers of the Bordeaux region, of Languedoc, Burgundy and the Loire. This drop, which had begun between 1770 and 1780, was a result of the development of viticulture. This had been subjected to severe restrictions; Colbert, in particular, had issued decrees strictly forbidding the planting of new vineyards. But the weak governments which had succeeded one another at Versailles ever since 1715 had failed to enforce these regulations. New vineyards had multiplied. To begin with these had proved profitable to the peasant, infinitely more so than if the same area had been planted with cereals. The landowner could get ready money, with which he had improved his dwelling and his food, buying meat regularly, which he had hitherto been unable to do. Vine-growing villages had a more prosperous appearance than the rest. With increasing wealth, the habit of discussing public affairs had developed. But from 1770 onwards over-production, following the difficulties encountered by the wine trade at this period, brought about a fall in prices. The vine-growers were

[1] See graphs nos. 1, 2 and 3, p. 13.
[2] J. Mistler, *Le 14 Juillet*, p. 10.

ruined, and the living standard which they had been at such pains to improve declined. Political discussions in their villages assumed a very bitter tone.

Stock farming suffered, too. The drought of 1775 had been disastrous for sheep, while cattle were affected by frequent epidemics.

Furthermore, the trade agreement with England seemed to hit French industry and industrial workers. Concluded, as we have said, in 1786, it lowered customs duty on English manufactured goods entering France and on French wines entering England. At the time, many people blamed this treaty for the economic crisis of 1789. It certainly played a part in this crisis, but only a contributory one, for two reasons: on the one hand, French industry was more seriously affected by the decrease in national consumption than by English competition. The rise in the price of bread obliged the mass of French consumers to reduce their purchase of manufactured goods, particularly textiles, and reserve the scanty funds at their disposal for buying foodstuffs. Secondly, the Eden Treaty had been so recently put into practice that its effects could hardly have been felt in 1788–89. Nevertheless it is clear that France had begun to be flooded with English manufactured articles, cheaper than her own because of the lead England enjoyed in the industrial field. On the other hand, the lowering of the English customs duty did not greatly increase the sale of French wines in Great Britain, since the English had already formed the habit of drinking Portuguese wines.

Such, then, was the atmosphere in which the elections took place. The common people, irritated by high prices and shortages, did not attribute these misfortunes to natural phenomena, to disastrous weather conditions. They needed a scapegoat, one or several individuals whom they could blame. Unemployed workers and artisans, shopkeepers whose trade was stagnant harboured resentment against the Government, which was responsible for the Eden Treaty. Casual labourers and manual workers, the unskilled and the jobless, seeing with despair that they could no longer buy the bread they needed to feed their families, accused the Government or the large-scale producers of hoarding grain. There was more talk of the 'famine pact'—the term used, by analogy with the 'family pact' between France and Spain, to describe a contract concluded by Louis XV's Government with the firm of Malisset for supplying Paris, but which had not produced the results hoped for.

Thinking people quite justifiably ascribed the rise in prices to taxation. For a good part of the taxes levied by the Government were indirect taxes bearing on staple foodstuffs, such as the salt tax or *gabelle*, the *aides* affecting wines, tolls and duties on most food products, dues that varied in different provinces, milling dues on cereals, an 'equivalent' tax on meat in Languedoc. Needless to say, feudal dues in kind, such as the *champarts* and tithes, which reduced the amount of agricultural produce available to the peasants, were the objects of fierce indictment, as were also the 'monopolies', the communal mill and bakehouse (*banalités*), which meant higher prices, and the hunting rights which damaged harvests and deprived the peasant of game. These taxes and dues aroused greater hatred in 1789, on account of the scarcity of food, than in a year when prices were normal.

2. The elections, the drafting of the *cahiers* and unrest in the provinces

The Electoral Statutes of January 24th, 1789, had not fixed one specific date for the elections throughout France, as is done nowadays, so that voting took place at times chosen by local authorities and dragged on, if we include the Paris elections (to be discussed later) until May 1789.[1] The state of unrest was thus kept alive throughout France by what might be called the electoral campaign and by the staggering of elections. In virtue of the Decree in Council of July 5th, 1788, which authorized all Frenchmen to express their points of view on the reorganization of the State, tracts and pamphlets poured forth in their hundreds, proposing remedies to the crisis and 'models' for the *cahiers*. Sieyès, for instance, published his famous pamphlets, *Essai sur les privilèges* and *Qu'est-ce que le tiers état?* But he also circulated a number of *Appeals* to the good folk of Normandy, Picardy, Languedoc, and so forth. The Government, for its part, remained neutral. In spite of Malouet's advice Necker refused to intervene, and the elections took place freely.

[1] On the year 1789 in general consult G. Lefebvre, *Quatre-vingt-neuf*, Paris, 1939; Id., *La Grande Peur de 1789*, Paris, 1932; F. Braesch, *1789 : l'année cruciale*, Paris, 1941; P. Frölich, *1789 : Die grosse Zeitwende*, Frankfurt-am-Main, 1957.

Electoral Excitement

In the villages, they were generally held on Sundays after mass. They bore little resemblance to modern elections.[1] Voters did not file past a ballot-box to put in their voting-papers, but forgathered in an 'assembly' which met and deliberated. The assembly generally met in the church. It is difficult to know from the reports what the state of the poll was, for the number of those present is not always noted precisely; abstentions seem to have been relatively few, though the most recent studies show that there was a fairly large proportion of them in the South, sometimes as many as half the electorate.[2]

The electoral assembly of the village met under the chairmanship of the seignorial judge. He was expected to prevent the peasants from expressing their hostility towards the 'feudal' régime. He was rarely able to do so. The anti-feudal feeling was so strong, even in the villages, that it was not easy to oppose it. The assembly would begin by drawing up its *cahier*. Methods varied widely. Sometimes the *cahiers* were the result of long preparatory labours, based on the tracts and pamphlets in circulation. This was the case at Brazey-en-Plaine, in Burgundy, where the successive drafts of the *cahier*, prepared by the village curé Pierre-Claude Perrot, have been preserved.[3] Sometimes the village assembly merely copied a model, adding its own particular grievances; sometimes, again, the entire *cahier* might be original. Subsequently the meeting elected its delegates to the *assemblée de bailliage* and commissioned them to insert the grievances of their parish in the *cahier* of the Third Estate for the *bailliage* or *sénéchaussée*. The complaints included in these rural *cahiers* are thus extremely diverse.[4] We find plans for a new French constitution, projects of

[1] On the elections of 1789, see A. Brette's *Recueil des documents relatifs à la convocation des États généraux de 1789*, Paris, 1894–1915, 4 vols., and A. Onou, 'Les élections de 1789 et les cahiers du tiers état' in *La Révolution française*, 1897, 1909, 1910; Ph. Sagnac, 'La rédaction et la valeur historique des cahiers de paroisse' in the *R.H.M.C.*, 1907; H. Sée, 'La rédaction des cahiers de 1789' in the *R.H.*, 1910.

[2] D. Ligou, *Cahiers de doléances du tiers état du pays et jugerie de Rivière-Verdun*, Gap, 1961.

[3] Jean Richard, 'L'élaboration d'un cahier de doléances: Pierre-Claude Perrot, curé de Brazey-en-Plaine' in *La Rèvolution dans la Côte-d'Or*, 1961.

[4] Many parish *cahiers* have been published, particularly by the *Commission d'histoire économique de la Révolution*, set up by the Government at the suggestion of Jean Jaurès in 1903. Consult Beatrice Hyslop, *Répertoire critique des cahiers de doléances pour les États généraux de 1789*, Paris, 1933, with a *Supplement* published in 1952; Id., *A Guide to the General Cahiers of 1789*, New York, 1936.

electoral reform, as well as discussions on free trade or the organization of justice. These refinements have obviously been borrowed from 'models' or inserted by educated editors, versed in the writings of the *philosophes* and in contemporary tracts. But the *cahiers* invariably contain protests, more or less violent according to the parish, against the 'feudal' régime, seignorial rights, the tithe, often against the division of common lands, enclosures and the burden of taxation. These complaints are obviously sincere. The peasants were seeking to free the land they tilled and to raise their own living standards by shaking off some of the burdens that weighed on them.

In the towns, elections often dragged on for several weeks. The trade guilds' assemblies had to be organized, then the assemblies of electors belonging to no guild, and finally the municipal assembly. In the towns, the number of educated voters was far higher than in the country, and their *cahiers* devoted a larger space to complaints of a general nature, bearing on the reorganization of the régime and administration of the whole country. However, arguments, which were sometimes very lively, took place within the trade guilds' assemblies, particularly on the problem (which had been much discussed ever since Turgot's time) of maintaining or abolishing *jurandes* and *maîtrises*.[1]

The general assembly of the *bailliage* or *sénéchaussée* was held at the principal town and comprised delegates from the villages and from the towns. Under the chairmanship of the *bailli* or *sénéchal*, it drafted the 'general *cahier*' and elected deputies to the Estates. In drawing up the 'general *cahier*' the townsfolk naturally tended to restrict the quota of complaints presented by the rural communes, and to devote most space to political, administrative, financial and judiciary demands. The assemblies of the clergy and nobility also met, it will be remembered, at the chief town of the *bailliage*. They, too, drew up *cahiers* and elected deputies.[2]

The *cahiers* drawn up by the electoral assemblies thus constitute a considerable body of documentation, providing a picture of

---

[1] Only a small number of *cahiers* drawn up by trade guilds have as yet been recovered. A. Perrier has recently published the 'Cahiers de doléances des corporations de la ville de Tulle' in the *Bulletin de la Société archéologique de la Corrèze*, 1955, pp. 43–76.

[2] The *cahiers généraux*, that is to say the *cahiers* drawn up by the assemblies of *bailliages* and *sénéchaussées*, have almost all been published in the *Archives parlementaires*, vol. I.

France as a whole, and each of its regions, in 1789. Of course, one cannot accept this picture without reservations. In general, it was painted in the blackest colours. However, the *cahiers* of the *bailliages* are unanimously hostile to the absolute power of the throne as then exercised, they all demand a written constitution on the pattern of the American constitution, with a legislative assembly and provincial assemblies, all elected, the former being responsible for establishing the budget and voting taxes, the second for the administration of the country. Most of these *cahiers* press for guarantees for individual liberty and the freedom of the press. None of them envisages the abolition of the monarchy. On the other hand they are sharply divided on the question of the liberty of conscience, on the initiating and sanctioning of laws, on the choice of Ministers, on the rights of peace and war, on an eventual reorganization of the Church. All the *cahiers* blame the Government for its 'wastefulness', in which they see the cause of financial difficulties, all hope that a new system of taxation will lessen the burden of each individual by means of a fairer distribution. Many of the Third Estate *cahiers* envisage the abolition of the feudal régime. And in spite of their sharply marked regional differences, they often insist on the need to unify the administration of the country, particularly in the field of legislation, in weights and measures, and in the customs system. On the other hand, if the Third Estate shows, on the whole, a marked hostility to the maintenance of orders and privileges, most of the *cahiers* of the nobility and clergy express a wish to preserve them. Thus the *cahiers* reflect that most violent and deep-rooted of the conflicts characteristic of the Revolution: the struggle for equality.

Given the nature of the demands and protests inscribed in the *cahiers* of the Third Estate, it is not surprising that many 'patriots' were elected by that order, but there were also quite a number of them (particularly parish priests) among the deputies elected by the clergy, and even some among those of the nobility. In the Third Estate, many 'men of law', doctors, and a few merchants represented the commoners; there was scarcely a single peasant or worker. Among the nobles there were a certain number of 'liberals' like La Fayette, whom the American war had made famous, or his brother-in-law the vicomte de Noailles. Another noble, well known both for his tumultuous life and his violent pamphlets against absolutism, Mirabeau, was chosen by the Third Estate of Aix-en-Provence. The abbé Sieyès, famous for his tracts, was elected by the Third Estate of Paris. Among the deputies of the clergy we note the cynical Talleyrand, bishop of Autun. Few of the deputies of the Third Estate were known outside their own province. The astronomer Bailly, deputy for Paris, was celebrated in the scientific world. Mounier had inspired the Assembly that met at Vizille. But Robespierre's notoriety had not spread beyond the region of Arras, where he was a brilliantly successful lawyer.

The excitement provoked by these manifold assemblies, the arguments over the drafting of the *cahiers*, the unprecedented competition for seats in the Estates-General—even though this was purely a matter of individuals, since there were no organized parties—were enough in themselves to create unrest. The rapid rise of prices, the prospect of shortages, indeed of famine, during the critical gap from June to August, between the moment when the stocks of last year's grain were exhausted and that when the new harvest could be consumed, intensified the unrest still further.

In the Northern region in March and April there were a number of attacks on bakeries and cornchandlers' shops: on March 13th at Cambrai, on March 22nd at Hondschoote, on March 30th at Hazebrouck and at Valenciennes, on April 6th at Bergues, on the 11th at Dunkirk, on the 29th at Lille. In Brittany the disturbances which had started in April 1788 went on unceasingly. The *intendant* Bertrand de Molleville was unable to rejoin his post and was replaced by Germain-François Dufaure de Rochefort. As soon as the *Result of the Council* of December 27th was made known, unrest was intensified. On January 9th the town hall at Nantes was invaded by rioters and bakers' shops were looted. When the electoral statutes were published on January 24th, trouble increased. On January 26th and 27th, a violent demonstration took place at Rennes. 'Domestic servants, chairmen and coachmen' demanded 'that the Breton constitution be respected' and clashed violently with the police. On learning this, the youth of Nantes set off for Rennes, but arrived only after peace had been restored. In April, rioting broke out, caused by food shortages, at Guingamp, Morlaix, Vannes, Josselin and Sarzeau. The rioters sought to hold up traffic in grain. At Landerneau, two granaries were plundered. The new *intendant* of Brittany wrote to Necker on April 6th: 'On arriving in Brittany I thought it right to call off the prosecutions

July 12th, 1789. An incident in the Tuileries on July 12th, 1789

engraving by Moreau le Jeune, Bibl. Nat., Print Room, Hennin 10 289

July 12th, 1789. Camille Desmoulins' proposal

Bibl. Nat., Print Room, Vinck Collection, 1503

July 12th–13th. Paris guarded by the people

Bibl. Nat., Print Room, Vinck Collection, 1526

begun in connection with the first riots that took place last October. I did not then imagine that they would recur, but it seems to me essential today to repress by a display of severity such unbridled licence and what appears to be a mutinous conspiracy against free trade in grain.'

In Franche-Comté, too, there was great unrest, particularly from March 30th to April 3rd. At Besançon, the rioters, led by a woman, fixed the price of corn. The home of Bourgon, a Councillor of the Parlement, was broken into, his furniture was smashed, his papers were torn up and thrown out of the window. In the corn loft were found two sacks of wheat and three of flour: a meagre booty! The house of Talbert, President of the Parlement, was also ransacked in search of corn, but without success. On the other hand 'a great deal' was found in the home of President Bouclans, and it was confiscated.

In the Alps, to the east of Gap, three villages of the valley of the Vance rose up in April against their lord, d'Espraux, Councillor of the Parlement of Aix. The peasants took back the grain they had paid in as *champarts* (feudal dues) in 1788. On Monday April 20th the peasants of the village of Avançon marched in an armed band down to Saint-Etienne-le-Laus and persuaded the inhabitants of that village to go with them to d'Espraux's château at Valserres. They invaded the château in the absence of the *seigneur*; but the *maréchaussée* (constabulary) intervened and, with the help of a troop of light cavalry, soon dispersed the demonstrators. In the same Alpine region the inhabitants of Le Passage (south of La Tour-du-Pin) decided to stop paying their feudal dues unless the lord produced the original act of concession.

Meanwhile unrest was spreading throughout the whole of Provence, in the towns as well as in the countryside, and assuming a definitely revolutionary aspect. It would seem that the disturbances began at Manosque where, on March 14th, the populace insulted and stoned the bishop, accusing him of favouring hoarders. On March 21st, at Marseilles, posters went up inciting those workers who paid no taxes to protest at being excluded from the franchise by the electoral statutes of January 24th. 'If you have courage, show it now,' urged the posters. Two days later, March 23rd, the demonstrators looted the home of the *directeur des droits affermés* and attacked that of the *intendant*. A 'council' of delegates of the three orders assembled forthwith and took over power from the municipality. It created a 'citizen militia', an important and characteristic gesture to be imitated later in Paris, though not until July 11th. The same day, at Toulon, workers at the arsenal demonstrated because they were owed two months' wages. On March 24th, disorder spread to Solliès, Hyères and La Seyne, where the electoral assembly was broken up by the insurgents. On March 25th there was a rising at Aix, due to the excessive price of bread. The first consul, who had refused for several days to fix the price of bread, was forced to agree to do so; in spite of which the rioters called him to account and he barely managed to escape through a window in the Hôtel de Ville. On March 26th Peyniers, Saint-Maximin, Brignoles, Barjols, Salernes, Aups, Pertuis, Riez, and Soleilhas were affected by the disturbances; the rioters pillaged barns and granaries, especially those belonging to monasteries and convents. At the same time they protested against the exclusion of poor workers from the electoral roll. Sometimes, as at Saint-Maximin, they nominated a new town council. They frequently attacked monastic buildings (the convent of the Ursulines at Barjols for instance), episcopal palaces (at Toulon and at Riez), châteaux (at Solliès and at Besse), mills (at Pertuis). Archives were seized and burned. At Aups on March 26th, one M. de Montferrat was killed. Everywhere, the demonstrators declared that they refused to pay any more tithes.

In Languedoc, on April 17th, the people of Agde went out into the countryside and carried off grain by force. On May 4th, 5th and 6th, in the little town of Limoux, south of Carcassonne, a crowd of seven to eight hundred people forced their way into the town hall and required the consuls (municipal authorities) to affix seals to the towns' granaries so that no corn could be removed. Next day the demonstrators demanded that a whole series of seignorial dues and indirect taxes should be abolished, that the price of corn and bread should be fixed and that these should be distributed gratis to the needy. The municipal authorities refused. The demonstrators then poured into the streets, forced their way into the tax-collector's offices, ransacked them and threw the account-books into the river Aude. On May 6th, the municipal authorities of Limoux decided, as those of Marseilles had done six weeks previously, to form a citizens' militia or *milice bourgeoise*, which restored order. In Guyenne, Bergerac had seemed threatened on April 22nd by a similar assault from the peasants of the neighbourhood, but these scattered before reaching the little town.

We read of similar disturbances in the Parisian region. In the neighbourhood of Chantilly the peasants took to hunting, in defiance of the Condé family's monopoly. On March 28th two guards who tried to put a stop to this were shot dead. The *sub-délégué* d'Enghien wrote that food shortages 'had driven the peasants nearly desperate'.

On April 15th riots broke out in the market place at Montlhéry, caused, so the *intendant* Bertier de Sauvigny wrote to Necker, by the peasants' refusal to give up their corn for less than 40 livres. In spite of the presence of ten brigades of the constabulary, corn was looted and its price fixed at 24 livres. There were similar scenes at Bray-sur-Seine on May 1st and at Rambouillet, where corn was priced at 24 livres and barley at 15 livres, despite the intervention of eight brigades of mounted constables, as well as Swiss soldiers and *gardes-chasses* (gamekeepers). On April 20th, on the road between Vatan and Poulaines, north of Châteauroux, 'fourteen woodcutters, penniless and starving', stopped and seized a convoy of corn. Elsewhere, townsfolk who were short of corn went out to commandeer some by force of arms in the neighbouring country-side; this happened on March 1st at Alençon, and in the beginning of April at La Ferté-Bernard.

These disturbances developed not only because unrest was as widespread as was the high price of grain and of bread, but also, as we have seen, because the forces of order acted halfheartedly. Their officers were afraid of being disowned or even punished by the authorities or by the Parlement, as had happened the previous year, if they should intervene forcefully. The non-commissioned officers were resentful of the decrees of 1781 and 1787 which, in practice, reserved commissions exclusively for the nobility and deprived them of any hope of promotion. They shared the ideas and the wrath of the common people, from whom they had sprung. Some of them, who had fought in America side by side with the colonial insurgents from 1778 to 1783, were not immune to the appeal of new ideas, to the glamour of the great principles of liberty and equality. And moreover the spread of unrest throughout all the regions of France, and its continuance, resulted in the splitting up of these troops into small detachments lacking any cohesion or discipline, and exhausted, furthermore, by continual alarms and excursions.

131

Thus the forces responsible for maintaining order frequently assumed a passive attitude when faced with insurrection. This was the case at Besançon from March 30th to April 3rd. According to a contemporary report,[1] 'on the Saturday evening, leaflets were distributed in the barracks warning the soldiers not to go where their assistance might be asked for. The Mayor went to find M. le marquis de Langeron, and found him already informed of the situation; he asked for orders, and was told by the *commandant* to wait and see.' While the private houses of members of the Parlement were being looted, the soldiers 'warned the rioters, out loud, not to break anything, but meanwhile whispered to them: courage, lads, courage!'

At Alençon, the *intendant* wrote on April 2nd: 'The *maréchaussée*, being just as unreasonable (as the crowd) and anxious to pay less for their bread, don't perhaps do all that they should to repress rebellion.' At Bellême, the sergeant of cavalry 'encouraged the excited populace by his words'.

Since the army failed them, local authorities formed citizen militias. We have already stressed the importance of the measure taken by the Council of delegates of the three orders at Marseilles on March 23rd. It was, however, by no means the first to follow this course. As early as April 1788 the municipality of Troyes had created a patrol of volunteers, intended to maintain order. On February 1st the town council of Gaillac, north of Toulouse, set up a *milice bourgeoise* to 'repress the excesses of malefactors', and a few days later the authorities of Mortagne, in Poitou, set up a 'voluntary patrol' to deal with smugglers. However, the example of Marseilles, in view of the importance of that town, seems to have promoted the growth of citizen militias or *gardes bourgeoises*. Such bodies were set up at Étampes on April 7th, at Caen on April 25th, at Orléans on the 27th and at Beaugency on the 29th. We have described the circumstances under which the citizen militia of Limoux was created on May 6th; Neuilly-Saint-Front followed suit on the 8th. Thus local authorities increasingly took over police duties, but with the obvious intention of using their powers only when the interests they represented, namely those of the bourgeoisie in its broadest sense, were threatened. By the end of April unrest in the countryside had in fact considerably reduced the authority of the throne, and seriously threatened the 'feudal'

[1] Bibl. nat., LB 39, 1486.

régime. But in Paris, too, the elections to the Estates-General had produced unrest and rioting.

3. The Parisian elections and the Réveillon riots

The elections in Paris were the last to take place. The electoral statutes of January 24th did not apply to the capital.[1] The preparation of the special rules for the Parisian elections gave rise to sharp controversy between the Lieutenant of Police and the *prévôt des marchands* (whose functions, at this period, were akin to those of a Mayor), as a result of which the latter resigned. The issue at stake was the question as to who should convoke the electors and who should preside over the electoral assemblies. A compromise was eventually reached, by which the *prévôt de Paris*, or *lieutenant civil du Châtelet*, subordinate to the Lieutenant of Police, would convoke the electors of the three orders in *Paris hors les murs*, that is to say the suburbs, and those of the two privileged orders in the capital, and would preside over their meetings. The *prévôt des marchands* would convoke the electors of the Third Estate of Paris and its faubourgs, and would preside over their meetings, but these would take place on days and at times fixed by the *prévôt de Paris*, April 20th for the nobility, April 21st for the clergy and the Third Estate. Furthermore, the statute laid down the conditions requisite for being an elector and for being eligible as a deputy. These were more restrictive than in the provinces. It was necessary not only to be a French national and over twenty-five years of age, but to provide proof of a civil function, or a University degree, or a commission, or a public office, or a diploma of mastership, or else produce a notice or a receipt of assessment for a poll-tax of over 6 livres. Those who had not the right to vote were forbidden to attend electoral meetings. As a result of this, the great majority of apprentices and journeymen were disfranchised. It was specified that meetings would open at 7 o'clock and that electors would be admitted until 9 o'clock. For electoral purposes, the city of Paris was divided into 60 'districts', a primary assembly of the Third Estate was to be held in each district, and each chairman was nominated by the *prévôt des marchands*.

These regulations promptly called forth a great many protests. Here is an extract from a pamphlet entitled: 'Reflections of a draper, addressed to the Third Estate of the city of Paris':

[1] Chassin, *Les Élections et les cahiers de Paris en 1789*, vol. I, Paris, 1889.

'Our deputies are not going to be our deputies. Things have been so arranged that we can have no part in choosing them, and the city of Paris, divided into sixty districts of people who do not know one another, will be in every respect like sixty flocks of sheep . . . Is it possible to take advantage of the credulity of a free people? The municipal officers, who are already betraying us, have agreed amongst themselves not to listen to us, not to let us deliberate, nor choose a chairman nor a clerk of the court, but to preside over us against our will, to listen to no protest, to force us to elect people we shall not know, and give us no sort of instruction. Shall we consent to be led like mere cattle?' Another pamphlet entitled: 'Election of the deputies of the town and viscounty of Paris, made free by simpler means than those of the Regulation', criticizes the statutes sharply: 'It is quite obvious that the sovereign, that is to say the King, will not allow the Nation, described as his subjects, to take part in any deliberation other than those he shall think fit to sanction.' Moreover, why the term *subjects*? 'It is a relic of the feudal era, which is the source of everything unjust and harmful, and that is why we should do well to destroy it, down to its slightest ramifications . . . The King is supposed to have said, in the opening words of the Regulation, that he wished all his subjects to be summoned to take part in the elections . . . All the priests have been summoned, all the nobles without exception; as for the Third Estate . . . only those who are inscribed on the tax-roll have been summoned . . . Those who are not thus inscribed have nothing against them but their poverty, this is a misfortune and by no means a reason for being deprived of the right of citizenship . . . Everything is sacrificed to the owners of property, particularly to the wealthy. It is right that they should have a reasonable influence on the commonwealth, since they have so large a share in it. But it is revoltingly unjust that they alone should be consulted, and that disdainful rejection should be the lot of those humble and useful men through whose labours they are able to subsist without needing to work, and who maintain them in luxury by improving their fortune.'

There was thus intense discontent among the people of Paris who, moreover, had caught that electoral fever which for the past three months had been sweeping through the provinces. The Government realized this and took certain elementary precautions: a few squadrons of cavalry were stationed around Paris, some 1,200 horsemen in all; the arms stored at the arsenal were transferred to the nearby Bastille for greater safety. Security measures were taken at the Invalides and at the École Militaire, where there were further stores of arms; the garrison of the arsenal, where a large quantity of gunpowder was kept, was reinforced by pensioners.

The elections began on the appointed days, but the drafting of the *cahiers* took a long time, and the meetings dragged on. The poll was very low, a total of 11,706 out of at least 150,000 potential electors. This may have been due to fear, or to inexperience. In fact these primary assemblies took place amid relative calm, and timid protests from disfranchised Parisians were heard only in the districts of Saint-Joseph, the Petits-Augustins and the Jacobins-Saint-André. Any such incidents were disregarded, and the primary assemblies elected 407 secondary electors, chosen entirely from the bourgeoisie. A classification of these electors by profession shows that they included 95 barristers, 75 lawyers of other kinds, 132 tradesmen, 32 civil servants, 12 academicians and 5 army men. This choice aggravated public discontent. Several pamphlets echo this, even though their authors were for the most part members of the bourgeoisie. Thus De Lahaie, a barrister and a member of the *parlement*, wrote in a pamphlet entitled: *Ce que personne n'a encore dit, je le dirai*[1] (I shall say what nobody has yet said): 'They were afraid of what is called *the populace*. They protected our assemblies with stout barriers, and manned these with armed soldiers . . . Have you not betrayed the people's trust? Have you at least responded to it? Which district has passed one motion in favour of this class, deserted by its fellow-citizens? . . . As I left the [district] assembly I was surrounded by several of these citizens, who had not been allowed to enter. They spoke with one voice: is anyone looking after our interests? Monsieur, are they thinking of lowering the price of bread? I have eaten none for two days, said one of those nearest me, it's so dear! . . . They make us pay fifteen sous for it now! . . . Ah, monsieur, don't forget us, we will pray God for you . . .' A 'Petition of 150 thousand Parisian workers and artisans addressed to M. Bailly, secretary of the Third Estate'[2] speaks in the same tone: 'Now that our fatherland is welcoming its children, why must 150 thousand persons who are useful to their fellow-citizens be thus repulsed? Are we not men,

[1] Bibl. nat., LB 39, 1661.
[2] Bibl. nat., LB 39, 1667.

Frenchmen, citizens? ... We can scarcely recognize, among 400 electors, four or five who know our needs, our way of life and our misfortunes, and can take a reasonable interest in them.' A certain Dufourny de Villiers published, in the same vein, the *'Cahiers du quatrième ordre.'*[1] 'Why is this immense class, made up of journeymen and wage-earners, the focus of all political revolutions, this class which has so many protests to make, the only protests which deserve, only too well, the degrading name of *doléances* (grievances), cast out from the bosom of the nation? Why has this order no representatives of its own? ... Why is it the only order which, in accordance with the old tyrannical customs of bygone barbarous and ignorant days, is not summoned to the national assembly, and is treated with as much scorn as injustice?'

Although the primary assemblies were able to proceed to their elections undisturbed, popular fury was shortly to break out, as often happens, in connection with a minor but characteristic incident: a wealthy industrialist of the faubourg Saint-Antoine named Réveillon declared, on April 23rd, to the electoral assembly of the Sainte-Marguerite district, which had met to draft its *cahier*: 'Bread is the foundation of our national economy. Let us insist ... that the fruit of our labours should no longer have its price settled at the gates of Paris and, when we have obtained satisfaction on these points, we employers can proceed to a gradual reduction of our workmen's wages, which will in turn produce a gradual reduction in the price of manufactured articles.'[2] In fact Réveillon proposed a whole series of reductions, which were not likely to affect the living standards of the working class. But the latter only took note of his proposal to lower wages. They were the more disturbed by this because at the assembly of the Enfants-Trouvés district, also in the faubourg Saint-Antoine, a certain Henriot, owner of a saltpetre works, made similar proposals. Immediately the faubourg Saint-Antoine was up in arms. This rising, known by historians as the Réveillon riot, is the most important of those that occurred in Paris prior to July 14th. It is worth pausing over this, in order to trace the conditions under which it developed, as well as its underlying causes.[3]

[1] Bibl. nat., LB 39, 1583.

[2] According to Montjoye, *Histoire de la Révolution en France*, Paris, 1791.

[3] The most detailed study of the Réveillon riots is by Jean Callot, 'L'affaire Réveillon', in the *Revue des questions historiques*, 1934, vol. CXXI, pp. 35–55. 1935, vol. CXXII, pp. 239–254.

The faubourg Saint-Antoine, one of the districts of Paris which had the largest working-class population, had been subject during the winter of 1788–1789 to a considerable influx of unemployed persons. The Lieutenant of Police, Thiroux de Crosne, who had succeeded Le Noir, had been disturbed by this fact, and had written to the Minister of War: 'We have in the faubourg Saint-Antoine more than 40,000 workmen, the high price of bread and other commodities might give rise to disturbances in this faubourg, where there has already been some unrest.'

Unemployed rural workers had come into the faubourg in hopes of finding work there more easily than elsewhere. For in this faubourg many workers did not belong to guilds, but worked at home, *en chambre* (and hence were known as *chambrelans*), or else were taken on by the few large recent factories which were not bound by guild laws. One such was the wallpaper factory set up by Réveillon. This was a flourishing industry at the time, owing to the new fashion for printed wallpaper combined with curtains of cotton material printed to match and known as *toile de Jouy* because they were made at Jouy-en-Josas, near Paris. Réveillon's works was the principal factory producing printed wallpaper in France on the eve of the Revolution. It stood at the crossroads of the rue Montreuil and the faubourg Saint-Antoine, in a large house or folly built by a big financier named Titon, who had ruined himself over it and then sold it to Réveillon. The latter had turned the ground floor into a wallpaper factory and kept the first floor for his own apartment, with all Titon's splendid furniture, valued at 50,000 livres—a large sum for those days. The house also contained well-stocked cellars, with many bottles of fine wine, a fact which was to prove important later. After the looting, to be described hereafter, 2,000 bottles were recovered intact. The whole property, house and garden, was known as Titonville. As for Réveillon, its owner, he was a self-made man, of working-class origin, who had begun as an apprentice paper-maker and had become a journeyman, then had left the paper-makers' guild, which was concerned with writing- and printing-paper, and had launched out into the production of wallpaper, an entirely new industry. He had soon become rich and had set up paper works in the provinces, at Courtalin in Brie for instance, where he manufactured vellum paper. In 1785, Réveillon had won the prize offered by Necker for 'the encouragement of the useful arts'. He succeeded in exporting his paper, even to England. He was an educated man, moreover, and in his house in the faubourg Saint-Antoine he had a library of over 50,000 books. As for his factory, it employed 350 hands. This was a large number for those days, when industrial concentration did not yet exist. Réveillon had the reputation of being a good employer and of paying his workers well, an average of 25 sous a day, which was quite a high wage when one considers that the average laid down by the Constituent Assembly a few months later was 20 sous for the whole of France. During the winter of 1788–1789, when Réveillon's factory was affected by the general unemployment, unlike most bosses he paid his unemployed workers at the rate of 15 sous a day, which was quite exceptional. Nevertheless he was an exacting and sometimes even a harsh master; in 1777, for instance, he had ruthlessly broken a strike at his Courtalin works.

Such, then, was the situation at the Réveillon factory when the incident referred to earlier took place at the electoral meeting of the Sainte-Marguerite district, on April 23rd. Réveillon's remarks about lowering workers' wages were immediately broadcast through the faubourg. A certain number of workmen seem to have been present at the district assembly. Information on this point is scanty, but a journalist, Montjoye, who in 1791 wrote a 'History of the Revolution' and collaborated in *L'Ami du Roi*, mentions a few details about the discussions at the Sainte-Marguerite meeting. He says that 'when it came to drawing up the *cahier*, everybody had some proposal to make, some motion to put forward. The coarsest, most ill-clad artisan sought to put forward his own, and in a way that implied that he knew very well that he had as much right to be heard as anyone else. These harangues, which dragged out the meeting, were listened to by the leading bourgeois with that air of superiority that results from education, enlightenment and wealth . . . The orators clearly noticed the effect their speeches produced. They mistook their listeners' lack of interest for contempt. When the *cahier* was almost completed, proposals poured in; those put forward by members of the common people were rejected. They persisted, imperiously demanding that their will, too, should be made known. They criticized the proposals of the bourgeois and could not conceive why these should be preferred to their own. The bourgeois, for their part, weary of all these delays, could not help showing impatience. Some of them indeed, thinking themselves unheard by those concerned, let slip the expression '*ces gens-là*', these fellows, instead of '*ces messieurs*', when speaking of the common people. All these trifles combined aroused considerable discontent among the working-class . . . All workers felt themselves humiliated by the behaviour of the bourgeois in Réveillon's district.'

On the evening of April 23rd, de Crosne, the Lieutenant of Police, sent a report to the Government on what had happened. He realized that trouble was brewing. 'Last night', he wrote, 'there was some unrest in the faubourg Saint-Antoine, but this was due to no general cause, it was merely the effect of the resentment shown by certain workmen against two factory owners [Réveillon and Henriot, the saltpetre manufacturer] who had made imprudent remarks at the Sainte-Marguerite assembly about the rate of wages. Calm was soon restored.'

On April 24th the Lieutenant of Police sent in a second report which was quite reassuring. 'The greatest calm prevails in the faubourg Saint-Antoine', he wrote, 'as well as in the rest of the city.' Meanwhile Réveillon had been elected deputy to the General Assembly of Paris, which was to meet at the palace of the archbishop of Paris, close to the Hôtel de Ville, behind Notre-Dame. On April 26th a new report from the Lieutenant of Police was sent to Louis XVI: 'All the information I received on my return [from Versailles] convinces me that complete calm has prevailed all day in the different districts of Paris, particularly in the faubourg Saint-Antoine.' Now it was precisely on that day that the riot began—the riots, rather, for several of them took place on the 26th, 27th and 28th of April. In this connection a question arises which is still unsettled, namely as to whether the rioters were Réveillon's own workmen or, on the other hand, workers from the trade-guilds who resented the competition offered by Réveillon, who signed on unemployed men and paid decent wages. On this point, documents are contradictory, while the many historians who have studied the question are divided. Some suppose that the disturbance started in the faubourg Saint-Marcel, the working-class district on the left bank of the Seine, largely inhabited by tanners, who treated their hides with the water of the river Bièvre. A witness named Guérin, himself accused, told the police: 'It was the people of the faubourg Saint-Marcel who started the trouble.' But the Lieutenant of Police always maintained that the workers of the faubourg Saint-Antoine were responsible. The reports of the *commissaires du Châtelet* disclose the addresses of 63 of those who were killed, injured, or arrested. Of these 63, only 6 lived in the Saint-Marcel district, and 32 in the faubourg Saint-Antoine, others in different parts of Paris, particularly in the Saint-Paul and Saint-Gervais districts, close to Saint-Antoine, towards the heart of the city. There were also a certain number of workmen living in the districts north of Paris, where during the eighteenth century factories had been set up employing workers who did not belong to guilds. The workers arrested included 16 masters or employers and 52 wage-earners, which proves that the rising was not solely caused by the unemployed.

In so far as these figures provide valid information about the social composition and local origins of the mass of the rioters, we may conclude that a good third of these were not Réveillon's workers and did not live in the faubourg Saint-Antoine, in the neighbourhood of his factory. Many of them came from the faubourg Saint-Marcel. And it seems, indeed, to have been in that district that the remarks made by Réveillon and Henriot, on April 23rd, caused most resentment. Already the workers of this district were uneasy because it had just been announced that the opening of the Estates-General, promised for April 27th, had been postponed to May 5th.

During the night of Sunday April 26th numerous groups hung about the streets of the faubourg Saint-Marcel, uttering threats against Réveillon and Henriot for 'speaking ill of the people' and saying that 'a worker could live on fifteen sous a day.' On Monday April 27th, about three in the afternoon, a column of demonstrators left the Saint-Marcel district and made their way towards the Seine, shouting: 'Death to the rich! Death to the aristocrats! Death to the hoarders! We want a penny loaf! *A l'eau les foutus prêtres!* Throw the damned priests into the river!' According to the bookseller Hardy, it was the workers from the neighbourhood of Notre-Dame who went in search of those of the faubourg Saint-Marcel, but this is not confirmed. At the head of the procession of demonstrators walked a drummer and a man bearing a gibbet from which hung two dummies representing Réveillon and Henriot. Behind them came another man carrying a placard with the words: 'By order of the Third Estate, Réveillon and Henriot are condemned to be hanged and burned in the public square.'

As the demonstrators marched past, tradesmen hurriedly shut up their shops and passers-by fled with shouts of 'It's a revolt! we're done for!'

The demonstrators appeared to be making for the Archbishop's palace, where the general assemblies of the clergy and the Third Estate were then being held. The electors took fright. Those of the clergy immediately announced that they had renounced their privileges, and asked for this to be made known to the populace. Those of the Third Estate delegated three of their members to make contact with the demonstrators. They met them in the place Maubert and addressed them in a lengthy harangue, urging them to disperse. This speech produced results, the column broke up, the bourgeois and shopkeepers in the square acclaimed the electors, but for fear of further disturbances they rushed to the bakers' shops and quickly emptied them.

De Crosne, the Lieutenant of Police, as soon as he heard about the demonstration, had summoned to his office Besenval, Lieutenant-General of the Swiss guards, and the duc du Châtelet, colonel of the *gardes-françaises*, to consider ways of restoring order. During their meeting they received contradictory reports, some implying that the demonstrators had dispersed, others that they had gone over to the Right Bank and were making for the Hôtel de Ville, others again that they were moving back towards the faubourg Saint-Antoine. De Crosne, while awaiting developments, confined his troops to barracks. He did not take these events seriously. In his report to the King he spoke of a 'contemptible masquerade' and added: 'It is clear that these people's sole object is to burn the effigy of M. Réveillon, which they have been parading through the streets; hitherto they have committed no sort of offence.'

Réveillon, warned of what was happening, felt himself to be in danger and asked the duc du Châtelet for protection. The latter sent fifty *gardes-françaises* under a sergeant to keep guard over Titonville. Réveillon protested against the inadequacy of such a force, to which the duke retorted: 'But, monsieur, we are not barbarians . . . Fifty grenadiers can easily deal with men who have no other arms than their bare fists. You wouldn't want us to send artillery?' At that very moment, the rioters were burning the effigies of Réveillon and Henriot in the place de Grève, and then moving on to the faubourg Saint-Antoine. The presence of the *gardes-françaises* prevented them from reaching the rue Montreuil, where Réveillon's house stood, and so they took the rue Cotte, which was unguarded, to get to Henriot's. The latter, on seeing them approach, fled in the disguise of a servant and took refuge in the citadel of Vincennes, while his wife and children found asylum with some friends. Their house was invaded and completely ransacked, the furniture and clothing taken to the Beauvau market-place and burnt.

The Lieutenant of Police was not informed of these happenings until eleven that night. He then summoned a battalion of *gardes-françaises*, the Paris guard, the watch, and a hundred horsemen of the Royal-Cravate regiment. A few hours later, he reported to the Minister of Justice on the success of his retaliation, and assured him that the demonstration was over, with no casualties. However, the Minister was less optimistic than the Lieutenant of Police, and told him: 'It needs great watchfulness to keep such discontent under control. It is fortunate that nobody was hurt.'

He was right, for on Tuesday April 28th, during the morning, fresh crowds began to gather in the faubourg Saint-Antoine. The Lieutenant of Police, who had been informed of the situation, took no sort of precaution. Meanwhile the Court, on the contrary, was growing anxious, and the King decided to relieve the Parlement of Paris of the task of investigating the demonstration of April 27th and entrust this to the *Prévôt's* court. This decision was probably due to the King's growing mistrust of the Parlement, which since 1787 he had begun to consider as partial to the insurgents. He thought, no doubt, that this rising, like others in 1788, had been provoked by the Parlement of Paris, and he imagined that the Parlement would be slow to investigate the affair. He therefore entrusted the enquiry to the *cour prévôtale*, whose loyalty was less suspect.

Meanwhile, on learning of the crowds that had gathered during the morning of April 28th, the Lieutenant of Police at last decided to send 350 *gardes-françaises* to the faubourg Saint-Antoine, between the fortress of the Bastille and the crossroads of the rue Montreuil, close to Réveillon's mansion of Titonville. This decision did not prevent the crowds of demonstrators from swelling. Those from the faubourg Saint-Marcel crossed the Seine and came to join those from the faubourg Saint-Antoine. It would seem that if proper precautions had been taken the Lieutenant of

Police would have put guards on the Seine bridges to prevent a meeting of the two groups. As they crossed the river, as they marched along the embankments, the demonstrators from the faubourg Saint-Marcel, the majority of whom were tannery workers, were joined by stevedores, by men employed on timber-floating and by the beggars who slept underneath the bridges; so that the crowd that eventually reached the faubourg Saint-Antoine was a considerable one. The demonstrators said to everyone they met: 'March along with us, do as we do, if we didn't rise up against the rich we should all be done for.' They swept along the workers from the Royal glass factory in the rue de Reuilly and repulsing the police, made their way into the rue de Montreuil.[1] They drove back the *gardes-françaises*, who made a stand in front of Réveillon's house and built barricades, with carts and rafters, to protect the entrance to the factory, which thus became a sort of fortress guarded inside by some fifty men. Soon a mob of demonstrators, roughly estimated at between five and ten thousand persons, thronged round the Réveillon works. That afternoon, April 28th, there was horse-racing at Vincennes. The intending spectators, members of the nobility and bourgeoisie, had to cross the faubourg Saint-Antoine. Their carriages had to force their way through the mass of demonstrators, who filled all the streets and who hurled abuse at any aristocrat reluctant to shout: 'Long live the Third Estate!' On the other hand, they cheered carriages bearing the arms of the duc d'Orléans, and the Duke himself was greeted with shouts of 'Long live d'Orléans, our father, the only true friend of the people!' The Duke, highly flattered, stopped his carriage, got out and harangued the crowd, saying: 'Now then, my friends, keep calm! take it easy! happiness is in sight.' This was an allusion to the meeting of the Estates-General, which had been scheduled for a week later. The people replied: 'But, monsieur, it's too long to wait, they've been promising us happiness for years now. Meanwhile we're dying of hunger, and those bastards of bosses are talking of reducing our wages to fifteen sous a day!' This shows how deeply Réveillon's remarks had stirred the workers. Then the duc d'Orléans took out his purse and emptied it among the crowd. Members of the nobility following his coach were somewhat shocked by this gesture. One of them, according to a police report, muttered: 'The Duke has come to review his

[1] Arch. nat., Y 15101, 13454, 13582, 12218. See also Hardy, Journal, *op. cit.*

troops. Now the big show can begin.' Many contemporary writings ascribed the responsibility for the events of 1789 to the duc d'Orléans; and the theory is by no means extinct. The Duke is held to have instigated the Réveillon riots, those of July 14th and of the night of August 4th, and the incidents in October.[1] He undoubtedly tried to take advantage of these, but it is extremely unlikely that he was at the bottom of them; in any case, even if he played his part, his efforts were an insignificant contribution to the vastly greater forces impelling Paris, France, indeed the whole Western world towards revolution.

Little by little the race-goers managed to get through the faubourg Saint-Antoine, and calm was restored. Meanwhile, however, the rioters had not moved, nor had the crowd of curious spectators. Besenval wrote in a brief report: 'One messenger after another went to try and get news, but we had to wait a long time for their return, the faubourg Saint-Antoine was so full of people that it was as hard to get through to the place where the disturbance was taking place as to come back and report on it.' In view of this mass demonstration, and the consequences that might ensue from it, the Lieutenant of Police decided, during the afternoon, to send horsemen from the Paris guard to the Trône *barrière* to divert traffic.

In front of Réveillon's works the situation remained unchanged. Fifty *gardes-françaises* were entrenched behind the barricades, with their guns loaded, ready to fire. The crowd had no firearms and was loth to join open battle with the troops. The situation would probably have continued thus until nightfall, and the crowd, from sheer weariness, might have dispersed, had not a fresh incident occurred: in spite of the horsemen keeping guard over the Trône *barrière*, the aristocrats who had been at the races insisted on returning through the faubourg Saint-Antoine, which was the shortest way. The duchesse d'Orléans, anxious to get back to the Palais-Royal, was one of those who most urgently demanded to be let through. So the horsemen of the Paris guard, in constant fear of being blamed, as they had been over the past two years, for harsh repression of demonstrations, allowed the duchesse d'Orléans and her train to pass through. Immediately disturbances broke out again in the faubourg. There is one point, however, that is not clear: why did the duchesse d'Orléans not continue

[1] See particularly B. Faÿ, *La Grande Révolution*, Paris, 1959.

July 13th, 1789. The plundering of St-Lazare

Bibl. Nat., Print Room, Vinck Collection, 1528

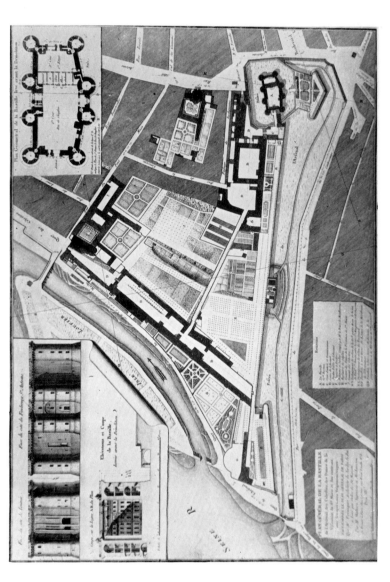

General plan of the Bastille, elevation and section, by Mathieu, architect

through the faubourg Saint-Antoine but, instead, take the rue de Montreuil? Those historians who support the hypothesis of the duc d'Orléans' 'plot' see in this fact the proof of some Machiavellian scheme. In any case, the duchess, passing along the rue de Montreuil, arrived in front of the barricades that had been set up round Titonville. The *gardes-françaises*, confronted by so important a personage, decided to open up the barricades to let her coach pass through. The coach was followed by an invading mob. The rioters assembled in the streets got inside the barricades; the *gardes-françaises* were completely overwhelmed; the crowd surged into the factory. Réveillon, his family and his household barely had time to escape through the gardens; the demonstrators did not pursue them. They sacked the place, as they had done Henriot's house the day before. In two hours Réveillon's home and factory were completely gutted. Furniture was thrown out of the windows. There seems to have been little looting, but three enormous bonfires were built in the gardens, and the paper and paint helped to set ablaze the furniture that was thrown on to them. Anything that could not burn, statues, the banister of the staircase, were torn down, mirrors and windows were smashed, the trees in the garden cut down; in a word, it was a holocaust. The well-known journalist Mallet du Pan, who was to become one of the chief oracles of the counter-revolution, wrote in the *Mercure de France*, of which he was chief editor: 'Huns, Vandals and Goths will not come from the North nor from the Black Sea, they are in our midst already.' The rumour ran, although the fact is not proved, that the crowd went on to rifle the shops in the rue de Montreuil and even in the Marais, particularly the bakers' shops. One fact remains certain: the entire contents of Réveillon's house and factory were destroyed.

When the Lieutenant of Police learned of these happenings, he tried to take action; he called up his reserve force, the *garde de Paris*, the men of the watch, the *gardes-françaises* and the Swiss guards. But it took time to assemble them. It was not until two or three hours after the end of the sack of Réveillon's factory that these troops reached the place de la Bastille, at the top of the rue de Montreuil. Cavalrymen from the Royal-Cravate regiment were also sent for. The demonstrators pulled them off their horses.

The infantrymen who came after them thought themselves threatened, and opened fire, at first with blank cartridges. This first volley sent the rioters surging back, but those who stood behind prevented those in front from retreating, and they poured into houses, climbed upstairs, reached roofs, and pelted the soldiers with tiles, slates, guttering, chimney-pots, stones, furniture, anything they could lay hands on. Shouts were heard of 'Liberty! murderers! we won't give way!' or else 'Long live the Third Estate! long live the King!' for the common people of Paris still believed that the King was sincerely anxious to reform the structure of the State. The troops gave way under this varied hail of missiles, which caused a fairly large number of casualties. Then the officers ordered their men to load their guns with bullets and fire a fresh volley, after which they were to shoot freely at anyone who appeared at windows or on roofs; many of the demonstrators were killed or wounded. Thus ended this day of riots; the forces of order remained in control, but there were a great many casualties both among the demonstrators and among those who were merely spectators or local people. That evening the Lieutenant of Police, de Crosne, wrote to the King: 'Although we fired repeatedly at half-past six in the evening, and some people were killed and others injured, we have not yet succeeded in becoming masters of the situation. We have brought forward the fifty men of the Royal-Cravate regiment who were at Charenton, a new battalion of the *gardes-françaises* are expected, the Swiss have set off from Courbevoie and 300 more cavalrymen have been sent for.' At eight that evening the *gardes-françaises* and the Swiss guards forced their way into Titonville and killed the rioters who were still there; many of these were drunk, for, as we have seen, Réveillon's cellar contained a great many bottles of wine. By 9 o'clock the regiment of Royal-Cravate, at full strength, was mustered at last, and scattered the last remaining rioters in the rue de Montreuil and the faubourg Saint-Antoine. At the same time, the Swiss guards brought their eight cannon into action and, on foot and on horse, they pursued stragglers up to the top of the Sainte-Geneviève hill and into the heart of the faubourg Saint-Marcel. The Lieutenant of Police, at this point, wrote to the King: 'I cannot yet give your Majesty an accurate statement as to the number of persons killed.' It seems unlikely that he ever did so, in fact, for the number remains unknown. Contemporaries, in particular the marquis de Sillery, who was moreover a supporter of the duc d'Orléans, and the bookseller Hardy, tried to estimate the number of casualties, but their conclusions vary widely.[1] The *commissaires du Châtelet* reckoned that 25 people were killed, while Sillery puts the number at 900! As for the injured, there were at least 300 of them. The only certain figure is that of the military victims: 12 soldiers were killed and 80 injured. The difference between the numbers of civilian and of military casualties is understandable, since the soldiers were killed by objects thrown from the rooftops, the demonstrators being unarmed, whereas on the contrary the troops fired bullets at the crowd. In any case it is certain that if we accepted the maximum (and doubtless exaggerated) figure of 900 dead, we could say that the Réveillon rising was the bloodiest of the whole Revolution up till the riot of August 10th, 1792, which brought about the fall of the monarchy, and indeed on that occasion the number of dead did not exceed a thousand. During the famous *journée* of 13 *vendémiaire*, Year IV, when Bonaparte swept with grape-shot the royalist demonstrators who were marching on the Convention to try and break it up and restore the monarchy, there were 300 fatal casualties. We must point out, moreover, that during the Réveillon riots it was chiefly the demonstrators who were killed, whereas on August 10th the dead consisted largely of Swiss guards and soldiers massacred after the capture of the Tuileries by *'fédérés'* from the Saint-Antoine and Saint-Marcel faubourgs. Pending the results of further research, we may take the mean figure of 300 dead for the Réveillon riots. The bodies of a certain number of victims were deposited in the catacombs of Paris. Some sixty skulls have been counted in the place where these bodies were laid. As other victims were buried, we may take the figure of 300 as valid. Nonetheless the Réveillon rising was one of the most serious in the whole history of the Revolution.

The Government was obviously forced to adopt a definite position, and this caused it considerable embarrassment because of the attitude it had maintained for the past two years. Was it to give complete approval to the action of the police, and declare that any further rising would be severely punished? Or was it, on the contrary, as it had done in the case of practically every previous riot since 1787, to disavow the police, proclaim that the shooting had been unauthorized, and blame Réveillon for suggesting a

[1] Arch. nat., KK 641. 'Le marquis de Sillery à ses commettants', Hardy, *op. cit.*, VIII, p. 313.

reduction of wages to 15 sous? Louis XVI was extremely hesitant. Necker, the principal Minister, did not want to take the responsibility for any categorical attitude on the eve of the meeting of the Estates-General. Louis therefore dared not take a decision. The result was that the Châtelet, the court of summary jurisdiction for Paris, did not venture to open an investigation into the causes and incidents of the rising on April 28th, 1789. It confined itself to passing summary judgment on a few looters caught redhanded, assuming that these examples would serve to deter the demonstrators. On April 29th, the day after the riot, it sentenced to death two demonstrators who had been caught looting, one Gilbert, who worked for a blanket-maker, and one Pourrat, a porter on the Seine embankment.[1] These two were hanged next day on the place de Grève, amidst an extraordinary deployment of troops, intended to intimidate the populace. Three weeks later, seven more individuals who had been caught redhanded were tried. One man, a public scrivener named Mary, was condemned to death and hanged. A pregnant woman, Marie-Jeanne Trumeau, was reprieved; five other demonstrators, workers from the faubourg Saint-Antoine, who had been found dead drunk in Réveillon's cellars, were condemned to the galleys for life. There were still twenty-six more prisoners, but their trial was adjourned; later, when the events of July 14th and the night of August 4th had taken place, the Réveillon affair seemed of lesser importance, and these 26 were released without trial. Thus we see that no serious attempt was made to discover the basic reasons for the riots. Fortunately we possess the reports drawn up by the *commissaires du Châtelet*, which reflect contemporary theories. These ascribe the rising to a wide variety of causes; some people thought the remarks attributed to Réveillon and Henriot were merely pretexts; a certain Le Blanc, arrested during the riot and questioned about his presence, replied that he had gone to watch the riot 'out of curiosity and because he got carried along by the crowd, that like other workers of the faubourg he bore a grudge against Mr Réveillon, who had said in the assembly of the Third Estate at Sainte-Marguerite that workers could live on 15 sous a day, while some of his own workmen earned twenty and had their pockets well lined and would soon be richer than he was.' Others, such as the bookseller Hardy, saw brigands behind the rising; as we shall

[1] Arch. nat., Y 10033, 13582, 15101. Commissaires au Châtelet.

see, this terror of brigands was to recur frequently during the summer of 1789. Hardy, in his *Mémoires*, declares that the demonstrators were 'stirred up by brigands' who had made their way into Paris. This hypothesis was echoed by Taine in his *Réflexions sur la France contemporaine*. It is not entirely baseless since, as we have seen, a great many unemployed labourers who could no longer earn a living in the country had come to town in the hope of finding work, as happened during every economic crisis. These workless peasants, ragged and destitute, often driven to theft in order to subsist, could easily pass for brigands. Other contemporaries believed that the aristocracy was behind the rising; witness the anonymous *Courtes réflexions sur l'événement du 28 avril*,[1] which declared: 'A great many workers of different trades were bribed, or forced, to follow this band of madmen.' The journalist Montjoye, already quoted, specifies that on every injured man taken to the Hôtel-Dieu there were found sums of from 12 to 36 francs, wrapped up in paper, as though they had just been distributed. However, on the 18 bodies taken to the Montrouge cemetery and searched by the *commissaires du Châtelet*, not a single coin was found. This legend of bribery recurs in connection with most subsequent riots during the whole revolutionary period; it is linked with the notion of an 'aristocratic plot'—the nobles were supposed to have taken brigands into their pay to protect their privileges. The theory makes its first appearance on the occasion of the Réveillon riots. Meanwhile the Paris police had arrested a certain abbé Roy, a personal enemy of Réveillon, who had accused him of swindling and blackmail. The abbé Roy was suspected of being one of the *agents provocateurs* of the riot, and of having handed out money from the nobility to certain agitators. Here we have yet another hypothesis, that of the responsibility of the clergy. We came across this in connection with the *Guerre des Farines* in 1775, and we shall meet it again in all the later riots of the Revolution. The police, after the arrest of the abbé Roy, investigated the activities of various ecclesiastics in Paris, but these enquiries led to nothing. As for the abbé Roy, he was released. Accusations were also levelled at the duc d'Orléans. We know that he had been warmly welcomed by the crowd as he passed through the faubourg Saint-Antoine, and that the crowd had invaded Titonville in the wake of his Duchess. But the police failed to secure any precise

[1] Bibl. nat., LB 39, 7158.

149

information about the Duke's activities. Until 1792 he was suspected of inciting every riot that took place in Paris.

It is curious, in any case, to note that the list of casualties and even that of arrests made during the riots include none of Réveillon's own workmen. These presumably formed only a minority of the demonstrators.

As for the sergeant in command of the *gardes-françaises* responsible for protecting Titonville, he was reduced to the ranks for having opened the barricades to let through the Duchess's coach. This punishment aroused great indignation among the non-commissioned officers of the regiment. They got up a 'solidarity fund' to provide their comrade with some compensation for his reduction in pay. The officers of the *gardes* publicly disavowed that one of their number who had given the order to fire. It would seem that from the time of the Réveillon riots the *gardes-françaises* began to criticize the Government and to side with the Parisian working class.

We have dwelt at considerable length on the Réveillon riots because we find here the same actors as on July 14th, with identical motives (apart from the particular causes of the taking of the Bastille). The workers came from the faubourgs of Saint-Antoine and Saint-Marcel, from the Halles and Hôtel de Ville districts; they were motivated by the fear of famine, provoked by the high price of bread and the alarming remarks of Réveillon and Henriot about a probable drop in wages; by the idea, still vague, of a struggle of the poor against the rich; and by hopes of an improvement in the lot of the working class, through the application of the great principles of liberty and equality of which they had heard talk, and which had been only too flagrantly violated during the Paris elections to the Estates-General.

The reactions of contemporaries were much the same as they were to be later, in July. Instead of seeking for the true underlying causes of the riots, they chose to see in them the result of a 'plot'; an 'aristocratic plot' according to the bourgeoisie, a 'clerical plot' or one involving the duc d'Orléans, according to the nobility. Nobody gave a thought to the sufferings of the working class.

Finally, although the Government reacted more vigorously than it was to do in July, although the forces of order had no scruples about firing, and although the Châtelet had men condemned and executed, we can none the less discern the first signs of slackening zeal. The Paris guards did not divert the traffic at the Trône *barrière*, the *gardes-françaises* allowed the Duchess of Orléans' coach to pass through, the Châtelet undertook no serious investigation of the rioters' case.

By the end of April, things had almost reached the point when the people of Paris would launch their assault on the régime, and the forces of order, disheartened, would no longer try to defend it.[1]

---

[1] We cannot close this chapter without mentioning what became of the chief protagonists of the Réveillon riots. The Lieutenant of Police, Thiroux de Crosne, was tried by a revolutionary tribunal on 9th Floréal, Year II (April 28th, 1794), condemned to death and guillotined. Réveillon took refuge from the angry populace in the Bastille, where he remained until shortly before July 14th. He emigrated to England and died there in 1794. Henriot went into hiding at Vincennes and was no more heard of.

VII

Between Hope, Hunger and Fear

The fact that the Réveillon riots died down during the night of April 28th must probably be explained not only by the repressive measures taken by the authorities but also by the imminent opening of the Estates-General. For a great hope had begun to dawn over Paris and over the whole of France. The Estates-General, so eagerly desired, so long awaited, were going to meet at last, and they would be able to remedy all the ills of which French citizens complained, to satisfy all the grievances presented to Versailles by their deputies!

1. The Estates-General from May 4th to June 27th, 1789

In spite of last-minute delays, the Estates-General opened at Versailles on May 4th, 1789.[1] The meeting began with a procession which has often been described, and which offended the Third Estate, because its deputies were forced to appear in deliberately modest dress in order to display to everyone the immense distance that separated them from the representatives of the privileged orders. This costume had been decided by the comte de La Galissonnière, deputy of the nobility of Anjou, at the request of Dreux-Brézé, grand master of ceremonies. The clergy wore their ceremonial dress, the high ecclesiastics in glittering robes, the deputies of the nobility wore silk coats and plumed hats, with swords at their sides, while the deputies of the Third Estate wore

[1] On the Estates-General, consult the collection of documents edited by Georges Lefebvre, *Recueil de documents relatifs à la convocation des États généraux de 1789*, Paris, vol. I, 1953; vol. II, 1963. See also G. Lefebvre, *Quatre-vingt-neuf*, Paris, 1939; J. Egret, *La Révolution des notables*, Paris, 1950; M. G. Hutt. 'The role of the curés in the Estates General of 1789', in *The Journal of Ecclesiastical History*, vol. VI, 1955, pp. 190–220.

the plainest of black coats. One of their number, Delandine, deputy for Montbrison, had protested against this discrimination, but he was not listened to. Needless to say the deputies of the Third Estate came at the tail of the long procession that marched from Notre-Dame to the church of Saint-Louis. Once they were all assembled, the twelve hundred deputies and the Court listened to a sermon preached by Monseigneur de La Fare, Bishop of Nancy. While insisting that religion was the basis of a nation's power and the inexhaustible source of its prosperity, while dwelling at length on the history of Clovis and of Saint Louis, the Bishop nevertheless implied that certain reforms were needed in the Government of France and that the two upper orders might graciously, and of their own free will, renounce certain of their privileges. He ended with a eulogy of the simple life, and in veiled and prudent terms stigmatized the luxury of the Court, contrasting it with the extreme poverty of the peasantry. Thus, in spite of the humiliation they had endured in the matter of dress, the deputies of the Third Estate remained full of hope and waited impatiently for the official speeches planned for the solemn opening session on the following day.

This took place on May 5th at the Hôtel des Menus-Plaisirs, in a makeshift hall of wood and stucco prepared for the occasion in an open coach-house, and where the acoustics were very bad. Here again the Third Estate were not spared humiliation. Whereas the deputies of the privileged orders were placed to the right and left of the Throne, those of the Third Estate had to sit on uncomfortable benches at the back of the hall. The King came in, took off his hat, sat down, and put it on again. The privileged orders followed suit. According to custom and protocol, the deputies of the Third Estate should have remained standing and hatless. To show their annoyance and their wish for equality, they did nothing of the sort, but imitated the privileged orders.

The King spoke first. His speech was brief and disappointing. Instead of setting forth the programme of thorough-going reform that was expected, instead of announcing that 'royal revolution', that 'revolution from above' that many people longed for, he confined himself to technical points. He spoke about the debt, which had been considerably swollen by France's participation in the American War of Independence, and he argued the need to pay it off by a fairer distribution of taxes. In this connection he referred, as the Bishop of Nancy had done, to the willingness shown by the two upper orders to renounce their privileges, but warned the Assembly against 'the exaggerated desire for innovation.'

Barentin, *Garde des Sceaux* (Minister of Justice), known for his hostility to innovation, spoke next. He justified all the King's actions since his accession. He dwelt on the need to vote new taxes. He granted that the Estates might debate the liberty of the press, the maintenance of public security, and certain changes in civil procedure and criminal legislature. But he too warned the deputies against the 'dangerous innovations which the enemies of the public welfare seek to confuse with those desirable and necessary changes that are to bring about our regeneration.' He closed with an appeal for unity: 'All titles,' he said, 'must be merged in the title of citizen,' and in the King's name he requested the deputies to meet next day in order to proceed to the confirmation of their credentials.

The next speaker was Necker, Director-General of Finance. His speech, unlike those of his predecessors, was long, very long, too long. It exhausted him so much that he could not finish reading it and had to pass the text to a subordinate with a monotonous and unpleasant voice. Consequently the deputies could not really take cognizance of its contents until they read it next day in the papers.

After the obligatory eulogy of Louis XVI, Necker launched into the technical problems of financial administration. He analysed, with a wealth of details, the structure of the budget for the year 1788–1789, and enumerated the 'anticipations' he had been obliged to make on the budget for 1790. He dwelt at length on the debt and on the payments which would shortly be due. Finally he suggested a remedy: a thoroughgoing alteration of the system of taxation, with the establishment of fiscal equality. Scarcely a mention was made of any other reform. Necker had merely referred to the suppression of the militia—which many parish *cahiers* had requested—and to the abolition of the *corvée*, both of these being replaced by a tax; to the desirable suppression of the negro slave trade—which only a few *cahiers* had asked for—and to the decentralization of the administration. Not a word about the 'constitution' which the 'general *cahiers*' had almost unanimously demanded, nor about the even more urgent and indeed paramount question of how voting should take place within the Assembly, which had been left undecided by the 'Result of the Council' of December 27th, 1788. And yet the success of the Estates-General, on which all the hopes of France were pinned, depended on whether voting should be *par tête* or *par ordre*.

On the morning of May 6th, as Barentin had ordered, the deputies met once more at the Hôtel des Menus-Plaisirs. Two special rooms had been put aside for the nobility and the clergy. The 600 deputies of the Third Estate, who were as numerous as those of the other two put together, had to debate in the main hall, which they promptly christened *salle nationale*. As soon as they had met, they began wondering whether to obey the orders of the Minister of Justice and proceed to the confirmation of their credentials. If the Third Estate were to confirm the credentials of its deputies in a separate chamber, was it not in danger of implicitly accepting the vote *par ordre*? On the other hand, if it refused to confirm these credentials separately, would it not be committing an initial act of insubordination which might alienate the goodwill of the Government? The deputies of Brittany and Dauphiné, still excited by the struggle they had been waging in their provinces for the past year against the royal authority, were in favour of immediate disobedience and confirmation of credentials 'in common', as a prelude to the vote *par tête*. The majority of the deputies were hesitant. After a long and confused debate, the point of view of the Bretons and Dauphinois prevailed. The Third Estate demanded 'the confirmation of credentials in common', and refused to 'constitute' itself in a separate Assembly with its own chairman and secretary, office and regulations. It merely sought to bring some sort of order into its debates by appointing a *doyen*, who was the famous astronomer Bailly, deputy for Paris. Finally, in imitation of the British Parliament and to make quite clear that it no longer recognized the existence of the three Orders, it assumed the name of *commons*.

This decision of the Third Estate started a crisis which was to last for fifty-two days and to have all-important consequences for France and for the whole world. Indeed, for over seven weeks the Estates-General were to be paralysed. The immense hope placed in their Assembly by the whole of France was gradually to fade away, turning into bitter disappointment and then into violent wrath. What was the point of the elections that had been held with such earnest fervour, and of the *cahiers* that had been drafted with such intense excitement, if the Estates could not even get started on their deliberations?

The attitude of the Third Estate did, indeed, encounter the immediate hostility of most members of the two privileged orders. On May 6th the chamber of the nobility voted by 188 to 46 against the Third Estate's proposal. It confirmed the credentials of its own members and, on May 11th, declared itself 'constituted'. The clergy, however, was much more divided. True, to begin with, under the influence of the higher clergy, the majority of ecclesiastical deputies were opposed to the confirmation of credentials 'in common'. But between 60 and 80 'patriot' *curés* met separately and unofficially, to study the possibility of a conciliation between the three orders. A proposal to this effect, made in the chamber of the clergy, won 114 votes, almost half the total number of deputies. Among those who voted in favour were a number of bishops or archbishops: Champion de Cicé (Bordeaux), Lefranc de Pompignan (Vienne), Lubersac (Chartres). In any case, unlike the nobility, the clergy did not declare itself 'constituted'.

Meanwhile the Third Estate was meeting every day. There was much argument and excitement. Certain deputies, Barnave, Mounier, Malouet, Sieyès, began to dominate their colleagues. The deliberations of the clergy were being closely followed. On May 7th Mounier proposed sending a deputation to the clergy inviting them to join the Third Estate. This met with no success. But on May 11th the clergy proposed to the other two orders to appoint representatives to discuss the situation. The Third Estate was uncertain: if it appointed representatives, would it not be admitting that it was 'constituted' as an order? if it refused to appoint any, would it not offend and alienate the clergy? After a long discussion, on a motion by the pastor Rabaut-Saint-Étienne, deputy for Nîmes, it decided to appoint representatives. But the conferences arranged between the representatives of the three orders could not begin until the 23rd. Meanwhile, on May 14th, Malouet, with a view to facilitating conciliation, invited the Third Estate to declare solemnly that it would 'respect the property, rights and prerogatives of the two upper orders', in exchange for which the latter would consent to the vote *par tête* on the fiscal question. Malouet's proposal was violently rejected. Conciliation was going to be difficult.

The meetings between the representatives of the three orders began on May 23rd and continued until the 27th. The Third Estate urged the clergy to side with it. But the influence of the bishops was still considerable, and they secured the postponement of the decision by suggesting that the King should intervene.

On May 28th, Louis XVI proposed a resumption of the conferences, this time in presence of the Ministers. They therefore began again on May 30th and concluded on June 4th with a compromise proposal: each order was to confirm the credentials of its own members, and any contested credentials were to be submitted to examination by the plenary assembly of the three orders. In case the compromise should not be accepted by each of the orders, the King was to decide.

Once again the Third Estate was most embarrassed. If it refused to accept royal arbitration, it would alienate the King, who was generally considered as the protector of the *Tiers* against the nobility. If, on the other hand, it accepted his arbitration, it might perhaps be forced also to accept the vote *par ordre*. It postponed its decision until June 5th. And on that same day the nobility virtually rejected the compromise, by limiting the confirmation in plenary assembly to the deputies elected by the three orders together (this was the case with the deputies from Dauphiné, who had been elected not by local assemblies but by the provincial Estates, revived in 1788). The nobility specified that as a general rule a deputy's credentials must be confirmed by the order which had elected him. The compromise proposal had come to nothing. The conference of representatives met for the last time on June 9th to sign a report on its failure.

Thus, one month after their inaugural meeting, the Estates-General were still at the same stage. Not a single step forward had been taken!

The French people were aware of this situation, for the liberty of the press had in fact been established, thus marking a first victory for the Third Estate. As early as May 4th Mirabeau, deputy of the *Tiers* for Aix-en-Provence, had planned to publish a *Journal des États-Généraux*. The Government forbade this by a decree in Council on May 6th and by a notification on May 7th. A motion of protest, proposed by Target, was passed by a unanimous vote of the electors of the Paris Third Estate, who were then still assembled. Mirabeau, on the strength of this attitude, circumvented the Government's ban by publishing his Journal in the form of 'Letters to his Constituents'. The Government could not stop a deputy from communicating to his electors an account of the discussions of the Estates-General. It was forced to give way, and granted permission to 'all authorized periodicals and news-papers to give an account of what takes place in the Estates-General, confining themselves to those facts on which they have accurate information, without permitting themselves any comment or reflection.' This almost amounted to the freedom of the Press. Letters from deputies to their constituents increased in number and were frequently printed. Thus the whole of France became aware of the *impasse* reached by the Estates-General. The dis-orders born of electoral excitement, which had somewhat subsided as the time for the Estates' meeting drew near, broke out again with renewed fury, as we shall see presently. The deputies of the Third Estate, meanwhile, were overwhelmed with letters adjuring them to stand firm and assuring them of the support of their constituents. Needless to say, developments at Versailles were closely and keenly followed in Paris. Every day, numbers of Parisians appeared at the *salle des Menus* and mingled with the deputies, encouraging them to resist; they could do so the more easily since for quite a long time there was no public gallery in the *salle nationale* and it was therefore difficult to distinguish specta-tors from deputies. The latter, outside their assembly room, tended to form groups according to their place of origin, their affinities or tendencies. Thus was formed the 'chamber of the province of Brittany' which soon became the 'Breton club', and, later, the Jacobin club. Certain deputies soon came to the fore during these interminable discussions; certain names became familiar, not only those of Bailly, Mirabeau and Sieyès, who were famous before the opening of the Estates-General, but those of Le Chapelier, Camus, Rabaut Saint-Etienne, Target, Mounier, Barnave and Malouet.

As early as the beginning of June Sieyès had declared: 'We must cut the cable', in other words abandon all concern for laws and regulations. On June 5th a deputy proposed that the Third Estate chamber should turn itself into a 'National Assembly', a term used by Necker in 1778 when he put forward his project of Assemblies. Malouet protested, but on June 8th he proposed the title of 'Legitimate Assembly of the representatives of the Commons'.

The report of the failure of the conciliation conferences was published on June 9th, and on the 10th Sieyès declared that it was high time to emerge from so long a period of inaction. Since the nobility rejected any sort of conciliation, the only course left the 'Commons' was to 'summon the other two orders to join with it to confirm the credentials of the representatives of the Nation'. The matter was debated at great length. It was decided by a majority of 247 votes that a deputation from the Third Estate should be sent to the nobility and clergy with an 'invitation' to join the Third Estate, and to proceed to a roll-call of deputies, by *bailliages* and *sénéchaussées*, without distinction of order; anyone who failed to appear would be considered a defaulter. However, the moderates, represented by Regnault de Saint-Jean-d'Angély, put through a motion that an 'address' should simultaneously be presented to the King.

The nobility and the clergy received the invitation on June 12th, and the King received the address on the same day. The privileged orders replied that they would discuss the matter. However, without waiting any longer, the Third Estate proceeded to the roll-call of deputies by *bailliages*. To begin with only those of the Third Estate answered and handed in their credentials.

The clergy had now embarked on a debate which was to be prolonged, since between June 13th and 19th 280 speeches were made. But already on the 13th three *curés* of the *sénéchaussée* of Poitiers, named Jallet, Ballard and Le Cesve, left the chamber of the clergy and went to join the Third Estate. But for the efforts of a certain canon Coster a far larger number of *curés* would have followed suit. The Government was not disturbed at this, and Barentin, Minister of Justice, remarked ironically to Bailly: 'My compliments on the conquest you have made.' To which Bailly replied: 'Monsieur, you may think it a petty conquest, but I can tell you, and you'll remember it, that it will be followed by many others.' And in fact on June 14th six more *curés*, including Grégoire, parish priest of Emberménil in Lorraine, joined the deputies of the *Tiers*; three more on the 15th; by the 16th there were nineteen of them altogether.

The nobility, on the other hand, remained unshaken. They merely proposed to the Third Estate that the King should decide the question of the confirmation of credentials, which the Third Estate refused to accept.

On June 17th, although it still comprised no more than 19 of the clergy, the Chamber of the Third Estate decided that it was time to adopt a title befitting its claims. Mounier suggested: 'Legitimate Assembly of the majority of the nation, acting in the absence of the minority.' This was far too long! and Pison du Galand's formula was little better: 'Active and legitimate Assembly of the representatives of the French nation'; nor was that of Barère, deputy for Tarbes: 'Representatives of the great majority of the French people in the National Assembly.' Sieyès's suggestion was clumsy: 'Recognized and confirmed representatives of the French people'. More satisfactory was Mirabeau's: 'Assembly of the representatives of the French people'; but the title finally adopted was that proposed by Le Grand, deputy for Berry: 'National Assembly', since, as Sieyès put it, the members of this Assembly 'represented ninety-six per cent of the Nation', and their credentials, and theirs alone, had been publicly confirmed and they were bound 'to fulfil the wishes of the Nation'. Thus the National Assembly denied the chambers of the other two orders the right to legislate, and even denied the King the right to use his veto. Sieyès's resolution was adopted by 491 votes to 89 and the deputies immediately swore 'to fulfil faithfully the functions entrusted to them'. To forestall any attempt at the use of force, the Assembly went on to pass a resolution proposed by Le Chapelier: it alone could authorize taxes, and it would *provisionally* allow the collection of taxes 'illegally established and levied', but only until the Assembly should break up. However it guaranteed the debts of the State with 'the honour and trustworthiness of the Nation', so as to reassure the *rentiers* and win them over to its side.

All these decisions made a profound impression on the other two orders. In the chamber of the nobility, the duc d'Orléans proposed uniting with the Third Estate, and he obtained 80 votes. This was insufficient, but it was a long way from the unanimous refusal of earlier days.

The clergy, on the other hand, was in favour of union, provided this did not entail voting *par tête*. Several bishops and archbishops, as well as a number of *curés*, spoke to this effect. The chairman, La Rochefoucauld, in great alarm, hastily adjourned the meeting and hurried to beg the King to intervene. But as soon as he had gone, voting took place and 149 deputies, the majority of those present, voted for union with the Third Estate. La Rochefoucauld refused

View of the Bastille

colour print by Pernet. Bibl. Nat., Print Room

July 14th, 1789. View of the Bastille from the
gallery facing the boulevards

*colour print, drawn by Pernet, engraved by Roger. Bibl. Nat.,
Print Room*

The Curé of St.-Etienne-du-Mont marching at the head of
his district to secure arms and munitions at the Invalides

colour print by Guyot. Bibl. Nat., Print Room

First attack on the first drawbridge of the Bastile

colour print by Guyot. Bibl. Nat., Print Room

to recognize this decision, which was nonetheless published with the 149 signatures of those who had supported it.

The Court, meanwhile, was preoccupied with a different matter. The Dauphin, eldest son of Louis XVI and Marie-Antoinette, whose birth had been so ardently longed for, had died on June 14th. His younger brother seemed sickly and there was anxiety about the succession to the throne. The royal family were heartbroken at their cruel bereavement. Louis XVI, by nature indecisive and easily influenced, was now, being obsessed by his personal grief, even more ready than usual to listen to those around him. Now the princes of the blood royal, the Queen, their friends, La Rochefoucauld and certain ministers considered that it was imperative to put a stop to the activities of the Third Estate. They did not go so far as to order the dissolution of the Estates, which had not yet had a single session, but they arranged for a 'royal session' to be held on June 23rd, where the King would make known his wishes, as in the *lits de justice* held in the Parlement. In the meantime the *salle des Menus* was closed, under pretext of reconstruction, so that the *Tiers* should not be able to go on meeting. Bailly, the *doyen* of the *Tiers*, was not even informed of these decisions, which were made known to the deputies by a notice posted on the door.

On the morning of June 20th, the deputies of the Third Estate made their way as usual to the '*salle nationale*'. Great was their surprise, and great their indignation, when they found it closed. Many believed that this was a prelude to dissolution. Most of them were in favour of holding their meeting all the same, in some other hall. Doctor Guillotin suggested the tennis court, the *salle du Jeu de Paume*, which was not far from the palace. Here the deputies forgathered, and here Mounier proposed the famous oath which was to avert any attempt at force from the throne:

'The National Assembly, considering that since it has been summoned to settle the constitution of the kingdom, bring about the regeneration of public order and maintain the true principles of the monarchy, nothing can prevent it from continuing its deliberations, in whatever place it may be forced to meet, and that in a word, wherever its members are assembled, there is the National Assembly, decrees that all the members of this Assembly shall instantly take a solemn oath not to separate, but to meet together wherever circumstances may require, until such time as

N

the constitution of the kingdom shall be firmly established on solid foundations, and all the said members and each of them individually will confirm by their signature this unshakeable resolution.'

577 deputies, including 7 from the clergy, signed immediately. Only one, Dauch, deputy for Castelnaudary, refused to sign because he did not want to commit himself to carrying out decisions which the King had not ratified. The other deputies of the *Tiers* and five more from the clergy signed on June 22nd.

That day the Third Estate sat in the church of Saint-Louis; it was joined by the majority of the deputies of the clergy and even by a certain number of nobles, especially those from Dauphiné and Guyenne.

Meanwhile the Government and the Court met at Marly on June 19th to prepare the declaration which the King was to make at the 'royal session'. The Council was divided; four Ministers, Necker, Montmorin, Saint-Priest and La Luzerne formed a 'progressive' party which accepted a National Assembly and, in certain cases, voting *par tête*. But three other Ministers, Barentin, Villedeuil and Puységur held out for tradition and the vote *par ordre*.

Necker proposed that the King should announce the abolition of fiscal privileges, equality of access to military rank for all Frenchmen and, in certain cases, voting *par tête*. Barentin, Minister of Justice, was opposed to all these projects of reform. The Minister for War, Puységur, indignantly rejected the proposal of equality of access to military rank. The King seemed already inclined to adopt their position, when the Queen intervened asking for the decision to be adjourned and for a new Council to be held on June 21st at Versailles.

This Council was attended not only by the Ministers but by the King's two brothers, the comte de Provence (the future Louis XVIII) and the comte d'Artois (the future Charles X). Necker declared that it would not do to 'exasperate the Third Estate, which was the more redoubtable in that it was the echo of public opinion.' Barentin retorted by insisting on the need to maintain the royal prerogative and the privileges of the two higher orders. He got the Council to declare that the resolutions taken by the *Tiers* since June 17th were null and void, that voting must be *par ordre*, except for the confirmation of contested credentials, and for certain matters such as the constitution of the orders, the rights of privileged members, the organization of future Estates-General, the abrogation of fiscal privileges decided solely by the privileged orders. Equality of access to public office was refused. Taxes would indeed be authorized by the Nation, that is to say by the three orders, but the King would decide on loans without consulting the Estates.

A new Council met on June 22nd to give final form to the speeches to be made by Necker, Barentin and the King. Mont-morin and Saint-Priest made a last attempt to persuade the King to make concessions. 'There's nothing permanent under the sun, Sire,' declared Saint-Priest, 'it's an old saying. It's necessary to change things when circumstances demand it. They are what really govern a State. The welfare of the people must be the sovereign law.' Necker said nothing; he foresaw catastrophe, and possibly had thoughts of deriving personal advantage from it. The King refused to reopen the discussion and said he would keep to the decisions that had been taken.

The session opened on the morning of June 23rd in the great hall of the Menus-Plaisirs, with the same ceremony as on May 5th. Necker, however, chose to show his disapproval by absenting himself. The decisions taken by the Council on the previous day had leaked out, and many deputies of the nobility and some Church dignitaries could scarcely conceal their delight. Louis announced, as in his *lits de justice*, that Barentin was going to 'make known his wishes'. The Minister consequently read out the conclusions reached by the Council on June 21st. Then the King spoke again, setting out his programme, the last programme of reforms he was to propose of his own free will, and one which was to remain for a long time that of the counter-revolution; it was to be resumed by Louis XVIII in 1795 and incorporated in the charter of 1814. Louis XVI had drawn it up with the help of his councillors, inspired by the ideas developed by Jacob-Nicolas Moreau in several works, particularly the *Principes de morale, de politique et de droit public puisés dans l'histoire de notre monarchie.*' (Principles of morality, politics and public law, drawn from the history of our monarchy.)[1]

Describing himself as the father of all his subjects, Louis declared that he sought their common happiness, but that he was the protector of the laws of the kingdom and in duty bound to

[1] J. Godechot, *La Contre-révolution*, Paris, 1961.

maintain them. Next he broached the burning question of the vote, and proposed the compromise reached at the Council of June 21st: confirmation of credentials would take place in separate meetings of the three orders, but if any deputy who had been excluded should protest, his case would be examined in a general assembly, by individual vote. If one of the orders should contest, by two-thirds of its votes, the decision taken by the general assembly, the King would decide the matter. A complicated solution, obviously, and likely to satisfy nobody.

As regards other questions, the King admitted individual voting (*par tête*) in matters of general interest, but voting *par ordre* would be retained for certain issues which he enumerated: the 'ancient and constitutional rights' of the three orders, the organization of the future Estates-General, which were to take place periodically, feudal and seignorial ownership, honorary privileges (particularly seignorial rights, the abolition of which was demanded by thousands of *cahiers*). The King declared that the clergy were prepared to make sacrifices to restore the finances of the State, on condition that nothing affecting religion should be altered without their consent, which implied the retention of tithes—so burdensome to the common people, and so violently attacked by them—since it was unlikely that the clergy would renounce these voluntarily.

All this part of the royal declaration was somewhat negative. But in the next part he promised certain positive reforms. He admitted that taxes—and in future, loans—should be voted by the Estates-General, which might also draw up the budget, in other words distribute State funds among the various public services, including the Court: which meant that the allowances granted to courtiers would henceforward be voted by the Estates. The King also agreed to fiscal equality, individual liberty and the freedom of the Press. He accepted the creation of provincial Estates throughout France, provided these were composed of representatives of the three orders, the Third Estate being doubly represented. The management of the royal domain was to be reformed; there were to be alterations in financial administration, particularly in the levying of the *gabelle* (the salt tax). Legal procedure might be reorganized; so also might the customs system. The *corvée royale* (forced labour on the roads) was to be abolished, as was the *mainmorte*, last vestige of serfdom.

Undoubtedly, this programme of reforms was not inconsiderable. But it was far from being a 'revolution from above', and still further from the demands contained in the vast majority of the electors' *cahiers*. The end of the King's declaration, moreover, presented this programme as the absolute maximum, and seemed to threaten anyone who might try to start a discussion to widen its scope: 'If you should abandon me in this noble undertaking,' said the King, 'alone and unaided I will provide for my people's happiness', which seemed to imply the dissolution of the Estates. He ended on a menacing note: 'Not one of your projects, not one of your resolutions can have force of law except by my special consent. I order you to separate immediately and meet again tomorrow morning, each in the chamber set apart for your order, to resume your discussions.'

A profound silence ensued. The nobility hastened to obey, and left the hall. The deputies of the Third Estate were dismayed; they were less impressed by the promise of reforms, which in fact were relatively numerous, than by the tone of the peroration, the atmosphere of the session, the display of force which surrounded them. After a few moments, dismay gave way to anger. The moderates either joined the extremists or were swamped by them. When the marquis de Dreux-Brézé, grand master of ceremonies, rose to call attention to the King's orders, Bailly, *doyen* of the Third Estate, retorted: 'The assembled Nation can take no orders'; and Mirabeau went even further in his famous apostrophe: 'We shall not budge from our places here except at the point of the bayonet.' Then Sieyès reminded the deputies: 'You are the same today as you were yesterday.' The Assembly, following the example so frequently set by the Parlements, decided to disregard these orders and to go on sitting.

Dreux-Brézé hurriedly informed the King of what had happened. Some courtiers suggested that the Army should be brought in. Then came a disquieting report of crowds gathering in the neighbourhood of the Hôtel des Menus-Plaisirs. '*Eh bien, foutre! qu'ils restent!* let them stay!' declared the King, thus abandoning at one blow the whole programme that he had just put forward, and admitting the victory of the Third Estate.

The latter took advantage of it. The deputies immediately resumed their discussions and, in the first place, confirmed their three fundamental decrees: the constitution of a National

Assembly, the oath taken in the Jeu de Paume, and the decision to cease payment of taxes should the Estates be dissolved. The *Tiers* moreover declared its members 'inviolable', indicting as 'infamous, disloyal to the Nation and guilty of a capital crime' those who should seek to prosecute them or arrest them.

The resolute behaviour of the *Tiers* impressed the other two orders. On the following day, June 24th, the greater part of the members of the clergy came to sit with the Third Estate and, through the mouthpiece of Lefranc de Pompignan, archbishop of Vienne, accepted the vote *par tête*. On June 25th a further group of ecclesiastics, as well as forty-seven deputies of the nobility, including Clermont-Tonnerre, the Lameths, Adrien du Port and the duc d'Orléans, entered the *salle nationale*, followed on June 26th by two more bishops, two *curés* and two nobles. The handful of clerics and those deputies of the nobility who had stayed behind in their separate chambers were hissed at by the crowd as they went in or out.

Could the King persist in his attitude? He was now bound either to carry out the threats made on June 23rd or to accept the 'National Assembly'. The Council, meeting on June 26th, admitted that for lack of troops resistance was out of the question for the time being. On June 27th, therefore, the King most unwillingly invited his 'loyal clergy and nobility' to unite with the Third Estate. The comte d'Artois, the King's brother, explained to the duc de Luxembourg, who presided over the nobility, that Louis had decided to take this step because 'his life was in jeopardy'. None the less it took a new, urgent letter from the King to bring the more unyielding members of the nobility to join the Third Estate in the *salle nationale*.

The conflict which had begun on May 5th seemed to have ended with the complete victory of the Third Estate. Was it to be a lasting one? This would depend on the attitude of the French people. We have said little about them, so as not to interrupt the account of the long crisis that marked the opening of the Estates-General. Yet if the deputies of the *Tiers* persisted in their defiant attitude it was because they received daily encouragement not only from the approval of the Parisians who flocked to Versailles but from the many letters they received from their constituents, showing that the provinces were in a ferment. Spurred on by hunger and by the fear of being cheated of their hopes by a

166

'nobles' plot', the masses were stirring, ready to oppose the authority of the throne.

2. Hunger

The meeting of the Estates-General on May 5th, 1789, had by no means put a stop to the economic crisis. The price of bread went on rising. True, the harvest of 1789 promised to be better than that of 1788, but owing to the wet, stormy spring it was likely to be a late one. Since in those days threshing, by flail, and grinding took a long time, there would certainly be a long and difficult interval before the harvest was secure. The Government, in spite of its financial difficulties, had bought grain in Holland and Poland; these countries, however, had also suffered from bad weather conditions in 1788, and their corn was scarce and dear. In any case, imports of foreign corn into France could only palliate the shortage in a few large towns, and did nothing to relieve country districts. The unrest in the markets was as great after May 5th as before it, even greater indeed, in so far as the problem of supplies became increasingly difficult.

On May 6th and 7th, violent riots broke out in the market of Cambrai, where customers thought the price of corn too high. Hungry crowds poured out of the town and, joined by unemployed peasants, went to plunder the granaries of the neighbouring abbeys of Vaucelles, Walincourt, Honnecourt, Mont-Saint-Martin, and Oisy-le-Verger, and those of the *seigneur* of Walincourt. In the markets of the Saint-Quentin region, similar gatherings imposed popular price control over grain. In June, the police claimed to have discovered a 'plot' aimed at plundering the granaries of the Carthusian monastery of Noyon. In the first fortnight of July rioting broke out in the market of Amiens.

Similar disturbances took place further North, on the 6th and 7th of May, in the markets of Valenciennes, Armentières, Hazebrouck and Estaires; on June 6th and 20th at Dunkirk; on June 30th at Valenciennes again. The peasants refused to pay their tithes.

In Normandy, on May 28th, grain was plundered on the market place of Rouen, and further looting took place on July 12th and 13th.

In Brittany, on June 9th and 10th, granaries were pillaged near Châteaulin. In the beginning of July, in the neighbourhood of

Fougères, seven or eight hundred agricultural labourers, armed with axes, sticks and scythes, stopped carts loaded with grain. On July 6th at Vitré the crowd gathered in front of the *sénéchal*'s house and that of his subdelegate, demanding that the price of bread should be dropped; stones were thrown at windows and several people were injured. The subdelegate of Ploërmel wrote on July 4th: 'Excitement has reached such a pitch that the threats I have heard uttered make me, and all sensible people, afraid of riots and terrible consequences when the time comes to collect the tithes . . . All the peasants of the neighbourhood and of my department are preparing to refuse their quota of sheaves to the tithe collectors, and even declare openly that no such collections shall take place without bloodshed, on the senseless pretext that the demand for its abolition having been included in the *cahier* of complaints, it has really come into effect.'

In the Alpine region, an agrarian rising took place on May 13th at Paladru, and another on June 28th at Thodure. President d'Ornacieux wrote in this connection: 'There is daily talk of attacking the nobility, of setting fire to their châteaux in order to burn all their title-deeds . . . In those cantons where unrest has been less sensational, the inhabitants meet daily to pass resolutions that they will pay no more rent or other seignorial dues, but fix a moderate price for the redemption of these, and lower the rate of the *lods*; endless hostile projects of this sort spring from that spirit of equality and independence which prevails in men's minds today.' At Crémieu, at the beginning of June, there was talk of burning and plundering the châteaux.

At Lyons, when it was learnt that on June 27th the King had commanded the three orders to debate in common, tumultuous gatherings clamoured for a reduction in prices. It was rumoured that the King had decreed 'three days of *franchise*' (exemption), during which food products would enter Lyons without paying duty. The crowd demanded the implementation of this decision, while in the countryside, here as elsewhere, peasants refused to pay tithes and objected to free trade in grain.

In Languedoc, near Montpellier, at Cournonterral, gatherings of armed peasants were reported at the end of May by the marquis de Pontalès. In the Uzès region they refused to pay tithes, and the bishop asked the King to give orders for armed forces to assist the tithe collectors. At Bagnols-sur-Cèze, confronted by the threatening attitude of his vassals who refused to pay seignorial dues, the lord consented to negotiate their redemption.

All round Paris, in an extensive area, identical scenes were taking place. At Vierzon, armed gangs ransacked granaries in search of corn. At Bar-sur-Aube, on June 24th, the municipal authorities had to take measures 'to ensure the safety of the shops in the town and to protect the inhabitants against the mobs from outside, who threatened to start fires on the pretext that there was not enough bread in markets.' At Sens, on July 13th, the 'rural population' captured the grain market. Everywhere the forces of order seemed powerless and the law was paralysed. Besenval, deputy commander of the troops in the Parisian region, wrote on June 19th: 'These incidents are unprecedented, and the people's licence increases daily; there is furthermore a very real danger of famine, and things may eventually reach a point where the troops will be unable to do more than, at best, defend themselves.'

3. Fear

It is very difficult to distinguish, among the motives that provoked the disturbances of spring 1789, between those due to the sharp rise in the price of bread and the prospect of famine, and those due to the disappointment caused by the stagnation of the Estates-General. The French people, as we have said, were kept informed of developments by their deputies, who unfailingly fomented their resentment, as may be judged by this extract from a letter addressed to his constituents on June 6th by Poncet Delpech, deputy for Montauban: 'You see, messieurs, that nothing important has yet been achieved; you can judge from the facts what causes prevent the execution of the great plans we have formed. This vexatious inaction is making us ill; we all wish we were still at home in our provinces in tranquil obscurity. People write to tell us they envy our position and wish to share it. We can truthfully say, with one of our poets: "We are envied elsewhere, but here we languish in distress".'[1] Hundreds of similar letters had increased the general disquiet. An 'observer'[2] wrote to Montmorin, Minister of Foreign

[1] G. Lefebvre, *La Grande Peur de 1789*, Paris, 1932; Daniel Ligou, *La Première Année de la Révolution vue par un témoin (1789–1790), Les 'Bulletins' de Poncet-Delpech, député du Quercy aux Etats généraux de 1789*, Paris, 1961.

[2] A. Brette, 'Relations des évènements depuis le 6 mai jusqu'au 15 juillet 1789. Bulletins d'un agent secret', in *La Révolution française*, 1892, vol. XXIII, pp. 348–368, 443–471, 520–547; 1893, vol. XXIV, pp. 69–84 and 162, 198.

Affairs, on May 15th: 'There is general anxiety about the results of the Assembly. People are astonished to see troops arriving every day in the neighbourhood of Paris, and they notice with resentment that most of these troops are foreigners.' On May 21st the same 'observer' notes that 'many people fear the dissolution of the Estates-General', and on June 3rd he writes: 'The general rumour today is that the Estates-General will not meet.' On June 13th, still according to the same witness, people are saying that 'the clergy, the nobility and the Parlement have combined to bring about the fall of M. Necker.' The 'observer' attributes these rumours to the deputies themselves: 'I am informed, and on good authority, that many deputies to the Estates-General, and *curés* in particular, render an exact account of their doings, that they keep up dangerous correspondence and endeavour to rouse the people against the nobility and the upper clergy; it might be possible to check this process, and I think it would be wise to do so. It is true that certain deputations have taken the precaution of sending couriers, but private individuals, to avoid this expense, merely use the ordinary post.' The Government does not appear to have attempted to introduce censorship to prevent the deputies from communicating with their constituents. By June 15th, in any case, it was too late, and rumours were already rife. More and more, the nobility were being accused of plotting against the Third Estate. On June 17th the 'observer' comments: 'The nobles are expected to mount their horses.'

The deputies, however, were not originally responsible for the notion of a plot against the Third Estate. There was an old and deep-rooted popular conviction that when things were going badly it could only be the result of a plot. We have seen how the Malisset contract had given rise to the idea of a 'famine pact', concluded in order to starve the people and reduce them to submission. On February 13th the bookseller Hardy noted in his *Journal*: 'Some people were heard to say that the princes had been hoarding grain on purpose to overthrow M. Necker ... Others were convinced that the Director-General of Finance was himself the chief and ringleader of all the hoarders, with the consent of the King, and that he encouraged and strenuously supported this process only so as to procure money for His Majesty more promptly and in greater quantity, and also so as to ensure payment of the revenue of the Hôtel de Ville' (i.e. the Municipal authority of Paris). On

May 20th a broadsheet was banned by the Châtelet of Orléans because it accused 'the princes, associated in their own interest with the nobility, the clergy and the Parlements, of having hoarded all the corn in the kingdom . . . Their abominable intentions are to prevent the meeting of the Estates-General, by reducing the whole of France to famine, and to make part of the people die of hunger and the rest rise up against their King.' On July 6th Hardy returns to the theory of a plot to starve the nation. It is considered 'quite certain', he notes, that the Government is responsible for hoarding all the grain supply and that the same thing will happen at the next harvest, in order to procure the money it needs 'in case the efforts of the Estates-General should come to nothing'.

An anonymous pamphlet entitled *Les vérités bonnes à dire* (Truths that ought to be told) ascribed the high price of grain and bread to the manœuvres of Necker's enemies. Should they succeed in driving him from the Ministry, 'the intention of this cabal was to deceive people for a brief moment about the reality and magnitude of their loss by throwing open the granaries they had kept closed and at the same time lowering the price of bread. Past centuries,' the author of the pamphlet exclaims, 'can show no precedent for so foul a plot as that which this dying aristocracy has been hatching against mankind.'

If the mass of the French people saw a conspiracy behind their food shortage, they could not fail to connect with this same plot the prevalence of brigandage in the countryside, which was a consequence of the growth of poverty and unemployment. From the time when the Estates-General first met at the beginning of May, gangs of brigands were reported from all over France, sometimes, it was said, reinforced by foreign soldiers. At Montpellier, in early May, the inhabitants asked for arms to repulse the brigands who were said to have landed at Sète from two foreign ships and to be threatening to set fire to the port. At Beaucaire, at the end of May, it was rumoured that brigands were laying waste the countryside and preparing to rob merchants on their way to the town's famous fair. In certain localities, the origin of the rumour is obvious. At Ribemont in Picardy some soldiers made their way into the abbey and forced the monks to serve them drinks. One terrified monk ran out screaming: 'The brigands are here!' The rumour immediately spread round the neighbourhood that brigands had taken possession of Ribemont; the peasants, armed with scythes and pitchforks, hurried up and forced the soldiers to evacuate the abbey. At Lyons, at the beginning of July, when the rumour (a false one) spread that for three days no dues would be levied on food products, the peasants of the surrounding countryside flocked into the town. They were mistaken for brigands or jailbirds. They were even said to have killed and injured three hundred people. This peasant movement may perhaps have been behind the rumour current at Bourg-en-Bresse on July 8th, that 600 brigands and vagrants had come from Savoy and overrun the region.

It seemed obvious that these brigands were under orders from the nobles whose obstructive tactics prevented the Estates-General from succeeding. How could the mass of the French people fail to connect three phenomena which were so noticeable in the spring of 1789: the high price and scarcity of bread and cereals, the spread of brigandage, the stagnation of the Estates-General? How could they help imagining that the nobility were deliberately seeking to bring about famine so that, with the aid of the 'brigands', they could more easily subdue those who had had the insolence to demand, through their *cahiers de doléances*, the abolition of that feudal régime which had prevailed in France for the past thousand years?

Towards mid-June the idea of an aristocratic plot had become widespread. The conviction that the privileged orders would defend themselves with the help of 'brigands' and even of foreigners was commonly held. The fact that the King had deliberately brought foreign troops into the neighbourhood of Paris was bitterly resented, as we have seen. And Frenchmen, if they had any sort of education, could not forget that the Genevan revolution of 1782 and the Dutch revolution of 1787 had been repressed with the aid of foreign troops. The notion of an 'aristocratic plot' involving the help of brigands or foreign troops was put forward in a large number of pamphlets, such as *La Conjuration découverte, La Découverte de la Conjuration, L'Avis aux bons Citoyens touchant la grande conjuration des aristocrates*, and many others.[1]

The reality of the plot seemed to be confirmed by remarks heard in the street and frequently distorted. Thus a certain

[1] See M. Tourneux, *Bibliographie de l'histoire de Paris pendant la Révolution française*, 1890–1915.

Perrot, secretary to the duc de Beuvron, *commandant* of Normandy, was reported to have said on June 23rd: 'I am firmly convinced that the *Intendant* and municipal officers [of Caen] are the chief agents of the monopoly.' If a man so highly placed used such terms, surely it meant that there really was a 'monopoly' aimed at starving the working class? In any case, great folk were indifferent to their poverty, to the famine from which they alone suffered while the rich went unscathed. People quoted the famous words attributed to Marie-Antoinette: 'If they have no bread, let them eat cake!' Some remarks were even more cruel. In the year II a former alderman was arrested at Orléans for having said in 1789: 'If all the little girls were to die, there would be enough bread', a remark which, when circulated, became: 'We should throw all the children in the river because bread is too dear.' Besides these remarks, which betray indifference, to say the least, on the part of the wealthy towards the sufferings of the poor, and at times suggest the existence of an actual plot to starve the people deliberately, we find others which seem to display a vindictive desire for bloodthirsty repression. During June, at Lons-le-Saunier, people quoted the comment of a councillor in the Parlement: 'We might hang half the inhabitants and spare the rest.' At Sarreguemines, at the beginning of July, a lieutenant in the Flemish *chasseurs* was said to have exclaimed: 'The Third Estate are a lot of *jean-foutres*, I could kill a dozen of them on my own, and I'd hang Necker.' Arthur Young reports that on July 9th, at Châlons-sur-Marne, an officer whose regiment had been summoned to Paris told him: 'Maréchal Broglio [de Broglie] was appointed to command an army of 50,000 men near Paris—it was necessary—the *tiers état* were running mad—and wanted some wholesome correction'.

Faced with these 'proofs' of a plot, what were the people to do? In the first place, they could write to their deputies to show them that they did not stand alone, that their constituents supported them. This they did not fail to do, and the deputies of the *Tiers* received large numbers of enthusiastic letters of approval. After the closing of the *salle nationale* at the Hôtel des Menus-Plaisirs on June 20th, the deputies of the Third Estate asked their constituents to combine in groups to send them 'addresses'. They received over three hundred.[1] The earliest of these support the Third Estate's

[1] These are preserved in the Archives Nationales, D XXIX.

resolution of June 17th, constituting itself a National Assembly. The others protest against what seems to them an attempted act of violence on June 20th. Thus the inhabitants of the region of Pontivy write on June 28th: 'The townspeople learn with the greatest dismay that the King's authority has made use of armed force to disperse the National Assembly by forbidding it the entry to the temple of the fatherland.' And the municipal authorities, the nobles, bourgeois and other inhabitants of Lannion write on June 27th that 'having first shown their grief and dismay by an expressive silence, they denounce as disloyal to their country those cowardly impostors who, for their base personal interests, attempt to deceive the faith and justice of a beneficent monarch.' Other addresses expressed approval of the Tennis Court Oath and of the meeting of the three orders. Finally those of the beginning of July warn the deputies against a possible act of force on the part of the King. The people of Thiaucourt in Lorraine, for instance, express apprehension lest 'the troops being assembled between Paris and Versailles may shackle the freedom of the Assembly.' These declarations came either from electoral assemblies of the *bailliages*, newly convened, or from general assemblies of townspeople, or from municipal authorities, sometimes reinforced by 'notables'.

Such 'addresses' served indeed to give moral support to the deputies. But if the 'plot' took the form of recourse to arms, there was no solution but to repel force by force and precipitate a general uprising of Frenchmen against the privileged classes and their defenders. True, the deputies, in their letters, had by no means sought to provoke such an uprising. While expressing their fears and anxieties, they did not ask their electors to take up arms.

The arming of the French people had been a spontaneous movement. It began, as we have seen, in April 1788, with the 'voluntary patrols' organized by the municipality of Troyes. It developed between February and July 1789 with the revival of the old *bourgeois* companies of *arquebusiers* or *francs-archers*, as at Etampes, Caen, Orléans and Beaugency, with the spread of 'voluntary patrols' as at Mortagne, Bar-sur-Aube, Sens and Amiens, or with the creation of *milices bourgeoises* (citizens' militias) at Gaillac, Marseilles and Limoux. Apprehension of famine made it seem advisable to protect the harvests against possible incendiaries, and from June onward the peasants took up arms, often with the agreement of official authorities, the *bailli*, the *sénéchal*, the *intendant* or the provincial *commandant*. Thus in June the *bailliage* of Douai authorized the arming of the peasantry to defend their harvests, and the *intendant* of Lille followed suit. In Gascony, too, the peasants were permitted to take up arms. On May 12th the peasants of Languedoc were armed by the *commandant* of the province, the comte de Périgord, while on the same day comte Esterhazy, in Hainault, took a similar decision. Thus by the beginning of July a large section of France was under arms, ready to give support to the deputies of the Third Estate in case of any attempt on the King's part to restrain or disperse them. At the same time the troops on which the Government might have depended had been undermined by popular propaganda. They were exhausted after six months constantly on the alert, obliged to send daily detachments to protect a bakery here, a granary there, a market elsewhere. Moreover they were disorganized; the regular units were completely dislocated. Battalions and squadrons had been broken up into an infinite number of small detachments under the command of non-commissioned officers or, at best, of a subaltern. Commanding officers had lost all authority over their men, who, being in permanent contact with the population, were growing increasingly susceptible to revolutionary propaganda. The non-commissioned officers were moreover dissatisfied, as we have shown, with the rulings of the War Minister, Saint-Germain, which debarred them from promotion. Private soldiers were irritated by other rulings of the same Minister, which introduced into France the Prussian style of discipline, including beating with the flat of the sword.[1] All the lower ranks were infected by that hatred of the privileged orders that inspired the Third Estate. Moreover, the Third Estate lavished attentions on the soldiers, as is proved by certain significant incidents occurring in Paris at the end of June.

On June 24th, two companies of *gardes-françaises* refused to perform their duties: following the events of the previous day at Versailles, disorders were feared in Paris, and these soldiers were unwilling to repress a possible Parisian uprising. On the 28th, other companies, to whom cartridges had been distributed in anticipation of disorder, flung down their weapons and munitions and hurried to the Palais-Royal to assure the crowd which was

---

[1] See for instance the *Avis aux grenadiers et soldats du tiers état par un ancien camarade du régiment des gardes-françaises.*

gathering there, excitedly discussing the news from Versailles, that they would not march against the people of Paris. Their colonel decided to punish this act of insubordination; he had fourteen grenadiers, considered as ringleaders, arrested and confined to the Abbaye prison. As soon as this event became known, the speakers in the Palais-Royal collected a crowd from those who were strolling in the gardens, and declared that the prisoners were going to be transferred during the night to Bicêtre and there 'hanged between the two wicket-gates'.[1] Three hundred people immediately rushed to the Abbaye, demanded and obtained the release of the *gardes-françaises*, and brought them to the Palais-Royal, where they were treated to supper. The duc d'Orléans ordered the gates of the Palais to be kept open all night, and the guards slept on mattresses in the Salle des Variétés Amusantes. A company of dragoons and one of hussars had meanwhile been sent to the Abbaye to prevent the grenadiers from leaving it. These were greeted by the crowd with cries of 'Lay down your arms, friends!' and treated to wine. According to the bookseller Hardy, the soldiers 'prudently sheathed their swords and held out their hands in token of friendship to their brothers.' However, he adds, peace-loving citizens 'felt a certain uneasiness . . . apprehending fatal consequences to an insubordination which was spreading to many members of society.' As for the *gardes-françaises*, lodging was found for them the following day in the Hôtel de Genève, in the Palais-Royal. They let down a basket from their window, into which passers-by put their contributions. The authorities, however, were anxious not to lose face. They had a notice printed saying that two of the soldiers arrested were thieves, three others were violent characters and the rest 'deserters and rascals'.[2] The bookseller of the Palais-Royal burnt the leaflet rather than sell it.

The Ambassador of the United States, Thomas Jefferson, wrote that in his opinion 'the French guards were . . . arrested under other pretexts, but in reality on account of their dispositions in favour of the national cause.'[3]

The electors of Paris intervened at the same time, appealing to

[1] Fournier 'the American', *Mémoires secrets*, Paris, 1890, pp. 5–8.
[2] *Etat des soldats du régiment des gardes-françaises qui ont été délivrés le mardi 30 juin des prisons de l'Abbaye de Saint-Germain-des-Prés*, Bibl. nat., Lb 39, 7340. See also Lb 39, 1880 and 1882.
[3] *The Papers of Thomas Jefferson*, vol. XV, pp. 284–291, Jefferson to John Jay, Paris, 19th July 1789. (Ed. J. P. Boyd, Princeton University Press, 1958.)

Third incident of July 14th, 1789. Brave Maillard walks the plank
over the moat of the Bastille to fetch the offer made by the besieged

Bibl. Nat., Print Room

The capture of the Bastille on July 14th, 1789. At Basset's, rue St-Jacques, Paris

the National Assembly in favour of the grenadiers. The Assembly approached the King; a compromise was reached, maintaining the authority of the law. The *gardes-françaises* would return to the Abbaye prison for twenty-four hours, after which they would be released and their names struck off the army list. This was done on July 6th; that same evening a collection was taken for them, which raised 4,000 livres, of which the grenadiers only got 22 livres 10 sous each owing to the dishonesty of those in charge of distributing the money.

The *gardes-françaises* were not the only soldiers to be affected by the movement of fraternization with the people. It even spread to the foreign troops. The log-book of the Swiss regiment of Salis-Samade[1]—the same which, as we shall see, provided a detachment for the Bastille—notes that on July 15th it lost 75 men, who let themselves be seduced by the inhabitants of Issy, Vaugirard and Sèvres, where they were billeted. 'It is remarkable', the document adds somewhat naively, 'that the loss sustained by the regiment on this occasion was chiefly caused by those soldiers whose loyalty seemed above suspicion, and almost entirely by sons of Swiss fathers, whether members of the regiment or other Swiss dwelling in France.' On the contrary, there is nothing surprising in this: the sons of Swiss fathers, of Swiss guards and of Swiss nationals domiciled in France had long shared the hopes and fears of all Frenchmen, they had been particularly susceptible to the effects of popular propaganda and appeals for fraternization, and it was natural that they should be the first to desert the regiment. Jefferson also notes 'that these troops show strong symptoms of being entirely with the people, so that nothing is to be feared from them.'[2]

Thus, at the beginning of July 1789, the French people, spurred on by hope and fear, were on the alert, armed, almost in a state of permanent insurrection; whereas the forces of order were dispersed, disorganized, undermined by propaganda, ready to fraternize. Circumstances thus hardly appeared favourable for a show of strength on the King's part. And yet, encouraged by an aristocratic coterie, he now attempted to take forceful action.

[1] Arch. de la Guerre, *Mémoires historiques*, vol. 619–626.
[2] *The Papers of Thomas Jefferson, op. cit.*, vol. XV, pp. 267–268, Paris, 11th July, Jefferson to Thomas Paine.

VIII

The Fall of Necker and the Rising in Paris

Was the King sincere when, on June 27th, he invited 'his loyal clergy and his loyal nobility' to join the Third Estate? Was it really his intention to let the National Assembly accomplish the reforms demanded by the *cahiers*, or was he merely hoping to gain time so as to assemble at Versailles the forces for lack of which, on June 20th and particularly on the 23rd, he had been unable to reduce the *Tiers* to submission or force it to accept his programme? The fact that on the 22nd he signed the first marching orders summoning troops to Paris, and on the 26th signed further, more important orders, seems to prove his duplicity and to show that his 'invitation' of the 27th was not a genuine one. Moreover, the major part of the nobility had not obeyed and had openly displayed their dissatisfaction. Only a minority of aristocratic deputies had joined the Third Estate and the clergy in the *salle nationale*; the others had abstained, on the pretext that their 'mandates' obliged them to sit in a separate chamber. And among those nobles who accepted union with the Third Estate, some refused to take part in the voting, again by virtue of the imperative mandates they had been given. The National Assembly, in order to make the nobility take a more effective share in its work, abolished these imperative mandates on July 8th, and the King authorized the deputies of the nobility to return to their *bailliages* in order to seek fresh credentials from their constituents. But all these measures were merely aimed at deceiving the public. A certain number of aristocratic deputies, supported by the King's brothers and the Queen's coterie, persisted in urging the King to take counter-revolutionary steps. Moreover, troops had begun to arrive in the neighbourhood of Paris.

The Fall of Necker and the Rising in Paris

1. The concentration of troops around Paris (June 22nd–July 10th)

We know about the concentration of troops around Paris through the marching orders which were given them and which have been preserved in the *Archives de la Guerre* at Vincennes.[1] The first orders were sent on June 22nd to the Swiss regiment of Reinach. It was due to leave Soissons on the 24th and to arrive in Paris on the 26th. At Soissons it was to be replaced on July 3rd by the regiment of Armagnac-Infanterie, 900 strong. The Government, in any case, could not have counted on the Reinach regiment for the session of June 23rd, and it probably did not expect the Third Estate to show any resistance until a few days later. When such resistance was, in fact, displayed on the 23rd, the Government no doubt assumed that its forces were insufficient to put up a fight. The King therefore decided to temporize with a pretence of goodwill, while he summoned fresh troops to Paris and Versailles. It was on June 26th, the day before he was to exhort the nobility and clergy to unite with the Third Estate, that the principal marching orders were given. These concerned three regiments of infantry, each 900 strong, and three of cavalry: the Bouillon-Infanterie, a German regiment, was to leave Valenciennes on July 1st to be in Paris by the 9th; the Nassau-Infanterie, also German, was to leave Metz on June 29th and reach Charenton by July 13th; the Provence-Infanterie was to abandon its garrison at Aire-sur-Lys on June 30th and station at Corbeil on July 12th. The cavalry comprised one foreign regiment, the Royal-Allemand, 400 strong, who were to leave Landrecies on June 29th and pitch camp at La Muette on July 7th, and two French regiments, each of 300 horse—the Dauphin-Dragons, who were to leave Metz on July 1st and reach Rambouillet by the 18th, stopping in the neighbourhood of Paris from the 14th to the 16th, at Luzarches, Pontoise and Mantes; and the Maistre de Camp Général de Cavalerie, who were to quit their garrison at Toul on July 1st and proceed to Meaux by the 14th and Marly by the 17th.

On June 29th and 30th, fresh orders were sent, proving that the King's plans were taking shape. The movements ordered on the 26th were altered so that the troops should station as close as possible to Paris, even within the city itself. The Provence-Infanterie was to make for Paris instead of stopping at Corbeil.

[1] Arch. de la Guerre, *Correspondance*, A 4, supplement 55, 1789.

The Bouillon-Infanterie was to await fresh orders at Louviers. The Nassau-Infanterie was to speed up its progress and, instead of reaching Charenton on July 13th, was to be at Choisy-le-Roi, closer to Versailles, on the previous day, July 12th. The Dauphin-Dragons was to halt at Senlis and await further orders there, while the Royal-Allemand was also to make for Choisy-le-Roi.

On July 1st these 2,700 infantrymen and 1,000 cavalrymen seemed insufficient, and the Government sent for fresh troops, a Swiss infantry regiment, the Castela, 900 strong, which was to leave Metz on July 6th and be in Paris by the 19th, and one battalion of Toul-Artillerie, garrisoned at Soissons, which was ordered to set out on July 4th and reach Paris by the 7th. On that date, fresh orders were given. Lauzun's hussars (300 horse) were summoned from Verdun to Marly-le-Roi, to be there by the 10th. The Bouillon-Infanterie, stationed at Louviers, were directed to Nanterre, while the Toul-Artillerie, presumably considered useless to cope with a Parisian riot, were sent back from the Invalides to Jouy. Including the troops already stationed in the Parisian region, there was thus a force of almost 30,000 men who on July 4th were placed under the orders of the seventy-year-old Marshal de Broglie, assisted by the Swiss general Besenval, who, in fact, directed operations and did so, as we shall see, very badly; he was said to be 'fitter for the service of Venus than for that of the army'.

In any case, the marching orders given to the troops prove that as early as June 26th the King had decided to take action around July 13th, since their concentration was to be completed at that date.

During these preparations, the National Assembly began its work. On July 3rd it appointed as its chairman Lefranc de Pompognan, Archbishop of Vienne, and on July 7th it decided to provide France with a constitution and assumed the definitive title of *Assemblée nationale constituante*. A Constituent Committee was appointed, and two days later Mounier presented to the Assembly a preliminary report on its behalf. On July 11th La Fayette tabled his draft for a Declaration of the Rights of Man, requesting that this should be set at the head of the Constitution. Until this date the Assembly had displayed great moderation. Needless to say, it had not for a moment called in question the monarchical character of the new regime. It took for granted that France was to remain a hereditary monarchy. It had not even discussed the royal prerogative, and did not envisage the possibility that the new constitution might be promulgated without ratification by the King. It thought of power as being wielded indivisibly by the King and the Assembly. The majority of the deputies had not yet adopted the theory developed by Sieyès in his famous essay *Qu'est-ce que le Tiers État?* which established the supremacy of the constituent power over all others. At this stage, in early July, the deputies do not seem to have had any intention of overthrowing all the old institutions and building an entirely new France on fresh foundations. After the conflict that began on May 5th and appeared to have been resolved on June 27th, between the Third Estate on the one hand and the King and the privileged orders on the other, an era of fruitful collaboration seemed possible. The arrival of troops in the Parisian region on and after July 7th, the rumours emanating from the Court, the self-assurance and arrogance of certain members of the nobility convinced the deputies of the *Tiers* that a *coup* was imminent. On July 8th a deputy spoke in the Assembly expressing concern about the movements of troops. Mirabeau then went up to the tribune and made a vehement speech denouncing the 'warlike preparations of the Court'. He foretold that the concentration of troops might drive 'the most prudent minds beyond the bounds of moderation' and that the people, in a frenzy, might commit 'excesses the original idea of which would have horrified them.' The Assembly voted an address to the King, drawn up by Étienne Dumont, Mirabeau's secretary, a Genevan exiled in France since the failure of the Geneva revolution in 1782. This address respectfully begged the King to withdraw the troops from the neighbourhood of Paris. It pointed out moreover that these troops might well be affected by the revolutionary fever then prevailing in Paris: 'the soldiers, being so close to the focus of discussions, may forget that a contract made them soldiers and remember that Nature made them men.'

Louis XVI did not reply until two days later, July 10th, by which time he had already taken all the necessary steps for his military *coup*. Needless to say, he refused to grant the Assembly's request, and justified the presence of troops in the Parisian region by declaring that 'they were only intended to repress, or rather to prevent, fresh disturbances, to maintain law and order, to ensure and even to protect the freedom which must reign in the deliberations' of the Estates-General. But he took advantage of the request

presented to him by the Assembly to try to realise part of his plan:
the removal of the Estates-General to the provinces: 'If nevertheless,' he said, 'the necessary presence of these troops in the
neighbourhood of Paris should still cause umbrage, I should
proceed, on the request of the Estates-General, to transfer the
Assembly to Noyon or to Soissons, and then go myself to Compiègne in order to maintain the necessary contact with it.' This
reply dismayed the Assembly and redoubled its apprehensions.

But the Assembly was not alone in its anxiety. There was unrest
in Paris too, as much on account of the continued rise in the price
of bread as of the bad news from Versailles. Montjoye wrote in
L'Ami du Roy,[1] in this connection: 'As regards bread, the experience of the people of Paris seemed to bear out M. Necker's
sinister prophecies, and the closer the 14th of July approached,
the greater grew the shortage. Every baker's shop was surrounded
by a huge crowd, to whom bread was distributed with the utmost
parsimony, and the distribution was always accompanied by
anxiety about the next day's supply. These fears were increased by
the complaints of those who, having spent an entire day outside a
bakery door, had come away empty-handed . . . And yet the bread
which was secured after such efforts was far from being wholesome
food; it was generally black, gritty and sour, causing sore throats
and colics. At the Ecole Militaire and elsewhere I have seen stores
of flour of the vilest quality, heaps of it, yellow in colour and foul-
smelling, clotting in hard masses that could only be broken up by
repeated blows of an axe.' The people of Paris concluded quite
rightly that one reason for the high price of bread was the duty
levied on its entry into the city. Crowds gathered at the *barrières*
(customs posts) of Paris and used force in an effort to get foodstuffs through without paying duty. On July 8th the prince de
Lambesc, commanding officer of the Royal-Allemand regiment,
was obliged to send his cavalrymen to the *barrières* to protect the
customs officers and force carriers to pay.

But there was great excitement, too, at the Palais-Royal, where,
apparently, news had come direct from Versailles. On July 6th
such violent speeches were made there that the duc d'Orléans felt
compelled to go in person to pacify the crowd. He went into the
garden and 'gently and politely invited all the people he had seen
forming groups or gatherings to be kind enough to separate or

[1] *L'Ami du Roy*, vol. III, pp. 38–39.

depart elsewhere.' In vain; he had to summon troops, but exhorted them to behave with restraint. The soldiers therefore, 'with great civility and consideration', besought the bystanders to go home, which they eventually did.

Two days later, on July 8th, a police spy tried to get a man arrested in the Palais-Royal whom he suspected of being an old offender. Immediately a crowd gathered, assaulted the informer and pursued him as far as the church of the Petits-Pères. Here they caught him, cut off his ear and brought him back to the Palais-Royal, where they ducked him in a pond, still belabouring him continuously.[1] The following day, July 9th, a 'woman of quality' was accused of 'spitting on the portrait of M. Necker'; she was whipped in public.[2]

The arrival in Paris of the first troops from the provinces resulted in a fresh bout of propaganda. The release of the *gardes-françaises* confined in the Abbaye jail, described in the previous chapter, had already made this regiment the ally of the people of Paris. Hardy notes in his *Journal*: 'Soldiers of the *gardes-françaises* from several barracks in the faubourg Saint-Marcel declared their intention of deserting, so irksome did they find the tasks expected of them daily; the officers of several companies of this regiment persuaded them to return from the Barrière-Blanche, where they had gone to celebrate their expected departure, each man paying his share.' But they were given free drinks in all the taverns of Paris on condition that they cried: *'Vive le tiers état!'*[3] Camille Desmoulins wrote to his father: 'The *gardes-françaises* would all sooner be hanged than fire on a citizen.'[4] According to the journalist Montjoye, a 'council of veterans' was set up within the regiment of *gardes-françaises*, whose members undertook not to participate in any action which might delay the work of the Assembly. But the troops arriving from the provinces were also won over. Montjoye writes, possibly with some exaggeration: 'All the troops that passed through Paris disbanded as soon as they came into the city and the soldiers rushed off to the Palais-Royal. Here Swiss guards, dragoons, hussars and artillerymen were welcomed with open arms; this motley crowd presented a spectacle which was most

[1] *La Mouche écrasée ou l'aventure du Palais-Royal.*
[2] *Dialogue entre un noble et sa femme qui fut fessée au Palais-Royal pour avoir osé conspuer le portrait de M. Necker.*
[3] Hardy, *Loisirs*, vol. VIII, p. 265.
[4] C. Desmoulins, *Lettres à son père, op. cit.*

encouraging to the innovators, but highly alarming for the Court
... The general officers themselves said that if the King should
try to interfere with the slightest action of the National Assembly,
he would be unable to count on the loyalty of a single regiment.'[1]
The officers, on the other hand, were frequently hooted at in the
Palais-Royal and in the Tuileries. We have seen that the log-book
of the Salis-Samade regiment admits to 75 desertions; actually the
date of this entry was July 15th. However, the rumour was
current in Paris that the soldiers of this regiment, which had
reached the city on May 13th, had sworn to dismantle their guns
if they were ordered to fire on the crowd. On July 6th, at Versailles,
some *gardes-françaises* came into conflict with hussars. The affray
may have been provoked either by *esprit de corps* or by an attempt
at enticement. But the *gardes-françaises* had the spectators on their
side, and the hussars were put to flight, 'biting their swords with
rage'.

On July 10th the artillerymen in the Invalides barracks mutinied;
80 of them leapt over the walls and rushed off to the Champs-
Elysées and the Palais-Royal, where they were treated to wine and
a ball was held in their honour.[2] Camille Desmoulins describes
this incident: 'Yesterday the men of the artillery regiment followed
the example of the *gardes-françaises*, they forced their way past the
sentries and came to mingle with the patriots in the Palais-Royal.
Most patriotic people do likewise. Everywhere you see working-
class people clinging to all the soldiers they meet: "Come on, *vive
le tiers état!*" and dragging them off to the tavern, to drink a health
to the Commons.'[3]

All these signs should have made the King and his circle
cautious. They had no such effect. On July 9th a meeting of the
King's Council was held, at which Necker was present, and at
which it was decided to bring in the baron de Breteuil to strengthen
the ministry. But no definite plan was put forward, because of
Necker's presence.

The baron de Breteuil, who was staying near Gisors, arrived at
Versailles on the 10th, and he immediately gave his approval to the
project of dismissing Necker. This was no new scheme. Louis XVI
had been bitterly offended by his Principal Minister's attitude on

[1] Montjoye, *Histoire de la Révolution*, vol. II, p. 118.
[2] Hardy, *op. cit.*
[3] C. Desmoulins, *op. cit.*

June 22nd and 23rd. There had been rumours of his dismissal at that date. But since June 27th Marie-Antoinette, the King's brothers and their set had been incessantly clamouring for Necker's departure.

To their great surprise, Louis consented to their request on July 8th; a letter from the baron de Staël, the Swedish ambassador, to his wife on July 12th, and a dispatch from the ambassador of Saxony, Salmour, on July 19th provide evidence that the royal decision was taken on that day, sooner than Necker's enemies had expected, since as we have seen the concentration of troops round Paris was not to have been completed until July 15th or 16th, although orders had been sent them on the 7th to speed up their march. Louis's decision seems to have been precipitated by the request to withdraw the troops presented him by the Assembly on the 8th. But it was kept secret, for the King was unwilling to act before securing the agreement of Breteuil, who was to be Necker's successor. Breteuil gave his approval to Louis's decision in the course of a lengthy conversation with the King on the morning of Friday July 10th. The following morning the King personally wrote a very curt letter to Necker, ordering him to leave Versailles secretly on the evening of July 11th and retire to Switzerland. Necker received the letter while he was at dinner. He replied courteously and assured the King that he would leave 'alone, without going through Paris, without saying a word to any member of his family.' And in fact he promptly set out for Brussels.

But a new Council had already met. It noted that the disturbances were increasing in gravity and in extent. The indiscipline of the *gardes-françaises* was alarming. It was now learnt that the electors of Paris, who had been meeting constantly ever since the election, in May, of their deputies to the Estates-General, had decided, following the example of Marseilles, of Limoux and many other towns, to form a citizens' militia which would clearly be independent of the King's authority. The Council therefore accepted the King's proposals, decided not to wait for the arrival of all the troops that had been summoned to the capital, and sanctioned the dismissal of Necker and of those Ministers who had supported his policy, Montmorin, Saint-Priest and even Puységur. La Luzerne tendered his resignation.

That same evening the news leaked out at Versailles, and a number of deputies who had played a prominent part since the beginning of June thought it wiser not to sleep in their own homes; they expected that during the night the King would order the arrest of the leaders of the Third Estate and the dissolution of the Estates-General. Nothing of the sort happened. Louis XVI had only vague ideas of what he would do after Necker's dismissal; for him, this was merely an incident like the fall of Turgot or that of Calonne. The next head of the Government would have the responsibility of taking action, as Clugny had done after Turgot, and Brienne after Calonne. But Breteuil had no plans. This became clear at the Council meeting held at Versailles on the morning of July 12th, and presided over by Breteuil. Those present were Barentin, Minister of Justice, and Laurent de Villedeuil, Minister of the King's household, the only members of the previous Government still holding office; Marshal de Broglie, commander of the troops stationed around Paris, who had been appointed War Minister and was wholeheartedly loyal to the King; the *intendant* Laporte, Minister of Marine, and La Vauguyon, who had accepted the Ministry of Foreign Affairs. But Breteuil had difficulty in finding a Finance Minister. The post had been refused by the *intendant* Foulon, who was unpopular because he was blamed for food shortages and high prices, and by d'Amécourt, Councillor to the Parlement; the duc de Castries, a former Minister, had also refused, despite his friendship with Breteuil, for he was unwilling to commit himself to so chancy an undertaking.[1] Finally Chaumont de La Galaizière, a former *intendant*, had accepted the post. The comte de Provence considered Breteuil 'the only man capable of saving France'. According to Mme de Staël, 'his loud voice suggested energy, he walked about noisily stamping his feet as though he wanted to bring an army out of the ground, and his self-confident manners deceived those who had faith in their own wishes.'[2] Breteuil set forth his ideas: he had aimed chiefly at coping with the financial difficulties which would inevitably arise from Necker's departure, the increased costs caused by the operations of the army, and perhaps the suspension of tax-collecting, if the Third Estate carried out its threat made on June 20th. He was supposed to have said that he needed 'a hundred million livres and a hundred thousand men.' As the hundred

---

[1] Duc de Castries, *Le Testament de la monarchie*, I; see also Arch. nat. K 163, no. 18.

[2] Mme de Staël, *Considérations sur la Révolution française*, vol. I, p. 212.

million livres were hard to come by, the Court was said to have secretly ordered the printing of paper money. At any rate Bailly asserts as much in his *Mémoires*,[1] though no documentary evidence has as yet been found. But while waiting for his money and his men, Breteuil had no plan of action; this passive attitude was to make possible the development of the Parisian rising.

2. The Parisian rising: Sunday July 12th

July 12th was a Sunday, a favourite day, as we have seen, for popular gatherings and mass demonstrations. The news of Necker's dismissal and his replacement by Breteuil became known towards nine in the morning, and was promptly broadcast through the Palais-Royal. It immediately aroused an intense emotional reaction. People assumed that Necker's dismissal would have threefold consequences: the transfer of the Assembly to the provinces and, presumably, its imminent dissolution; a still higher rise in the price of grain and bread, since Necker was considered as the man who held food-hoarders at bay; and finally, national bankruptcy, as a consequence of which investments would cease to pay. Thus, apart from the privileged classes, almost the entire French nation was disturbed about the fall of Necker: all those who hoped for reforms and saw their hopes fading, all those who dreaded famine and saw their fears being realized, all those who apprehended ruin and felt themselves threatened by it. It is unnecessary to postulate a plot, whether Masonic or Orléanist, to account for the uprising of Paris, and indeed of the whole country, at the news of Necker's fall. We need only remember that the mass of the French people felt personally injured by the departure of the Director-General of Finance. And it is easy to understand how, hungry for news, and at leisure since this was a Sunday, Parisians flocked to the Palais-Royal. Soon the trees were bending 'under the weight of the people perched on them'. Impromptu speeches were made, suggesting methods of organizing resistance and calling the people to arms. The orator who drew the largest audience was undoubtedly Camille Desmoulins. Climbing on to a table, he uttered a passionate harangue: 'Citizens, you know that the Nation had asked for Necker to be retained, and he has been driven out! Could you be more insolently flouted? After such an act they will dare anything, and they may perhaps be

[1] Bailly, *Mémoires*, vol. I, pp. 325–331.

planning and preparing a Saint-Bartholomew massacre of patriots for this very night!... To arms! to arms! Let us all wear green cockades, the colour of hope... The famous police are here; well, let them look at me, observe me carefully! Yes, I call on my brothers to seek liberty!' And, raising a pistol, Desmoulins exclaimed: 'At least they will not take me alive, and I am ready to die a glorious death! I can only meet with a single misfortune, and that would be to see France in bondage!' Other orators made similar gestures, but their names have not survived. Poupart de Beaubourg, for instance, tells us: 'I hurried to the Palais-Royal where, climbing on to a table, I moved a number of proposals all aimed at repelling force by force, at defending our homes against the fury of a threatening army of mercenaries.'

As it was a Sunday, the theatres were all going to hold performances in the afternoon. But could such festivities be tolerated when a catastrophe threatened the Nation? Groups were quickly formed, and hurried to the theatres to force the directors to close their doors in token of mourning and refund the price of tickets to those who had reserved seats. At the Opera over 3,000 people invaded the house, 'uttering fearsome cries'. They forced the director to reimburse the spectators who had already taken their seats. On their way down the boulevard du Temple, one group broke into a museum of waxworks owned by one Curtius, of German origin. Here were displayed models of famous people; the demonstrators demanded the bust of Necker. Curtius handed it over to them, declaring: 'My friends, he is ever in my heart, but if he were indeed living there I'd cut open my bosom to give him to you. I have only his likeness, it is yours.' They also carried off the bust of the duc d'Orléans; which was not surprising, since it was in his residence, the Palais-Royal, that the demonstration had begun.

Preceded by the images of Necker and the duc d'Orléans, a procession of five to six thousand people carrying black banners in token of mourning formed, and marched along the boulevards, the rue Saint-Martin, the rue Saint-Denis and the rue Saint-Honoré. On reaching the place Vendôme they encountered a detachment of dragoons, who not only proved unable to disperse the crowd but were promptly swamped by the demonstrators. The prince de Lambesc, commanding the Royal-Allemand regiment, which had massed on the place Louis XV (the present place de la Concorde),

ordered his horsemen to charge, rescued the dragoons and
brought them back to the place Louis XV, while the demonstrators
made for the Tuileries, which were soon swarming with people. As
the crowd surged into the gardens, they clashed with the troops.
François Pépin, a pedlar, who was carrying the bust of the duc
d'Orléans, was dragged to the foot of the statue of Louis XV, where
he was stabbed in the breast 'by a sword, a sabre, or a bayonet'.
The excited demonstrators picked up stones from a nearby building site, climbed on to the terrace overlooking the place Louis XV
and pelted the cavalrymen.

The time had come for the officer in command of the Paris
troops to take a decision. Besenval had just replaced Marshal de
Broglie, who had been appointed War Minister. He ordered the
Prince de Lambesc to clear the Tuileries. It was this order which
was to turn the demonstration into an insurrection.

The Royal-Allemand regiment formed a column and entered
the Tuileries by way of the swing-bridge connecting the garden to
the square. The crowd retreated, but the most heterogeneous
collection of objects, including many chairs, continued to rain
down from the terrace onto the horsemen. Lambesc, afraid lest his
soldiers should be submerged by the crowd, ordered them to
withdraw. But they had to cut their way with drawn swords over
the swing-bridge. Several civilians were injured, and one old man
may possibly have been killed, although there is no proof of this.
Lambesc, in any case, succeeded in regrouping all his men on the
place Louis XV. He reported to Besenval that he had been unable
to perform his mission, and asked for reinforcements.

During this time the rumour spread through Paris that the
Royal-Allemand had massacred peaceful strollers in the Tuileries.
Immediately the *gardes-françaises*, who had sided with the people
of Paris since the events of June 30th, and were extremely hostile
to foreign regiments, left their barracks and made their way,
armed, to the Tuileries, where they clashed with the Royal-
Allemand and put one detachment to flight.[1] The people of Paris,
in search of weapons, broke open and looted armourers' shops,
and disarmed a patrol of the watch near the Hôtel de Ville. The
detachments of infantry and cavalry stationed in various parts of
Paris were surrounded or driven back towards the place Louis XV.

[1] M. Civrays, 'Lettre d'un garde-française sur la prise de la Bastille',
(*A.H.R.F.*, 1924, pp. 464–465).

The Fall of Necker and the Rising in Paris

It was a matter of urgency to respond to the prince de Lambesc's appeal and to bring up the reinforcements which were massed at the Invalides, the Ecole Militaire and the Champ-de-Mars. Four Swiss regiments—Salis-Samade, Reinach, Diesbach and Châteauvieux—had been stationed at the Champ-de-Mars since June 5th; the log-book of the Salis-Samade regiment has been preserved.[1] On the evening of the 12th it received orders from Besenval to proceed to the place Louis XV. It would have been logical to send it along the left bank and across the Pont Royal—the Pont de la Concorde did not then exist—and then up the right bank to the place Louis XV. It is unlikely that an unarmed crowd, however dense, would have been able to oppose such an operation. But Besenval saw the mission entrusted to the Swiss regiments as a military operation, the crossing of a river in presence of the enemy. The engagement of the Swiss regiments thus became an excessively lengthy process, out of keeping with the urgency of the situation. 'Orders were given to embark the regiment on the two ferries lying on the Seine, opposite the Hôtel des Invalides. The regiment set forth with its [mounted] gun [the other three cannon of its regulation equipment had been lent to the Reinach regiment to defend the Saint-Cloud and Sèvres bridges]. The men crossed the Seine in detachments, since the two ferries could only take 80 and 100 men respectively. One company of grenadiers and one of fusiliers, with the [mounted] gun, formed the vanguard. The rest of the regiment stood in battle array on the left bank of the Seine. The crossing took two hours. The regiment was fortunate not to be attacked on either bank, as might have been feared, particularly since a number of *gardes-françaises* were quartered close to the place where the crossing was made, and these soldiers had also taken up arms to resist the King's troops. A few companies of this corps even crossed the Seine at the same time as the Salis-Samade regiment and intermingled with them on landing. The night being extremely dark, the Salis-Samade regiment did not reach the place Louis XV until after ten. The cannon and the two companies of grenadiers were placed in battle order in front of the balustrade facing the Tuileries, with a few companies on their flanks and the rest of the first battalion behind the grenadiers; the second battalion had its right flank lined up against the Place and its left extending at right angles down the Champs-Elysées, with

[1] Arch. de la Guerre, Mémoires historiques, vol. 619–626.

the Seine behind the front; three battalions of Swiss guards were drawn up in the Champs-Elysées, to the left of the second battalion of Salis-Samade, the detachments of cavalry formed by the regiments of Esterhazy, Bercheny, Royal-Dragons, Royal-Cravate and Royal-Allemand were scattered along various avenues, along the bank of the Seine, in the rue Royale and on the boulevards . . . The baron de Besenval was in command of these various troops. The Royal-Allemand regiment came under fire from the *gardes-françaises* on the boulevards, a number of men and horses being killed and wounded. About half an hour after midnight the entire body of cavalry hurried up behind the Salis-Samade regiment, and the officers warned the Chevalier de Bachmann [in command of Salis-Samade] that they were no longer in a position to resist the rebels, who were bringing up vastly superior forces. Since the baron de Besenval had gone off to give orders somewhere else, the chevalier de Bachmann assumed responsibility for changing the original plan and making others which would enable him to defend himself in case of attack. While he was making these arrangements the entire body of cavalry left the neighbourhood of the place Louis XV. About one o'clock the baron de Besenval returned to the Place. The chevalier de Bachmann tried to explain the changes he had made to the original plan, but M. le baron ordered him to withdraw to camp with his regiment immediately. The chevalier de Bachmann thought it best to cross the Seine at Sèvres, since both the Pont Royal and the Tuileries were guarded by the rebels and it was no longer possible to use the ferries. The regiment of Salis-Samade retreated in perfect order to Sèvres, crossed the Seine there and followed the other bank of the river as far as their camp, which they reached at five o'clock on the morning of the 13th.'

There is no reason to doubt the truthfulness of this logbook. M. Jean Mistler has recently written that it brings out the 'extremely suspect attitude of the baron de Besenval'.[1] Already at the time of the Revolution Royalist writers had tried to make a scapegoat of Besenval. In my opinion there is no reason to suppose that he wanted to promote the rebellion. At most, one might criticize his inefficiency, or rather point out that he manœuvred his troops as though in a struggle between two regular armies, whereas it was simply a matter of restoring order. In any case, it

---

[1] J. Mistler, *Le 14 Juillet*, p. 44.

was not he, as M. Mistler asserts, who took the decision of sending Salis-Samade back to the Invalides by way of the Sèvres bridge, but the chevalier de Bachmann, commanding officer of the regiment. It was Besenval, however, who by wasting the two last precious hours of daylight in sending his troops across the Seine by ferry instead of by the Pont-Royal had allowed the insurgents to strengthen their position in the Tuileries and on the place Louis XV. What emerges with more certainty is the passivity of the officers, shackled by military regulations and alarmed by the rebellious attitude of the *gardes-françaises*. By the time the troops were massed on the right bank, the night was 'extremely dark'. Paris, at this time, was badly lit, as we have seen. The leaders of the various units greatly exaggerated the number and strength of the rebels. It was only during the course of the night that the latter began to obtain weapons by plundering armourers' shops.[1] It is possible that if energetic action had been taken during the evening of the 13th, and the military had occupied the Hôtel de Ville, the rebellion might have been nipped in the bud, but it is far from certain. By now other elements had gradually joined the fray: the victims of food shortage, fearful lest it should develop into famine, the electors of Paris who were seeking to organize the uprising, the bankers and *rentiers* who wished for the return of Necker, the National Assembly itself at Versailles, and behind it the whole of France. On Monday July 13th the action of these various elements combined became obvious to all eyes.

3. Monday July 13th

For the majority of Parisians, the eviction of Necker meant above all a rise in the price of bread, and an intensification of the food shortage, amounting perhaps to famine. Everything must be done, therefore, to avoid such a catastrophe. Now one cause of the high cost of living was thought to be the notorious wall which had surrounded Paris since 1785. As soon as the King's troops had evacuated Paris and withdrawn to their camps at the Invalides and the Champ-de-Mars, which happened about midnight on the 12th, a crowd of Parisians made their way to the *barrières* (customs posts) where dues were levied on goods entering Paris; forty of these fifty-four customs posts were set on fire during the night of July 12th–13th, the Clichy post being the first destroyed, before

[1] Restif de la Bretonne, *Les Nuits de Paris*, vol. I, Paris, 1788.

The capture of the Bastille

from Les Révolutions de Paris, *engraved by Dupin*

Seventh incident of July 14th, 1789.
Death of M. de Flesselles, Prévôt des marchands

Bibl. Nat., Print Room

The fall of the Bastille

colour print (Image d'Epinal), Bibl. Nat., Print Room

The taking of the Bastille

English print, Bibl. Nat., Print Room

midnight. The *mur d'octroi*, the surrounding wall, was itself demolished in a number of places. Montjoye describes the attack on the customs post of the Chaussée d'Antin: 'While the rabble hacked, tore up, threw down and burnt the barriers of the Chaussée d'Antin and the railings, offices and registers of the customs officers, the *gardes-françaises* came up to stand between the fire-raisers and the spectators, leaving the former free to act.'[1] His story is confirmed by the report drawn up by the *prévôt* of Belleville after the burning of the customs post of La Courtille: 'About eight o'clock [on July 13th] a crowd of poorly-dressed people arrived and lighted a fire opposite and quite close to the said *barrière* of La Courtille, and broke and tore down the planks of the doors of this *barrière* and the two adjacent to it, throwing the said planks on to the said fire, broke down the doors of the house adjacent to the said *barrière*, which serves as a courtyard for the employees of the Customs office, went up into the rooms of the said house, and flung on to the fire the said planks and all the mattresses, bedsteads, registers, papers, etc.'[2]

The burning of the *barrières* went on all day on July 13th. However, when the fire threatened to spread to nearby houses the rioters called a halt to their destructive activities. Thus, after long argument, they decided not to burn the Saint-Maur customs post, because the fire might destroy a neighbouring porcelain factory. The *barrière* of La Folie-Méricourt was also spared, because an adjacent house, full of casks, might have caught fire.

An enquiry was held on the burning of the *barrières*, and 81 witnesses were heard between March 29th and April 29th, 1790. They gave evidence about the burning of 31 out of the 40 customs posts destroyed, and described some of the incendiaries. There were among these 'a few well-dressed persons' who, however, seem not to have played a leading role; they were adventurers, such as a certain Mosquinet de Saint-Félix, or idle spectators, 'two well-dressed individuals', a man 'in a blue coat, carrying a gold-headed stick', or another 'riding a white horse'. But the great mass consisted of working-class people, who had come to attack the customs posts in order to bring down the price of bread, wine merchants for whom the *barrières* represented heavy duties on wine and spirits, and smugglers who did not realize that by

---

[1] Montjoye, *L'Ami du Roy*, III, p. 53.
[2] Arch. nat., Y 9999.

destroying the customs posts they were putting an end to their own livelihood. Out of 80 rioters who were arrested, 15 (including three women) were 'professional' smugglers, 15 wine-merchants, 5 self-employed artisans; the rest were coopers (in Montmartre), masons (in Le Roule), weavers (in La Rapée), porters or unemployed workers who had been given jobs at the charity workshop of the Saint-Martin *barrière*. Among the persons brought to trial we find three wage-earners (one grocer's assistant, one porter, one stonemason). All in all, insofar as the data we possess are representative of the bulk of the rioters, we may conclude that this consisted mainly of workers, convinced that the destruction of the *barrières* would bring about a lowering of prices.[1]

In the meantime, they hoped to restore abundance by taking possession of the foodstuffs they believed to be hoarded in certain buildings. The monastery of Saint-Lazare was one such. It was said that the monks had laid up enough corn to last several years. In fact, this monastery also served as a prison where youths arrested for misconduct were confined, and the monks had to feed five hundred persons a day, not to mention the poor and the unemployed who came to beg a bowl of soup at their door. However, they had already been indicted for 'hoarding', and the previous June 'the *commissaires de police* had visited all the store-rooms and taken away 900 *setiers* of grain, which the brotherhood had sold them at a loss of 12 livres on every *setiers*.' This search and the ensuing sale had given credence to the idea that the monastery contained an enormous stock of provisions. And in fact the Saint-Lazare brotherhood was rich, owned great estates, levied considerable tithes and stored the fruits of these.

The monastery was attacked very early in the morning of July 13th and almost completely ransacked. According to the monks' sworn evidence, given three days later, the rioters had taken away 76 *muids* of Burgundy each worth 200 livres (the *muid de Paris* being equal to 268·82 litres), 18 *muids* of Roussillon wine at 210 livres apiece, 600 bottles of wine including 350 of Greek wine at 3 livres the bottle and 150 of Burgundy at 30 sous, 8 barrels of beer at 30 livres apiece, 3 *muids* of vinegar at 60 livres, a cask of oil worth 1,800 livres, two barrels of oil at 140 livres each, 25 Gruyère cheeses worth 812 livres 2 sols, 5 barrels of melted butter at 700 livres, and 53 cartloads of corn which were taken to the Halles to

---

[1] G. Rudé, *The Crowd in the French Revolution*, op. cit.

be sold. The wine seems to have been drunk by those who had seized it. The rioters also laid hold of silver and books and smashed a great deal of furniture. The total loss was reckoned at 22,700 livres. Nevertheless not everything had been taken, for, after the departure of the rioters, there were still left in the house 4 *muids* of Burgundy, 2 of Roussillon, 4 casks of beer, 2 casks of olive oil, 24 *setiers* of corn and 3 of flour.[1] A certain number of rioters were arrested and brought before the Lieutenant of Police between July 20th and 30th, 1790; these were chiefly local workers and tradesmen. The enquiry showed that those responsible for seizing and removing 53 cartloads of corn and for releasing the prisoners were chiefly petty bourgeois and artisans, assisted by the *gardes-françaises*. The ransacking of the rooms in the monastery, the looting of wine, the theft of silver and the destruction of the furniture were the work of labourers and unemployed men, sometimes those who had been assisted by the monastery, together with small shopkeepers and market porters. Out of 23 persons arrested, 16 were wage-earners, the rest were master artisans of the humblest category: cork-makers, market stallholders (including six women). It was undoubtedly hunger that drove these indigent or semi-indigent persons to robbery. The bourgeois were concerned with the general welfare and took the corn to the Halles.

The prisoners of Saint-Lazare had been set free, but what about other prisoners? Already, as we have seen, the gates of the Abbaye jail had been forced open on June 30th and the imprisoned *gardes-françaises* released. During the day of July 13th, after burning the customs posts and plundering Saint-Lazare, the mob rushed to the prisons. At La Force, a captain and fifty soldiers were guarding the gates. When he saw the procession of demonstrators approaching, the captain sent a message to Besenval asking for reinforcements. Besenval replied that the soldiers must withdraw to the interior of the prison and protect it against invaders, but that no reinforcement could be sent. Concluding that defence was out of the question, the captain hurriedly put on civilian clothes and went home, the soldiers dispersed, the porter opened the gates and the prisoners were set free. The crowd went off to demonstrate outside the other prisons, but refused to visit Bicêtre and the Châtelet because these jails were reputed to contain 'dangerous criminals'. Meanwhile the rumour that the prisons had been

[1] Arch. nat., Z 2, 4684 and 4691.

opened reached the prisoners in the Châtelet. They mutinied at half-past nine that morning, and armed with paving-stones and planks of wood they tried to break the doors and to subvert their guards. But a patrol that happened to be passing restored order, with the aid of onlookers. A few volleys of gunfire brought the mutineers to heel; two of them were killed outright and two fatally wounded; a score of others, less seriously injured, were taken to the infirmary.[1]

Paris seemed given over to anarchy. Could the municipal authorities and the bourgeoisie remain unmoved? The chief *de facto* authority was at that time the assembly of 'electors', that is to say those who had elected the Parisian deputies to the Estates-General. They had been meeting regularly ever since the end of the belated Parisian elections. On Saturday July 11th they had met once more at the Hôtel de Ville and decided, following the example of several provincial towns, and although they as yet knew nothing about the dismissal of Necker, to set up a citizens' militia. One of the electors, Leutre, had proposed a permanent session of their assembly, 'or else the 13th of July this year', he said, 'may be even more catastrophic than the 13th of July last year', when a violent storm had destroyed the meagre harvest which had managed to survive a particularly disastrous spring, and had proved the climax to the nation's economic difficulties. But the majority of the electors had not considered the danger so imminent, and the assembly had adjourned until the 13th, two days later.

Meanwhile, however, when the news came of Necker's fall, a certain number of electors had spontaneously made their way to the Hôtel de Ville, during the afternoon of Sunday July 12th. At eleven in the evening, they organized a limited session with Delavigne as chairman. But besides the electors, the hall was thronged with spectators making clamorous suggestions of every sort. Amid the hubbub, it was decided to summon the people of Paris to the headquarters of each electoral district next morning, Monday, at five o'clock. This could obviously only be achieved at such short notice by recourse to such exceptional measures as the ringing of the alarm-bell and the firing of cannon, while drums were beaten in the streets to rouse the people.

Thus Paris awoke that Monday at five in the morning, not only amid the smoke of the burning customs posts, but to the sound of

[1] Arch. nat., Y 9999.

the tocsin and gunfire, the typical atmosphere of the great revolutionary *journées*. It seems to have been chiefly the electors,
rather than the whole population of Paris, who made their way to
the district assemblies. Those who had not voted in April
abstained, or arrived later. The numbers varied widely, according
to district; only 4 persons at Les Minimes, but 1,200 at Le Petit-
Saint-Antoine. The latter was one of several districts which
decided of their own accord to form a *garde bourgeoise*: citizens
promptly formed armed groups, organized posts and patrols.

The electors soon made their way to the Hôtel de Ville, and
their session opened early in the morning. Two important decisions
were taken: the formation of a permanent committee, and the
creation of a citizens' militia. The Assembly of Electors was clearly
too large and too unruly a body to be effective. A smaller permanent
committee was formed under the chairmanship of Flesselles, who
was *prévôt des marchands*, the senior City magistrate under the
ancien régime. The *milice bourgeoise*, the citizens' militia, was first
designed to consist of 200 men for each of the 60 districts, a total
of 12,000 men, but these numbers were considered inadequate and
raised during the afternoon to 48,000, or 800 per district. Only
'recognized citizens' were to be accepted, which, in practice,
meant electors. But a considerable number of volunteers offered
themselves, and in most districts were unquestioningly accepted.
The duc d'Aumont had been suggested as chief of the militia. He
refused. The marquis de La Salle accepted. To recognize each
other, the militiamen adopted a distinguishing badge, at first a
green cockade like that which Camille Desmoulins had made out
of chestnut leaves in the Palais-Royal and which was believed to
be the colour of Necker's livery. But it was also that of the comte
d'Artois. When this was discovered, the green cockade was
abandoned and replaced by another, red and blue, the colours of
the city of Paris.

The militia needed arms as well as cockades. The looting of the
armourers' shops had only produced a small quantity. Parisians
rushed to the Arsenal, but it was empty, powder and arms having
been removed to the Bastille. Then they flocked to the '*garde-
meuble*' in the place Louis XV. There were indeed arms here, but
they were museum pieces, medieval armour, lances, halberds,
crossbows, old muskets, a sword 'which had belonged to Henri IV'
and a small cannon inlaid with silver which had been presented to

Louis XIV by the King of Siam. These were seized; but they could hardly suffice to arm the citizens' militia, which was now reinforced by the former company of '*arquebusiers*'. The crowd therefore returned to the Hôtel de Ville and demanded arms from Flesselles. This caused him much embarrassment. It was true that he had not a large supply of weapons at his disposal. But he was probably reluctant to arm this militia, which was still somewhat of an unruly mob. Flesselles tried to gain time, thus giving an impression of duplicity and untrustworthiness for which he was to pay with his life. He first declared that he would send for arms and hand them over later. The crowd dispersed, but presently returned; faced with its clamorous demands, Flesselles was obliged to hand out the 360 guns that were kept at the Hôtel de Ville. These were insufficient. Cases were fetched from the arms factory at Charleville, which were labelled 'Artillery'. When opened, they were found to contain nothing but old rags. There were shouts of 'treachery!' Flesselles then declared that there were guns and cartridges at the Carthusian monastery near the Luxembourg, and signed an order to the prior to hand them over. The crowd hurried to the monastery; they found no arms there, and were convinced that Flesselles had betrayed them once more. He then decided to appeal to the governor of the Invalides, where in fact there was a considerable store of arms. The committee of electors therefore sent a deputation to Besenval and to Sombreuil, governor of the Invalides, asking for arms to be distributed to the newly-formed militia. Sombreuil was as embarrassed as Flesselles had been. He replied that he must seek instructions from Versailles. The delegation returned empty-handed to the Hôtel de Ville, but by now the people knew that there were firearms at the Invalides and powder in the Bastille.

Meanwhile they waited patiently. And in fact a boat laden with powder had just been seized at the Port Saint-Nicolas. The 35 barrels of powder were taken to the Hôtel de Ville, and an elector, the abbé Lefèvre d'Ormesson, spent the whole night distributing powder to those who had guns.

Thus armed, the militiamen began to patrol the streets. It seemed best to provide them with an escort of experienced soldiers. The *gardes-françaises* had, on the previous day, given unequivocal proof of their feelings by firing on the Royal-Allemand regiment. Four electors were sent to their barracks to ask them to come to the Hôtel de Ville so as to provide an escort for the militia of each district.

During the evening of Monday July 13th, the first patrols of the militia were active and efficient. They disarmed vagrants, the '*gens sans aveu*'. It is easy to imagine how the disturbances of the previous night had brought into the streets of Paris not only the workless and the hungry but also professional thieves and bandits. The number and importance of these is variously assessed by witnesses, according to whether they seek to show the Parisian insurrection as the work of the 'purest' section of the population, or of a gang of brigands and assassins. Restif de la Bretonne, the celebrated author of the *Nuits de Paris*, is inclined towards the second interpretation. During the night of July 12th to 13th, he tells us, he met a number of hostile groups in the streets. 'The rue des Petits-Champs was full of armed brigands . . . fighting or pretending to fight . . . At the entry to the rue des Vieux-Augustins I was nearly killed by a pistol-shot. I made my way to the Halles. This was like hell itself . . . I escaped amid manifold dangers and reached the rue des Prouvaires at midnight. There, someone grabbed me by the collar. "Here's an abbé!" "No, no, my friends, I have children and grandchildren." "He's too old!" said someone else. The brute who was holding me pushed me down into the mud, and left me alone.' On the bridge of Notre-Dame, he was once more stopped by 'brigands'. 'My goodnatured attitude disarmed them and I was able to get home.' Next day he saw 'the bandits of the faubourg Saint-Marcel' going past his door to 'join up with the bandits of the faubourg Saint-Antoine. These bandits were the lowest of ruffians; together with the horrible fellows that haul floating timber, they made up a formidable rabble which seemed to say: "Today's the last day for the rich and well-off; tomorrow it'll be our turn, tomorrow we shall lie on feather-beds".' Many Parisian bourgeois undoubtedly saw things in the same light as Restif. The militia they had created had a twofold aim, to protect the rich and to frighten the King. It is not surprising therefore that during the night of July 13th to 14th the militia arrested and hanged thieves caught redhanded (the number of whom is not known). They also made householders and tenants show lights in their windows, so as to counteract the darkness which, the previous night, had obstructed the efforts of the royal troops. In any case, there is considerable evidence that order was more or less maintained during the militia's first night of activity.[1]

While the assembly of electors, the permanent committee and the *milice bourgeoise* had taken measures to maintain a certain degree of order, while the mass of the population had sought to avert famine by burning the customs posts and plundering the monastery of Saint-Lazare, the bourgeois, and particularly the *rentiers* and the bankers, were now anxiously anticipating the financial consequences for themselves that the departure of Necker might entail: it seemed imperative to force Louis XVI to recall him.

It has been said recently that the role of financiers and bankers in the rising of July 14th has been exaggerated.[2] A. Mathiez was the first to point out that they had given the rising not only their approval but their active help.[3] This was something unprecedented, for it is not usual to see bankers, stockbrokers and leading financiers contribute to a revolution. No doubt the 'capitalists' played a smaller part than the electors of Paris or the *gardes-françaises*, yet they hold an important place among those who contributed to the fall of the Bastille.

There are many proofs of the distress felt by 'capitalists' at the dismissal of Necker. The *bailli* de Virieu writes: 'The dismissal of Necker struck a blow at credit, and the Caisse d'escompte [which was then the principal bank in Paris] might well go bankrupt.' Bailly notes that at the news of Necker's fall 'the brokers got together to discuss the likely consequences on trade and finance of this blow. They decided that, to avoid disclosing the complete discredit of all bills, the Bourse would be closed on Monday [July 13th]; they hurriedly sent one of their number, M. Madimer, to Versailles to get news and to discover the state of affairs.' And in fact, during the single day of July 13th, 5,000-livre bills on the Caisse d'escompte, whose value was 4,265 livres, dropped to 4,165 livres. Moreover, the closure of the Bourse allowed brokers, and especially their clerks, to join the insurgents; this was the case with Charles-Alexis Alexandre, who was to play an important part during the *journées* of June 20th and August 10th, 1792, and later,

[1] See Morellet, *Mémoires*, Paris, 1821; Mathieu Dumas, *Souvenirs*, Paris, 1839, and the letters written to their respective Governments by various foreign ambassadors in Paris.

[2] Jean Mistler, *Le 14 Juillet*, p. 49.

[3] A. Mathiez, 'Les capitalistes et la prise de la Bastille' (*A.H.R.F.*, 1926, pp. 578–582).

as military *commissaire* under the Directoire,[1] he immediately enlisted in the Saint-Magloire battalion of the citizen militia. A deputy to the National Assembly, Lofficial, wrote that the *rentiers* envisaged the bankruptcy of the throne and their own certain ruin. It seemed impossible, in fact, for the new Government to resolve the financial crisis except by bankruptcy.

The Royalist pamphleteer Rivarol was probably the only person at the time to accuse the bankers of having actually bribed the rioters. He specifically mentions the bankers Laborde de Méréville, Boscary and Dufresnoy. He was in fact not wholly mistaken. Delessert, when arrested during the Terror, made a statement to the Comité de Sûreté Générale on May 8th, 1794 (19th floréal, Year II), setting forth the services he had rendered on July 14th, 1789. He said that at this time 'his whole household, children, servants and clerks took up arms in defence of the Revolution, and went to the Invalides to collect weapons, even one of his sons, then aged sixteen, who though he had an injured leg and was limping, went there bareheaded . . . and that on the day the Bastille fell his house was an arms factory, where they were melting down lead for bullets so as to join the citizens of that section [actually that district, for sections did not yet exist], anxious to repel the satellites of despotism who were plotting at the Champ de Mars; that he provided his neighbour, the caterer Courbet, for several days, with all the foodstuffs he had at home to help him feed the Saint-Eustache battalion, billeted on the said Courbet; that he and the citizen Prévôteau [another banker] had for over a month advanced the necessary funds to provide pay for this battalion, as he could prove by the sergeant-major's receipts; and that at least ten persons from his household had served continuously in the National Guard.'[2] The broker Nicolas Coindre took part in the capture of the Bastille.[3] The banker Boscary—one of those mentioned by Rivarol—declared that ever since the beginning of July he had exercised important functions which proved that his feelings in favour of the Revolution were unmistakable.[4] Chol, his

[1] J. Godechot, *Fragments des mémoires de Ch.-A. Alexandre sur sa mission aux armées du Nord et de Sambre-et-Meuse*, Paris, 1941; Id., 'Fragments des mémoires de Ch.-A. Alexandre sur les journées révolutionnaires de 1791 et 1792' (*A.H.R.F.*, 1952, pp. 113–251).

[2] Arch. nat., F 7, 4667.

[3] Arch. nat., F 7, 4650.

[4] Arch. nat., F 7, 4609.

associate, took part in patrols during the night of July 12th to 13th. Without any doubt, this attitude of the bankers and financiers had a considerable influence on that of their neighbours and friends. It helps to explain why Paris was practically unanimous in its attitude during those hectic days of July, 1789.

But Paris had the backing of the whole of France. And in the first place, that of the National Assembly at Versailles. No session had been arranged for Sunday, July 12th. However, on learning the news of Necker's dismissal, a number of deputies had met at the Hôtel des Menus-Plaisirs. They held some discussion, but in the absence of their chairman they broke up without deciding anything. Next day, July 13th, in the morning, an anxious crowd of deputies met and decided to send a delegation to the King immediately, with Bailly at its head, to inform him that Necker's dismissal was deplored by the whole nation, that the change of government was the cause of its existing misfortunes, that the Assembly wished the troops to be withdrawn from Paris and order ensured there by a *milice bourgeoise*. Louis XVI replied curtly: 'I have let you know my intentions regarding the measure which the disturbances in Paris have forced me to take. It is for me alone to judge of their necessity, and I can make no change in this connection. Some towns are able to protect themselves, but the size of this capital does not permit of that kind of surveillance.' He concluded by forbidding the delegation to go to Paris; he still believed in the success of his plans.

And yet throughout France the news of Necker's fall had aroused the keenest emotion. At Lyons, where people learned of it on July 17th—before they knew what had happened on the 14th—the electors declared that 'personal responsibility for present and future misfortunes lay with the ministers and councillors of the King, of whatever rank, condition or function they might be', and took possession of armouries to arm a citizen militia. Again, at Dijon by July 15th, and at Rennes by the 16th, the armouries had been ransacked and their contents distributed among the militia in process of formation. Sometimes the banks were taken over in order to paralyse the Government: this happened at Nantes, Bourg-en-Bresse and Château-Gontier. At Le Havre and at Honfleur, stocks of grain intended for Paris were seized, so that the troops stationed around the city could not be provisioned. At Nîmes, where Necker's dismissal was only learnt on the 20th, the assembled electors declared that they considered as 'infamous and disloyal to their country all agents of despotism and abettors of the aristocracy, all general officers and soldiers, both foreign and national, who should dare to use against Frenchmen the weapons they had received only for the defence of the State.' They urged all Nîmois in the army 'to disobey the atrocious order to shed the blood of their fellow-citizens, if they should receive such orders.'

Throughout France a formidable reply to the dismissal of Necker was in preparation: but it was the savage Parisian *journée* of July 14th which was to mark the decisive triumph of the Revolution over the 'feudal' régime.

IX

The Fourteenth of July

On the evening of July 13th, there was every sign of an imminent clash between the people of Paris and the Government forces. But there was no indication of where or when it would take place. Would it be in connection with the search for the arms stored in the Invalides or the powder stocked in the Bastille? It seemed more likely that a struggle would break out between the Parisians, who were more or less adequately armed, and the troops massed round Paris, which had remained inactive during the day. Through the night of July 13th–14th, Paris lived in fear of a counter-attack. At two in the morning, somebody came to tell the Permanent Committee at the Hôtel de Ville that 'all was lost', that 15,000 soldiers were advancing along the rue Saint-Antoine towards the place de Grève. The news was untrue; but it was repeated several times during the night. At seven in the morning fresh rumours arose: that the Royal-Allemand was in battle array at the Trône *barrière*, that other regiments were advancing through the faubourg Saint-Antoine and that those stationed at Saint-Denis had moved forward as far as La Chapelle. This was not so; nonetheless the Permanent Committee took precautions, assembled all the *gardes-françaises*, who had gone over to the side of the Parisians, and raised barricades in the streets. All vehicles entering or leaving Paris were brought to the place de Grève, in front of the Hôtel de Ville, so that the square looked like an enormous market-place where provisions of every description were mingled in confusion with fabrics, old iron and the barrels which had contained the powder distributed during the night by the abbé Lefèvre d'Ormesson. The banks, particularly the Caisse d'escompte and the Royal Treasury, were guarded by the militiamen and a few *gardes-françaises*. A south-west wind was blowing, and heavy clouds drifted over Paris. It was not very warm (22° [72°F] at midday) but rain seemed likely before night. The atmosphere was very tense, and many Parisians thought the day would be a decisive one.

1. Historical documents referring to July 14th

How do we come by our knowledge of the events of this day, which was of such capital importance in the history of the Revolution? Before relating its manifold episodes, it is necessary to consider the sources of our information, so as to assess the value to be attributed to each testimony. These sources have already been described in great detail by Flammermont in 1892;[1] since that date a handful of fresh documents have come to light. Contemporary sources can be divided into four categories: official documents, eye-witness accounts, letters and newspaper articles. To these contemporary documents may be added the accounts published in the few months following the capture of the Bastille, and the reports drawn up not too long after by witnesses or reliable authorities.

There are three official documents, two coming from the electors of Paris and the third from the *gardes-françaises*. The most definitely 'official' of these is the *procès-verbal* (minutes) of the meetings of the second-degree electors of Paris.[2] It begins with their first meeting on April 26th, and describes the election of the twenty deputies of the Third Estate of Paris, then the meetings which took place, in defiance of regulations, after these elections. From June 27th onwards the electors had formed the habit of meeting every day at the Hôtel de Ville, and thus formed a sort of clandestine power by the side of the official authorities of the *ancien régime*, by which Paris was still administered. We have referred to the evening session of Saturday July 11th, and to the spontaneous meeting of a few electors on Sunday July 12th. On July 13th and 14th the assembly of electors played an important role. However, it kept no minutes of its meetings until July 18th, because it had

[1] J. Flammermont, *La journée de 14 juillet 1789, fragment des mémoires inédits de L.-G. Pitra, électeur de Paris en 1789*, Paris, Société de l'Histoire de la Révolution, 1892. See also F. Funck-Brentano, *Bibliographie critique de la prise de la Bastille*, Paris, 1899.

[2] *Procès-verbal des séances et délibérations de l'Assemblée générale des électeurs de Paris réunis à l'Hôtel de Ville de Paris, le 14 juillet 1789, rédigé depuis le 26 avril jusqu'au 21 mai par M. Bailly et depuis le 22 mai jusqu'au 30 juillet 1789 par M. Duveyrier*, Paris, Baudouin, 1790, 3 vols. 8vo.

not appointed a permanent secretary. It was when the Assembly began to keep regular minutes that it felt the need to extend them to include its earlier sessions. Bailly, the Chairman, was therefore instructed to write up a report of the first meetings, from April 26th to May 21st, and the lawyer Duveyrier to describe those held between May 22nd and July 18th. These reports were not drawn up until September, having been reconstructed from the accounts given by electors who had been present, from newspaper articles and other evidence. For a further safeguard, the reconstructed minutes were read, criticized, discussed and finally approved by the assembly of electors. They were published in three volumes on July 13th, 1790, for the anniversary of the fall of the Bastille. In spite of the care taken in the reconstruction of the minutes, they contain mistakes and serious lacunae. They are therefore not to be trusted entirely, and moreover they naturally provide information only about what took place within the assembly and very little about the events that occurred in Paris.

One of the electors who was among the delegation sent to the Bastille (to be referred to later) was careful to set down the very next day, July 15th, the conversation that took place with the Governor, de Launey.[1] But the author shows an uncritical attitude and seems convinced of the Governor's 'treachery'. Another elector, Dusaulx, made an official speech in the National Assembly on February 6th, 1790, about the taking of the Bastille. It was published separately.[2] Dusaulx was known as a translator of Juvenal and author of a book on 'the passion for gambling'. He was fairly prominent in the Assembly of Electors and seems to have had some influence. He had a certain sense of history, but his style is declamatory, as was common at the time. His speech is preceded by an Introduction relating what took place during the week of July 7th to 14th. The whole thing is fairly accurate, but very incomplete.

The mouthpiece of the *gardes-françaises* was the journalist

---

[1] *Relation exacte de ce qui s'est passé dans la députation en parlementaire à la Bastille et de tout ce qui l'a précédé*, n.p., n.d. (Paris), 'written on July 15th by a citizen elector and eye-witness', 8 pp.

[2] Dusaulx, *De l'insurrection parisienne et de la prise de la Bastille, discours historique prononcé, par extraits, dans l'Assemblée nationale par M. Dusaulx, de l'Académie des belles-lettres, l'un des électeurs réunis le 14 juillet 1789, représentant de la Commune de Paris et l'un des commissaires actuels du Comité de la Bastille*, Paris, Debure l'aîné, 1790, pp. XVI–269.

Beffroy de Reigny, known by the name of Cousin Jacques, from the title of one of his books, *Les Lunes du Cousin Jacques*. Beffroy de Reigny explains that he has written his account 'in the presence of all the *gardes-françaises*, the sergeants and all the leading citizens who were at the siege of the Bastille' very soon after July 14th, in order to make known the part played by the Gardes in the capture of the fortress.[1] However, the author was not an eyewitness of the facts he relates; he merely questioned the *gardes-françaises*. His story, immediately on its publication, called forth protests from many who had taken part in the events of July 14th and had been 'forgotten', and he therefore published a 'supplement' on July 24th,[2] which he further enlarged in two later editions.[3] The first version, however, is the best and most reliable.

Eye-witness accounts of the taking of the Bastille are not numerous, and are provided chiefly by those who took part in the siege; we have only a single report by one of the besieged, which however is of some value.

One of the besiegers, Thuriot de la Rozière, a member of the district of Saint-Louis de la Culture, seems to have been the author of two anonymous accounts of the taking of the Bastille, which describe the events as a whole, and were written on August 15th and 16th, 1789.[4] A certain Pitra, born in Lyons in 1736 and living in Paris since 1766, was a draper by trade but also a professional *feuilliste*, supplying news, in manuscript, with some regularity to certain correspondents; a few months after the event he wrote an account of the fall of the Bastille for a German correspondent. It first appeared in German,[5] and was later (in

[1] *Précis exact de la prise de la Bastille, rédigé sous les yeux des principaux acteurs qui ont joué un rôle dans cette même expédition, et lu le même jour à l'Hôtel de Ville,* n.p., 1789, 10 pp.

[2] *Supplément nécessaire au Précis exact de la prise de la Bastille, avec des anecdotes curieuses sur le même sujet, par le Cousin Jacques,* n.p., n.d., 8pp.

[3] *Histoire de France pendant six semaines ou Précis exact des faits relatifs à la Révolution, du 20 juin au 30 juillet 1789, avec anecdotes soigneusement recueillies et des réflexions sur l'état actuel de la France, fait d'après des dépositions et des certificats authentiques par un Français impartial,* Paris. 1789; and *Histoire de France pendant trois mois ou relation des évènements qui ont eu lieu à Paris, à Versailles et dans les provinces depuis le 15 mai jusqu'au 15 août 1789, avec des anecdotes qui n'ont point encore été publiées, et des réflexions sur l'état actuel de la France, et suivie d'une épître en vers à Louis XVI,* Paris, 1789.

[4] *Récit relatif à la prise de la Bastille,* Paris, Cailleau, 16pp., and *Deuxième récit explicatif de la prise de la Bastille,* Paris, Cailleau, 4pp.

[5] The MS is preserved in the library of Oldenburg, in the Correspondence of Grimm and Meister. Pitra repeatedly replaced Meister. The first German

1892) published in a French translation by Flammermont.[1]
Pitra is a good eye-witness, but quite devoid of any critical
sense. Another witness, Boucheron, was careful to have his story
confirmed by those whom he accompanied during the negotiations
with the Governor of the Bastille.[2] This was also the case with
Humbert, who claims to have been the first to climb one of the
towers of the Bastille. He got five witnesses to countersign his
narrative, on August 12th, 1789.[3] Cholat's account is less reliable;
though fifty years old, he could neither read nor write, and
dictated his recollections to a public scribe.[4] His evidence is
interesting, however, for he had operated the cannon in front of
the Bastille. He claims moreover to have arrested Governor de
Launey. He, too, got five witnesses to confirm his story. Curtius,
the director of the waxworks museum, who on July 12th lent the
busts of Necker and the duc d'Orléans to the demonstrators,
joined the citizens' militia on the 13th. He was to reach the rank
of captain. He wrote and published his recollections, but he did not
personally participate in the taking of the Bastille; when he
arrived in the faubourg Saint-Antoine, the fortress had already
fallen. Curtius's account is interesting, none the less, and it, too,
is confirmed by a number of witnesses.[5] Pannetier, on the other
hand, was one of the first to penetrate into the outer court of the
Bastille, the cour du Gouvernement, and by lowering the drawbridge he enabled the crowd to enter; his evidence is of considerable value.[6] There are other accounts of the taking of the

---

edition appeared at Brunswick in 1793 under the title *Authentische Nachricht von
den ersten Auftritten der Französischen Staatsumwälzung von einem mitwirkenden
Augenzeugen aus einer Französischen Handschrift des Herrn Pitra*. It was edited
in 1865 by Paul von Bojanowski: *Die Estürmung der Bastille am 14 Juli 1789 nach
einer handschriftlichen Mittheilung*.

[1] Flammermont, *op. cit.*
[2] Boucheron, *Récit de ce qui s'est passé sous mes yeux le 14 juillet 1789, à onze
heures du matin*, n.p., n.d., 15pp.
[3] *Journée de J. B. Humbert, horloger, qui le premier a monté sur les tours de la
Bastille*, Paris, Volland, 1789, 16pp.
[4] *Service fait à l'attaque et à la prise de la Bastille et autres, pour la cause
commune, par le sieur Cholat, marchand de vins, rue des Noyers au coin de celle des
Lavandières, le 14 juillet 1789*, Paris, Brunet, Desenne, 1789, 27pp.
[5] *Service de Pierre Curtius, vainqueur de la Bastille, depuis le 12 juillet jusqu'au
6 octobre 1789*, Paris, 1790, 27p.
[6] Arch. nat., C 35, no. 298. *Hommage à l'Assemblée nationale. Tableau du
commencement du siège et de la prise de la Bastille par une patrouille commandée par
Jean-Armand Pannetier, citoyen du faubourg Saint-Antoine, soldat de la milice*

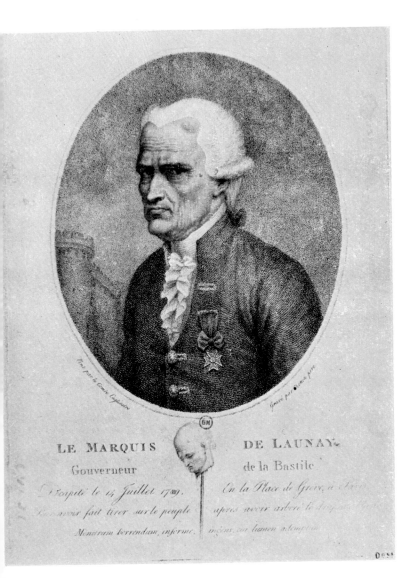

LE MARQUIS DE LAUNAY
Gouverneur de la Bastile

Décapité le 14 Juillet 1789. En la Place de Grève, à Paris

Pour avoir fait tirer sur le peuple après avoir arboré le drapeau blanc

Monstram terrendam, informe, ingens, cui lumen ademptum.

The Marquis de Launay

Bibl. Nat., Print Room

Portraits of Humbert and Harné

colour print, Bibl. Nat., Print Room

A woman of quality being whipped for having spat on
Necker's portrait

Bibl. Nat., Print Room

Bastille written by besiegers, but these are either not by eye-witnesses or are unreliable.[1] A few documents have been published recently, but they add little to our information.[2]

The defenders of the Bastille have left only two accounts. One comes from the *invalides*, or pensioners, who formed the largest section of the garrison, the other from Lieutenant Deflue, who was in command of the detachment of the Salis-Samade regiment of Swiss guards sent to reinforce the Bastille on July 7th. The account written by the *invalides* is intended to vindicate them by showing that they refused to fire on the people and did their best to bring about the surrender of the Bastille. It is a synthesis of the questions put, from July 15th onwards, to the pensioners, porters and jailers who were in the fortress on the 14th. This report was first published in September 1789 in an anonymous work entitled *La Bastille dévoilée*.[3] As for Lieutenant Deflue's story, there are three versions of it, which complement one another. The oldest seems to be one which was inserted into the log-book of the Salis-Samade regiment, preserved in the Archives de la Guerre at Vincennes, under the title: *Précis de ce qui est arrivé au régiment de Salis-Samade pendant la campagne de* 1789.[4] It is a strictly objective

---

parisienne, marchand épicier de Paris, établi rue du Faubourg-Saint-Antoine, vis-à-vis de celle de Reuilly.

[1] See Santerre's story in Arch. nat., C 134, no. 2. Santerre reached the Bastille after its surrender. The three following reports are declamatory and frequently inaccurate: Palloy, *Relation sur la prise de la Bastille*, Paris, 1790. viii–50; P. Rousselet, *Détail intéressant et jusqu'à présent ignoré sur la prise de la Bastille à un de ses amis, blessé au même siège*, n.p., n.d., 32pp.; *Récit fidèle non publié jusqu'à ce jour de la prise de la Bastille*, by a former officer of the *gardes-françaises* (the Marquis de Sainte-Fère), Paris, 1833.
[2] The report of Sublieutenant Elie, who played an important part in the final assault, was published by Tourneux in the *Mémoires* of Marmontel, Paris, 1891, 3 vols. See also: L.-G. Pélissier, 'Une nouvelle relation de la prise de la Bastille', in the *Bulletin de la Société de l'histoire de Paris et de l'Ile-de-France*, 1899, pp. 107–112; 'Lettre d'un officier aux gardes-françaises (14 juillet 1789)' in *La Revue rétrospective*, 1899, vol. II, pp. 26–28; M. Civrays, 'Lettre d'un garde-française sur la prise de la Bastille' in the *A.H.R.F.*, 1924, pp. 464–465; V. Gastebois, 'Les Argentanais à la prise de la Bastille' in *La Révolution française*, 1934, pp. 345–350.
[3] *La Bastille dévoilée*, Paris, Desenne, 1789. This account was republished shortly afterwards under the title *Attaque, défense et reddition de la Bastille*, Paris, Brunet, 1789, then reprinted by M. Cottin under the title *Relation inédite de la défense de la Bastille par l'invalide Guyot de Fléville*, Paris, n.d. (1885), pp. viii–35 8vo.
[4] Arch. de la Guerre, *Mémoires historiques*, vols. no. 619 to 626.

military report. It was published in 1854 by E. Fieffé,[1] with certain errors. In addition, Deflue described the taking of the Bastille in a letter in German sent on September 2nd, 1789, to two of his brothers in Switzerland. This letter, which Flammermont translated into French and published in 1886,[2] is more subjective than the report, but it seems to have been written later. Finally a third version, possibly intended to be published in the *Mercure de France* (it never was), was discovered among the cabinet documents of Louis XVI and published in 1834.[3] It is of a later date, less precise and less objective than the two others. In view of the paucity of information provided by the besieged, the evidence of Lieutenant Deflue is of capital importance.[4]

The inhabitants of Paris wrote a great many letters describing the events of July 14th. But naturally most of these have escaped historians, although one turns up from time to time. The only letters to have been recovered in their entirety, and in many cases published, are those sent by foreign ambassadors resident in Paris.[5] These letters are all the more interesting for being written immediately after the events and referring to recent recollections or evidence. The Duke of Dorset, British ambassador, wrote on the 16th; Mercy-Argenteau, Austrian ambassador, on the 17th and again on the 23rd;[6] Simolin, the Russian minister, on the 19th;[7] the marquis de Circello, Neapolitan ambassador, and the comte de Fernan Nuñez, Spanish ambassador, on the 20th;[8] the marquis de

[1] E. Fieffé, *Histoire des troupes étrangères au service de la France*, Paris, 1854, vol. I, pp. 349–356.

[2] *Obwalden Volksfreund*, 1886. French translation by Flammermont, *op. cit.*, pp. lxvii–lxviii and ccxxxiii–ccxxxv.

[3] The original is preserved in the Arch. nat., K. 164, no. 5; it was published by Taschereau in the *Revue rétrospective*, 1834, vol. IV, pp. 285–298.

[4] J. Suratteau has published 'Deux documents sur les débuts de la Révolution française et le 14 juillet vus par un officier d'un régiment suisse', *A.H.R.F.*, 1957, pp. 358–362, but it is chiefly concerned with July 16th and 17th.

[5] De Grouchy, 'Le 14 juillet raconté par des diplomates étrangers', in the *Nouvelle Revue rétrospective*, 1898, vol. IX, pp. 1–28.

[6] Letters published by Flammermont in the *Bulletin mensuel de la Faculté des Lettres de Poitiers*, 1885.

[7] Letter published by Feuillet de Conches in *Louis XVI et Marie-Antoinette*, vol. I, p. 476, and republished in the *Revue de la Révolution*, 1886, vol. VII, documents, pp. 1–8.

[8] The marquis de Circello's letter was published by M. Pellet in *Le Temps*, July 7th, 1892. The comte de Fernan Nuñez' correspondence, edited by A. Mousset, was published as *Un témoin ignoré de la Révolution, ambassadeur d'Espagne à Paris (1787–1791)*, Paris, 1923, 356. See the review by A. Mathiez in the *A.H.R.F.*, 1924, pp. 171–172.

Cordon, Sardinian ambassador, on the 17th and 20th;[1] the comte de Salmour, ambassador of Saxony (and nephew of Besenval) on the 16th;[2] the Portuguese ambassador, Vicente Souza Coutinho, and the Venetian ambassador, Antonio Cappello, on the 20th.[3] Count von der Goltz, the Prussian minister, in a dispatch written on July 24th described not only his own impressions but those of his colleagues.[4] Jefferson, ambassador of the United States, wrote a number of letters to his friends; a long letter written on July 19th to John Jay, President of the Supreme Court, is of particular interest because it reports a conversation with Ethis de Corny, the head of the delegation which, as we shall see, tried to negotiate with de Launey, Governor of the Bastille.[5] Jefferson's successor, Gouverneur Morris, who was in Paris on the 14th, wrote to George Washington from Dieppe on the 31st giving an account of the events he had witnessed.[6] The baron de Staël, ambassador of Sweden and son-in-law of Necker, seems to have written no report until September 13th.[7]

The deputies to the National Assembly wrote a great many letters, but as they were all at Versailles on the 14th their accounts of what happened in Paris that day are based on hearsay. However Maillot, deputy for Toul, came to Paris on the evening of the 15th, and the letters he wrote on the 16th and 18th are of interest.[8] The marquis de Sillery, husband of Mme de Genlis and deputy for the nobility of Rheims, wrote to Bertier de Sauvigny on the evening of the 17th; his letter provides valuable information, but chiefly about the events of that day.[9] There are a far greater number of

---

[1] Unpublished, in the Archivio di Stato, Turin.

[2] Unpublished.

[3] The Portuguese Ambassador's dispatch is unpublished; that of Antonio Cappello is preserved in the Bibl. nat., MSS, *fonds italien*, vol. 1988, p. 236.

[4] Unpublished.

[5] Published in *The Diplomatic Correspondence of the United States of America*, 2nd series, 1783–1789, Washington, 1837, and republished in *The Papers of Thomas Jefferson*, edited by Julian P. Boyd, vol. XV, (March 27–November 30 1789), Princeton University Press, 1958, XL -677, 8vo.

[6] Published by Jared Sparks, *The Life of Gouverneur Morris, with selections of his correspondence and miscellaneous papers*, Boston, 1832, pp. 78–81. A new and more accurate edition: *Gouverneur Morris, A Diary of the French Revolution*, was published by B. C. Davenport, Boston, 2 vols., 1939.

[7] Published by Léouzon Le Duc in *La Correspondance diplomatique du Baron de Staël-Holstein*, Paris, 1885, pp. 115–125.

[8] Published by A. Denis in *Les Annales de l'Est*, 1891, vol. V, p. 532 ff.

[9] Arch. nat., KK 647.

inaccuracies in the letters of Barnave, deputy for the Dauphiné,[1] Gautier de Biauzat and Huguet, deputies for Clermont-Ferrand,[2] and the deputies for Anjou[3] and Strasbourg.[4]

Among the letters of Parisians who had no official status, those of Camille Desmoulins[5] are of particular interest, as are also those of Gudin de la Ferlière, a cashier of Beaumarchais,[6] whose son took part in the attack on the Bastille, and those of Paré.[7]

Foreign visitors passing through Paris could not but be vividly impressed by what was happening there. Some of them, for instance the Englishmen Huber and Dr Rigby[8] and the German Campe,[9] described these events in letters to their families and friends.

Newspapers were still scarce; their number increased after July 14th. All made it a point of honour to publish accounts of the great events of early July, but many of these are full of inaccuracies, for instance that in *Les Révolutions de Paris* of July 17th, which none the less had an enormous success because it praised the attackers of the Bastille in a dithyrambic panegyric. The account by Rivarol, published in the *Journal politique national*, is interesting

[1] Published by J. de Beylié in the *Bulletin de l'Académie delphinale*, Grenoble, 1905, pp. 279–305.

[2] Published by Francisque Miège, *Vie et correspondance de Gautier de Biauzat*, Paris, 1890, 2 vols., 8vo.

[3] *Correspondance de MM, les députés des communes des provinces d'Anjou avec les commettants*, Angers, 1789–1790, vol. I, pp. 376–377.

[4] Published by R. Reuss, 'Correspondance des députés de Strasbourg avec les commissaires de la bourgeoisie de cette ville' (*Revue d'Alsace*, 1889).

[5] Camille Desmoulins, *Oeuvres complètes*, edited by Jules Claretie, Paris, 1874, 2 vols.

[6] Published by Begis in the *Revue rétrospective*, July 1889, p. 9 ff.

[7] Letter from Paré, published in *La Révolution française*, 1902, pp. 175–176. See also J. Faurey, 'Relation inédite des journées de juillet 1789' in *La Revue des Études historiques*, 1930; J. Marchand, 'Journal inédit de Creuzé-Latouche sur juin et juillet 1789' in *La Revue des questions historiques*, 1935, and separately, in its entirety, Paris, Didier, 1946; R. Bouis, 'Grégoire et la crise de juillet 1789', in the *A.H.R.F.*, 1948, pp. 179–180; J. Palou, 'Un document sur les évènements de juillet 1789', *ibid.*, 1948, p. 358; G. Rudé, 'Un témoignage oculaire sur les évènements des 12 et 13 juillet 1789', *ibid.*, 1953, pp. 73–75; R. Garmy, 'Encore une lettre sur les évènements de juillet 1789', *ibid.*, 1954, pp. 171–173; R. Gandilhon, 'Cinq lettres sur les évènements parisiens' August 30, 1788–August 2nd, 1789, *ibid.*, 1956, pp. 267–278.

[8] Huber's letters were addressed to Lord Auckland (William Eden, who negotiated the trade treaty of 1786) and published in the *Journal and Correspondence of William, Lord Auckland*, London, 1861, 4 vols. Dr Rigby's letters were published in London in 1880 as *Letters from France*.

[9] L. W. Cart: 'Trois semaines à Paris pendant la Révolution. Impressions du voyageur allemand Campe', in *La Révolution française*, 1910, vol. LVIII, pp. 31–51 and 97–116.

because the author indicts de Launey, Governor of the Bastille, as responsible for its rapid capitulation. 'He had lost his head,' says Rivarol, 'before having it cut off.' As for the people of Paris, they 'took few risks' and committed many atrocities. The article by Mirabeau published in *Lettres à mes commettants* (Letters to my constituents) on July 24th contains few details about the fall of the Bastille, but some far-sighted opinions as to its consequences. The article by Mallet du Pan in the *Mercure de France* of July 24th is unusually dull; that of Gorsas in the *Courrier de Versailles à Paris* of July 15th is objective and, on the whole, accurate. Among French papers printed abroad the *Gazette de Leyde* is undoubtedly the one which devotes most space (the whole of the issue of July 24th) to the account of the *quatorze juillet*; however, this version contains many inaccuracies. Most foreign papers describe the fall of the Bastille, but without contributing any fresh information.

There is not much to be got from the innumerable pamphlets which appeared during the second fortnight of July. Their aim was propaganda rather than documentation.[1]

The first works having any pretension to be serious historical studies, making use of sources and comparing evidence, appeared at the end of 1789. They bring the historian little unfamiliar information about events, but their interpretations are of interest. Galart de Montjoye's book,[2] of which we have already made considerable use, is full of matter and well documented; Restif de la Bretonne's,[3] which we have also utilized, is definitely hostile to

[1] See for instance: *Il était temps ou la Semaine aux évènements*, n.p., n.d., 15 p.; *Les Lauriers du faubourg Saint-Antoine ou le Prix de la Bastille renversée*, Paris, July 20th 1789, 8pp.; *Historique de la Journée parisienne ou Triomphe de la France*, Paris, July 17th 1789; *Paris sauvé ou Récit détaillé des évènements qui ont eu lieu à Paris depuis le dimanche 12 juillet 1789, une heure après midi, jusqu'au vendredi suivant au soir*, n.p., n.d. (written between July 17th and 21st); *Révolutions de Paris ou Récit exact de ce qui s'est passé dans la capitale et particulièrement de la prise de la Bastille, depuis le 11 juillet 1789 jusqu'au 23 du même mois*, by M.D.C., 1789, 40pp. See M. Tourneux, *Bibliographie de l'histoire de Paris pendant la Révolution*, Paris, 1890–1913, 5 vols.

[2] Galart de Montjoye, *Histoire de la Révolution de France et de l'Assemblée nationale pour former, avec le journal intitulé* L'Ami du Roy, *commencé le 1er juin 1790, un cours complet d'histoire du temps actuel*, Paris, Gattey, 1792.

[3] Restif de La Bretonne, *Semaine nocturne, sept nuits de Paris, qui peuvent servir de suite aux CCCLXXX déjà publiées; ouvrage servant à l'histoire du jardin du Palais-Royal*, Paris, Guillot, 1790, in-12. See on this subject Jacques Pinset, 'Les origines instinctives de la Révolution française', in the *Revue d'histoire économique et sociale*, 1961, pp. 198–228.

the Revolution; the studies by Ducray du Mesnil and by 'two friends of Liberty' are fairly objective.[1]

Memoirs and recollections are extremely numerous, but their value depends on the part played by the author and the date at which they were written. We have often referred to the journal of the bookseller Hardy, the major part of which is still unpublished.[2] This journal, in spite of appearances, was not written day by day but generally after a certain lapse of time. Its author, who had had a good secondary education, was shrewd enough at judging events, but he is more inclined to note in his journal the trivial items of news, the brawls and scandals of his neighbourhood—the Saint-Jacques district—than events of national importance. Moreover, he was a prudent, not to say a timid man, who avoided leaving home when there were disturbances in the city and only described them by hearsay.

The Company of the *Arquebusiers* of Paris, which, as we have seen, joined the militia and, with the *gardes-françaises*, provided its officers with a sort of escort, kept a log-book about the events of July 14th. It was published that same year, and is a rich source of information.[3] Besenval, commander of the royal troops for the neighbourhood of Paris, wrote some memoirs which were published in 1805, after the death of their author (which occurred in 1791). Their authenticity was once questioned, but is now well established. They are of great value. But as in any work of this sort, the writer's primary aim is to vindicate himself and to blame his superior officer, the Marshal duc de Broglie, for any mistakes committed. As these Memoirs were published after the death of de Broglie,[4] the latter was never able to answer the charges. The Mayor of Paris, Bailly, also wrote memoirs, early in 1792; they

[1] Ducray du Mesnil, *Les principaux évènements de la Révolution de Paris, et notamment de la semaine memorable, représentés par figures, avec un récit lapidaire, historique, fait sur les extraits et les rapports les plus authentiques, suivi de la liste alphabétique des citoyens qui se sont distingués au siège de la Bastille*, Paris, 1789, 187pp.; *Histoire de la Révolution de 1789 par deux amis de la liberté*, Paris, 1790–1803, 20 vols. See also the definitely counter-revolutionary *Histoire authentique et suivie de la Révolution*, published in Paris and in London from Sept. 29th 1789.

[2] Hardy, *Mes loisirs ou Journal d'évènements tels qu'ils parviennent à ma connaissance*, MS in the Bibl. nat., *fonds français*, 6680–6687, 8 vols., from 1764 to 1789. Only vol. I (1769–1773) has been published; edited by Tourneux and Vitrac, Paris, 1912.

[3] *Journal de la compagnie des Arquebusiers royaux de la ville de Paris sur la Révolution française*, Paris, 1789.

[4] *Mémoires de M. le baron de Besenval*, Paris, 1805, 3 vols. 8vo.

were published in 1821.[1] The existence of the manuscript proves their authenticity; however, on July 14th, Bailly was at Versailles, and only came to Paris on the following day, when he was elected Mayor. His memoirs are therefore only of value for the period following July 14th. There are other memoirs, but they are either by people who played only a secondary role, or else written too long after the events to provide worthwhile information.[2]

2. The attack on the Invalides

The whole day of July 13th had been devoted to the search for arms to equip the citizen militia. It will be remembered that this search had not been fruitful: a queer collection of old armour unearthed at the Garde-meuble, a few hundred muskets discovered at the Hôtel de Ville, the barrels of gunpowder taken off a boat at the port Saint-Nicolas, the contents of which had been distributed by the abbé Lefèvre d'Ormesson; there was not nearly enough to arm some 48,000 men. It was thus indispensable, in order to arm the militia, to take possession of the 32,000 muskets stored at the Invalides, and the cartridges which had been transferred from the Arsenal to the Bastille. It will be remembered that on the evening of July 13th a delegation of electors had requested Sombreuil, Governor of the Invalides, to hand over arms to the militia. He had referred the matter to Besenval, who, to gain time, had replied that he would seek instructions from Versailles. As was to be expected, the delegation, followed no doubt by a crowd of demonstrators, returned on the morning of the 14th to repeat its demands. Looting of arms seemed likely to ensue; to prevent this from being effective, Besenval had decided to put the guns out of action by removing their ramrods and unscrewing their hammers. Twenty pensioners were put to this task. But as their sympathies were with the insurgents they worked with extreme reluctance, and in six hours they only unscrewed some twenty hammers! Thus by far the greater part of the guns were intact on the morning of July 14th.

By six in the morning a huge crowd of citizens, their hats

[1] *Mémoires de Bailly*, Paris, 1821.
[2] Marmontel, *Oeuvres posthumes*, Paris, year XII, republished and edited by Tourneux, Paris, 1891; Duc des Cars, *Mémoires*, Paris, Plon, 1890, 2 vols.; *Souvenirs du général Mathieu Dumas*, Paris, 1839, 3 vols.; Chancelier Pasquier, *Mémoires*, vol. I, Paris, Plon, 1893, pp. 51–52; Barras, *Mémoires*, edited by G. Duruy, vol. I, Paris, 1895; *Souvenirs du général baron Thiébaut*, Paris, 1895–1896, 5 vols.

decked with red and blue cockades, thronged the parade ground of the Invalides, demanding arms. On learning of this development the Assembly of Electors, which had been sitting all night at the Hôtel de Ville, decided that the *procureur du roi*, Ethis de Corny, should be sent to the Invalides. He set off in his carriage, and with great difficulty made his way through the crowd to the gate of the Invalides; it was opened to let him in, and immediately closed behind him. The governor, Sombreuil, received him and told him that the expected reply from Versailles had not yet arrived. Increasingly violent clamours arose from the crowd, which was estimated by some at eighty thousand people, by others at forty thousand. Sombreuil then advanced, opened the gate and tried to explain to the demonstrators that he had as yet received no orders. But immediately the shouting broke out again and before Sombreuil had time to go in and close the door behind him, the crowd poured in on his heels. Other demonstrators, who had gone down into the moat, climbed up the parapet and entered the Invalides that way. And yet there were loaded cannon there, and behind each of them were pensioners with lighted matches ready to fire. But they were reluctant to do so, being of a like mind with those who had been instructed to dismantle the guns. Besenval wrote: 'Far from resisting the invasion, the soldiers of the Hôtel [des Invalides] supported it, and the Governor, about whom these fellows had no complaint to make, narrowly escaped being hanged from the entrance-gate.'[1]

It is more surprising that Besenval did not send for the troops—infantry, cavalry and artillery—that were encamped close by, on the parade-ground of the Invalides. Rivarol asserts that he would not allow the cannon to be fired for fear of damaging a house which he owned in the neighbourhood and had recently had done up. The researches we have made in the central records book of the notaries of Paris have yielded no result, and Rivarol's accusation seems unfounded. In fact Besenval considered taking action, and quickly summoned a council of commanding officers. But these declared that they could not count on their troops. One colonel, 'with tears in his eyes', asserted that his regiment 'would refuse to march'. Salmour, the ambassador of Saxony, an eye-witness and moreover well-informed, being Besenval's own nephew, wrote to the Court of Dresden on July 16th: 'Having witnessed this operation [the

[1] Besenval, *Mémoires*, vol. III, p. 415.

capture of the Invalides], which took place with astonishing rapidity, I made my way to the nearby camp, where the sight of downcast and dispirited troops who had been shut up in a narrow space for the past fortnight, struck me as very different from that of the venturesome and courageous men I had just left. The generals agreed thenceforward that it was impossible to bring Paris to heel, that retreat was the only prudent policy.' This evidence is corroborated by the *Procès-verbal des électeurs*,[1] which asserts that during the morning of the 13th 'a large number of soldiers, dragoons, infantrymen from the various regiments encamped round about Paris . . . appeared with their arms and baggage . . . and declared their intention of serving the Nation'. The passive attitude of the troops encamped on the Champ-de-Mars also surprised Jefferson, who wrote to John Jay on July 19th: 'It was remarkable that not only the Invalides themselves made no opposition, but that a body of 5,000 foreign troops, encamped within 400 yards, never stirred'.[2]

In short, after the invasion of the Invalides and the clear proof that the troops could not act, the victory of the Parisian insurrection was assured, and the capture of the Bastille might well be considered as a symbolic episode which made little difference to the situation.

But to return to the Invalides: the crowd which had poured into the buildings went down into the cellars and seized the thirty to forty thousand muskets, which were then distributed to all and sundry amid the utmost confusion. Thus, for instance, weapons were handed to two servants of the Duke of Dorset's, who were merely there as onlookers. The demonstrators seized not only firearms, but a dozen pieces of ordnance, ten-, eighteen- and twenty-four pounders, and a mortar. At ten o'clock, Ethis de Corny returned to the Hôtel de Ville on foot and gave an account of these happenings to the Permanent Committee. The latter immediately gave instructions for the distribution of arms to proceed in an orderly fashion, but this proved practically impossible. The evidence given by Humbert, a watchmaker, and Desnots, a cook, shows that people came to the Invalides and seized whatever weapons they liked, and that very few muskets were carted off to the Hôtel de Ville. The citizen militia was thus

[1] *Procès-verbal* . . . vol. I, p. 227.
[2] The Papers of Thomas Jefferson . . ., vol. XV, pp. 284–291.

most inadequately armed. Moreover the muskets were not much use without powder or shot; only a very small quantity of these had been found at the Invalides. Both powder and cartridges had been stored at the Arsenal and in particular in the Bastille, where they had been taken during the night of July 12th–13th. After the capture of the Invalides, the goal of the Parisian rioters was therefore inevitably the Bastille.

3. The attack on the Bastille

On the morning of the 14th, while a huge crowd was marching towards the Invalides, another almost equally dense crowd was making its way towards the Bastille, to demand arms, powder and bullets from the Governor. But this was a more anxious crowd than that surrounding the Hôtel des Invalides. The latter building was a sort of great barracks, with a few cannon protecting it, indeed, but which presented no great threat to the population of the neighbourhood. The Bastille, on the other hand, was a fortress, and for the past week its Governor, de Launey, seemed to have been strengthening its defences. His garrison of 82 *invalides*—easy-going fellows, well-known figures in the faubourg Saint-Antoine—had been reinforced on July 7th by a detachment of 32 Swiss soldiers from the Salis-Samade regiment, commanded by a sergeant and by Lieutenant Deflue (who had in fact been promoted Captain a few weeks previously, although he had not yet been given a company). Now the Bastille was equipped with efficient artillery, fifteen eight-pounder cannon (firing eight-pound cannon balls) standing on the towers and inside at the foot of the walls, but mounted on naval gun-carriages which were difficult to manœuvre, three eight-pounder field cannon ready for action in the large inner courtyard, pointing towards the entrance gate, and twelve rampart guns each firing balls weighing a pound and a half. The Governor had reinforced the defences, built a second wall behind the garden wall (which was not very high and might have allowed attackers to find their way in), widened the embrasures to give the cannon more range, repaired the drawbridge to make it harder to force, and removed its parapet so that attackers could be more readily flung into the moats. A load of six cartloads of paving-stones and old iron had been taken up into the towers on July 9th and 10th so that, as in the Middle Ages, they could be hurled at the assailants. Tongs had also been taken up there, which could be used to break down the chimneys and make additional missiles out of the débris. Loopholes and windows which served no useful defensive purpose had been blocked up with solid pieces of wood, and new slits had been opened on the sides which were not threatened.

True, de Launey had not stocked up with provisions; he had only one day's supply of meat and two days' supply of bread, and moreover there was no drinking water inside the fortress. But, bearing in mind the experience of the Réveillon riots of April 28th, de Launey may legitimately have thought that if he were attacked by an unarmed or ill-armed crowd the assault would not last longer than one day and that at nightfall the rioters would disperse; or that if they attempted a siege the Bastille would soon get help from the many troops which had been assembled around Paris since the beginning of July.

It would thus have been easy for a determined leader to resist an attack. But Governor de Launey was no such thing. Lieutenant Deflue describes him thus:[1] 'The Governor of this fortress, the comte de Launey, was a man without much knowledge of military matters, without experience and of little valour. As soon as the disturbances began, he appealed to the generals in command of the army and asked them to reinforce the garrison, which consisted only of eighty-four veterans. His request was refused, because the authorities did not believe that the rebellion would become so violent or that anyone would think of trying to seize the Bastille. He renewed his request. Finally I was detailed off with thirty men and sent to the Bastille on July 7th. The very day after my arrival I got to know the man, through all the preparations he was making for the defence of his post, in which there was neither rhyme nor reason, and I could clearly see, from his perpetual uneasiness and irresolution, that if we were attacked we should be very badly led. He was so terrified that at night he mistook the shadows of trees and other objects around him for enemies, and on this account we had to be on the alert all night. The staff officers, the *lieutenant du roi*, the regimental adjutant and I myself often argued with him, on the one hand to reassure him about the weakness of the garrison, of which he complained constantly, and on the other to induce him not to bother about insignificant details while neglecting important

[1] Letter from Deflue to his brothers, published by Flammermont, *op. cit.*, pp. lxvii–lxviii.

matters. He would listen to us, and seem to agree with our advice; then he would do just the reverse, then a minute later he would change his mind; in a word, his whole behaviour gave proof of the utmost irresolution. Although he had decided with his general staff and the officers of the garrison to defend the outer buildings as long as possible if they should be attacked, on the evening of July 12th he ordered us to withdraw within the fortress and to abandon the outer buildings, where the entire garrison had been stationed until then, and from which considerable resistance could be put up. We were forced to obey. We then found ourselves behind walls eighty foot high and fifteen foot thick, which inspired us with greater confidence than did the talents of the Governor.'

What Deflue does not mention is the attitude of the pensioners and even of the Swiss soldiers. The pensioners were most reluctant to fire on the people, and we have seen that on July 15th there were 75 deserters from the Salis-Samade regiment. It needed a resolute leader to restore the morale of the soldiers, rather than this timorous governor.

As soon as the news of the disturbances of July 12th reached him, de Launey was seized with terror. His assistant, the *lieutenant du roi* du Puget, who was also commander of the nearby Arsenal, then asked for the powder in the Arsenal to be transferred to the Bastille. The 250 barrels, containing 30,000 pounds of powder, were taken thither during the night of July 12th–13th by Swiss soldiers, and placed under inadequate covering in the rear court-yard. Then, when the customs posts were seen to be ablaze on July 13th and on the morning of the 14th, the Swiss soldiers carried the heavy barrels down into the cellars; the Governor gave them each two louis by way of bonus for the job. However, 'these soldiers were very tired by the morning of the 14th. They had not slept all the previous night. The crowd had begun to gather under the walls of the Bastille on the evening of the 13th; during the night several shots—seven, according to one report—were fired in the direction of the fortress. The alarm was sounded repeatedly, and on each occasion the garrison took up their posts on the towers and curtains.'

During the morning of the 14th, while the militia were demand-ing arms at the Hôtel de Ville, the inhabitants of the quartier Saint-Antoine conveyed to the Assembly of Electors their anxiety about the warlike preparations being made by the Governor of the

Bastille. The guns that were pointing at them through the embrasures seemed to have an aggressive as well as a defensive significance. The electors, on whose behalf Ethis de Corny had gone to the Invalides (he had apparently not yet returned) decided to send a delegation to the Bastille. The delegates got there at about ten o'clock. De Launey received them in friendly fashion at his residence, the 'Gouvernement', and as it was lunch time (for in France in those days *déjeuner* was eaten about half past ten, a tradition which was maintained until quite recently in barracks and monastic houses) he invited them to share his meal. There was apparently no question of distributing to the population the firearms and munitions stored in the Bastille, but the chief point at issue was the withdrawal of the guns that seemed levelled at the faubourg. The object of the demonstration began to change, and was to alter still further, for already people might be heard in the crowd talking about taking the Bastille. As Dusaulx wrote in his account: 'The purpose of marching on the Bastille was solely to secure arms and munitions there. Little by little, more was ventured. The people . . . soon came and demanded from us the capture of this fortress . . .'[1] But the delegation did not go so far; it merely asked the governor to take such measures as might allay the people's fears. De Launey assured the delegates that he would do no harm to the quartier Saint-Antoine, and gave orders for the guns standing on the towers to be withdrawn and for the embrasures to be blocked with planks of wood.

During the time that this luncheon, and these talks, were going on—an hour to an hour and a half—the crowd had increased considerably and was thronging in the cour du Passage, in front of the porte de l'Avancée which, it will be remembered, gave access to the Governor's courtyard (cour du Gouverneur or du Gouvernement.)

What did this crowd consist of? We can form some idea from the social structure of the group of 954 persons who, in June 1790, were awarded the title of *vainqueur de la Bastille*—the men who took the Bastille.[2] The professions of 661 of these are known. By far the greater number were artisans; in the first place, workers in the furniture industry from the faubourg Saint-Antoine, 49 joiners, 48 cabinet-makers, 41 locksmiths, 9 *tabletiers* (workers in ivory,

---

[1] Dusaulx, *De l'insurrection parisienne, op. cit.*
[2] G. Durieux, *Les Vainqueurs de la Bastille*, Paris, 1911.

inlay, etc.), 11 engravers, 28 odd-job men, more or less casually employed (though only four admitted to being *chômeurs*, out of work). Then we find 28 cobblers, 27 'carvers', 23 workers in gauze, 14 wine merchants, 9 jewellers, 9 hatters, 9 nailsmiths, 9 monumental masons, 9 tailors, 9 dyers; a total of 332. But there were also some bourgeois: 4 tradesmen, 3 industrialists, one brewer—the famous Santerre—35 various 'merchants', 4 'bourgeois', that is to say *rentiers*, of independent means; 80 soldiers or officers; and the rest belonging to widely varying professions. Their ages range from 72 for the oldest—citizen Crétaine, a Parisian bourgeois—to 8 for the youngest, the boy Lavallée, who was one of the first up the towers. The index of professions is not enough to give an idea of the socio-economic group to which any one individual belongs. We should have to know his financial position. Such research, which is quite possible, would take a long time and has hitherto not been attempted. The 332 artisans include masters and journeymen, between whom it is impossible to distinguish. It may be said, however, if we add to the 332 artisans the 202 citizens of various professions, that five-sixths of the 'conquerors'—and presumably of the crowd thronging beneath the walls of the Bastille—were artisans, masters or journeymen; the remaining sixth consisted of bourgeois.[1]

These demonstrators were undoubtedly all Parisians, the great majority of them (425 out of 602) from the faubourg Saint-Antoine, another fifty from the faubourg Saint-Marcel, and some more from the Halles. None of the 'conquerors of the Bastille' lived further than two kilometres from the fortress. But most of them had only recently become Parisians; if we study the references to their birthplaces, we find that 345 of them came originally from the provinces. The accompanying maps show the distribution of the 'conquerors' according to birthplace. The region of the Seine leads, naturally, with 244. But it is interesting to note that two other regions of France provided a quite considerable proportion of 'conquerors'; the region between Paris and the northern frontier, where six departments (Seine-et-Oise, Nord, Oise, Aisne, Somme, Ardennes) provided more than ten each, and the eastern region, where the same is true of five departments (Côte-d'Or, Haute-Saône, Haute-Marne, Bas-Rhin, Moselle). This is easy to explain,

[1] G. Rudé, 'La composition sociale des insurrections parisiennes de 1789 à 1791', in the *A.H.R.F.*, 1952, pp. 256–288.

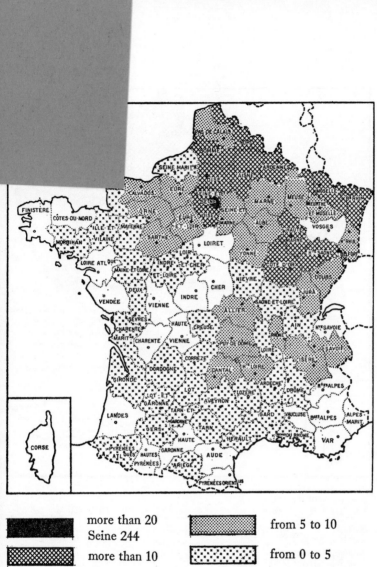

▇▇▇	more than 20 Seine 244	▦▦▦	from 5 to 10
▩▩▩	more than 10	░░░	from 0 to 5

other *départements :* nil

(b) Map I of the 'Vainqueurs de la Bastille', 1789

Division of the 'Vainqueurs de la Bastille' into the *départements* they came from: in absolute terms

223

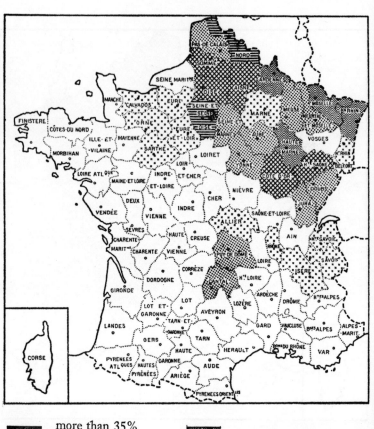

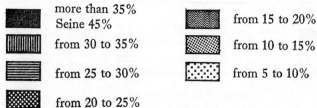

	more than 35% Seine 45%		from 15 to 20%
	from 30 to 35%		from 10 to 15%
	from 25 to 30%		from 5 to 10%
	from 20 to 25%		

(c) Map II of the 'Vainqueurs de la Bastille', 1789

Division of the 'Vainqueurs de la Bastille' into
the *départements* they came from: percentage

July 14th, 1789. The memorable *journée* of Tuesday, July 14th, 1789

Bibl. Nat., Print Room

July 14th–15th, 1789. Alarum during the night of July 14th–15th

the northern departments being affected by the proximity of Paris, the eastern ones by the relatively large number of soldiers and ex-soldiers who took part in the assault on the Bastille. Five other regions provided a somewhat smaller quota of insurgents (between 5 and 10 per department): the north-eastern region (Eure, Eure-et-Loir, Calvados, Orne and Sarthe), the east of the Parisian basin (Meuse, Marne, Aube and Yonne), the Jura (Doubs and Jura), the Lyonnais region (Rhône, Isère), the central and eastern parts of the Massif Central (Allier, Puy-de-Dôme, Cantal and Haute-Loire). Thus it is not really accurate to say, as does Albert Mathiez,[1] that the Fourteenth of July was a Parisian *journée*, while August 10th 1792 involved the whole of France. True, on the latter occasion the '*fédérés*' from Marseilles and Brest played an important part, but on July 14th at least half of the demonstrators were provincials who had only recently come to Paris. Moreover foreigners also took part in this *journée* and helped to give it an international character. Among the 'conquerors of the Bastille' we find 13 Italians (six of them, however, being from Savoy, which was then subject to the King of Sardinia), 12 Germans, 12 Belgians, one Dutchman and one Swiss. Some of the men who captured the Bastille were already revolutionary veterans, having taken part either in the American Revolution or in that of Geneva. Citizen Crétaine had lost two sons in the American War of Independence, Pierre Delauzière had been through the campaigns of 1780–1783 in America, Second Lieutenant Elie, of whom we shall speak again later, had served in Savannah as a sergeant under Admiral d'Estaing, François Folitot had fought in the same war as a corporal in the Cap regiment, Jean Founitillat as a sailor in d'Estaing's squadron, Abraham Pélerin as cabin-boy on a privateer which was captured by the English, and Jean-Georges Richard as marine gunner. Louis La Reynie, who played a notable part on the 12th, 13th, and 14th of July had even been aide-de-camp to the American General Schuyler. Two 'conquerors' had taken part in the Genevan revolution; the watchmaker Humbert, who was the first insurgent to climb up on to the towers of the Bastille, had had to leave Geneva after the defeat of the democrats in 1782; and the famous Hulin, whom we shall meet again, had performed the functions of *adjudant-major de la place* in Geneva after its revolution. He had then had occasion to witness the results of the

[1] A. Mathiez, *Le dix août*, Paris, 1931, p. 43.

aristocratic reaction of which he had been an involuntary agent. He had subsequently, but in vain, tried to enlist in the Belgian army raised in revolt against Joseph II.

Of the men who were later to play a political role during the Revolution, very few were present. Stanislas Fréron, one of the most prominent members of the Convention during Thermidor, declared that he was one of the first to enter the Bastille, but no witness confirms his claim. When Camille Desmoulins and Danton arrived at the Bastille, the fortress had already fallen; Danton, who was captain of the militia in the Cordeliers district, was even appointed provisional commander of the Bastille after its fall. The marquis de la Salle, who had been appointed head of the citizens' militia by the electors on July 13th, was present at the siege and protected the prisoners.

Such was the social structure of the body of men who took the Bastille, and it probably reflects fairly closely the structure of the crowd that gathered towards noon under the towers of the fortress. We must doubtless assume the presence of a number of vagrants, homeless persons and former jailbirds, who would not be anxious to claim the title of 'conqueror' because it might have brought them into contact with the police.

This crowd was closely watching what went on at the top of the towers. When it saw the cannon being drawn back it assumed they were going to be loaded, for the delegation of electors, still in conference with the Governor, had not yet reported on the result of their negotiations. Moreover, when the delegates failed to reappear, it was assumed that they were being held as hostages. Panic seized the demonstrators, who hurried to the headquarters of the neighbouring district, the church of Saint-Louis de la Culture, declaring that the Governor of the Bastille had given orders to fire on the people. Immediately the members of the district decided to send a deputation to de Launey, led by the lawyer Thuriot de la Rozière, who was later to be a member of the regicide Convention, and moreover to make his name as President of the Assembly on 9th Thermidor and as such to be in part responsible for the fall of Robespierre. Thuriot and his companions left immediately for the Bastille, which was close by; they went into the cour du Gouverneur and then into the Governor's residence, where they met the deputation of electors, who had just finished their lunch and were leaving the fortress. Thuriot set forth the apprehensions of the people and asked de Launey not only to withdraw the cannon from the embrasures, but also to agree to the occupation of the Bastille by the citizens' militia. De Launey reassured his interlocutors, and as Thuriot had frequently visited the Bastille, where one of his clients, the forger La Corrège, was imprisoned, de Launey invited him to enter the fortress himself to make sure that the guns had been withdrawn from the embrasures and were not loaded. Lieutenant Deflue relates the incident thus: 'M. de Launey came into the interior of the fortress with a person . . . who had already been into the Bastille several times (having permission to visit prisoners); when I went up to them I learnt that this person was asking, in the name of the city, that the guns should be withdrawn from the towers and that no resistance should be offered in case of an attack on the fortress; he said that it was pointless to shed the blood of citizens and wrong to make war on the Nation, that after a great many people had been killed we should still be obliged to yield the fortress. This person also demanded that a citizens' militia should be allowed in to guard the stronghold, in conjunction with the garrison . . . The Governor replied that he could not yield the fort to anyone whatsoever and that he would defend it as long as he was able, that he was answerable for it with his life, and nevertheless, to set the citizens' minds at rest, he had had the guns withdrawn, that the delegate could reassure his constituents on this point, and that he gave his word of honour that he intended no insult to anyone, provided no attempt was made to seize the stronghold or to attack its bridges or gates'. He even took Thuriot to the top of the towers to show him the condition of the guns, so that he might give a more accurate account of the Governor's intentions. During his visit Thuriot spoke to the Swiss soldiers and the pensioners, and repeatedly asked them to reach an agreement with the people. De Launey meanwhile urged them to swear 'that they would not fire nor use their arms unless they were attacked', to which they readily agreed.

Up on the towers, Thuriot observed that the cannon had indeed been withdrawn, that they were not loaded, and that the embrasures had been concealed with wooden panels. As he went down again he once more exhorted the garrison to surrender, but Deflue and the officers of the staff declared that it would dishonour them to give in without fighting. The pensioners seemed inclined to yield, but de

Launey was hesitant, torn between the reproaches of his officers and the attitude of the pensioners. The sight of the ever denser crowd gathering in front of the Bastille and in the cour du Passage strengthened his will to resist. He therefore confined himself to repeating that he would only give orders to fire if he were attacked. Thuriot left; his mission had been a partial failure. He was therefore hooted at by the crowd, which had hoped that as a result of his efforts the citizens' guard would be able to enter the citadel. On all sides the cry was now not merely 'Withdraw the guns!' but 'We want the Bastille! Out with the troops!' It was now half-past twelve.

Without addressing the crowd—probably because he would have met with a hostile reception—Thuriot went off to the district headquarters to give an account of his interview with de Launey. The situation seemed serious, and Thuriot was next sent to the Hôtel de Ville to report developments to the permanent Committee of Electors, which decided that Ethis de Corny, who had been successful enough at the Invalides, should accompany Thuriot; together, accompanied by a trumpeter, they would endeavour to acquaint the crowd with the Governor's promise that the garrison of the Bastille would fire only if it were attacked.

They were just setting forth when the sound of a violent explosion rent the air. At first this was thought to be from the cannon in the Bastille; soon afterwards was heard the crackle of musket fire, and a few minutes later an injured man and a fatally wounded *garde-française* were carried into the Hôtel de Ville, while the crowd protested loudly that they had been betrayed. What had happened?

After the departure of the delegation led by Thuriot, the crowd displayed mounting impatience, and the latest arrivals pushed those in front up against the first gate, the porte de l'Avancée, the two drawbridges of which were raised, but guarded by a single unarmed pensioner. From the towers, the pensioners urged the crowd to retreat, knowing that an attack on the gate might provoke gunfire from the citadel. But as they were aware that their voices might perhaps not be heard twenty-five metres lower down, they began to gesticulate and wave their hats. Did the demonstrators misunderstand the meaning of these signals? Did they think the pensioners were encouraging the crowd to come in? At all events, they prepared to force the doors and drawbridges of the forecourt.

The Fourteenth of July

Two men, Davanne and Denain, climbed on to the roof of a perfumer's shop, one of those built up against the rampart-walk, and thence got down into the cour du Gouvernement. They were followed by others, notably a grocer named Pannetier, a carter, Tournay, and a soldier, Bonnemère. As soon as they were in the court they entered the guardhouse to get the keys of the gates and drawbridges. Not finding these, they seized axes and sledge-hammers and smashed the pulleys to which the drawbridge chains were fastened; the bridges crashed down, killing a man who was standing too close to the moat, and injuring another. The gates, too, they hacked down.

Then the crowd rushed in. It was half-past one by some accounts, three o'clock by others. There is equal uncertainty about the firing of the first shots. The attackers all declare that as soon as they entered the cour du Gouvernement the garrison fired at them with muskets and even with the cannon, this being the explosion heard by Thuriot and Ethis de Corny as they left the Hôtel de Ville. According to Lieutenant Deflue, 'the Governor had forbidden his men to fire on the besiegers before calling on them to withdraw, which was out of the question as they were too far away', and the besiegers then 'fired the first shots at those who were on top of the towers, as had already been done the day before by various troops passing through the neighbourhood ... The assailants were asked what they wanted, and the general demand was for the bridges to be let down [i.e. the drawbridges allowing access to the fortress]. They were told that this could not be done and that they must withdraw, or else they would be fired on. They renewed their cries of 'Down with the bridges!' Then the order to fire was given to thirty *invalides* stationed in the embrasures on either side of the gates.'

In any case, the immediate response to this volley and the single cannon-shot that accompanied it was a shout of 'Treachery!' The assailants, those at least who were not in the front rank, believed that de Launey had had the bridges lowered and the gates of the *avancée* opened so as to allow the crowd to pour into the cour du Gouvernement, and had then ordered his men to fire on the people the better to massacre them. This legend of de Launey's 'treachery' was rapidly propagated, and figures in most of the accounts given by the besiegers. Flammermont's detailed study of the various statements has unanswerably demonstrated the

229

senselessness of this hypothesis.[1] There are still several points to be elucidated, however. Did de Launey personally give the order to fire? Deflue writes: '. . . the order to fire was given.' But by whom? The pensioners, in their apologia,[2] declare that it was the Swiss soldiers who forced them to fire, under threat of being themselves shot, and this assertion is quite plausible. But did the garrison fire to prevent the assailants from lowering the bridges of the fortress itself, as they had just lowered those of the *Avancée*? Or did de Launey give the order to fire to prevent them from plundering his residence in the cour du Gouvernement, as was suggested by some witnesses? This accusation would in fact contradict Rivarol's assertion that de Launey—like Sombreuil—had refrained from firing the cannon so as not to damage a house he had just bought in the vicinity of the Bastille. If we have been unable to verify Rivarol's charge in Sombreuil's case, that of de Launey is somewhat different. An examination of the notaries' records shows that de Launey owned two houses, one in the rue Saint-Louis-au-Marais (the present rue de Turenne), some 1,800 metres from the Bastille, the other in the rue Saint-Sauveur, a little further off, about 2,000 metres from the fortress.[3] These houses were in any case out of range of the Bastille guns and, it would seem, not within the axis of their fire. It does not appear therefore as if de Launey had let himself be influenced by his ownership of property in the vicinity of the Bastille to order or not to order fire. A single question remains unanswered: was it he or Deflue who gave the order to shoot? The fact that Deflue endeavours to prove that the assailants fired first, by referring to the shots of the previous night, leads one to think that on the 14th, about one o'clock in the afternoon, it must have been the Swiss who, on seeing the attackers approaching the principal drawbridge of the Bastille, fired on their own initiative.

The besiegers were not slow to reply. They were, however, unorganized, they had no leader, only a handful of them were armed, and those who had firearms often lacked powder or bullets. Witness the case of Humbert, the watchmaker, whom we have already mentioned. He had taken a musket, with bayonet attached,

---

[1] Flammermont, *Le 14 Juillet*, op. cit.
[2] *La Bastille dévoilée*, op. cit.
[3] I am grateful to M. Pierre Rouleau, archivist in the Archives nationales, for providing this information from the record-books of the notaries of Paris.

from the Invalides, but he had neither powder nor shot. Hearing that powder was being distributed at the Hôtel de Ville, he went there, 'I was given a quarter of a pound', he says, 'but they gave me no shot, for they said they had none. As I left the Hôtel de Ville I heard someone say that the Bastille was being besieged. My regret at having no shot prompted an idea which I immediately carried out, namely to buy some small nails, which I got from the grocer's at the *Coin du Roi*, on the [place de la] Grève. As I was leaving the shop and was just about to load my gun I was accosted by a citizen who told me they were handing out shot at the Hôtel de Ville. So I hurried there, and was given half a dozen pellets of buckshot. I immediately set off for the Bastille, loading my gun as I went. I joined a group of people preparing to go to the siege. We found four footsoldiers of the watch, armed with muskets; I urged them to come to the siege; when they replied that they had neither powder nor shot, we clubbed together to give each of them enough for two shots. Then they followed us willingly. As we went past the Hôtel de la Régie [the excise office], somebody had just broken open two cases of bullets which were being freely handed out. I filled my coat pocket with them so as to give them to those who were short.'[1]

These besiegers, thus unconventionally armed, started sniping at the towers and curtains of the Bastille, and the garrison fired back. The besiegers took refuge from these answering shots in the kitchens which stood to the right of the bridge, in the cour du Gouvernement. At one point they attempted a sortie, and tried to get near the drawbridge again, but they were driven back by a volley from the garrison. However, to guard against an attack on the drawbridge and gate of the Bastille itself, de Launey had posted the Swiss detachment and about ten pensioners opposite the gate, in the main courtyard of the fortress. 'I had behind me,' writes Deflue, 'three two-pounder pieces of ordnance which were to be served by twelve of my soldiers to protect the entrance to the fortress in case the doors should be forced. As the besiegers seemed bent on carrying out this project, we tried to make it harder for them, after their second attack, by piercing two holes in the bridge, in which we intended to place two of these cannon, but since we could not bring them close enough because of the counterpoise of the drawbridge, we replaced them with two rampart guns of the

[1] *Journée de J.-B. Humbert, op. cit.*

sort known as *amusettes*, which were loaded with grapeshot, but these were scarcely used.' For the fact was that the besiegers, seeing that they could not get up to the walls of the Bastille in the open, had had recourse to an old-established military stratagem. They had fetched from the Santerre brewery two carts loaded with straw or stable-litter, brought these into the court and set fire to them. They intended to reach the gates under this smoke screen. And indeed Deflue tells us that as soon as the straw caught fire his soldiers could no longer see their assailants.

While all this was happening, the permanent committee at the Hôtel de Ville was taking steps to try and put an end to the bloodshed. It was decided to send a new delegation to the Bastille, led by Delavigne, president of the Assembly of Electors, and consisting of three members, one of whom, the abbé Fauchet, was later to play a considerable part in the Revolution as president of the Cercle Social and as journalist. The delegation was to ask de Launey to order a cease fire, to hand over to the people the arms stored in the Bastille and to take on a detachment of the militia as part of the garrison of the fortress. He was to be presented with an order couched in the following terms: 'The Permanent Committee of the Militia of Paris, considering that there must be no military force that is not under the control of the City, instructs the deputies whom it is sending to M. de Launey, commander of the Bastille, to enquire whether he is willing to accept in that fortress the troops of the Parisian militia, who will guard it in conjunction with the troops at present stationed there, and who will be under orders from the City.' Thus the Permanent Committee was, from now on, to act as the authority legally representing the City of Paris and directing the insurrection of its inhabitants.

It was about two o'clock when the delegates reached the cour de l'Orme. The firing was so loud that they could not make themselves heard. They pulled out white handkerchiefs and waved them in the hope of stopping the firing: 'We made several signals, both with our hands and with our handkerchiefs, using these as a white flag to inform the garrison, and thus the Governor, of our function and mission, which were further implied by our dress and our confident bearing in the face of danger. We do not know whether our signals were noticed and understood, but the firing never ceased.' The delegates then tried to reach the door of the Bastille, but were prevented by another volley. A further attempt was made from the rue Saint-Antoine, but here too 'a great number of citizens in arms ... without any sort of cover or protection, were exchanging shots with the garrison of the fortress, who were also firing great pieces of ordnance, as far as we could judge by the noise and the effect of the discharge. We went up to these citizens and made ourselves known to them, and at the same time informed them of the object of our deputation, urging them to suspend hostilities in order that the garrison should also cease fire when we repeated our signals, and that after making ourselves known at the gate we should be taken before the Governor to call upon him to surrender the fortress or to accept a municipal garrison. As our mission required, the citizens accepted the truce; they observed it, but although we renewed our signals of peace, the garrison went on firing at us and we had the painful experience of seeing several citizens, whose struggle we had interrupted, collapse at our sides. The attackers gathering in the rue Saint-Antoine therefore resumed their fire with as much courage as indignation. Our remonstrances, our prayers could no longer halt them; they no longer needed any deputation; the siege of the Bastille, the destruction of that horrible prison, the death of the Governor, this was what they loudly clamoured for.' The delegation therefore made its way back towards the Hôtel de Ville.[1]

But while Delavigne's delegation was trying to get into the Bastille, the electors and their Permanent Committee had carried on discussions. The bodies of the dead and wounded were constantly being carried into the Hôtel de Ville. Demonstrators from the Bastille came to demand arms and munitions; all described how de Launey had trapped them by dropping the drawbridges of the *avancée* and letting the crowd into the cour du Gouvernement, so as to shoot them down more easily. Everyone was convinced of de Launey's supreme treachery, and many thought that Flesselles too was betraying them, when he told those who came to get arms, powder and shot that he had no more to give them. It was imperative to act, and to stop the firing at the Bastille completely, if the people's anger were not to be directed against Flesselles. As there was no sign of Delavigne's delegation returning, it was decided to send another, led this time by Ethis de Corny, who at half-past one that afternoon had already been sent to the Bastille together with Thuriot, but whose mission had

---

[1] *Procès-verbal des électeurs*, vol. I, p. 330 ff.

remained unaccomplished because the fighting had broken out. This delegation was to present Governor de Launey with the order which had already been entrusted to Delavigne. But in order to secure the attention of the defenders of the fortress, the five electors took with them a drum-major of the *gardes-françaises* and a flag.

Like its predecessor, Ethis de Corny's delegation reached the cour de l'Orme. The drummer sounded a roll, the flag was waved, and two members of the delegation, Boucheron and Piquod de Sainte-Honorine, made their way into the cour du Passage. 'Here we found a number of persons', writes Boucheron, 'armed with guns, axes, sticks and so forth. I announced that we had come as deputies from the City, to parley; I begged them to break off their fighting. They heard my request. We passed over the main drawbridge, which we found lowered. I went up to the foot of the citadel, to the second drawbridge, which was raised; I took off my hat and shouted with all my might that the City had sent a deputation to parley, that they must all cease fire and lay down their arms. A person in a coloured coat, in the midst of a group of pensioners, all holding their hats in their hands, answered me from the summit of the citadel that he was willing to receive the deputation, but that the crowd must withdraw. We went into the second court, known as the cour de l'Avancée. We begged the people who were there in great number to withdraw, explaining that only on this condition would the deputation be received. Some of them were influenced by our entreaties; others went on aiming their guns. We left the Bastille with them.'[1] They rejoined Ethis de Corny, who had stopped in the cour de l'Orme with the other members of his delegation. These all declared that they had seen 'a white flag flying from the platform of the Bastille, and that the soldiers who were carrying muskets had turned their weapons upside down, and responded to our appeals and signals of peace by waving their hats,' but that just as the firing broke off the deputies 'suddenly saw a cannon levelled at the cour de l'Orme, and at the same time received a volley of musketry that killed three persons at their feet; that one citizen who was speaking to a deputy had his hat pierced by a bullet, while another bullet tore off the epaulette of M. de Beaubourg, one of the deputies.' Who had given the order to fire on the delegates? Since Deflue was in the courtyard of the castle it

[1] Boucheron, *Récit . . . op. cit.*, p. 4 ff.

can only have been de Launey, who must have been the 'person in a coloured coat' whom Boucheron had seen at the top of the tower.

The *invalides*, in their account, assert that they saw the deputation, heard the drum-roll and noticed the flag. This was why some of them waved their hats and reversed their muskets; the garrison was on the point of ceasing fire. But de Launey intervened—on this point the pensioners are quite explicit—and declared that this was not a real deputation from the City but a trick of the attackers. This time de Launey's responsibility is flagrant and his 'treachery' unmistakable, although the pensioners declare that they did not aim at the delegates and that the firing was not resumed until after their departure. In any case it certainly seems as if, to echo Rivarol's remark, de Launey had really lost his head this time. But his 'treachery' infuriated all those who were in the cour de l'Orme. Moreover their fury was partly directed against the delegates from the Hôtel de Ville, whom they accused of having encouraged the assailants by means of their drum-beating and flag-waving to go unsuspecting into the courtyard, where, unprotected, they had been fired at. Several of the insurgents, says Ethis de Corny, were so infuriated that they surrounded the deputies, thrust bayonets against their breasts and swords against their heads, saying: 'You are traitors too; you brought us into this courtyard to be killed.' Ethis de Corny replied: 'If your friends, if the deputies sent by the City to succour you, could be suspected of so heinous and detestable a project, they would be unwilling to stand by your side, in your midst, exposed to the same dangers. Moreover I make myself your hostage, your prisoner; go with me to the City and you will be convinced of the truth.'[1]

The fourth delegation to be sent to the Bastille that day thus retraced its steps to the Hôtel de Ville, its mission unfulfilled. Nobody knew how things would end, when on their way back Ethis de Corny and his companions met a detachment of about 100 *gardes-françaises* 'marching in order, at the double, telling everyone they were going to besiege the Bastille.' The detachment was followed by a number of armed citizens and, as well, by four cannon and a mortar which had been seized that morning at the Invalides. This intervention by the *gardes-françaises* and the guns from the Invalides was to prove decisive.

[1] *Procès-verbal des électeurs*, vol. I, p. 336 ff.

4. The fall of the Bastille

What happened to bring about the intervention of the *gardes-françaises* and the artillery?

As soon as he heard that the deputation led by Ethis de Corny had been fired at, the second-in-command of the citizens' militia had given orders for some of the twelve cannon which had been taken from the Invalides that morning to be brought to the Bastille. At the same time Hulin, director of the Buanderie de la Reine (the Queen's Laundry), at La Briche, near Saint-Denis, was asking for help from the *gardes-françaises*. We have already mentioned this man, who was to win a sorry fame under the Empire. Born in Paris in 1758, he had spent his childhood with the regiment, had served as soldier and then sergeant in the Swiss guards, and had then become an official in the service of Geneva where, as we have said, he took part in the revolution of 1782–3. On July 12th he, like Camille Desmoulins, had harangued the crowd in the Palais-Royal and incited them to insurrection. He was personally acquainted with Necker, having met him in Geneva. On the morning of Monday July 13th, he met Mme. de Staël at the home of a neighbour of his at La Briche, named Fournier; and then, in spite of her entreaties, apparently, he decided to return to Paris immediately, declaring: 'I want to avenge your father on the bastards who are trying to murder us.' During the night of July 13th–14th Hulin was on patrol with the militia of his district, and then went home. On the morning of the 14th he went to the Invalides, and it was on his way back that he came into contact with the *gardes-françaises* for the first time. According to Pitra's memoirs,[1] as Hulin was returning from the Invalides he met in the place Dauphine 'two companies of *gardes-françaises* surrounded by citizens. He recognized among these several officers of that regiment, in civilian dress, who were trying to persuade their soldiers to follow them and desert the people's cause. Hulin soon got rid of these officers by loudly exposing the motives that had brought them there.' He then, apparently, sent the *gardes-françaises* off to the monastery of Saint-Lazare, where renewed looting was rumoured to be in progress. He eventually reached the Hôtel de Ville, where he intended to report his activities to the Electors. On the place de l'Hôtel de Ville he 'found the grenadiers and fusiliers

[1] *Mémoires inédits de L.-G. Pitra,* published by Flammermont, *op. cit.,* p. 35 ff.

of Lubersac and of Ruffevielle (the *gardes-françaises*) drawn up in
battle array . . .' Hulin vainly attempted to go up on to the perron.
He had managed to climb up a few steps of the main stair when a
crowd came pouring out and swept him down, bringing him face
to face with the two companies, which seemed by their very
immobility to share his rage and despair . . . 'He paused before
them for a moment, swept his gaze over all the soldiers and, raising
his voice, in accents which proclaimed the intensity of his emotion:
"Are you citizens, brave *gardes-françaises*, and can you listen to
these cries?" he said to them. "Don't you hear the cannon . . . with
which that villain de Launey is murdering our parents, our wives
and children, gathered unarmed around the Bastille? Will you let
them be massacred, while you have guns and strength available?
My friends! good people!" (and tears were streaming from his
eyes) "*gardes-françaises*! Parisians are being slaughtered like sheep,
and will you not march on the Bastille? won't these sergeants, men
of high renown, take the lead and bring you thither?" Immediately
the *gardes-françaises* fell into line, the sergeants took the lead, and
all shouted: "March on and we'll follow you." Hulin hesitated to
do so. "Lead us, good fellow," the sergeants told him, and themselves gave the order to march.' It was in this fashion that Hulin—
whose role may perhaps have been somewhat embellished in the
reports of Pitra and of 'Cousin Jacques'—led the *gardes-françaises*
up to the Bastille. He was subsequently to become a general, and
to preside over the council of war which condemned the duc
d'Enghien to death.

It was about half-past three in the afternoon when Hulin at last
reached the Bastille, followed, not by two whole companies of
gardes-françaises but by precisely thirty-six grenadiers of Ruffevielle's company, twenty-one fusiliers, two corporals, two artillerymen of Lubersac's company, Sergeant La Barthe and a crowd of
three or four hundred armed citizens, together with four of the
five cannon that had been brought to the Hôtel de Ville. At the
same time another column of armed citizens arrived under the
command of Second Lieutenant Elie, standard-bearer of the
regiment of La Reine-Infanterie. This man was one of the few
officiers de fortune, in other words risen from the ranks, still
to be found in 1789. He had recently been promoted second
lieutenant at the age of forty-one, after twenty-two years of
service!

The character of the battle now changed. Whereas hitherto the besiegers had shot at random, leaderless and in the most total confusion, the presence of Hulin and Elie completely altered the situation. They were accepted as leaders and assumed control of operations. Hulin had a cannon brought into action in the first court, the cour des Salpêtres. A few shots were fired against the towers, but proved totally ineffective. Hulin's column then moved forward into the cour de l'Orme, where the cannon was once more brought into action, but with no greater effectiveness, while the *gardes-françaises* opened fire on the pensioners posted on the towers. No result having been obtained, the cannon were now brought into the cour des Casernes and the rue du Petit-Musc. The cannon-balls did not even shake the thick walls. It was obvious that to achieve any decisive result the gates of the Bastille themselves would have to be shattered by cannon fire. But this had been impossible because of the carts loaded with blazing straw which had been placed in front of the gate to cover the advance of the besiegers. These must now be removed, which was a perilous operation. Second Lieutenant Elie undertook it himself and, with the help of Reole, a haberdasher, nicknamed *Vive l'Amour*, and a few more citizens, he dragged the carts out of the cour du Gouvernement. A couple of citizens were killed in the course of this manœuvre. Two cannon were then brought into this court, which was no easy task; they had to be dismounted, then re-assembled on the gun-carriages and placed on the stone bridge about thirty metres from the drawbridge and gates of the fortress. 'When [the cannon] were back on their gun-carriages,' writes Humbert the watchmaker, 'we all with one accord formed ranks of five or six and I found myself in the front row. In this array we marched up to the drawbridge of the castle . . . We levelled the guns; the bronze one was pointed at the great drawbridge and a smaller one of iron inlaid with silver at the small bridge.'[1]

This manœuvre settled the fate of the battle. It was a daring one, for behind the drawbridges three cannon manned by Swiss guards stood ready for action, and if these had been fired they would have wrought havoc among the *gardes-françaises* and the citizens who had brought their cannon on to the stone bridge. But in any case they would only have been able to fire a single volley,

[1] *Journée de J.-B. Humbert*, op. cit., p. 11.

and the mass of besiegers would have swept in through the gates of the Bastille while these cannon were being reloaded, just as, that very morning, they had invaded the parapet of the Invalides before the artillerymen had been given the order to fire. The bravery and daring of the attacking crowd is thus not in doubt, and the counter-revolutionary authors of *La Bastille dévoilée* have paid due tribute to it; 'Never', they declare, 'have more courageous actions been witnessed in an unruly crowd. It was not only the soldiers, the *gardes-françaises*, but townspeople of all classes, simple working men of every description, who, with inadequate weapons or none at all, defied the gunfire from the ramparts and seemed to mock at it. They did not shelter behind retrenchments; they stood in the very courts of the Bastille and so close to its towers that M. de Launey himself repeatedly made use of the paving-stones and other debris that he had had brought on to the platform. It cannot be denied that there was much confusion and disorder. Every man was his own leader and followed his own impulse. There were individuals from all districts, several of whom had never handled arms, and yet the pensioners, who had been through many sieges and many battles, have assured us that they never saw such musketry fire as that of these besiegers; they dared not raise their heads above the parapets of the towers.'[1]

No doubt this was what Governor de Launey must have been thinking. Should he allow the cannon to breach the gate, and then return fire? The victory of the assailants seemed probable, and would doubtless entail the slaughter of the entire garrison. The pensioners, moreover, were making the same reflections and urging the governor to capitulate. Their reports and that of Lieutenant Deflue differ in some respects. The former describe events as follows: 'Towards four in the afternoon, the Governor, whose non-commissioned officers were earnestly beseeching him to surrender the Bastille, realizing himself that he could not stand the siege much longer for lack of provisions, took the match of one of the guns in the inner court to set fire to the powder stored in the Tour de la Liberté, which would inevitably have blown up part of the faubourg Saint-Antoine and all the houses in the neighbourhood of the Bastille, had not two non-commissioned officers prevented him from carrying out his plan; they forced him to withdraw at the point of the bayonet. A certain Ferrand drove the Governor back

---

[1] *La Bastille dévoilée, op. cit.*, 2nd instalment, p. 129.

from the entrance to the *sainte-barbe* (the gun-room) and he then went down to the Tour de la Liberté, from which he was also repulsed by a certain Biquard.

'Then M. de Launey consulted the garrison as to what action he should take, seeing no alternative but to blow up the fortress rather than risk being slaughtered by the people, from whose fury there was no escape; he urged them to go up the towers again and keep on fighting, and then blow themselves up rather than surrender. The soldiers replied that it was impossible to fight any longer, that they would accept anything rather than cause the death of so large a number of citizens, and that it would be more advisable to send a drummer up on to the tower to beat the recall, fly a white flag and capitulate. The Governor, having no such flag, gave them a white handkerchief. Two men, Rouf and Roulard, went up on to the towers, flew the flag, and walked three times round the platform with the drummer beating a retreat, which took about a quarter of an hour; the people kept up continuous fire and paid no attention to the flag nor to the drum-roll.

A quarter of an hour after the pensioners and the drummer had come down again, the besiegers, seeing that firing had ceased from all parts of the Bastille, advanced as far as the inner bridge, still firing and shouting: Lower the drawbridge! The Swiss officer spoke to them through a sort of slit beside the drawbridge and asked leave to go out with the honours of war. They refused his request. The said officer then wrote out a capitulation and passed it through the slit, saying that the garrison was ready to yield and lay down its arms, provided [the besiegers] would promise not to massacre them; there were cries of 'Lower your drawbridge and no harm will be done you.' On receiving this promise the Governor handed over the key of the small drawbridge, which he had in his pocket, to Corporal Guiard and N.C.O. Perreau, who then opened the gate and lowered the bridge.'[1] In the account prepared for his regimental log-book, Deflue is more laconic, but there are differences between his version and that of the *invalides*.

'M. de Launey', he writes, 'seeing these preparations [i.e. the two cannon levelled at the gates of the Bastille] from the top of the tower, without warning or consulting either his general staff or his garrison, caused the drummer who accompanied him to beat a recall; on this signal I myself went to the battlements and into the

---

[1] *Ibid.*, pp. 104–108.

July 15th. Louis XVI leaving the National Assembly

Bibl. Nat., Print Room, Vinck Collection, 1731

July 15th–17th. Demolition of the Bastille

rooms to order a cease fire; the crowd then came nearer and the Governor offered to surrender, but they would not hear of surrender and renewed their cries of "Down with the bridges!". This was all the answer to be got from them. Then M. de Launey came down from the tower, went into the Council Chamber and wrote a note informing the besiegers that he had ten thousand pounds of powder in the fort, that if they would not accept his offer of capitulation he would blow up the fortress, the garrison and the whole neighbourhood. He gave me this note with orders to transmit it. I went to the gate and passed the note through the slit I have already mentioned. I handed it to an officer of the Queen's regiment, or at any rate to someone wearing that uniform, who had had a plank brought so as to cross over; but the note had no effect. The shouts of "no capitulation!" and "let down the drawbridges!" were the only reply. I went back to the Governor and reported the state of affairs to him, and then immediately rejoined my company, who were drawn up, by my orders, to the left of the gates. I was expecting the Governor to keep his word and blow up the fort, but to my great surprise I saw four pensioners go up to the bridges, open them and lower them, and then the crowd came rushing in.'[1] In the letter to his brothers, which may be subsequent to this report, Deflue definitely states that he tried to prevent de Launey both from signing the capitulation order and from blowing up the Bastille. 'I took the liberty of pointing out to him that it was still unnecessary to take such extreme measures. I told him that the garrison and the fortress had suffered no damage, that the gates were still intact and that we had the wherewithal to defend ourselves; for we had had only one pensioner killed and two or three wounded. He did not seem to like my arguments; I had to obey.'[2] Since this intervention of Deflue's is mentioned in only one of the three versions he has given of his role at the Bastille, it is by no means certain that it represents the truth. It is more likely that de Launey yielded to pressure from the pensioners. In any case, we possess an old copy of the note written by de Launey and passed through the Bastille gate: 'We have twenty thousand pounds of powder, we shall blow up the garrison and the whole neighbourhood unless you accept our capitulation. From the Bastille, at five in the evening, July 14th, 1789, Launey.'

[1] Arch. de la Guerre, *Mémoires historiques*, vol. 619–626.
[2] Flammermont, *op. cit.*, p. ccxxxv.

The besiegers tell roughly the same story. The clockmaker Humbert asserts that the two cannon drawn up before the gate each fired about six shots; this is unlikely. Or, at all events, they failed to destroy the gate, since Deflue asserts that it was intact when he passed de Launey's note through one of the slits which he himself had made to shoot through. When the attackers saw the paper being waved in front of the gate, they were perplexed as to how they could cross the moat to get it.[1] A clerk at the Mont-de-Piété (the pawn office), named Ribaucourt, went to fetch eleven planks from the carpenter Lemarchand's shop in the rue des Tournelles. The longest was placed across the moat, several men stood on one end of it to hold it down, while a cobbler named Michel Bezier advanced over the void to seize the paper. But he lost his balance and fell into the moat, where he was not killed, as has been said, but injured; he broke his elbow.[2] We have seen that according to Deflue it was an officer of the Queen's regiment, presumably Elie, who followed him and took the paper. But Maillard, son of an usher in the Châtelet, who, in 1792, was to play an infamous part in the September massacres, claims to have seized it himself. The point is unimportant. The note was transmitted to Hulin. In view of the shouts of the crowd, who refused to hear of capitulation, he was about to order the cannon to fire at the drawbridge, when the latter were suddenly lowered. Then the crowd rushed in. Meanwhile some besiegers, who were still outside the cour du Gouvernement and had not been informed of the surrender, went on firing. Several of the attackers were thus killed as they came out on to the towers.

'They disarmed us immediately', writes Deflue, 'they took us prisoner, each of us having a guard, they went into the apartments, they took possession of the arms, they flung our papers and records out of the windows and plundered everything; those of our soldiers who had not got their kitbags with them lost all their clothing, and I myself all my possessions.'

The seven prisoners who were in the Bastille were of course set free; later that evening they were to be carried in triumph through Paris. As for the powder, the assailants seized part of it and the rest was taken back to the Arsenal.

---

[1] Réole's account in *La Bastille dévoilée*, 2nd instalment, p. 107.
[2] Durieux, 'La capitulation de la Bastille', in the *Bulletin du Comité de travaux historiques*, 1925.

It is difficult to estimate the casualties suffered by the attacking force. According to the report of 'Cousin Jacques', there were thirty dead; according to '*Deux amis de la Liberté*', forty. Deflue says that there was talk of 160 casualties, dead and wounded, but the figure seemed to him an exaggerated one, 'to judge by the small amount of firing that came from the fortress'. According to various more detailed estimates, it seems that 83 of the attackers were killed on the spot and 15 died from wounds; a total of 98 dead, probably less than during the Réveillon riots on April 28th. To these must be added 60 injured and 13 badly disabled, that is to say another 73 victims. On the defenders' side, there had been only one pensioner killed and three wounded. The Swiss detachment had suffered no casualties. But several of the defenders of the Bastille were to be massacred during the evening. Public anger, paradoxical as it may seem, was not directed particularly against the Swiss. Deflue, however, tells us how he escaped from death: 'After many threats and much ill-treatment, the first fury of the crowd subsided a little and I was taken to the Hôtel de Ville, together with part of my company which, in the mêlée, had remained at my side. All the way there we were met with threats and insults, and a clamour from the whole mob that we ought to be hanged. I firmly believe that but for the efforts of an officer of the *Arquebusiers*, named M. Riccard, to protect the prisoners I should not have reached the Hôtel de Ville alive.'[1]

Du Puget, the *lieutenant du roi*, managed to escape by wearing his coat inside out; he was mistaken for one of the attackers. Governor de Launey was arrested by Maillard and a *garde-françaises*. His sword and cane were snatched from him; around him, on all sides, there were shouts of *A mort!* (Kill him!). But Hulin and Elie managed to protect him, and he was taken on foot to the Hôtel de Ville. On the way there he was constantly subjected to insults, blows and injuries. Near the church of Saint-Louis the crowd got hold of de Launey and tried to kill him, but Hulin succeeded in rescuing him. On reaching the Hôtel de Ville the Governor was once more torn from his protectors and was killed by an unemployed cook named Desnot, who later, in 1792, boasted of his 'exploit'. Desnot's story is well known, but despite its horror it must be retold here, for it illustrates certain sides of the popular mentality. 'At this moment several people refused to

[1] Arch. de la Guerre, *Mémoires historiques*, vols. 619–626.

let de Launey be taken to the Hôtel de Ville, some saying "Off with his head", others "Hang him", others "tie him to a horse's tail". Desnot pointed out to his neighbours that the Governor was already seriously wounded and that it would be better to take him to the Hôtel de Ville, where his fate would be decided. One man, a tall and striking individual, supported this suggestion, but at that moment the wretched de Launey, flinging his arms out wide, rolling his eyes and grinding his teeth, cried out: "Let me die!" As he struggled, the Governor kicked Desnot, who received the blow in his private parts and called out: "I'm done for!" Immediately somebody stabbed de Launey in the stomach with a bayonet; several others followed suit, the Governor fell and was dragged as far as the gutter. Here they stabbed him repeatedly with bayonets and swords, and fired pistol shots to finish him off, saying: "*C'est un galeux* (he's a mangy dog), a monster who has betrayed us, he must be destroyed." When de Launey was dead, the people said: "The Nation requires that his head be shown to the public, so that it may know his guilt." Someone standing near Desnot handed him a sword and said: "Here, since he hurt you, you cut off his head." And he did so, not with the sword, which he could not manage, but with his pocket knife.'[1] Three officers of the staff of the Bastille and three pensioners were also massacred. Finally Flesselles, *prévôt des marchands*, also fell victim to the conquerors of the Bastille. They had been saying all day that he had betrayed them by refusing to arm the people. When he left the Hôtel de Ville to go to the Palais-Royal, where he wished to vindicate himself against his accusers, he was brought down by a pistol shot. His head was cut off and carried, along with de Launey's, through the streets of Paris.

We are not seeking to justify these massacres, far less to extol them, but to explain them. No one has done this better than Babeuf, the future 'tribune of the people'. In fact, he did so in connection not with the murder of de Launey and Flesselles but a few days later, when he watched the people carrying through the streets the severed heads of Bertier de Sauvigny, *intendant* of Paris, and of Foulon, who had both been murdered on July 23rd. He wrote to his wife on this occasion: 'When I arrived [in Paris] I

---

[1] Flammermont, *op. cit.*, pp. ccxl–clvli, quoting the examination of Desnot by the *commissaires au Châlet*, published by I. Guiffrey in the *Revue historique*, vol. I, pp. 497–507.

found everyone talking about a conspiracy led by M. le comte d'Artois and other princes, and aimed at exterminating the major part of the population of Paris and subsequently reducing to slavery all those who, throughout France, had only escaped being massacred by humbly submitting to the will of the nobility, and holding out their hands, without a murmur, for the shackles prepared by the tyrants. If Paris had not discovered this hideous plot in the nick of time, all would have been lost; no more heinous crime could ever have been perpetrated. The people's sole thought was to wreak a signal revenge for such a betrayal, unprecedented throughout history. Their minds were made up, and they would spare neither the principal authors of the conspiracy nor their adherents. The executions began to take place, yet failed to assuage a resentment that was only too well founded. The wrath of the people is far from being appeased by the death of the Governor of the Bastille'. And after describing the parade of severed heads through Paris, amid applause from the beholders, Babeuf exclaims: 'Oh, how painful I found all this joy! I was at the same time satisfied and vexed, I said so much the better! and so much the worse! I can understand the people taking the law into its own hands, and I commend such rough justice when it is satisfied by the destruction of the guilty, but how can it fail today to be cruel? Cruel punishments of every sort, quartering, the rack, the wheel, the stake, the whip, the gibbet, so many tortures everywhere have taught us such wicked ways! Our masters, instead of civilizing us, have made us barbarous because they are barbarous themselves. They are reaping what they have sown, and they will go on reaping it; for all this, my poor wife, will have terrible consequences, it seems; we are only at the beginning.'[1] Loustalot, in *Les Révolutions de Paris*, expressed a similar idea: 'Frenchmen, you are destroying your tyrants! Your hatred is shocking! it is horrible . . . But you will be free at last! I feel, o my fellow citizens, how much these shocking scenes distress your souls; like you I am deeply distressed by them. But think how ignominious it is to live a slave!'[2] And Creuzé-Latouche writes: 'In spite of the ferocious acts which the people have committed . . . they have maintained a certain respect for justice and an aversion for what is vile . . . One has a general sense that under existing circumstances all that is needed, to

[1] Babeuf, *Pages choisies*, edited by M. Dommanget, Paris, 1935, pp. 73–75.
[2] *Les Révolutions de Paris*, no. 2, July 18th to 25th 1789.

allay the fury of the people, is a tribunal in which it can have confidence.'[1]

From its origins, the Revolution was influenced both by the ideals of liberty and equality inherited from the *philosophes*, and by the cruelty which resulted from the violence and arbitrary rule of the *ancien régime*. But Paris was more conscious, on the night of July 14th, of the victory which seemed to promise it liberty and equality than of the massacres which heralded the Terror. A general joyfulness prevailed; everyone kept repeating: 'The Bastille has fallen, its gates are open!' Some people, Camille Desmoulins among them, wanted to take advantage of the victory to march on Versailles immediately and force the King to dismiss de Broglie's ministry and recall Necker. But was this possible? A large number of troops were still encamped at the Champ-de-Mars and stationed in barracks at the Ecole Militaire. Others were defending the bridges of Sèvres and Saint-Cloud. Was it not wiser to wait and see what the King would decide? This attitude prevailed. The significance of the victory that had been won was still unknown. While awaiting a morrow that was rich with promise but also heavy with threats, people were content to keep on patrolling Paris all night, to the sound of the tocsin, which incessantly reminded them of danger, and to the sound of the volleys fired by the artillery, celebrating the victory, but also warning Versailles of the resolution of the people of Paris.

[1] Creuzé-Latouche, *Journal, op. cit.*

X

The Abdication of the *Ancien Régime*

The rain which had been threatening all day on July 14th finally fell in torrents during the evening, forcing the demonstrators and militiamen to go home and even the regular troops to take shelter in houses. It was possible at last to take stock of the day's happenings.

Of these happenings, which was really the most important? The taking of the Bastille? No doubt most Parisians, and before long, indeed, most people in France and abroad thought that the fall of the Bastille constituted the decisive factor in the events of the Fourteenth of July. It would be truer to call it the symbolic factor. The fall of that symbol of all that was arbitrary and anachronistic about the feudal régime was in itself a symbol. But in fact an event of even more crucial significance was the council held that morning, at ten o'clock, by Besenval with his army leaders, during which, as we have said, it was admitted that the troops would 'refuse to march'; in consequence of which Besenval was unable to make use of his forces, which were considerable, to relieve the Hôtel des Invalides, and during the afternoon made no attempt to free de Launey at the Bastille. Du Puget, the *lieutenant du roi* at the Bastille, accused Besenval of conniving with his compatriot Necker, 'the secret agent behind the riots, unwilling to deliver the Court from the anxiety which these caused it.'[1] In fact a certain credence can be given to this rumour if we consider that Necker was to do his utmost, when restored to power, to secure the release of Besenval, who had been arrested after July 14th. Necker admitted moreover that Besenval reported all his decisions directly to himself as well as to the Minister for War. But it should

---

[1] *Mémoires des faits authentiques, op. cit.* The charge has been repeated by Jean Mistler, Le 14 Juillet, op. cit., p. 116.

not be forgotten that de Broglie, at first as general in command of the troops in Paris and Besenval's superior officer, and later as Minister for War, showed the most complete confidence in his subordinate. It is inconceivable that Besenval should have refused to order his troops to march, unless he had been convinced that they would defect. Already several regiments had passed over to the insurgents, or had given unequivocal proofs of their frame of mind:[1] the *gardes-françaises*, ever since the release of fourteen of their number from the Abbaye prison on June 30th; the hussars and dragoons who had been sent that very day to the Abbaye to disperse the crowd of demonstrators and had gone over to their side; the regiment of La Reine-Infanterie to which Second Lieutenant Élie belonged; the pensioners at the Bastille, who forced de Launey to capitulate; and many others. Even the foreign regiments were not to be relied on, as is proved by the desertion of 75 soldiers of the Salis-Samade regiment on July 14th and 15th, and of 19 others between the 16th and the 25th. Under such conditions, what commander would have risked engaging his troops, in a city of 600,000 inhabitants? Now the state of mind of the soldiers was the consequence, not of the dismissal of Necker and his ministry, but of two years of disturbances, two years of contact between the people and the small military detachments employed to restrain them, two years of official repudiation of those leaders who had sought to take action, together with the influence of the subversive propaganda of the *philosophes*, which had ample opportunity for pin-pointing the latest mistakes of the *ancien régime* in military matters, such as the introduction of 'Prussian-style' disciplinary beatings with the flat of the sword, and the denial of promotion to noncommissioned officers. The defection of the troops was not a specifically Parisian incident, it was a national event which made possible the free development of the Parisian insurrection.

Under these conditions, did it make any difference whether the Bastille held out for a long or a short time? Suppose de Launey, like Sombreuil at the Invalides, had allowed the crowd to seize the arms and munitions in the Bastille during the morning, would things have turned out very differently? Suppose, on the other hand, de Launey had not capitulated, and the Bastille draw-

---

[1] On the army's morale on the eve of the Revolution, see: Captain Latreille, *L'Armée et la Nation à la fin de l'Ancien Régime*, Paris, 1914.

bridges had not been lowered by the pensioners, with or without orders from the Governor; the cannon brought up by the *gardes-françaises* would no doubt before long have brought down bridges and gates, and the attackers would have invaded the fortress an hour or so later. July 14th thus marks the culmination of two great currents, the uprising of the people of Paris, which was one aspect of the great national uprising that had been under way for several months, and the defection of the troops, another aspect of the same national insurrection. The capture of the Bastille served as a marvellous symbol, for France and for the world, of the triumph of this insurrection. Nevertheless it was some time before the King and the Court became aware of this.

1. July 14th at Versailles

Despite the significant events of the 12th and 13th of July in Paris, the King was confident. His diary is significant. It reads: 'Tuesday 7th: Stag-hunt at Port-Royal, killed two. Wednesday 8th: nothing. Thursday 9th: nothing. Deputation of the Estates. Friday 10th: nothing. Replied to the deputation of the Estates. Saturday 11th: Nothing. Departure of M. Necker. Sunday 12th: Vespers and *salut*. Departure of M. de Montmorin, Saint-Priest and La Luzerne. Monday 13th: Nothing. Tuesday 14th: Nothing.' Various witnesses, including Bailly, tell us that Breteuil and the King were planning to hold a 'Royal session' of the Estates-General on July 16th, at which the Estates would have been asked once again to accept the programme of June 23rd; if they refused, the Assembly would have been dissolved. The disturbances that had arisen in Paris since the 12th had brought about only one minor change in this programme. Marshal de Broglie, Minister for War, had been ordered to prepare for military intervention against Paris, to begin during the night of the 14th so that the Royal Session could take place on the morning of the 16th. In fact, no documentary evidence of such a project remains, but it is mentioned by Bailly, by the marquis de Ferrières, deputy of the nobility to the Estates, by Miot de Mélito and by the ambassador of Saxony, Salmour. These all tell us that on the evening of the 14th two German regiments were inspected and harangued at the Orangerie at Versailles by the comte d'Artois and the duchesse de Polignac, who were still unaware of what had been happening in Paris that day. It is possible that these intentions or preparations may have given rise to the rumour current in Paris on the evening of the 14th: an attack by the troops from Versailles was expected, and the militia moved towards the bridges of Sèvres and Saint-Cloud to repel it if it came. The Assembly, meanwhile, had taken different steps.

We have seen that the National Assembly had decided, on learning the news of Necker's dismissal, to sit in permanence. However, apprehending a possible *coup de force*, its secretary, the abbé Grégoire, had put the archives in safe keeping.[1] The Assembly continuously discussed how to get the King to recall the troops. On the evening of July 14th, the vicomte de Noailles, newly arrived from Paris, told the Assembly about the fall of the Invalides and the Bastille, and the murder of de Launey. Immediately the Assembly sent a deputation to Louis XVI to inform him of the state of things in Paris. The King, relying perhaps on the counter-attack being prepared by de Broglie, sent a non-committal written reply. He declared that he had given orders for the generals to take command of the *milice bourgeoise* and for the troops encamped on the Champ de Mars to leave Paris. It was obvious that he did not yet realize the importance of the events which had taken place in Paris and of the enormous consequences which they must inevitably entail. However, no doubt in the hope of restoring calm to Paris, Dupont de Nemours, deputy to the National Assembly, immediately left for the city. He arrived at the Hôtel de Ville at two in the morning of July 15th and repeated to the electors what the King had told the deputies. To make assurance doubly sure he even set down the King's answer in writing; the document is at present preserved among the Dupont de Nemours papers at Wilmington, Delaware, U.S.A. It reads as follows: 'July 15th, at a quarter past two in the morning, M. Dupont, deputy for Nemours, arrived at the Hôtel de Ville and said that a deputation from the National Assembly having approached the King on the previous evening, His Majesty replied: "I have arranged with the *prévôt des marchands* for the establishment of the *garde bourgeoise*. I have commissioned two general officers to assist it with their experience. I have given orders for my troops which are in the Champ-de-Mars to withdraw. The cause of your anxiety is one which must move the hearts of all good citizens and has deeply touched my own." He signed this Du Pont.'[2]

[1] R. Bouis, 'Grégoire et la crise de juillet 1789' (*A.H.R.F.*, 1948, pp. 179–180).
[2] Wilmington (Delaware, U.S.A.), Eleutherian Mills Historical Library.

The Abdication of the Ancien Régime

While the deputation from the Assembly was conferring with the King, two electors, sent by the Permanent Committee from the Hôtel de Ville, appeared in the salle des Menus-Plaisirs and confirmed the report made by de Noailles. The Assembly decided to send a second deputation to the King, led by the Archbishop of Paris. It left as soon as the first had reported on its mission. Louis XVI, having heard what the deputation had to say, replied: 'Messieurs, you distress me increasingly by the story you tell me about the misfortunes of Paris; it is impossible to believe that these are the result of my orders to the troops. You know the answer I made to your previous deputation, I have nothing to add to it.' This was very curt. Louis XVI had obviously not yet understood what the success of the Parisian uprising implied. He lacked one essential factor: a knowledge of the state of mind of the army. Besenval, in his memoirs, declares that before his arrival at Versailles 'nobody had wanted to tell the King the whole story of this disastrous day, so that he was only informed of events through fragmentary accounts which left him in a state of uncertainty.' He adds that Louis learnt from him 'all the facts and all their sinister implications for the present and the future.'[1] This statement must be interpreted as follows: Louis XVI knew of the taking of the Invalides and the Bastille, and of the murders of de Launey and de Flesselles, but he was unaware of the state of mind of his troops, which was a far more serious matter than the invasion of two military buildings by the people of Paris, since it obliged the King to renounce his project of a counter-offensive against Paris, and a Royal Session to be held on July 16th.

It was doubtless this state of mind of the King's that gave rise to the well-known story which is probably as legendary as others of the sort. The comte de La Rochefoucauld-Liancourt, in his Life of his father, written in 1827, tells how the duc de Liancourt woke up Louis XVI during the night of July 14th to tell him what had been happening in Paris. 'Why, it's a revolt', the King is supposed to have said, to which the duke replied: 'No, Sire, it is a revolution.' The anecdote had been current as early as 1789; the comte de La Rochefoucauld-Liancourt claims to have found it written down among his father's papers, and Bailly repeats it in his memoirs. But as we have seen, Louis XVI had already been informed of events by two delegations from the National Assembly.

[1] Besenval, *Mémoires*, vol. III, p. 417.

251

It is possible that the duc de Liancourt may have been the first to enlighten him as to the consequences to be expected from the events in Paris.

Besenval, moreover, had anticipated these consequences on the evening of the 14th by ordering the troops stationed in Paris to withdraw towards the bridges of Sèvres and Saint-Cloud; the order had, as we have seen, been confirmed by the King. The log-book of the Salis-Samade regiment, which we must quote yet again, gives us a detailed picture of this manœuvre: 'The news of the capture of the Bastille having reached our camp [the Champ-de-Mars], the generals summoned the corps commanders and informed them of the necessity of evacuating this post and leaving the precincts of the city; since it was impossible to provide transport for our equipment, all our belongings were deposited at the École Militaire, the camp remained pitched and, at nine in the evening, the infantry took up arms, the cavalry mounted their horses and dispositions were taken up for the withdrawal to Versailles. The *barrières* in this region were all on fire, and guarded. It was decided to force a way through, if necessary. The grenadiers of the three regiments were ordered to form the rear-guard, the Salis-Samade regiment took the head of the column, which proceeded towards the *barrière* of the Grenelle plain. This *barrière* had been set on fire during the daytime and was at this time completely abandoned. Consequently the troops met with no obstacle to their passage. The column reached Sèvres between midnight and one a.m. and the mounted troops were quartered in the park of Saint-Cloud. The infantry stopped in the village and the regimental commanders were ordered to provide shelter for their troops as best they could. The Salis-Samade regiment went to the further end of Sèvres, in the direction of Versailles; the terrified inhabitants refused to open their doors. As the night was very wet we forced open some of these and took up makeshift lodgings for that night, in the hopes of being more decently accommodated next day.'[1] Contact with the inhabitants on whom they were billeted increased the tendency of the troops to insubordination and defection. The author of the log-book goes on to say: 'The events of the 15th were disastrous for the Salis-Samade regiment and the other regiments that had been sent to Sèvres. The districts which our regiment had previously occupied around

[1] Arch. de la Guerre, *Mémoires historiques*, vols. no. 619 to 626.

Paris being contiguous to Sèvres, and the soldiers having formed strong attachments to their former hosts and hostesses, who came over to Sèvres in crowds to invite them to take refreshment and rest at their homes, a considerable number of men accepted these invitations unsuspectingly, and the more eagerly because they were most uncomfortably situated at present, and because having left a large proportion of their belongings in these villages they intended to remove these before being sent even further away. They were so generously entertained in their former quarters at Issy, Vaugirard and Vanves that they were made completely drunk, and were then carted off to Paris, several who did not submit willingly being forced to follow their guides with pistols aimed at their throats.' It was on this occasion that 75 soldiers of this regiment deserted. It is probable that similar desertions took place from other regiments.

At all events, on July 15th Marshal de Broglie had to admit that the soldiers 'would not fight against their fellow-citizens'. Gouverneur Morris, the future United States Ambassador in Paris, concluded that the troops 'would not serve against their country . . .' and that consequently the King's plans 'could not be carried into effect.'[1]

2. The King's capitulation

It was not until the morning of the 15th that the King became aware of the situation. He seems to have been deeply impressed by Liancourt's account of the deaths of de Launey and Flesselles.[2] Liancourt then convinced him that it was imperative for him to approach the Assembly, and even perhaps the insurgent authorities in Paris. The King consented to visit the Assembly, and Liancourt went off to warn the deputies of his coming.

It so happened that they had been debating the events in Paris and had just decided to send an address to the King asking him to get rid of those who had advised him to dismiss Necker, 'that virtuous minister who had dedicated himself to his [the King's] glory and the welfare of the Nation.' The chosen deputies were about to leave when Mirabeau addressed them in words that have become famous: '*Eh bien*, tell the King that the foreign hordes by

---

[1] Gouverneur Morris, *Diary and Letters*, I, p. 151.
[2] *The Papers of Thomas Jefferson*, vol. XV. Jefferson to John Jay, Paris, July 19th, pp. 284–291.

whom we are surrounded were visited yesterday by princes, princesses, favourites of both sexes, who made much of them, exhorted them and gave them presents; tell him that all night long these foreign satellites, gorged with gold and wine, foretold in their impious songs the enslavement of France and with savage vows called for the destruction of the Assembly; tell him that in his very palace courtiers danced to this barbarous music, and that a scene such as this preceded the massacre of St Bartholomew. Tell him that Henri IV of blessed memory, that ancestor of his on whom he sought to model himself, conveyed provisions into insurgent Paris while himself besieging it, whereas our King's ruthless councillors deny entry into the loyal and starving city of the flour brought thither by lawful trade.' The delegation was about to set forth after his speech when the duc de Liancourt announced the King's arrival. Loud applause broke forth, but Mirabeau silenced it by resuming his speech: 'Wait until the King has let us know the friendly intentions which we are led to expect from him; let a bleak respect be our first greeting to our monarch in this distressful moment . . . The people's silence is a lesson for kings.' In fact, the King's intentions were not as favourable as the deputies had hoped. Louis announced neither the dismissal of Breteuil's ministry nor the recall of Necker. He confined himself to denying the project of violent action against the Assembly and its members which had been imputed to him, and ended by saying: 'I have ordered the troops to withdraw from Paris and Versailles; I authorize you, nay I invite you to inform the capital of my intentions.' Bailly notes that Louis used for the first time the expression *Assemblée nationale* instead of the term *États*. However, in his diary, the King notes for July 15th: 'Session at the Salle des États, returning on foot.' In fact he did return to the Palace on foot, accompanied by a large number of deputies, and amid a cheering crowd. The Queen herself appeared on the balcony of the Cour de Marbre, and was greeted with applause. In any case, if the King had accepted the withdrawal of the troops from Paris, as ordered by Besenval, he had as yet given no order for these, or those quartered at Versailles, to return to their provincial garrisons. None the less Jefferson considered the King's action, and his speech to the Assembly, as 'a surrender at discretion.'[1] After the King's departure the Assembly proceeded, in accordance with his request, to appoint a

[1] *Ibid.*, Jefferson to John Mason, Paris, July 16th 1789, p. 278.

delegation for the purpose of conveying his assurances to the people of Paris. Eighty-eight deputies were appointed, and instructed to do their utmost to restore calm in the capital, to strengthen the civic guard and to proclaim everywhere that the King had guaranteed the withdrawal of the troops from Paris.

The arrival of this considerable deputation from the National Assembly produced excellent results. The Parisians as yet knew nothing of the King's intentions, except what Dupont de Nemours had told them at two o'clock in the morning. They were not clearly aware of the attitude of the troops. We have seen that during the whole of the night of July 14th they had apprehended a counter-offensive by the troops from Versailles, and these fears had by no means been dispelled by the morning of the 15th. People were still tearing up paving stones and building barricades. The workers had not resumed work, and indeed many workshops were closed. On the 15th the Permanent Committee opened a fund to subsidize *ateliers de charité* (charity workshops). Moreover the food situation in the capital had not improved since Sunday the 12th, in spite of the burning of the customs posts. We have seen how Mirabeau contrasted the attitude of Henri IV, who allowed foodstuffs to be smuggled through to the beleaguered Parisians, with that of Louis XVI, who deliberately starved the capital. At the Hôtel de Ville, it was reckoned that Paris had only enough food for three days. And so the announcement of the arrival of a large deputation from the National Assembly was greeted at first with incredulity, and then with joy.

The delegates drove off from Versailles 'in a large number of carriages', as Bailly tells us, 'while all Versailles gathered round to watch our departure, which was like a public festival. We left in splendid weather and our journey was a continuous triumph. At several spots we encountered troops which were withdrawing, the road was crowded with people, and everywhere cries of *Vive la Nation!* greeted us as we passed. We thus made our way to the place Louis XV, where we alighted to cross the Tuileries.' Further on, in the streets of Paris, 'an immense crowd ... every window crammed, everything very orderly, and on all sides unfeigned and open enthu-siasm, greetings and blessings as we passed, tears and cries of *Vive la nation! Vive le roi! Vive les députés!*' Red, blue and white cock-ades were handed to them; they were surrounded and embraced.'[1]

[1] Bailly, *Mémoires*, vol. II, pp. 17–18.

At the Hôtel de Ville, La Fayette, vice-president of the National Assembly, declared that the King had been misled, but was now undeceived. He read the speech that Louis had made that morning. Moreau de Saint-Méry, a former member of the *Conseil supérieur* of San Domingo and now second President of the Electoral Assembly, answered, bidding La Fayette convey to the King the respect and loyalty of the Assembly. The latter, which had definitely assumed the role and functions of a municipal authority, acclaimed Bailly 'Mayor' of Paris and La Fayette general of the Parisian citizens' militia, which was soon to take the name of National Guard.

Deputies and electors then made their way to Notre-Dame, where a Te Deum was sung at which the Archbishop of Paris officiated. But the people who lined the streets did not seem satisfied with the King's promises, of which they had just been informed; they loudly clamoured for the dismissal of Breteuil's government and the recall of Necker.

At Versailles, moreover, the National Assembly, whose earlier enthusiasm had cooled, was expressing similar wishes. Barnave, deputy for the Dauphiné, put forward a motion demanding the departure of the ministers and the return of Necker. He declared that the honour of the Assembly required it to anticipate the people of Paris, who would shortly make known their demands. Mirabeau supported Barnave, but Clermont-Tonnerre asserted that 'on so happy a day, the King must be allowed to enjoy in silence the happiness of ruling over so loyal a nation. God forbid', he said, 'that I should try to defend such ministers, God forbid that I should seek to prevent their indictment, but on so happy an occasion it does not become the dignity of the Assembly to concern itself with so despicable a set of ministers.' The discussion was therefore adjourned to the next day.

July 16th was to be the day of the King's decision, for in spite of the assurances he had given on the morning of the 15th he had as yet taken no resolution, and he by no means considered himself defeated. The Court, of course, had learnt on the evening of the 15th of the clamours arising in the streets of Paris and of Barnave's motion in the Assembly. On the morning of the 16th, when the Assembly resumed its discussions about the Government, Louis XVI was presiding over an important council.

In the Assembly, Mirabeau began by reading the draft of an

July 17th, 1789. A memorable day

Bibl. Nat., Print Room, Vinck Collection, 1733

July 17th, 1789. Louis XVI at the Hôtel de Ville

Bibl. Nat., Print Room, Vinck Collection, 1744

address demanding the dismissal of the ministers. Barnave proposed to add: 'and the recall of M. Necker'. Lally-Tollendal won general support when he declared: 'Messieurs, as we have seen and heard, in the streets and squares, on the *quais* and market-places, the cry was "Bring back Necker". The whole vast population was begging us to ask the King for M. Necker. The people's request is an order. We must therefore demand the recall of M. Necker.' For the first time in any French assembly, the theory of Parliamentary rule had thus been suggested.[1] But before the Assembly had time to vote, the results of the Council held by the King were made known.

This Council had been attended by the Queen, the Counts of Provence and Artois and all the ministers. At the King's suggestion they had first examined the possibilities of resistance. The Minister for War, Marshal de Broglie, then informed them of the attitude of the troops and the impossibility, for the time being, of reconquering Paris. Failing this solution, could not the King take refuge in some provincial stronghold, protected by loyal troops, and have the Estates-General transferred thither? Such a project had already been considered on June 23rd. Marie-Antoinette insisted that the King should settle at Metz, under the protection of the army.[2] But Marshal de Broglie declared that he could not guarantee the safe passage of the royal family through a country the whole of which was in a state of insurgency, escorted by troops that were ready to side with the rioters. Later, after his emigration, de Broglie denied having opposed the plan of moving to Metz. But Louis XVI himself declared to Fersen, when in February 1792 he was considering a plan for escape: 'I know I missed my opportunity; that was on July 14th. I ought to have gone away then, and I wanted to, but what could I do when Monsieur [i.e. the comte de Provence] himself begged me not to leave, and the maréchal de Broglie, who was in command, replied to me: "Yes, we may go to Metz, but what shall we do when we get there?" I missed my opportunity, and I've never found it again.'[3] The King's younger brother, the comte d'Artois, did not miss his. He left Paris during the evening of the 16th, accompanied by his wife, his mistress, the

---

[1] On this subject see R. K. Gooch, *Parliamentary Government in France, 1789–1791*, Ithaca, 1960.

[2] *Mémoires de Mme Campan*, vol. II, pp. 52–53.

[3] Ferson's *Journal*, published by Klinckowström in *Le Comte de Fersen et la Cour de France*, Paris, 1878, vol. II, p. 6.

Polignacs and the abbé de Vermond, Marie-Antoinette's confidant for the past twenty years.

Resistance on the spot and departure for the provinces being equally out of the question, there was nothing for it but to submit. In the words of Joseph de Maistre, which have often been repeated: 'Few battles are lost physically. Defeat is almost always a matter of morale. The real victor, or the real loser, is the man who believes he has won or lost.'[1] Until that Council meeting on the morning of July 16th Louis XVI had not believed himself to be defeated. He was now convinced of his defeat, and he had to accept all the consequences of it, to drink the bitter cup of capitulation. The first step, which was promptly taken, was to inform the Assembly of his decision to dismiss the Government and recall Necker, and to prevent the deputies from voting on the motion put forward by Barnave, Mirabeau and Lally-Tollendal. The Assembly greeted the King's news with loud applause. Next he must recall Necker; the comte de Provence, who was at this time trying to play a revolutionary hand,[2] was entrusted with this mission. Finally he must give the order to withdraw the troops concentrated around Paris and Versailles. This order, which is preserved among the War Archives, is in fact dated July 16th.[3] It orders 6 regiments of French infantry, 9 regiments of foreign infantry, 5 of French cavalry, 2 of foreign cavalry and 2 battalions of artillery to leave Paris and its neighbourhood on July 16th and 17th and make for garrisons on the frontier: Arras, Nancy, Givet, Saint-Avold, Verdun, Philippeville, Metz, Douai, Saint-Omer, Sarrelouis, Montmédy, Toul, Condé-sur-Escaut, Maubeuge, Rocroy, Charleville. The War Minister, Marshal de Broglie, himself left Versailles on the evening of the 16th, and on the 17th led a column of 4 Swiss regiments, together with the Royal-Allemand, skirting Paris on their way north through Saint-Denis.[4]

The dismissal of the Ministers, the withdrawal of the troops and the recall of Necker were not enough to reassure the people of Paris. They wanted the King himself to come, and by his presence confirm the victory of the Revolution and the defeat of the old régime. As the Duke of Dorset, the British ambassador, informed

[1] Joseph de Maistre, *Correspondance diplomatique*, for the year 1812.
[2] Gérard Walter, *Le Comte de Provence*, Paris, 1950.
[3] Arch. de la Guerre, A 4, 55.
[4] Arch. de la Guerre, *Mémoires historiques*, vols. 619–626. Log-book of the Salis-Samade regiment.

his government on July 16th, the King's failure to appear that day was attributed to indisposition. But the people were not convinced, and it was generally believed, according to the ambassador, that a troop of armed citizens some 50,000 strong would go to Versailles to bring him back by force.[1] This was not to take place until some two and a half months later. But we have seen that on the morning of July 15th the duc de Liancourt had tried to urge the King to go to Paris, which, on the 17th, he decided to do. Fearing lest an attempt might be made on his life during the journey, or lest he should be seized as a hostage, he said his prayers before leaving, and handed over full powers, during his absence from Versailles, to the comte de Provence, with the title of Lieutenant-general of the Kingdom. He left, accompanied by a few officers of his household, a few bodyguards, 32 deputies selected by lot, and a huge crowd of working-class people, 'Savoyards [chimney-sweeps], beggars and fishwives.'[2] The procession moved slowly and took four hours to reach the *barrière* of Chaillot. A delegation of electors, led by Bailly, was awaiting the King. Bailly made a short speech in which he said that 'Henri IV had won back his people, whereas now the people had won back their King.' Then the procession resumed its march through the place Louis XV and the rue Saint-Honoré as far as the Hôtel de Ville. 'The way was lined on both sides', writes Bailly, 'by national guards armed with guns, swords, pikes, lances, scythes, sticks, etc. There were women, monks and friars all carrying guns! The utmost order was maintained everywhere, nobody broke ranks or stepped out of line, although an immense crowd of spectators was standing behind. The air rang with continuous shouts of *Vive la Nation! Vive le Roi! Vive Messieurs Bailly, La Fayette, les députés, les électeurs!* and these cries mingled with the sound of trumpets, of military music, and of gunfire wherever the artillery were placed.'[3] Jefferson comments: 'A more dangerous scene of war I never saw in America than what Paris has presented for five days past. This places the power of the States General absolutely out of reach of attack, and they may be considered as having a carte blanche.'[4] Barère, who was in the procession, notes that there were many hostile cries as

[1] See J. Flammermont, *Relations inédites de la prise de la Bastille . . ., op. cit.*
[2] *Journal de M. de Gauville*, pp. 12–13.
[3] Bailly, *Mémoires*, vol. II, p. 57 ff.
[4] *The Papers of Thomas Jefferson*, vol. XV, Jefferson to Thomas Paine, Paris, July 17th, p. 279.

well as cheers: 'Before we got to the Hôtel de Ville we had great difficulty, in certain districts, in restraining the indignation of citizens provoked beyond measure by the serious motives that had caused their insurrection.'[1] The Austrian ambassador, Mercy-Argenteau, also notes the hostility of the King's reception: 'It is certain that during his journey there were very few cries of *Vive le roi*, and that even in the city it was seldom heard, whereas on all sides there were shouts of *Vive la Nation*.'[2]

At the Hôtel de Ville the King was received 'with solemn severity; when the people is in an angry and threatening mood, it does not pay court or flatter.' Bailly offered the King the tri-coloured cockade which, since July 16th, had become the emblem of the insurgents; when it was learnt that the King was withdrawing troops from Paris, the white of the Bourbon monarchy had been added to the red and blue that were the colours of the city of Paris. 'Sire', said Bailly, 'I have the honour to offer your Majesty the distinctive emblem of the French nation.' The King accepted it with good grace and placed it in his hat: the new national emblem was born, as a result of the revolution of July 14th.

Next the King mounted the stairs, under an arch of steel formed by the bared swords of the national guards; this arch has been interpreted as a Masonic symbol, but it had probably become a traditional habit with no very precise meaning attached to it. When he came into the main hall, the King listened to a number of speeches. Then he tried to speak himself, but he was not accustomed to impromptu oratory. He mumbled a few words: 'You can always rely on my affection . . . I am most satisfied, I agree to the establishment of the citizens' guard . . . Monsieur Bailly, I am very glad that you should be Mayor and M. de La Fayette commander-in-chief. . . .' Next Louis, wearing the tricolour cockade in his hat, appeared on the balcony and was greeted with cheers. He then began the return journey, following the same route, and reached Versailles at ten in the evening. 'He was conducted by a *garde bourgeoise* to his palace at Versailles', writes Thomas Jefferson, 'and thus concluded such an *Amende*

---

[1] Barère, *Mémoires*, Paris, 1842–1844.
[2] See J. Flammermont, *Relations inédites de la prise de la Bastille . . . op. cit.*, letter from Mercy-Argenteau dated July 23rd. Cf. a letter from Jefferson to John Jay on July 19th.

honorable as no sovereign ever made, and no people ever received.'[1]

The excitement aroused by the victory of the French people and the King's humiliation was immense. The foreign ambassadors and travellers visiting France were the first to realize this and to spread the news in their own countries. On July 16th the British ambassador, the Duke of Dorset, wrote to tell the Foreign Minister in England that the greatest revolution known to history had taken place with relatively little bloodshed, that France was now a free country where the King's powers were limited and the nobility was on a level with the rest of the nation.[2]

On July 23rd the comte de Mercy-Argenteau informed the Austrian Minister, Kaunitz: 'However unbelievable the Revolution that has just been accomplished may appear, it is none the less absolutely certain that from now on the city of Paris has assumed the role of a King in France, and that it can, if it pleases, send an army of forty to fifty thousand citizens to surround the Assembly and dictate the laws to it.'[3] The Ambassador of Saxony, Salmour, writes on July 19th of 'this important and extraordinary revolution which cannot fail to bring about a considerable change in the political system of France.'[4] The Portuguese Ambassador declared on July 20th that 'in all the world's annals there is no mention of a revolution like this one . . . If he had not witnessed it he would not dare to describe it, for fear the truth should be considered as a fable. A King of France in an army coach, surrounded by the bayonets and muskets of a huge crowd, finally forced to display on his hat the cockade of liberty.'[5] The Russian Minister, Simolin, asserted: 'The Revolution has taken place in France and the royal power no longer exists.'[6] As for Gouverneur Morris, he wrote to Washington on July 31st: 'You may consider the Revolution as complete; that is to say, the authority of the King and of the nobility is completely subdued.'[7] Among private observers, an English doctor named Rigby who happened to be in Paris at the

[1] *The Papers of Thomas Jefferson*, vol. XV, pp. 284–291. Jefferson to John Jay, July 19th 1789.
[2] See Flammermont, *Relations inédites . . .*, op. cit., p. 20.
[3] *Ibid.*, p. 20.
[4] Dresden Archives, Salmour to Stutterheim, July 19th, quoted by J. Flammermont, *Le 14 Juillet*, op. cit., p. cclxxiii.
[5] Archives of the Ministry of Foreign Affairs in Lisbon. Dispatch from Don Vicente Souza Coutinho, quoted by J. Flammermont, *ibid.*, p. cclxxxiii.
[6] Feuillet de Conches, *Louis XVI et Marie-Antoinette*, vol. I, p. 476.
[7] Gouverneur Morris, *Diary and Letters*, I, p. 143.

time is one of the most perspicacious. He writes to his wife: 'I have been witness to the most extraordinary revolution that perhaps ever took place in human society. A great and wise people struggled for freedom and the rights of humanity; their courage, prudence and perseverance have been rewarded by success, and an event which will contribute to the happiness and prosperity of millions of their descendants has taken place with very little loss of blood, and with but few days' interruption to the common business of the place.'[1]

Foreign newspapers carried many accounts of the taking of the Bastille, particularly in the United States, Holland, Germany and even Russia.[2] In fact, as the German Heinrich Steffens put it, 'it was not merely a French revolution but a European revolution.'[3] For those who did not read the papers because they were illiterate, stage plays and even dumb shows served to reveal the importance of July 14th and to reconstitute, in *tableaux vivants*, its principal episodes, which were further popularized in countless pictures, drawings and engravings. In France, at least three plays were based on the fall of the Bastille: *La Prise de la Bastille ou la liberté conquise*, a 'national' play in four acts by P. David, performed in 1790 for the anniversary of the event; *La Prise de la Bastille*, described as a 'hierodrame', with words and music by M.-A. Désaugiers, written 'by order of the National Assembly' and performed on July 13th, 1790; and *La Prise de la Bastille*, 'a historic event, in Three acts, in prose interspersed with songs, words by P.-M. Parein, music by M. . . . A. . . .', Paris, 1791.[4] In England and in Ireland, between 1789 and 1793 at least two plays and one dumb-show performance are recorded.[5] For France and for the whole world, the *journée* of July 14th, and that of July 17th which profited from its results, signified the end of the 'feudal' régime—which was shortly to be known as the *ancien régime*—and the advent of a new society for which the National

---

[1] *Dr Rigby's Letters, op. cit.*, p. 28.

[2] See M.-N. Strange, *La Société russe et la Révolution française*, Moscow, 1961, pp. 54–56.

[3] Quoted by Oncken, *Das Zeitalter der Revolution*, p. 210.

[4] See J.-A. Rivoire, *Le Patriotisme dans le théâtre sérieux de la Révolution*, Paris, 1950.

[5] J. H. Stewart, 'The Fall of the Bastille on the Dublin Stage', in *The Journal of the Royal Society of Antiquaries of Ireland*, 1954, vol. LXXXIV, pp. 78–91.

Assembly was to have the dangerous duty of planning the structure and establishing the laws.

3. The destruction of the Bastille

We cannot close this study without telling what happened to the Bastille and its inmates. We have said that the prisoners were set free by the besiegers as soon as the latter had penetrated the fortress. The insurgents, indeed, were greatly surprised to find so few prisoners. Many of them believed that there were others hidden in secret underground dungeons. The engineer of the City of Paris was sent to visit the vaults and cells. He found that these were empty and that no secret subterranean passage existed. On July 18th the four jailers of the Bastille were interrogated separately. They confirmed that on the 14th the Bastille had held only seven prisoners: Solages, Whyte, Tavernier, Béchade, La Corrège, Pujade and Laroche. The four latter, common law prisoners accused of forgery, quickly disappeared and were never found again. The comte de Solages had been shut up at the request of his family. He was transferred to the Oratoire district, 'where he expressed his gratitude in the most touching terms', and installed in the Hôtel de Rouen, lodged and fed at the expense of the district; he soon left Paris, however, and returned to Languedoc. Whyte was an Englishman, who was a little mad. He was wearing a long beard on July 14th, and when he was carried through Paris in triumph with the rest of the prisoners, he was greeted as another Latude, the representative, in a way, of all those who had spent long years in the dungeons of despotism. But once the parade was over, his insanity had to be admitted, and on July 15th he was confined to Charenton. Tavernier was also mad, but this was only noticed five days later, on July 20th, when he too was sent to Charenton.

The reality was far removed from the sinister descriptions published by Linguet and Latude. However, people sought to add a romantic note—and the word is scarcely anachronistic, in connection with their period—by describing to the public, with a wealth of horrible details, the stench of the dungeons furnished only with a few bundles of damp straw, the iron chains and instruments of torture. A suit of fifteenth-century armour, found in the Bastille, was christened 'iron corset intended to maintain prisoners in total immobility'. A toothed wheel was presented as having served to torture prisoners: it was actually a printing press, confiscated in 1786. Bones were also found on the cellar floors when the fortress was demolished. These were possibly the remains of prisoners who had died in the fifteenth or sixteenth centuries, or of soldiers killed during one of the many sieges to which the Bastille had been subjected: by the Armagnacs in 1413, by the Burgundians in 1418, by the King of France in 1436, by Condé in 1565, by the Catholic League in 1591, or during the Fronde, in 1649 and 1652, by the royal troops. But they were said to belong to a prisoner who had died in an oubliette, possibly the man in the iron mask! Many prints were produced to illustrate the stories.

What was to be done with the Bastille? As we have seen, there had been proposals to destroy it several years previously, because it was too expensive to keep up and served no useful purpose.

A contractor named Palloy had already offered his services before 1789 to the city of Paris. Needless to say, he promptly renewed his offer on July 15th, claiming (quite unjustifiably) that he had played an important part in the previous day's events. On July 16th the Permanent Committee, at the Hôtel de Ville, decided that 'the Bastille should be demolished without delay, after a visit by two architects entrusted with this operation, under orders from M. le marquis de La Salle, responsible for taking the necessary measures to prevent accidents. And in order to give notice of the present decree, four electors, accompanied by two deputies to the National Assembly now in session at the Hôtel de Ville, shall immediately make their way to the Bastille.' The demolition operation was entrusted to Palloy, who henceforward assumed the title and signature of 'the patriot Palloy'. He signed on more than a thousand workmen, including a large number of unemployed. The demolition of the Bastille thus helped to relieve, to some extent, the economic crisis that was brewing. The first step was to remove the powder, arms, furniture and archives still stored in the Bastille; these were transferred to the Arsenal. Then the demolition began. On February 6th, 1790 the last stone of the Bastille was presented to the National Assembly.

But what was to be done with the demolished remains? Here Palloy had an inspiration. Instead of transporting them to some rubbish dump, he bought them very cheap and began to transform every stone, every scrap of old iron into 'souvenirs of the Bastille', which he then sold. The stones were carved so as to represent a relief plan of the fortress; the first model thus produced was presented to the Constituent Assembly on September 2nd, 1790. The new local authorities created by the Assembly proved ready customers. The carved stones were transported into the provinces by certain more or less authentic 'conquerors of the Bastille' who called themselves 'apostles of Liberty'. They also took along with them a paving-stone from a cell, a map with the description of the fortress, a ball-and-chain and a cuirass found in the Bastille, the Life of Latude and Dusaulx's *Oeuvre des sept jours*, which as we have seen had become the official story of the revolution of July 14th, a picture representing the skeletons found during the destruction of the fortress, and another showing its demolition, with, in the background, Palloy hanging the portrait of Bailly on the pedestal of Louis XVI's statue, in the presence of La Fayette. A first consignment consisted of 246 parcels, three for each department. At the principal town of each department a grand demonstration was organized to welcome the 'stones of the Bastille'. These were presented gratis to the authorities, who however had to pay the cost of transport, calculated so as to ensure a handsome profit for Palloy. The 'apostles of Liberty' thus travelled through the whole 'French empire' during the year 1791. Other carved stones were sold to the numerous new local authorities which were constantly being created: new magistracies, district and departmental tribunals, municipal administrations, district administrations and so forth. It must be remembered that in 1790 France comprised 83 departments, 547 districts and 6,000 cantons.

Palloy had the 'irons' of the Bastille made into medals, dice-boxes, snuff-boxes, paper-weights, sweetmeat-boxes, inkpots, keys and lock-plates; the paper found in the Bastille was used to make packs of cards, or fans on which were painted the scenes of July 14th.

Proposals had already been made before 1789, as we have said, to erect a monument on the site of the Bastille. Palloy drafted several designs; the column that was eventually set up there after 1830 was inspired by one of his suggestions.

Under the Empire, Palloy became a conspicuous supporter of the régime, which did not prevent him from rallying to the

Bourbon cause in 1814 and that of Louis-Philippe in 1830. He died, practically ruined, in 1835.[1]

The besiegers of the Bastille were duly rewarded. On June 19th, 1790, the National Assembly passed the following decree: 'Stirred by legitimate admiration for the heroic intrepidity of the conquerors of the Bastille, and wishing to give public recognition in the name of the Nation, to those who have exposed and sacrificed their lives to shake off the yoke of slavery and bring freedom to their country, the Assembly decrees that each of the conquerors of the Bastille who is able to bear arms shall receive, at public expense, a coat and a complete set of weapons, according to the uniform of the Nation; that on the barrel of the gun and on the blade of the sword there shall be engraved the escutcheon of the Nation, with an inscription that these arms have been given by the Nation to so-and-so, conqueror of the Bastille, and that the coat shall be embroidered with a crown, either on the left sleeve or beside the left lapel; that to each of the said conquerors there shall be sent an honourable certificate describing his services and the gratitude of the Nation, and that in any deed he may sign he shall be entitled to assume the title of Conqueror of the Bastille . . . An honourable certificate shall similarly be sent to those conquerors of the Bastille who are not capable of bearing arms, to the widows and children of those who have died, as a public record of the gratitude and honour due to those who have brought about the triumph of liberty over despotism'. We have seen that 954 citizens were declared to be 'conquerors of the Bastille'. Many enrolled in the National Guard, and later formed part of the national gendarmerie. They were to form the shock troops of the Revolution, to remain vigilant guardians of the country's newly-acquired liberty, and resist any attempted return of despotism.[2]

[1] G. Dubois-Desaulle, 'L'entreprise de démolition de la Bastille', in *La Revue Blanche*, 1902, vol. XXVIII, pp. 401–412. H. Lemoine, 'Les comptes de démolition de la Bastille', in the *Bulletin de la Société de l'Histoire de Paris et de l'Île-de-France* 1929, pp. 77–83; Id., *Le Démolisseur de la Bastille, son histoire de 1789 à nos jours*, Paris, 1930; Romi, *Le livre de raison du patriote Palloy*, Paris, 1962; Id., 'La méprise de la Bastille' in *Le Nouveau Candide*, no. 167, July 8th and 15th, 1964.

[2] J. Durieux, *Les Vainqueurs de la Bastille, op. cit.*

XI

Conclusion:
The Significance of the Taking of the Bastille

What is the real meaning of the events that took place in Paris during that memorable week, July 11th to 17th, 1789? Those who, at the time, took an over-simple view of things—and there were many such, as there are today, in every social class and in every political party—interpreted these events as the result of a plot. The partisans of the monarchy denounced a conspiracy of free-masons or *philosophes*, or else of supporters of the duc d'Orléans. This idea found expression as early as 1789 and was later developed, particularly by the abbé Barruel.[1] The theory attracted many people, and still finds its adherents today. It is based on arguments which seem well-founded. Did not the Parisian uprising begin, on July 12th, in the Palais-Royal, property of the duc d'Orléans, Grand Master of French freemasons? Did it not conclude, on July 17th, with Louis XVI's forced passage up the staircase of the Hôtel de Ville, under the 'Masonic' arch of steel? Everything would seem to have been contrived by the Freemasons, carrying out the ideas of the *philosophes*. But this theory ignores the fact that French masonic lodges at the end of the eighteenth century were composed of nobles, members of the clergy and of the upper bourgeoisie, and included none of those working class people who formed the overwhelming majority of the Parisian insurgents in July.[2]

[1] Abbé Barruel, *Mémoires pour servir à l'histoire du Jacobinisme*, Hamburg, 1798, 5 vols., 8vo. But Barruel had expounded his thesis as early as 1789 in *Le Patriote véridique ou Discours sur les vraies causes de la Révolution actuelle*. See J. Godechod, *La Contre-révolution*, Paris, 1961, pp. 46–53.
[2] Alain Le Bihan, *Francs-maçons parisiens du Grand-Orient de France*

Conclusion : The Significance of The Taking of the Bastille

Recognizing the truth of this objection, certain authors, at the end of the eighteenth century and later, reduced or eliminated the role of freemasonry and interpreted the rising of July 14th as a riot instigated by the duc d'Orléans. Strange stories were told, mysterious remarks reported which implied an invisible leader behind the Parisian insurrection. The Venetian envoy, Antonio Capello, wrote of the duc d'Orléans on July 6th: 'His intentions are suspect, and his tolerance towards what takes place in his residence [the Palais-Royal] is condemned by all persons of good sense.' He added that the orators who harangued the people in the gardens of the Palais were 'certainly in the pay of this unworthy man'. Similarly the *bailli* de Virieu, Minister of Parma, asserted on July 13th: 'It has been conjectured, not without good reason, that the disturbances have been provoked by a person of the highest rank. We blush to name him. He is a disgrace to the Nation and to the blood that flows in his veins. The vile creatures that serve as his tools were at first paid thirty sous a day, now they can be got for twenty.' Later, in connection with the enquiry into the origin of the events of October 5th and 6th, when the King and Queen were brought back to Paris by force, three deputies to the National Assembly, Tailhardat de la Maisonneuve, Dufraisse (both from Riom) and Guilhermy, of Castelnaudary, repeated a conversation they claimed to have heard between Malouet and Coroller, deputy for Hennebont: 'You would have achieved nothing,' Malouet is supposed to have said, 'without the defection of the *gardes-françaises* and the troops.' 'We were sure of the troops,' Coroller replied, 'we had had contacts in every regiment for a long time past.' 'Nonetheless you would certainly have failed, if the Court had not made the mistake of dismissing M. Necker.' 'That event only speeded up our achievement. We were assured of arming Paris, and to that end the Palais-Bourbon was to be set on fire.' While according to another statement made during this enquiry, Mirabeau declared: 'His [the duc d'Orléans'] timidity made him miss great opportunities; he was to have been made Lieutenant-general of the kingdom; it was entirely up to him, he had been told what to say.' Mounier, who had emigrated to Geneva, declared in July 1790 that a 'faction' existed which sought to give the throne to the duc d'Orléans. All these comments, which in fact refer to

(Commission d'Histoire économique et sociale de la Révolution française, *Mémoires et documents*, vol. XIX, Paris, 1966.

the events of October rather than to those of July, are unimportant.[1] Nevertheless there are still some people who are convinced of the considerable, and even essential, role played by the duc d'Orléans and his circle.[2] In actual fact the great objection to be made to the thesis of a Masonic or Orleanist plot is that the Parisian revolution was not an isolated phenomenon. It was only a link, although an important one, in the chain of revolutionary events that had been taking place in France since 1787 and that were to go on after July 14th. But for the revolt in the French provinces, from 1787 onwards, there would surely have been no Fourteenth of July, and but for the capture of the Bastille the peasant rising of July–August 1789 would probably not have taken place.

But supporters of the plot theory are not to be found only among the adversaries of the Revolution. Certain historians who are sympathetic towards it also seek to account for the Parisian rising by a conspiracy: the 'nobles' plot', which was aimed at preventing the Revolution. The Parisian insurrection, according to this view, was an answer to this conspiracy. The idea of a 'nobles' plot' had, as we have seen, been spreading throughout France since the middle of May, when the Estates-General had seemed smitten with paralysis. The closing of the salle des Menus-Plaisirs on June 20th, the Royal Session of June 23rd, the mustering of troops, particularly foreign troops, around Paris at the beginning of July, and finally the dismissal of Necker, had all given further plausibility to the theory. But can we believe that the Court, Marshal de Broglie, Besenval and the *intendant* of Paris, Bertier de Sauvigny, had formed a plot to attack Paris and gain possession of the city by force? This was asserted by the Committee set up in August by the *commune* of Paris to investigate the 'conspiracy of the preceding months of May, June and July'. Their report even asserts that 'at Versailles, people had seen the gridirons for heating the cannon-balls' which were to set the capital ablaze. In fact there never was a nobles' 'plot' in the usual sense of the word. Louis XVI, the Queen, the princes and their entourage wanted to close down the Estates-General, by virtue of their traditional right, when they saw that this purely consultative assembly could no longer continue its sessions owing to disagreement between the three orders. But what had seemed legal in 1614 no longer appeared so in

[1] They are quoted by J. Mistler, *Le 14 Juillet, op. cit.*, pp. 31–36.
[2] See particularly B. Faÿ, *La Grande Révolution*, Paris, 1959.

Conclusion : The Significance of The Taking of the Bastille

1789. The Estates-General was by now considered not as a body representing 'orders' but as an assembly of the deputies of the whole nation. Any attempt to interfere with its meetings seemed a plot against the Nation. But public opinion, which readily accepted this interpretation, could scarcely imagine that the King, the Princes and even the nobility would do so too. So that the victory of July 14th not only did not invalidate the idea of a plot, it even strengthened it. Since the King and the nobility had not been powerful enough to oppose the popular rising in July, they were assumed to have sought foreign allies to defeat the Revolution. The examples of the Genevan patricians in 1782, and of the stadthouder of the Netherlands in 1787 justified this belief. We read in the *Mémoire des faits authentiques*:[1] 'How did it happen that the finest monarchy in the world . . . was suddenly shaken and overthrown even to its foundations? . . . For . . . Louis XVI is now merely his people's plaything, a mere stage king . . . How is it that Spain and the other branches of the House of Bourbon, which in spite of their professed renunciation have an interest in preventing the dissolution of the French monarchy, and the Emperor, who must wish to avenge his sister's injuries, and the King of Sardinia, to protect the honour of his son-in-law, have not all combined in a common cause and sent formidable armies against the rebels?' This was what many Frenchmen thought, and dreaded. The idea of an aristocratic plot, reinforced by a foreign plot, was to provoke many other popular movements in France during the revolutionary period, and to generate many risings. But there was in fact no plot, either aristocratic or Masonic, either foreign or Orleanist. The explanation of events by a conspiracy has always appealed to the masses because it seems a simple one. But things are always infinitely more complicated—particularly revolutions, which involve so many people and such diverse interests.

If the uprising of July 14th was not the result of a plot, if it was not the reaction to a plot, neither was it a violent riot by the Parisian population alone. As we have said, it takes its place in the context of an infinitely wider revolutionary movement. Under these conditions, can one wonder, as P. Chauvet has done,[2] if the

[1] *Histoire authentique et suivie de la Révolution de France ou Correspondance avec un étranger*, 'Mémoire des faits authentiques concernant la Bastille', letter 1, September 29th 1789.
[2] P. Chauvet, *L'Insurrection parisienne et la prise de la Bastille*, Paris, 1946.

Conclusion : The Significance of The Taking of the Bastille

Parisian proletariat, which provided the bulk of the rioters, failed to take advantage of the rising to seize power? Let us first point out that the term *proletariat* is ambiguous with reference to 1789. It is quite true, as we have seen, that some five-sixths of the insurgents consisted of artisans, workers who were independent but poor, if we are to judge by the analysis of the social structure of the 'conquerors of the Bastille'. It is moreover certain that the Permanent Committee and the Assembly of Electors endeavoured without delay, after July 14th, to keep power out of the hands of this class. On the 15th, the Assembly of Electors gave strict orders for the re-establishment of entry duties, under supervision by the Parisian militia. Thus it nullified what the Parisian workers had sought to achieve when they burnt down the customs posts. The Assembly, furthermore, took steps to disarm these workers. It offered to buy up all available muskets, hoping that this financial bait would induce the many *gens sans aveu* (vagabonds) who had got hold of firearms to hand these over. Thus, on July 18th, it 'invited workers to resume their tasks, and fixed the price to be paid them for the arms they brought back, provided they could show a certificate from the master for whom they had resumed work.' It cannot be doubted that the bourgeoisie lost no time in trying to appropriate the victory won by the workers of Paris. But could the latter have seized power themselves? True, the Réveillon riots on April 28th had looked like a revolt of the poor against the rich. But the Parisian 'poor' were not organized. At that period one cannot speak of classes, nor of the class struggle. In 1793 the *sans-culottes*, who were to be for a time masters of Paris, did not form a social class, but a group that included both proletarians and independent artisans owning their own business, and this group had taken shape after 1791, particularly as a result of the formation of 'sectional assemblies' and popular clubs.[1] Now in 1789 the 'poor' of Paris had no class consciousness, whereas the bourgeois and the well-off artisans possessed the nucleus of an organization, thanks to the electoral assemblies of each district, from which the poor, as we have seen, were excluded, and the assemblies of second-degree electors, which met at the Hôtel de Ville. Moreover it must not be forgotten that in nations which had already achieved a degree of solid unity, as was the case with France by the end of the eighteenth century, national solidarity

[1] See A. Soboul, *Les Sans-culottes parisiens en l'an II*, Paris, 1958.

took precedence, on certain important occasions, over solidarity between 'classes', orders or other social groups. This was the case on July 14th, 1789, as it was to be on other occasions, such as August 2nd, 1914.

The rising of July 14th was in fact a truly national rising. It was prepared by a gradual and deep-rooted movement of international character, which by its very amplitude precludes any notion of conspiracy.

The revolutionary movement, throughout the Western world, was the result of demographic and economic upheavals, of the rise of the bourgeoisie and the spread of 'philosophic' ideas. It had made itself felt in North America, in England, the Netherlands and Switzerland before any signs of it were perceptible in France. It acquired its impetus, in France itself, from the Assembly of Notables; but the Parisian rising could not have taken place without the *journée des Tuiles* at Grenoble on June 7th, 1788, or the affray at Pau, nor above all without the manifold riots which took place throughout almost the whole of France from January 1789 onwards, some of them provoked by the economic crisis and others arising from the elections to the Estates-General. One can surely not imagine that the troops which were brought into Paris caught the 'revolutionary' spirit and tended to fraternize with the rioters after only a few days' stay in the capital. They acquired this attitude of 'sympathy with the *Tiers État*' after weeks and months of contact with the leaders of the Third Estate in the provinces. The countless minor local risings, and the consequent division of the army into small detachments sent to suppress or prevent these, played a fundamental role in the victory of the Parisian insurrection. The institutions created in Paris as a result of the rising were not themselves original. Citizens' militias or *gardes bourgeoises* had been set up, as we have seen, in several provincial towns, notably Marseilles, Gaillac, Limoux and Orleans, before being introduced in Paris, and revolutionary authorities had seized municipal power in certain towns, such as Agde, Autun, La Ferté-Bernard, before doing so in the capital. The Parisian insurrection thus represents, as it were, the peak of the national insurrection. It was with good reason, therefore, that the three colours adopted as their badge by the Parisian insurgents on July 14th became the national emblem, and that the anniversary of this rising was chosen for the day of national celebration. It was the national character of the rising of

Conclusion : The Significance of The Taking of the Bastille

July 14th, 1789, which conferred on the fall of the Bastille prison an importance incomparably greater than that of other events of the sort, such as the attack on the Old Bailey in London on June 5th, 1780.

But if the Parisian rising of July 14th represents the peak of the national rising, it also marks a stage in it. Until July 14th the handful of revolutionary institutions set up in the provinces were disparate and isolated. Henceforward most of the towns and many of the villages of France were to imitate Paris with extraordinary swiftness. During the weeks that followed the fall of the Bastille there arose everywhere revolutionary Town Councils of permanent committees,[1] and citizen militias which soon assumed the name of national guards. But the dread of an aristocratic plot, which had been felt in Paris and which was already latent in many regions of France, soon spread, and finally took the form of an immense *grande peur*, a panic which brought the majority of the French peasantry out in arms by the end of July.[2] Once armed, these peasants attacked their lords' châteaux just as the Parisians had attacked the Bastille. They seized and burned the old charters on which feudal rights were inscribed. The people of Paris, by taking the Bastille, had destroyed the symbol of the feudal régime; the peasants, by attacking the châteaux and burning the seignorial papers, sought to destroy the feudal régime itself. And they succeeded, for the National Assembly realized that only the official abolition of this detested régime could re-establish order and peace in France. That is why, on the night of August 4th, it solemnly proclaimed the abolition of feudalism. Two weeks later, when on August 26th it voted the *Déclaration des droits de l'homme et du citoyen*, it laid the foundations for the new régime.

Thus the Parisian rising of July 14th, resulting from the provincial insurrectional movements which had begun the previous January, provoked in its turn a great national revolutionary impulse which irrevocably overthrew the *ancien régime* and gave France a new aspect. The Fourteenth of July is indeed one of the great days that made France.

---

[1] See on this subject D. Ligou, 'A propos de la révolution municipale', in the *Revue d'histoire économique et sociale*, 1960, pp. 146–177.
[2] G. Lefebvre, *La Grande Peur*, Paris, 1932.

Appendices

The Evidence of one of the Besiegers: The *Journée* of J. B. Humbert

The Fall of the Bastille

Frenchmen, my compatriots, I am a native of Langres, I learnt watch-making in Switzerland, particularly in Geneva, where I was working as a journeyman when that Republic lost its liberty.

I was peacefully asleep on a camp bed in a guardhouse when the French troops seized the town, the gates of which had been opened for them by a handful of traitors.

I witnessed the dismay of the townspeople, and I heard the curses they uttered against a certain Minister of France, who, they said, had deceived my King; I heard so many sighs, complaints and regrets, that for a long time I bore in my heart something of the same feeling towards that Minister as the unfortunate people of Geneva.

I returned to Paris in 1787; there I grew accustomed to bearing, with ease, the yoke that seemed so heavy to many of my compatriots, the brave people of Paris.

Like them, on July 12th, on hearing the news that the armed populace was attacking the Bourgeois instead of defending them, I made my way to St-André-des-Arts, to offer my services, assuming that I belonged to that district; the attack on the Tuileries by the Prince de Lambesc, and several other circumstances that are well known to everyone, having heightened the fears of the bourgeois and determined them to take up arms, I submitted to the commanding officers whom they appointed.

In all my endeavours I so firmly believed that I was only doing my duty that I sought to gain neither glory nor profit therefrom,

JOURNÉE

D E

JEAN-BAPTISTE HUMBERT,

HORLOGER,

Qui, le premier, a monté sur les Tours de la BASTILLE.

· Il est glorieux de s'arracher à un lâche repos : de s'exposer aux dangers, de ne fuir ni la douleur ni la mort, de chercher les nobles aventures, de purger la terre des monstres qui la désolent, & de la rougir de leur sang.

WIELAND.

À PARIS,

Chez VOLLAND, quai des Augustins, N. 25.

1789.

3

AVERTISSEMENT.

FRANÇAIS, mes Compatriotes, je suis natif de Langres, j'ai appris l'horlogerie en Suisse, & notamment à Genève, où j'étois Compagnon, quand cette République perdit sa liberté.

Je dormois tranquillement sur un lit de camp dans un corps-de-garde, lorsque les troupes Françaises s'emparèrent de la Ville, dont plusieurs traîtres leur avoient ouvert les portes.

Je fus témoin de la consternation des Bourgeois, & confident des imprécations qu'ils firent contre un Ministre de France, qui, disoient-ils, avoit trompé mon Roi : j'entendis si souvent des soupirs, des plaintes & des regrets, que je gardai long-temps dans mon cœur, pour ce Ministre, une partie des mêmes sentimens qu'avoient pour lui les malheureux Genevois.

Je revins à Paris en 1787; là, je

A 2

and was happy to earn six francs a day in my profession until I should have established myself, but happier still to have helped France to recover her liberty, and to have given some pleasure to my relatives by the story of my actions.

These relatives having learnt from a notice that the municipal authorities, seeking to learn which citizens had distinguished themselves in the taking of the Bastille, wished me to go and give an account of my conduct to the *Commissaires examinateurs* at the Hôtel de Ville. I prefer to make this statement to the public, and I do not want the town of Langres to give any credence to the information given by my relatives until I have the signatures of all those whom I mention in my statement; I invite all of them to give me the lie or to confirm what I say. I have the honour to request these gentlemen of the Bureau de l'Hôtel de Ville to undertake the enquiries I suggest before formally accepting any of the facts concerning myself, or giving me any of the rewards with which they honour those who have served their country.

Certain citizens who fought for liberty have already recognized me, with my coat and cartridge-pouch, and have done me the honour of signing my declaration, on my reading it to them; this I accept, but it is not enough. There were witnesses to everything that I have alleged, and so I need the signatures of all these witnesses.

The *Journée* of J. B. Humbert

Who was the first to climb on to the towers of the Bastille

My name is J. B. HUMBERT, and I am a native of Langres, working and living in Paris, at Monsieur Belliard's, watchmaker to the King, rue du Hurepoix.

Assuming that I belonged to the district of St-André-des-Arts, I went to that Parish on Monday morning with the rest of the citizens, and patrolled the streets with them all that day and night, armed with swords, the District having no firearms or only a few.

Overcome with weariness and lack of food and sleep, I left the District at six in the morning. I learned during the course of the morning that arms for the various Districts were being distributed at the Invalides; I promptly went back to inform the Bourgeois of

Saint-André, who had gathered together at about half-past twelve. M. Poirier, their Commander, understood the importance of this news, and was preparing to lead some of the citizens thither, but he was unable to set forth, being detained by various people making requests; as these matters seemed to me of very little weight compared to the advantage of procuring arms for the citizens, I seized hold of M. Poirier and took him off, as though by force, together with five or six of the townsfolk. We reached the Invalides at about two o'clock, and we found there a great crowd, which forced us to separate. I do not know what became of the Commander or his company.

I followed the crowd, to get to the cellar where the arms were kept.

On the staircase leading to the cellar, seeing a man armed with two muskets, I took one from him, and went up again; but the crowd at the top of the stair was so great that all those who were climbing up were pushed down again, and fell right down into the cellar. Since I was only shaken and not injured by the fall, I picked up a musket which was lying at my feet, and immediately handed it to somebody who had none.

In spite of this horrible tumble, the crowd persisted in going down the stairs, and as nobody could get up again, there was such a crush in the cellar that people were shrieking and gasping for breath.

Many people had fainted; so all those in the cellar who were armed followed the advice someone gave and forced the unarmed crowd to turn and go back, threatening them with the points of their bayonets. The advice succeeded, and as the crowd drew back in terror we took advantage of this moment to form a line and force the people up the stairs.

The crowd went up again, we managed to carry up the people who had fainted, and lay them on a piece of grass near the dome and the moat. After helping and protecting the removal of these people, since my presence seemed superfluous, armed with my gun I searched in vain for my Commander, and then set off for my own District.

As I learned on the way that they were handing out powder at the Hôtel de Ville I hurried thither, and was given about a quarter of a pound, but they gave me no shot, saying that they had none.

Appendices

As I left the Hôtel de Ville I heard someone say that the Bastille was being besieged. My regret at having no shot prompted an idea which I immediately carried out, namely to buy some small nails, which I got from the grocer's at the *Coin du Roi*, place de la Grève.

There I fixed up and greased my gun.

On leaving the Grocer's, as I was about to load my gun, I was accosted by a Citizen who told me that they were handing out shot at the Hôtel de Ville. So I hurried there, and was given half a dozen pellets of buckshot.

I immediately set off for the Bastille, loading my gun as I went.

I walked along the embankment as far as the second court of the Arsenal, and there joined a group of people who were preparing to go to the siege.

We found four foot-soldiers of the Watch, armed with guns, and I urged them to come to the siege; as they replied that they had neither powder nor shot, we clubbed together to give each of them enough for two shots. Then they followed us willingly.

As we were passing in front of the Hôtel de la Régie [the Excise Office] they had just broken open two cases of bullets, which were being freely handed out, and I filled one of my coat pockets with them to give to anyone who was short. I still have over three pounds left.

A few paces away I heard a woman calling for help, I promptly went up to her and she told me that *they were setting fire to the saltpetre store.* She added that this was unfair, *because the store had been thrown open and put at the disposal of the citizens as soon as they had asked for it.* I got this woman to take me to the store, and there I found a Barber, *holding a lighted torch in each hand,* with which he was in fact setting fire to the place. I rushed at this Barber and thrust the butt of my gun violently against his stomach, knocking him over. Then, seeing that the barrel of saltpetre had caught fire, I overturned it and succeeded in smothering the flames.

Meanwhile the household staff came to beg me to help them drive out certain ill-intentioned people who had forced their way in and broken into the documents room; I followed them and drove out of the place several individuals who had already smashed some cupboards on the pretext of looking for powder.

Then I left the house, amid general thanks; and having re-joined the soldiers of the Watch to whom I had given powder and shot, I persuaded one of these to stand sentinel in front of the door.

I immediately made my way to the Bastille, passing through the courtyard of the Arsenal; it was about half-past three; the first bridge had been lowered, and the chains cut; but the portcullis barred the way; people were trying to bring in some cannon which had previously been dismantled; I crossed over by the small bridge and from the further side helped to bring in the two guns.

When they had been set up on their gun-carriages again, everybody with one accord drew up in rows of five or six, and I found myself in the front rank.

In this array we marched to the drawbridge of the fortress; on either side of this I saw two dead soldiers lying; the one on my left was wearing the uniform of the Vintimille regiment; I could not make out that of the soldier lying on my right.

The cannon were then levelled: the bronze gun at the large drawbridge and a small iron one, inlaid with silver, at the small bridge.

This operation forced me to fall out of line; and as we wanted to know whether any offers of peace were forthcoming from the garrison, I undertook to survey the terrace.

While I was occupied with this mission, it was decided to start the attack with musket fire; I hurriedly returned to my post; but my way being blocked by a crowd of people, in spite of the peril I returned by way of the parapet, and resumed my post; I was even forced to step over the body of the soldier from the Vintimille.

We each fired half-a-dozen shots. Then a paper was thrust through an oval gap a few inches across; we ceased fire; one of our number stepped forward and went to the kitchen to fetch a plank so as to collect the paper; this plank was laid on the parapet; many people stood on it to weigh it down: one man started out along it, but just as he was about to take the paper, he was killed by a shot and fell into the moat.

Another man, carrying a flag, immediately dropped his flag and went to fetch the paper, which was then read out loud and clearly, so that everyone could hear.

The contents of this message, which offered capitulation, proving unsatisfactory, we decided to fire the gun; everyone stood aside to let the cannon-ball pass.

Just as we were about to fire, the small drawbridge was lowered; it was promptly filled by a crowd of people, of whom I was about tenth. We found the gate behind the drawbridge closed: after a couple of minutes a Pensioner came to open it, and asked what we wanted: *Give up the Bastille*, I replied, as did everyone else: then he let us in. My first concern was to call for the bridge to be lowered; this was done.

Then I entered the main courtyard (I was about eighth or tenth). The Pensioners were lined up on the right, the Swiss guards on the left; we shouted: *lay down your arms*, which they did, except for one Swiss officer. I went up to him and threatened him with my bayonet, repeating: *lay down your arms*. He appealed to all present: '*Gentlemen, please believe me, I never fired.*'

I immediately said to him: '*How dare you say you never fired, when your lips are still black from biting your cartridge?*' As I said this, I pounced on his sword; another fellow did the same; as the two of us were arguing as to which should have the sword, I happened to glance at a staircase on my left, and I saw three citizens who had gone up five or six steps and were hurrying down again; I immediately left the sword and, armed with my rifle, which I had never abandoned, I rushed over to the staircase to help the citizens, whom I assumed to have been driven back; I rapidly climbed up to the keep, without noticing that nobody was following me; I reached the top of the stairs without meeting anyone either. In the keep I found a Swiss soldier squatting down with his back to me: I aimed my rifle at him, shouting: *lay down your arms*; he turned round in surprise, and laid down his weapons, saying: '*Comrade, don't kill me, I'm for the Tiers État and I will defend you to the last drop of my blood; you know I'm obliged to do my job; but I haven't fired.*'

While he was speaking thus I picked up his rifle, then, poking him in the stomach with my bayonet, I ordered him to hand over his cartridge-case and sling it round my neck, which he did.

Immediately afterwards I went to the cannon that stood just above the drawbridge of the Bastille, in order to push it off its gun-carriage and render it unusable. But as I stood for this purpose with my shoulder under the mouth of the cannon, someone in the vicinity fired at me, and the bullet pierced my coat and waistcoat and wounded me in the neck; I fell down senseless; the Swiss soldier whose life I had spared dragged me on to the staircase, still clutching my gun, so he told me, though I had dropped the one I had taken from the Invalides.

When I recovered from my swoon I found myself sitting on the stairs; the Swiss guard had been shaking me to restore me to consciousness, and he had tried to staunch the blood that was pouring out of my wound with a piece of linen he had cut off my shirt.

Finding myself very weak I decided to go downstairs, asking the Swiss to support me, which he willingly did.

Half way down the stairs we met a number of townsfolk coming up, some in armour and others not; seeing me covered in blood, they assumed that the Swiss must have wounded me, and tried to kill him; I opposed this, and explained the situation. They fortunately took my word for it, and I went my way downstairs, still leaning on him.

When we reached the courtyard together, the Swiss was not allowed to leave, so I was obliged to go out by myself; people made way for me on seeing my blood and my wound.

On the way to the Bastille kitchens I met an army surgeon, who urged me to show him my wound; when he had examined the place, he told me I had a bullet in my neck which he could not extract by himself, and persuaded me to go to a hospital to get it seen to.

On my way there I met somebody who had just been to the Minimes monastery to have a sprained wrist attended to. He immediately took me to the Minimes, where they readily attended to my wound. No bullet was found in it.

As I was seized with a violent thirst they gave me a pewter bowl full of wine and water, which restored my strength. Then I got up joyfully, intending to hurry back to the Bastille.

I immediately got dressed again, I picked up my gun and my cartridge-pouch, but the Minimes who had dressed my wound begged me to change my mind. They assured me that movement would be very bad for my wound, and made me promise to go back home and have some rest, which they thought absolutely indispensable. They offered to take me home, but I refused with thanks.

On my way home I remembered some friends who lived in the rue de la Ferronnerie; I had left them that morning, and they had seemed anxious about the dangers which they foresaw my zeal might lead me into; I went to their house, and four armed Bourgeois escorted me to the rue du Hurepoix. I was greeted with praise wherever I went; but when we reached the Quai des

Augustins, we were followed by a crowd of people who mistook me for a malefactor, and twice attempted to put me to death; as I could not explain things to everyone, I was about to be *seized*, when I was recognized by a Bookseller on the Quai, who rescued me from the hands of the crowd and took me into his own home; I was put to bed there and given all the care I needed.

I rested until about midnight, when I was woken by repeated cries of *to arms! to arms!* Then I could not resist my longing to be of some further use; I got up, armed myself and went to the guard-room, where I found M. Poirier, the Commanding Officer, under whose orders I remained until the following morning.

We, the undersigned, certify that the details related in this account, which consists of 16 pages, are correct as regards the fall of the Bastille. Paris, August 12th, 1789.

DUCASTEL, Gunner; MAILLARD, RICHARD, DUPIN, GEORGET

APPENDIX 2

The Defence of the Bastille:
Log-book of the Salis-Samade Regiment
(Archives de la guerre, Vincennes, Mémoires historiques,
vol. no. 619–626)

A. A summary of what happened to the Salis-Samade
   regiment during the campaign of 1789

Account of the Fall of the Bastille

The regiment received orders to leave Arras on May 3rd for Beauvais, which town it reached on the 6th of that month. The disturbances occurring in the capital had decided the Government to bring the regiment to Paris. It left Beauvais on May 11th and took up quarters in Vaugirard, Issy and Vanves.

The admirable order maintained by this regiment on its way through the capital from the *barrière* of St-Denis to that of Grenelle won it general admiration and praise, and a few days later two of the seven companies quartered at Issy received orders to pitch camp at Clamart. On June 14th Monseigneur le comte d'Artois inspected the regiment on the Champ de Mars and it subsequently performed manoeuvres before this prince with such perfection that His Highness expressed his satisfaction in the most flattering terms to the Chevalier de Bachmann and all the officers and soldiers of the regiment; next day, June 15th, it was dispersed among 9 districts, as follows: 5 companies at Vaugirard, 4 at Issy, 2 at Vanves, 2 at Clamart, 1 at Le Châtou, 1 at Le Peq, 1 at Poissy, 1 at Claye and 1 at Meudon and at Belleville.

The Revolution that threatened the Kingdom was about to break out, and the regiment of *gardes-françaises* having shown itself in its true colours towards the end of June, the regiment of Salis-Samade was in a very awkward position, seeing that crowds of soldiers of the *gardes-françaises* frequented the taverns of Vaugirard, in which 5 companies of the Salis-Samade regiment were quartered; the *gardes-françaises* carried indiscipline to the point of trooping to Vaugirard with drums beating and swords bared to establish themselves there, posting sentries and beating hourly tattoos. Since the soldiers of the Salis-Samade regiment had been forbidden to fraternize with those of the *gardes-françaises*, the latter took their revenge for this order by behaving with the most shocking licence.

On the night of June 30th, M. le duc du Châtelet sent orders to the regiment to move to Paris with the four pieces of ordnance it had borrowed from the Swiss guards' regiment, for the purpose of preventing the rebels from seizing the Abbey of St-Germain; this *coup* had already been accomplished before the arrival of the regiment, the advance-guard of which had just reached the boulevards when it was ordered to return to its quarters; the same night it received a second order to send 2 Companies of grenadiers and 100 fusiliers to the corner of the Boulevards between the

Précis de ce qui est arrivé au Régiment de Salis Samade pendant la Campagne de 1789

Invalides and the Grenelle *barrière*, which order was subsequently renewed every night until the regiment left for Camp.

On July 1st the companies that had been sent to Poissy, Le Peq, Châtou and Meudon rejoined the regiment, leaving these posts to be occupied by the Reinach regiment; only the Company of Akerman l'Aîné, which had been sent to Claye, was not recalled; the defence of the bridges of St-Cloud and Sèvres was entrusted to the Reinach regiment; for which purpose the Salis-Samade regiment sent to the Reinach regiment 3 pieces of ordnance and kept only one for itself; the regiment was to appear at the Champ de Mars on July 8th, but as the behaviour of the *gardes-françaises* grew daily more unruly, it was thought prudent to make the regiment evacuate its quarters during the night of July 4th and proceed to the Champ de Mars, where it bivouacked, since its camp equipment could not follow it until the 5th. The regiment pitched camp on the 5th but only left some guards there while it spent the night in the buildings of the Ecole Militaire, on the 6th it was joined in Camp by the Châteauvieux regiment and the second Battalion of the Diesbach regiment, the first Battalion only arriving on the 7th. Room was left for the Vigier regiment, which was due to arrive on the 17th, Captain Buxdorf of the Salis-Samade regiment was appointed *aide major général* of the army and performed the functions of that post with uncommon intelligence until such time as the troops were dispersed. On July 7th the Chevalier de Bachmann was asked for a detachment of 33 men with an officer of his own choice, to reinforce the garrison of the Bastille, which consisted only of 70 Pensioners; Lieutenant Louis Deflue was chosen for this mission (this officer's account of the surrender of the Bastille may be read in the ensuing pages).

Nothing very remarkable occurred in the Camp until the 12th, when the Salis-Samade regiment was ordered to proceed to the place Louis XV; the order specified that it should embark on the two ferries lying on the Seine opposite the Hôtel des Invalides; the regiment set forth with its single cannon at 8 in the evening and crossed the Seine in detachments, since the ferries could only hold 80 and 100 men respectively; 1 company of grenadiers and 1 of fusiliers, with the cannon, formed the advance guard, the rest of the regiment was drawn up in battle array on the left bank of the Seine, the crossing took two hours, the regiment was very fortunate not to be attacked on either bank, which was the more to be apprehended in that a number of *gardes-françaises* had their quarters within reach of the crossing, and that the soldiers of this regiment had taken up arms to oppose the King's troops; a few companies of them had even crossed the Seine at the same time as the Salis-Samade regiment and mingled with our men on disembarking, the night being extremely dark. The Salis-Samade regiment did not reach the place Louis XV until after ten o'clock, the cannon and the 2nd company of Grenadiers were drawn up in battle order in front of the balustrade that faces the Tuileries, a few companies on either flank and the rest of the 1st battalion behind the Grenadiers, the 2nd battalion having its right flank up against the square and its left projecting at right angles along the Champs-Elysées, with the Seine behind its front. Three battalions of Swiss guards were stationed in the Champs-Elysées, on the left of the second battalion of Salis-Samade: the detachments of horse consisting of the regiments of Esterhazy, Bercheny, Royal Dragons, Royal Cravatte and Royal Allemand were drawn up partly along different avenues, either beside the Seine or down the rue Royale, and partly along the Boulevards. Before the arrival of the Salis-Samade regiment, the Royal Allemand regiment had made a charge in the Tuileries, having been fired on there with muskets and pistols; the baron de Besenval was in command of these various troops. On the Boulevards, the Royal Allemand regiment received a volley from the *gardes-françaises* which killed and wounded several men and some horses of this regiment. About half an hour after midnight all the cavalry drew up behind the Salis-Samade regiment and the officers warned the Chevalier de Bachmann that since the rebels were coming up with greatly superior forces, the mounted troops were no longer in a position to oppose them. The Baron de Besenval having gone elsewhere to give orders, the Chevalier de Bachmann assumed responsibility for altering the original plans and making others which might provide him with some means of defence, should he be attacked. While he was occupied in drawing up these plans the entire cavalry vacated the neighbourhood of the place Louis XV. About one o'clock the Baron de Besenval returned to the square, and the Chevalier de Bachmann tried to explain the changes he had made to the original plan, but M. le Baron ordered this Officer to withdraw to camp with his regiment without delay. The Chevalier de Bachmann chose to cross the Seine at Sèvres, since the Pont Royal as well as the Tuileries was guarded by the rebels, and crossing by means of ferries was no longer possible. The Salis-Samade regiment withdrew in perfect order to Sèvres, crossed the Seine there and marched up the river on the further bank as far as its camp, which it reached about five in the morning of July 13th. That day, the troops encamped on the Champ de Mars were under arms almost uninterruptedly, and again the following night and the next day, July 14th.

During the morning of the 14th the soldiers of the *gardes-françaises* and other rebels seized the arms and cannon of the Invalides, this post being guarded by no regular troops was captured or surrendered without a single blow being struck, and the muskets and artillery seized there were used for the attack on the Bastille that same day.

Here follows the account of the capture of that fortress and its means of defence, and of what happened there between the arrival of the detachment of the Salis-Samade regiment and its surrender.

B. An account of the surrender of the Bastille, given by Louis Deflue, Lieutenant of Grenadiers in the Regiment of Salis-Samade, holding the rank of Captain

Following the orders I had received the previous day from M. le Baron de Besenval, I left the Champ de Mars on July 7th, 1789 at nine in the morning, with a detachment of 32 fusiliers and a sergeant. I crossed the city of Paris without difficulty and arrived at the Bastille, where I was allowed to enter although unrecognized, my men were stationed in an armoury above the rooms of the Pensioners in the first Court.

The first day after I entered this fortress, M. de Launey, the Governor, showed me over it, particularly the places he thought the weakest and most liable to attack; he showed me the precautions he had taken to protect himself, which consisted in blocking up a few loopholes and windows, both in his own house and in the Bastille, through which he was afraid of being shot at, in opening up other loopholes which he thought more useful for defence purposes, in reinforcing a wall in one wing of the bastion of the Governor's garden, through which he was afraid of being attacked, in having a few cartloads of paving stones brought up on to the towers, and tongs made to pull down the chimney-pots; he frequently complained of the weakness of the garrison and the impossibility of saving it in case of attack, he even allowed me to express my own opinion on these precautions. I pointed out to him, as did M. du Pujet, the *lieutenant du roi*, that his fears were ill founded, that the fortress was strong enough in itself, and the garrison adequate if every man was willing to do his duty defending it until outside help could be provided.

Towards evening on the 12th we learned in the Bastille that they were threatening to attack the powder-magazine in the Arsenal. M. du Pujet, *lieutenant du roi* in the Bastille and also officer in command at the Arsenal, being unwilling to relinquish the powder stored there, and considering the garrison of the Arsenal, which consisted of one company of Pensioners, too weak to be able to defend it, persuaded M. de Launey to take this powder into the Bastille; M. de Launey having consented, my detachment was employed during the whole night of July 12th–13th in transporting this powder from the magazine into the Bastille; it was stored in the rear courtyard, inadequately covered; that same night the Governor gave orders for the whole garrison to retire inside the Castle, being unwilling in case of attack to defend the exterior of the fortress, although he had previously decided to the contrary with his staff and the officers of the garrison, and arrangements had been made accordingly; it was pointed out to M. de Launey that he had no provisions in the fort, my detachment having only bread enough for three days and meat for one, and the Pensioners lacking both; in answer to which protests the Governor had two sacks of flour brought in. The munitions of war consisted of 3000 cartridges specially made and a few hundreds of big-gun cartridges. The many fires that could be seen blazing from the top of the Bastille during the day of July 13th made us aware of the danger to which this powder would be exposed, should such fires be started in the neighbourhood of the fortress; I therefore sought a safer hiding-place for the powder; having discovered an underground cell, I showed it to M. de Launey and du Pujet, who considered it suitable, and my detachment spent the morning of the 14th putting all the powder away safely. M. du Pujet gave my soldiers a bonus of 2 louis to reward them for their work.

It was learnt during this same morning of July 14th that the people in the neighbourhood of the Bastille, and the townsfolk in general, were alarmed at seeing the cannon of the Bastille pointed at the city, while a *garde bourgeoise* [citizens' militia] was known to be keeping watch over public safety, and this militia could not perform its duties confidently while threatened by the cannon from the fortress; on hearing which rumours the Governor ordered the cannon to be lowered and withdrawn, and even had the gun-slits blocked up with boards and sticks.

About midday a detachment of about 40 armed townspeople made their appearance, they stopped in the first court, and the leader of the troop asked to speak to the Governor, who took him into the Government house. I do not know what form their conversation took, since I was inside the fortress during this interview. After half an hour M. de Launey came inside the fortress with a certain individual who, I was told on enquiring, had already been several times to the Bastille with permission to visit prisoners there. I joined them, and learned that this person was asking on behalf of the City that the cannon should be taken down from the towers and that no resistance should be offered in case of an attack on the fort, on the grounds that it was useless to shed the blood of Citizens, and wrong to make war on the Nation, and that after a great many people had been killed we should still have to surrender the fort; this person furthermore demanded that a citizens' militia should be admitted to keep the fort, in conjunction with the garrison (I have since learnt that the said person was the *procureur du Roi* of the City of Paris).

The Governor replied that he could not yield the fort to anyone whatsoever, that he would defend it as long as he could, that he was answerable for it with his life, and that nevertheless in order to allay the fears of the townspeople he had already had the cannon lowered and withdrawn, that he gave his word of honour to that effect, as the visitor might assure those that sent him; he intended no insult to anyone, provided no one tried to take possession of the fort nor to attack its bridges or gates, he even took this person to the top of the towers to show him the state of the guns, so that he might give a more exact account of the Governor's intentions; when they came down again the Governor told us he thought things had been settled and he hoped there would be no attack, however the delegate left in some dissatisfaction.

About three in the afternoon a troop of armed townspeople

among whom were a few *gardes-françaises* appeared and sought entry; they came into the first court without difficulty, by way of the Arsenal and the Cour de l'Orme, seeing that the gate was guarded only by a single unarmed pensioner; this band of men then moved towards the bridge that protected the Cour du Gouvernement; the drawbridge being raised, they cut the weights of the counterpoise from their chains, and the bridge dropped; this operation was made easier by the fact that the Governor had forbidden us to fire on the besiegers without first calling on them to withdraw, which owing to the distance was impossible; during this exploit, the besiegers fired several shots at those who were at the top of the towers, as had also been done the previous day by different troops passing in the neighbourhood. After breaking down the bridge, they easily hacked their way through the gate, and the crowd poured into the Cour du Gouvernement and on to the stone bridge running alongside the kitchens to the main building of the fortress. We asked the attackers what they wanted, there was a general cry of 'lower the bridges'. We replied that this could not be done, that they must withdraw or else they would be fired on, they renewed their cries of 'down with the bridges', on which a company of pensioners stationed at the loop-holes on either side of the gates were ordered to fire; the Governor had gone up on to the towers with some thirty other pensioners; the besiegers in their turn fired at the loop-holes and at those who were on the platforms; presently they withdrew into the kitchens, which are on the right of the bridge and in the Cour du Gouvernement, behind the walls of the parapet-walk, from whence they went on firing on the fort through the slits in this wall and the windows of the kitchens; they returned a second time to the attack and were driven back in the same way. I was posted with my detachment and a dozen pensioners in the courtyard of the Bastille itself opposite the gate; and I had behind me three pieces of ordnance firing two-pound balls; these were to be manned by twelve of my men to protect the entry to the fort in case the besiegers should force the gates; as they seemed bent on this project, we endeavoured to thwart it, after their second attack, by piercing two holes in the bridge, which was raised, in which we intended to place two of the cannon, but being unable to get near enough on account of the bascule of the drawbridge, we replaced these by two rampart guns of the sort called *amusettes*, which were loaded with grapeshot, but little use was made of these because the besiegers were no longer appearing in large numbers and moreover had brought up a cart loaded with burning straw and placed it at the entry to the bridge, which prevented my men from seeing them.

The besiegers, seeing that this method was unsuccessful, had set up three eight-pounder guns and a mortar in the garden of the Arsenal, from which they fired a few ineffective shots at the fort, and our cannon replied with a few shots.

The besiegers, having conceived the plan of forcing the gates by gunfire, brought their cannon into the Cour du Gouvernement and placed them at the entry to the bridge, levelling them at the gates without firing them.

M. de Launey, seeing these preparations from the top of the towers, without warning or consulting his staff or his garrison, had the drummer who accompanied him sound the recall; on this signal I went myself to the loopholes and rooms to order a cease-fire; the crowd then drew near and the Governor asked them to accept capitulation, but the people would not hear of such a thing and redoubled their shouts of 'down with the bridges'; this was all the answer to be got from them; then M. de Launey came down from the towers, went into the council chamber and wrote a note in which he warned the besiegers that he had 20 thousand pounds of powder in store and if they would not accept his capitulation he would blow up the fort, the garrison and the entire neighbourhood; he handed me this note with orders to transmit it. I went to the gate and passed the note through one of the holes I have mentioned; an Officer of the Queen's regiment, or at any rate someone wearing that uniform, having had a plank fetched so as to cross the moat, was the person to whom I handed this note, but it had no effect, the shouts of 'no capitulation' and 'down with the bridges' were the only reply; I returned to the Governor and reported the state of things to him, and I immediately rejoined my troop, which I had drawn up to the left of the gate; I was waiting for the Governor to keep his word and blow up the fortress, but greatly to my surprise I saw four pensioners go up to the bridges, open and lower them; then the crowd rushed in; they immediately disarmed us and seized hold of us, each of us being given a guard; they went into all the apartments and rifled everything, taking possession of weapons, throwing papers and records out of the windows; everything was pillaged, those of my soldiers who had not their kitbags with them lost their clothes, and I myself lost all my possessions. After many threats and considerable ill-treatment, the first fury was somewhat allayed, and I was taken with some of my men, who had stayed by my side during the mêlée, to the Hôtel de Ville; all the way there we were subjected to threats and insults and a general cry from all the people that we deserved hanging. I really believe that but for a *chevalier* of the Arquebuse, named M. Riccard, who endeavoured to protect the prisoners, I should not have reached the city alive; as we drew near the place de Grève they brought along a head at the end of a stick.I was told it was that of M. de Launey. In the mêlée I had lost sight of the Governor and did not know what had become of him; the Major and his aide, an officer of the Invalides and two pensioners, one of whom had been wounded in the head by gunfire, were hanged or executed on the place de Grève that same evening. When we got to the Hôtel de Ville I was brought before a Committee in session there, and to allay the fury of the crowd and save myself and the remnants of my company from execution I declared myself willing to surrender to the city and the nation; my offer was accepted and we were led in triumph to the Palais-Royal, where after taking us all round the garden they brought us up into a room, a collection was then made to provide us with supper, after which there came an order to bring us back to the Hôtel de Ville. When we got there we were allotted to various districts; I was sent with my sergeant and one soldier to St-Jean-en-Grève, where we spent the night in the Church, which was being used as a guardroom. Next day, July 15th, my fate did not seem too sure as the *gardes-françaises* came to fetch me with many threats, assuring me that I should not escape the gallows, since the pensioners had levelled many indictments at me, accusing me of being primarily responsible for the losses suffered by the besiegers. About noon M. Riccard, Chevalier of the Arquebuse and Elector, had obtained an order from the city to accept me in his company, so he came to fetch me and lodged me in his own home, while some of my soldiers who had also been attached to the same company were lodged close by in an inn where they were provided with food during the whole time they served in the city.

During the action there was only one pensioner killed on top of the towers and three or four wounded; I have since learned that two of my soldiers were massacred by the populace on their way to the Hôtel de Ville. I could not discover the exact number of casualties among the besiegers; it has been put as high as 160 killed and wounded, but this number seems exaggerated considering how little fire there was from the fortress.

From this exact and truthful report it will be possible to judge the different accounts that have appeared dealing with this event, and it will also be easy to assess the acts of bravery and heroism on which several people pride themselves in this connection.

It only remains for me to express my surprise at the general cry of treachery and at the cruel penalty inflicted on M. de Launey; I do not think this Governor can be considered as a traitor towards the nation because he handed over to it a fortress which he might have held a good deal longer, and could have defended at the cost of thousands of citizens' lives.

As for the story which someone invented and which was generally believed, that M. de Launey had the drawbridges lowered and then raised again, having allowed a number of people to come in, and then fired at them, as for this story, I say, I declare that it is false and without foundation, and the more unbelievable since it is obviously impossible to raise a drawbridge in front of a crowd that is hurrying across it, half of it on the bridge and the other half already over it; I will also point out that it would have been impossible for the garrison to fire on those who had crossed the bridge, since all the soldiers were disarmed as soon as the first besiegers entered the fortress.

I am convinced that those who disarmed that section of the garrison which was in the courtyard will of their own accord pay tribute to the truth and will testify that they found the men standing at ease, in no position to fire their weapons; I do not deny that there were many people killed after the surrender of the fort, because the assailants had started shooting as soon as they were masters of the place without caring where or at whom they were firing.

Another charge is also levelled at M. de Launey, namely that he had a white flag hoisted from his towers but carried on firing despite this signal. I cannot give an opinion on this question, since from the courtyard where I was stationed I could not see what was happening on the platforms, but I suppose that the Governor may in fact have hoisted this flag, but that those who were stationed in the rooms on either side of the gates, being unable to see it, may have gone on firing. I cannot see why they should be accused of treachery on this account.

I think myself in honour bound to do M. de Launey the justice of saying that if he deserved the penalty he endured on account of his behaviour on this occasion, it is certainly not because of any treachery towards the citizens and the nation.

To return to the troops encamped on the Champ de Mars, of which the Salis-Samade regiment formed part. The news of the surrender of the Bastille having reached the Camp, the generals summoned together the commanding officers and informed them of the necessity of evacuating that post and leaving the precincts of the city; being unable to provide carriages for the transport of their equipment, their belongings were deposited at the Ecole Militaire, the camp remained pitched and at nine that evening the infantry took up their arms, the cavalry mounted their horses and dispositions were taken up for the withdrawal to Versailles; the customs posts in this area being all ablaze and guarded, it was decided to force a way through if necessary; the grenadiers of the three regiments were ordered to form the rear guard, the regiment of Salis-Samade took the head of the column, which made its way towards the *barrière* of the Grenelle plain; this *barrière* had been set on fire during the day and was at the moment completely abandoned, consequently the troops met with no obstacle to their passage; the column reached Sèvres between midnight and one o'clock, and the mounted troops were placed in the park of St Cloud.

The Infantry arrived in the village and the officers were ordered to provide shelter for their troops as best they could.

The Salis-Samade regiment went to the further end of St Cloud in the direction of Versailles; the inhabitants refused to let them in; as it was a very wet night, the men had to break open some of the doors and spend that night in makeshift lodgings, hoping to find more tolerable quarters the next day; the 15th proved disastrous for the Salis-Samade regiment as well as for the other regiments that had been flung into Sèvres. The districts that the Salis-Samade regiment had previously occupied in the neighbourhood of Paris were practically contiguous to Sèvres, and the soldiers had been very familiar with their former landlords and landladies, who came over to Sèvres in throngs to invite them to their homes for rest and refreshment. A large number of men accepted this invitation unsuspectingly, and the more readily because they were extremely uncomfortable in every respect in their present situation, and because having left a large proportion of their clothes and belongings in these villages, they hoped to get them back before being sent even further away; and they were so generously treated in their former quarters at Issy, Vaugirard and Vanves that their hosts were able to make them completely drunk and then convey them to Paris in carts; several who were unwilling were forced to follow with pistols at their throats. In this way the regiment lost 75 men during the days of July 15th and 16th, a few of whom deserted the flag voluntarily; adding to this number the 33 men who were taken prisoner at the Bastille, the regiment lost 108 men between the 14th and the 16th, and between then and the 25th some 19 more who joined the Parisian troops, which brings the total to 127. It is remarkable that the greater part of the regiment's losses on this occasion consisted of the men who had been considered the most reliable, particularly the Swiss, 'children of the regiment' and other Swiss natives living in France.

On the 16th, towards seven in the evening, all the troops quartered at Sèvres received marching orders, the cavalry forming the advance guard, followed by the infantry. It is probable that the regiment was intended to cross the Seine towards St Germain. When the head of the column of infantry, led by the Salis-Samade regiment, arrived level with the palace of Marly, the column was stopped and the three Swiss regiments were ordered into the precincts of the château, together with the Royal Allemand regiment; the latter stabled their horses in such a way as to leave the remaining 6 battalions only room for a single battalion under cover, the rest spent the night bivouacking in a courtyard, on wet grass; straw was distributed to them, but in very small quantities. As it was pouring with rain, the superior officers and some officers of the Salis-Samade regiment bought wood in a neighbouring village to enable the troops to get dry, they also bought some bread and ordered some to be baked for the regiment, for the soldiers had no bread left at all.

We set off again towards five in the morning, contending for the passage of the Seine with the mounted troops who had formed the advance guard on the previous day. The Salis-Samade regiment, followed by the Diesbach, Châteauvieux, and Reinach regiments, took the head of the column, the cavalry followed the column of

infantry, the Seine was crossed at Le Peq without hindrance, and a
halt was made in the woods between Le Peq and Châtou, where
these troops were joined by the Nassau and Bouillon regiments,
Lauzun's hussars and a considerable train of artillery come from
Versailles.

Marshal de Broglie, who had been appointed by the King
Commander-in-chief of the army, which was to assemble in the
neighbourhood of Paris, also came to join this body of men at the
same rendezvous, and led them to St-Denis where they arrived at
four in the afternoon, and occupied different camps; the four
Swiss regiments found theirs pitched in the precincts of the
Abbey garden. Before nightfall, the different units received orders
to march to their respective garrisons on the following day,
leaving the time of departure to be decided by each regiment.
Consequently, the Salis-Samade and Diesbach regiments left
St-Denis on the 18th at five in the morning to go to Arras, the
Diesbach regiment by way of Senlis, the Salis-Samade regiment
by way of Pontoise. However, the latter regiment was held up by
a new order from the Marshal, forbidding any troops to leave
St-Denis before him. The regiment was unable to get going until
nine in the morning, and only reached Pontoise at three, the
Company which had remained at Claye served as escort to Marshal
de Broglie's train as far as Meaux, where it turned back and took
the road to Arras; on arriving at Amiens it received orders to
march to Albert, where it stayed until August 7th.

Next day, July 19th, the Salis-Samade regiment left Pontoise to
take up quarters at Chaumont, but on its way there it was over-
taken by a courier bringing an order signed by the King personally
to return to Pontoise and stop there on the 19th and 20th. This
town having been threatened with pillage, a considerable gang of
malcontents appeared there on the following day, July 20th; the
regiment took up arms, and the Chevalier de Bachmann prepared
to deal with the rebels, although it was evening before these could
be dispersed. Monsieur de Boccard, Captain of Grenadiers,
placed with his troop outside the gate of the bridge over the Oise,
which separates the town from the suburb of St Ouen l'Aumône,
had great difficulty in restraining the crowd which had thronged
thither, and only succeeded in doing so by dint of coolness,
firmness and patience. The town of Pontoise which, as is well
known, is the granary of Paris, recognized the important service

rendered to it by the Salis-Samade regiment, and expressed its gratitude to the Chevalier de Bachmann, offering the regiment a Certificate to this effect.

On the 21st, at three in the morning, the regiment took up arms to continue its march towards Arras, but a second courier arrived at that instant from Versailles, ordering it still to remain at Pontoise until the 26th. During this stay both the officers and the soldiers used the most prudent, gentle and humane methods to ensure the safety of markets and shops, to preserve the town from attack by ill-intentioned persons and to maintain order there. It is not irrelevant to mention here a surprising fact, namely the extreme suspicion of the inhabitants of Pontoise towards the regiment, this aversion became even more obvious when there arrived in Pontoise a detachment of the Paris militia, who delighted in fomenting and and even increasing this mistrust, which in turn provoked the resentment of the soldiers against the inhabitants, but particularly against this troop from Paris, consisting of *gardes-françaises*, surgeons' apprentices and other undisciplined and ill-educated young men.

On the 26th the regiment assembled once more at three in the morning to continue its journey towards Arras. A third Courier, sent from Versailles, arrived just as the regiment was leaving, with orders for it to go to Mantes that very day. The regiment therefore took the Mantes road instead of the Chaumont road. Just outside Mantes, they found the inhabitants of the *faubourgs* assembled, who protested to the Chevalier de Bachmann about the arrival of the regiment, which they strongly resented, refusing to provide lodging for the men; the Chevalier de Bachmann, by fair words, persuaded them to give his soldiers shelter for at least one night. He then went to the town hall to make his protests to the assembled committee, and it was agreed that a courier should be dispatched to Versailles immediately, on behalf both of the regiment and of the town, to explain the impossibility of keeping the regiment at Mantes or even providing it with bread for the next day. The Chevalier de Bachmann in his letter to M. de St Priest, seconding the request of the town of Mantes, expressed the hope that that Minister would agree to let the regiment make its way to Arras at last, which was all the more desirable since the regiment's equipment had been left on the Champ de Mars and the officers had no other belongings with them but those they were wearing on the

14th, when the troops first withdrew. This courier returned at six o'clock the following morning, but the Minister's reply was not favourable to the regiment, which received orders to return to Pontoise until further notice, the day being a very wild one, the by-ways being very hard going and spoilt by the rain, and the soldiers having received no food, a request was made for some bread, which was however not obtained until about eleven o'clock, and the regiment set off at noon in horrible weather. It would take too long to describe in detail the rude and inhuman way in which the regiment was received and treated at Mantes; indecent remarks and insults of every sort were the only things of which it was not deprived; stones were even thrown at the soldiers' lodgings during the night.

The regiment only arrived at Pontoise at nightfall, and its friendly reception there was largely due to the following incident: that same day, July 27th, a rumour had spread through many provinces simultaneously that a gang of bandits several thousand strong was laying waste the countryside and plundering the harvest. Everyone rushed into the fields, and when the regiment arrived in Pontoise the town was practically deserted, this circumstance altered people's attitude and ensured a most friendly reception for the regiment from the inhabitants of Pontoise. Good relations have subsequently been uninterrupted between these townspeople and our men.

The Chevalier de Bachmann having learnt that the Committee of the town was hard put to it to supply arms for its newly-formed civic militia, offered them, with the consent of his officers, 60 surplus muskets belonging to the regiment. The Comte Chevalier de la Motte, colonel of this militia, who was returning to Versailles, was commissioned to ask for the consent of the Minister, which was granted. The regiment formed several detachments jointly with the militia of Paris to safeguard the grain supply. It was to be feared that this combination might have undesirable results, since these militiamen, inspired by a spirit of mutiny, did their utmost to debauch our soldiers, who steadfastly resisted their enticements. This militia was so averse to discipline that it felt bound, on principle, to provide an example of licence and unbridled freedom. It delighted in roaming through the countryside, shooting game and doing such considerable damage to property that the magistrates of Pontoise were forced to complain to the Marquis de La

Fayette, Generalissimo of these troops. On August 3rd the Chevalier de Bachmann was told that the regiment would that same day receive orders to march to Chartres. On this news, the Committee of Pontoise decided to send a deputation of 3 of its members to the Chevalier de Bachmann, offering him as a token of gratitude from that town the national cockade, which was accepted and worn from that day forward by the officers and men of the regiment. The order to leave for Chartres did not arrive, however, until the following day. Meanwhile just before nightfall a Government courier brought orders to the Chevalier de Bachmann to leave 5 companies at Pontoise and set off immediately for Ecouis with the rest of the regiment, reaching Magny that same day; it was thought best to obey these orders, seeing that they were dated later than the order to go to Chartres, which arrived after them. Since it was impossible to obtain the horses and carts necessary for the equipment of the troops, and since nobody at Magny had been warned of the arrival of the regiment, the Chevalier de Bachmann decided to postpone the departure of the troops until the following day, hoping to be able to speed up their march so as to arrive at Ecouis on the 5th as ordered, but having fifteen leagues to go between Pontoise and Ecouis, he did not get there until the morning of the 6th; only 4 companies could be stationed at Ecouis, the others were quartered in neighbouring villages.

The regiment, worn out by very arduous duties and by a march of 15 leagues in less than 24 hours, was looking forward to a breathing space, when, that same night, it received orders from the Marquis d'Harcourt, Commanding Officer in Normandy, to make all haste for Rouen, where disturbances were rife; the regiment arrived there, after an extremely hurried march, about four that same day. When this destination was reached, the Marquis d'Harcourt informed the Chevalier de Bachmann of the duties intended for the regiment, and gave him to understand, in presence of a great number of officers of his own and other regiments, that the safety of France had been entrusted to the Salis-Samade regiment, that Paris was living from hand to mouth, that if it should go short of bread for one single day the people would invade the provinces and plunder the whole kingdom. In order, therefore, to prevent the bread supplies of the capital from running short, it was thought essential to protect from pillage those supplies coming from maritime regions, and entrust them to a body of men long inured to unshakable discipline and loyalty, able to resist temptation as well as fatigue, and led by officers who were experienced, zealous and intelligent.

The escorts provided hitherto had proved unsatisfactory, and it was presumed that the Salis-Samade regiment would acquit itself honourably of this arduous and important task; those who entrusted this task to it did not find their confidence misplaced, since out of the immense number of boats and carts escorted by the regiment not one failed to reach its destination. The Marquis d'Harcourt kept 7 companies at Rouen and next day detached the staff officers with 2 companies of grenadiers to Yvetôt, 1 company of fusiliers to Caudebec, 1 to Boulle and 1 to Quillebeuf at the mouth of the Seine. The troops sent to Yvetôt met with a very hostile reception there, and in order to gain the friendship of the inhabitants they were obliged to spend part of the night on guard duties dictated by circumstances and necessity; they were ordered to escort the convoys of grain from Le Havre on the road to Rouen, while the companies that remained at Rouen provided escorts up the Seine as far as Conflans; these detachments usually remained 10 to 12 days on the boats and then returned by land to Rouen in 4 days; this type of duty, as wearisome for the soldiers as it was burdensome for their officers, often reduced the Rouen companies to such an extent that they could not have a single sentry at their quarters, everyone being employed on escort duty by land and by water.

On August 16th the company of Nicodème Deflue, stationed at Caudebec, detached Lieutenant Blumer, with a sergeant, 19 fusiliers, and as many horsemen of Royal Champagne and volunteers from Caudebec, to the Old Port, to seize a ship loaded with grain and a sum of money of about 42,000 livres resulting from the sale of 3 boatloads of grain, also two persons who had led a gang of several hundreds of armed peasants to take possession of it. This mission was effectively performed and the box containing the sum of 42,000 livres was entrusted to the Sergeant, who kept the keys of it and who, accompanied by 6 of his soldiers, took it over to Caudebec next day, August 17th, and handed it to the officers of the permanent Committee of that town. Gugger's Company, detailed to Quillebeuf, had great difficulty in maintaining order there, since this place had no armed militia and since as much prudence as firmness was required to restrain certain ill-disposed inhabitants and particularly a large number of sailors of all nations.

The extent to which the regiment was scattered can be judged from the following table:

Provinces:		
Île-de-France	5 Companies at Pontoise	
Normandy	7 Companies at Rouen	
	1 Company at Quillebeuf	
Cau	2 Companies and staff officers at Yvetôt	
	1 Company at La Bouille	
	1 Company at Caudebec	
Picardy	1 Company at Albert	
Artois	1 detachment of 50 men at Arras	
Alsace	1 Captain and 35 recruits at Belfort	

In spite of this dispersion and the soldiers' excessive fatigue, not one deserted the flag, and since July 25th the regiment did not lose a single man. On August 17th the company detached to La Bouille received orders to rejoin those at Rouen.

At the beginning of August, the Company detailed to Albert received orders to move to Arras, and during the same month the soldiers who had been taken prisoner at the Bastille managed to rejoin their companies, as did several of those who had been forcibly removed. On September 10th the Company and the ordnance that had been left at Arras, also the staff officers and the companies who had been detailed to Yvetôt, received orders to go to Rouen. The latter arrived there the same day and the detachment from Arras, with the equipment, arrived on the 17th. It must be pointed out that the Yvetôt Committee made the most pressing efforts to keep that very detachment which it had been so reluctant to receive; 3 members of the Committee were successively sent to the Marechal d'Harcourt to press this request, and the Chevalier de Bachmann received a further deputation from the same Committee during the night of September 9th, begging him to prolong his soldiers' stay. The companies at Pontoise, Caudebec and Quillebeuf remained at their posts, since the inhabitants of these places made the most pressing requests for them to stay.

The regiment was exceedingly ill bestowed at Rouen, a few companies occupying the barracks of Martainville outside the town, and 5 companies being quartered in a few monastic houses.

The Salis-Samade regiment went through the whole of this campaign, ever since July 14th, without equipment, the baggage that had been left on the Champ de Mars had been taken to Arras, but the things that the troops from Paris had removed at Vaugirard, Issy and Vanves had been deposited at the Hôtel de Ville and the church of St Jean, where they were left, partly plundered; the remnants of these effects were not returned to the regiment until . . . and then only after repeated requests and protests. This campaign was exceedingly ruinous for the captains and all the officers of the regiment, their clothes were completely worn out by the end of September, the arms and leather equipment stored in the quarters that the regiment had occupied were removed and kept by the troops from Paris, as well as 94 men. The way this regiment was driven from pillar to post ever since July 14th, the high cost of provisions and the difficulty of procuring any, the transport of equipment from Arras to Paris, from Paris to Arras, from Arras to Rouen, the loss of part of the regiment's effects and above all the loss of its permanent establishments, caused incalculable expense and damage to the regiment. These disasters were unable to discourage it or diminish its constant zeal for the public welfare. In the course of this unfortunate campaign the regiment frequently found itself in very difficult situations, from which it always extricated itself with honour and without shedding the blood of a single citizen, it preserved the Capital from famine and from all the ills that might have ensued therefrom; it never assumed that it, or any of the other Swiss regiments, had any other function than to forestall and restrain the disturbances occasioned by insubordinate assemblies, which it has always succeeded in quelling by means of patience, gentleness and prudence. This wise and temperate conduct did not protect the regiment from receiving the most unseemly treatment, suggested by unfair prejudice or provoked by those who lacked all spirit of patriotism. The inhabitants of all the places where this regiment has stayed, either as a unit or in detachments, render justice and homage to it, and will be ready to prove to prejudiced or ill-disposed minds that all the individuals of the Salis-Samade regiment have in this campaign acquired the most legitimate rights to the gratitude of any Frenchman who has his country's welfare at heart, and that they have never ceased to display, in an exceptionally zealous, constant and disinterested fashion, feeling of true brotherhood, such as the French nation was entitled to expect from her oldest, most loyal and most faithful allies.

APPENDIX 3

Eye-witness Account: Extracts from the Memoirs of Pitra, one of the 'Electors' of Paris

The Events of July 14th, 1789

M. de Flesselles, who had somewhat recovered his presence of mind, proposed sending a new deputation to M. de Launey to persuade him, by arguments which he expounded convincingly, to receive in his fortress a certain number of citizens to guard it in conjunction with his soldiers. 'In this way he cannot plead his oath to the King,' said M. de Flesselles, 'in this way we shall make sure of the fortress and shall have nothing to fear from it.' I supported his arguments, adding: 'In this way, with a little intelligence we shall take possession of it.' The Permanent Committee immediately appointed a deputation to convey this resolution to the Governor of the Bastille. M. de Flesselles invited two deputies from the Palais-Royal to accompany it; they refused, and the deputation left immediately. These deputies stayed behind, insistently demanding that the *Prévôt des marchands* should come to vindicate his actions at the Palais-Royal, or at any rate in the main hall. It was at this moment that M. de Flesselles, going up to take a glass of water from a small fireside table, said to me in a low voice: 'What can I do, Monsieur Pitra? I'm done for!' I made no reply; indeed, I was alarmed at his having spoken to me thus, in full view of the crowd. The Committee, during these deliberations, maintained a silence which boded ill for the *Prévôt des marchands*, who was still being urged to appear at the Palais-Royal. He replied that at such a moment he could not leave the Hôtel de Ville to go to the Palais-Royal, but that he would go into the main hall, where people could wait for him, thus making room for the district deputies who could not approach the Committee directly. 'Come, gentlemen,' I said, 'let us go into the main hall, and leave the Committee to do its work.' I went out at once, accompanied only by a handful of spectators, but since several of these were armed this made it easier for me to enter the hall.

Meanwhile M. Clouet, the controller of the powder magazines of the Arsenal, returning from a visit to the Intendant of Finance concerned with this department, wearing a blue coat with gold braid, had been mistaken by the populace in the rue Saint-Antoine for the Governor of the Bastille; they had pulled him from his horse and were dragging him to the Hôtel de Ville. He would never have reached it alive but for the courage and devotion of M. le Chevalier de Saudray, who dashed out into the square to rescue him from the mob which was seeking to tear him in pieces.

At the same time the crowd, uttering terrible cries, was dragging to the Hôtel de Ville three pensioners of the Bastille garrison, having seized hold of them as they left a nearby tavern and were trying to return to the fortress by way of the small drawbridge of the Avancée. The mob accused them of having fired on the citizens, and clamoured loudly for their death; and the unfortunate wretches only owed their lives to the presence of mind of an elector who said that these pensioners must be questioned so as to secure information about the state of the Bastille, and kept as hostages for the behaviour of the Governor, to whom a deputation had just been sent, requesting him to accept a citizens' guard for the fortress along with his garrison.

I cannot attempt to describe the scene in the main hall. The amphitheatres and the rows of seats all round it were filled by a crowd of people armed with guns, pikes, swords and even sticks with knives fastened to them; others, who by their atrocious expressions even more than by their dress resembled the brigands we had disarmed only the day before, filled the centre of the hall; they were armed, for the most part, with old-fashioned or foreign axes which they had taken from the Garde-meuble; some of them, shoeless and almost without breeches, were armed only with stonemasons' hammers. They were loudly clamouring for the electors, who stood in a tiny group at the far end of the hall, unable to find seats, and trying in vain, through this terrifying tumult, to obtain silence.

I had at last succeeded, with the greatest difficulty, in making my way into this hall, and I was trying to reach that part of it where the electors stood, when I was met by four armed citizens from my district, who had been sent to fetch me. The news of what had happened at the Bastille had reached my district, and my fellow-citizens there were in the greatest ferment of excitement. However, when I told them that every minute brought news of fresh attacks on different faubourgs, particularly the faubourg Saint-Honoré, they realized their personal danger, and were persuaded to send representatives to the Hôtel de Ville to find out for certain what was happening at the Bastille and to bring me back to my district. I made haste to follow them and was on my way out with them, when we encountered on the staircase the new deputation which the Permanent Committee was sending to the Bastille. While I was in the main hall, where despite the terrifying hubbub the shouts of the people on the Place outside could still be heard, a crowd of citizens came up to announce to the Committee, in tones of mingled fury and despair, that the Bastille was still firing on the people. They brought along with them a young man who had had his arm broken in front of the fortress. These infuriated citizens were demanding arms, cannon, and gunpowder, and wanting to march off and besiege the Bastille. They accused the Committee, which included the majority of the Electors, and above all the *Prévôt des marchands*, of all that day's misfortunes, and they threatened to make them suffer for these.

It was in this highly dangerous and alarming situation that the Committee, having received no news of the deputation it had sent to the Bastille, and realizing that it had no distinctive mark which would enable it to approach the fortress, decided to send another preceded by a white flag, a drum and some soldiers from the city. M. de Corny, *procureur* of the King and of the City, was at the head of this deputation, whose purpose was to arrange a parley, to persuade the citizens to leave the Bastille and return to their districts, and to order M. de Launey to receive in his fortress a certain number of citizens who should guard it along with the garrison.

But before describing the adventures of these two deputations and my own return to my district, I must give some account of what had taken place in the Bastille after M. de Launey's imprudent admission of the citizens into the Avancée and the still more imprudent military action which was its unfortunate sequel.

The mob which had rushed into the Avancée as soon as M. de Launey had the drawbridge lowered had been, as I have said, driven out by musket shot, and a burst from the cannon charged with grapeshot, killing or wounding many citizens outside the Avancée, caused the crowds surrounding the Bastille to draw back. But this first impulse of panic had quickly been replaced by that of revenge; the people soon gathered together again, in even greater numbers than before the first cannon shot had announced the opening of hostilities. All those citizens of the Saint-Antoine district and the others closest to the Bastille who had fire-arms and a share of the powder which had been seized and taken to the Hôtel de Ville on the previous day, had flocked thither.

This disorderly rabble had taken up its stand all round the fortress, wherever it was sheltered from the garrison's fire; the greater part under the archway between the rue Saint-Antoine and the Arsenal; they stood at the entrance to this archway, facing the Bastille, and fired at the fortress whenever they caught sight of a soldier on the walls; others, stationed in the many shacks surrounding it, kept up a continuous fire which, however, did little harm to the garrison, merely enabling it to aim more effectively at those who emerged from these houses to shoot unavailingly at the soldiers on the top of the towers. The garrison would not have lost a single man in this sort of attack had not one individual, who lived in a nearby house roughly the same height as the Bastille, decided to go up on to his roof and shelter behind a chimney, from which vantage-point he aimed at the gunners as soon as they emerged unprotected on to the platform to man their cannon. He killed and wounded several of them, while they, being fired at on all sides, could not guess whence came these more deadly shots. Meanwhile the cannon fire from the Bastille raked the rue Saint-Antoine, where it caused more terror than damage, although the balls flew as far as the place Royale.

This sporadic cannon fire did not prevent a vast crowd of citizens, most of them moved solely by curiosity, from making their way to the Bastille either along the rue Saint-Antoine or the boulevard leading into it, which had also been subjected to a number of volleys.

At the same time, another crowd of citizens was moving through the garden of the Arsenal to the gate that divided it from the Bastille: this multitude, armed only with pitchforks, scythes and other agricultural implements, came from the faubourg Saint-Marceau. It was led by a brewer named Acloque; and this man, who showed great courage during the Revolution, had much difficulty in making the assailants stay behind the trees and the Governor's house so as to be sheltered from the shots being fired from the Tour de la Comté and raking this part of the Arsenal garden. But from that part of the faubourg Saint-Antoine that skirts the Bastille and leads to La Rapée, another brewer named Santerre, at the head of a crowd of inhabitants of that district, was firing at that part of the fortress that faces it. To shield himself and those of the citizens who were stationed in the neighbouring houses, M. Santerre had set fire to several cartloads of manure, the smoke from which was driven by the wind directly on to the Bastille, hiding him and his troop from the besieged garrison.

It was amid this tumultuous attack that M. de la Vigne, President of the Electors, at the head of the first deputation sent, as I have told, by the Permanent Committee, got into the Cour de l'Orme and came within a hundred yards of the Bastille. From here, these emissaries had seen the soldiers of the garrison, scattered about the platform, firing and aiming at the very court in which they were. They had tried in vain to make signs, which had not been recognized either by the garrison or by the citizens who surrounded the Bastille. Unable to make their way to the Porte de l'Avancée through here, the delegates had gone round by the rue de la Cerisaie, hoping to reach the archway of the Arsenal which opens on to the rue Saint-Antoine; but this side was even more inaccessible; the whole of this vast space was full of a crowd of people, of armed citizens led by brave Lieutenant Elie, who had returned in uniform and assembled them around this part of the Bastille, from which, unprotected, they kept up uninterrupted fire on the fortress, the only advantage thus gained being to drive the garrison a few feet back from the parapet. Finding themselves unable to make their way through this crowd of attackers or persuade these to listen to them, the delegates had returned to the Cour de l'Orme by way of the rue de la Cerisaie; here they succeeded in obtaining a cease-fire in this part of the siege by announcing to the citizens that they had come on a mission of peace. They had reached a point not far from the Avancée, and in the same way had got the citizens to cease firing from the arch of the Arsenal; but their repeated signals were unavailing, the garrison appeared not to see them and went on firing volleys which killed several citizens before their eyes; one bullet pierced the cloak of the abbé Fauchet, a member of the deputation. The assailants, seeing that the emissaries were being fired on in spite of their signals, which they thought must surely be seen from the top of the fortress, then gave vent to cries of indignation; the delegates were thrust aside, the crowd had no further use for parleying: they clamoured for cannons, they wanted to seize the Bastille and put to death the infamous Governor and his garrison. Such was the report that the delegation was obliged to make on its return to the Hôtel de Ville.

A considerable crowd followed the delegates, demanding vengeance and asking for cannon to besiege the Bastille. Just at this moment (it was about two o'clock), when a disorderly and un-armed mob was surging round the Bastille on almost every side, when the wounded men being brought into the Hôtel de Ville and the lack of success of this first deputation intensified the fury and vindictiveness of the crowd that filled the place de Grève, a hitherto unknown individual appeared at the head of two com-panies of *gardes-françaises*, the same companies which had been that morning to the Trône *barrière* and which those at the Bastille had sought to retain, but which had subsequently remained drawn up in battle array on the place de Grève. Cheers, which rang out as far as the Hôtel de Ville, announced their departure, and they soon appeared followed by pieces of ordnance and by other troops of armed citizens who joined their ranks. The staff officers gave these companies and the people who accompanied them the bullets and the scanty amount of powder still in stock at the Hôtel de Ville.

It was at this moment that the second deputation, which had been sent bearing a flag of truce, returned to the Hôtel de Ville. This deputation had at first won some sort of success, for when the flag was seen from the Bastille, the standard-bearer and the drummer had been able to approach the drawbridge of the Avancée; presently a white flag was seen flying from the platform, the soldiers of the garrison had reversed their arms, and they and the attackers were waving their hats at one another in token of peace, for the sight of the flag of truce had produced this effect on both sides. Already the emissaries had succeeded in persuading those of the attackers who were able to hear their words to move aside, thus enabling the Governor to open the Avancée for them, and themselves to fulfil a mission which was to bring peace; they stepped confidently forward, expecting to see the drawbridge lowered, when in spite of the white flag which was flying from the walls of the Bastille, all of a sudden the soldiers lined up there, who had been holding their weapons reversed, fired a volley that prostrated several citizens beneath them and tore the epaulette of M. de Beaubourg, one of the delegates. This fact, confirmed by a thousand witnesses, occurred because the attackers on the faubourg Saint-Antoine side, who could not see the white flag flying on the tower of La Basinière on the Arsenal side, fired a volley against the Bastille. The Governor may have thought that they were trying to surprise him from one side while pretending to parley on the other. This may perhaps have been the cause of an event which had such dire consequences for M. de Launey; it is one of those whose true cause will never be known. The moment which was to cost the life of this man, as imprudent as he was unfortunate, was drawing near; but I must now break off the story of the attack on the Bastille to describe what was happening at the Hôtel de Ville.

The news of the return of the emissaries with their flag of truce, and the story they told, soon spread through the place de Grève; indignation and rage possessed every heart. The roar of the Bastille cannon could be heard, while the *gardes-françaises* attacked the citadel; the crowd in the Place displayed a most ominous distrust of the *Prévôt des marchands* and the electors, accusing them of conniving with M. de Launey, and of being traitors, who must be sacrificed to the vengeance of the citizens they had betrayed; finally the populace that filled the place de Grève and thronged around the Hôtel de Ville clamoured to set fire to it and to burn the *Prévôt des marchands*, the aldermen (*échevins*) and the Permanent Committee with it. These were undoubtedly in greater danger, at this juncture, than the Governor of the Bastille and its attackers. Soon after, when I was at the head of the Provisional Committee, I had some citizens beg favours from me as a reward for having restrained the fury of the people on this occasion and at the risk of their own lives opposed attempts to set fire to the Hôtel de Ville. Several of them told me how they had argued with the infuriated multitude, pointing out that they would cause the death of three or four thousand innocent persons who happened to be assembled in the hall, the courtyard and the corridors of the Hôtel de Ville, including maybe their own fathers, brothers or

Appendices

children. Two individuals assured me that in the neighbourhood of the rue de Mouton they extinguished a lighted candle with which a young man was preparing to set fire to a bundle of straw he held under his arm. Finally I am convinced that it was one of that day's miracles that the Hôtel de Ville was not burnt down and all those within it slaughtered, and that this shocking misfortune was only averted because the crowd that was thronging around it prevented those who, like the above-mentioned young man, were provided with fire and combustible material, from getting near to it.

While these ominous cries rang through the square, the Permanent Committee, installed at the far end of the Hôtel de Ville where it could not hear them, but accused and threatened at every instant by the crowd that filled the place, sent two Electors to Versailles to report to the National Assembly about the situation in Paris and to ask for arms. This resolution, recorded in the *Procès-verbal des électeurs*, is perhaps, considering the moment when it was taken, one of the most remarkable tributes to the courage of those who made up the Permanent Committee.

It was during this time of terror that a man was brought into the Hôtel de Ville bearing a packet addressed to M. du Pujet, *major* of the Bastille. This packet contained a letter which ran as follows:

'I am sending you, my dear du Pujet, the order which you think necessary.

Paris, July 14th. Signed: Besenval.'

This letter enclosed another addressed to M. de Launey:

'M. de Launey is to hold firm to the end; I have sent him sufficient forces.

July 14th, 1789. Signed: Baron de Besenval.'

It is clear from this order addressed to M. du Pujet that he doubted whether M. de Launey was prepared to resist to the end, and that he had asked M. de Besenval for this order so as to force him to do so. We have the more reason to believe this, in that an officer of the Invalides who was in the Bastille told me and some other people next day that on Monday 13th, at midday, M. de Launey had held a council of war or staff meeting of the officers in the garrison, in which he had made clear his intention of surrendering if he were attacked, in view of the inadequate help to be expected from the company of pensioners which was then the sole garrison of the Bastille, since the forty Swiss guards did not arrive until Monday night.

In any case, these letters, when read aloud to the Committee before the throng that filled the hall, inflamed men's minds still further; there were murmured accusations against the *Prévôt des marchands* of having encouraged the Governor to prolong the resistance required of him, by omitting and even obstructing preparations to seize the Bastille. M. de Flesselles, who like the Permanent Committee knew nothing about the departure of two companies of *gardes-françaises* because they had left from the back of the Hôtel de Ville, gave strength to these suspicions by spending what seemed an endless time to the impatient crowd, listening to the suggestion made by a carpenter for breaching the Bastille by means of a catapult, the appearance and use of which he described at great length. He was also tactless enough to listen to proposals made by Major de Caussidière for a regular siege of the fortress, with open trenches.

These proposals and the discussions they involved exacerbated people's impatience, and increasingly inflamed suspicions which they seemed to justify. The crowd that filled the Committee rooms was expressing its fury against the Governor of the Bastille, and openly displaying its suspicion of the *Prévôt des marchands* and the Permanent Committee itself, when an old man called out: *'My friends, why waste time over these traitors? Let's march on the Bastille . . .'* and the mob followed him.

While the Permanent Committee breathed freely for a moment, having got rid of the crowd which had flocked after the old man, citizens who had been injured before the Bastille were being carried up to the Military Committee, which was stationed below the Hôtel de Ville. The mob that filled the courtyard of the Hôtel de Ville, inflamed by the sight of these poor wretches, rushed up to the hall where the Permanent Committee sat; finding it closed, they forced open the doors, uttering curses against all its members, whom they accused of hiding there so as to betray the city more irrevocably. I was told by one of the clerks who were at this door that they were flung to the ground and dragged by the hair by this maddened mob. The *Prévôt des marchands*, aware of his danger, tried to speak, but was shouted down with insults, cries of treachery, and demands that he should go to the Palais-Royal or into the main hall to vindicate himself.

Finally, in the midst of this terrifying tumult, M. de Flesselles, despite warnings of the even greater danger he would run in the main hall, and despite the efforts of M. l'abbé Fauchet to dissuade him, rose to go thither, saying: 'Since they insist, let's go.' He left the Committee, with the crowd following close on his heels. The main hall was so full of a dense mob, swaying hither and thither, that de Flesselles' arrival was unnoticed until he had taken his place at the desk. Several persons immediately aimed their guns at him; and if he survived a few minutes longer, with the anguished apprehension of death clearly legible on his features, he owed this misfortune to the fear, imparted to these madmen by their neighbours, of harming those electors who had followed M. de Flesselles and were standing beside him around the desk.

While the attack on the Bastille was proceeding and the life of the *Prévôt des marchands* hung in the balance, I had gone to my own district; I had found it in a state of extreme ferment; the news of the first civilian casualties at the Bastille had just reached it; people wanted to set forth immediately to be avenged on the Governor for his perfidy in firing on those to whom he had opened the Avancée, under pretext of giving them arms. I had great difficulty in allaying the citizens' excitement and in dissuading them from marching on the Bastille forthwith. I announced, and I was supported by the evidence of the four citizens who had come to the Hôtel de Ville to fetch me, that a new deputation had just been sent to the Governor of the Bastille urging him to accept a certain number of townspeople into the fortress to guard it in cooperation with the garrison. I added that I had no doubt but that M. de Launey would accept a proposal which safeguarded us against any infringement of the decision we had taken the previous day, by which we had sworn not to attack the King's property, and that above all we should not expose the lives of the brave citizens of the district, which were my particular concern. 'But', said I, 'if M. de Launey should not surrender, if he should fire on the citizens again, I will march at your head with a cannon.' And I proposed that horses should be harnessed to this cannon forthwith. I have found it indispensable to give an account of this fact, which concerns myself alone and has little connection with the absorbing stories which I have interrupted, because my supposed refusal to march to the Bastille when asked to do so was one of the chief heads of the indictment levelled against me a few days later.

For that matter, the horses had barely been harnessed to the piece of ordnance when the news of M. de Launey's second act of apparent treachery, the shots fired on the second deputation with its flag of truce, reached my district and revived the popular fury. I did not hesitate, because I partook of the general indignation; I seized a musket from a citizen, who tried in vain to wrest it back from me, and soon I set forth at the head of a hundred armed citizens, taking a cannon along with us; flying rather than marching, we made our way towards that Bastille whose name we uttered with a sort of fury, along the rue Saint-Honoré and the rue de la Verrerie. We presently reached the place Baudoyer, where confused shouts informed us of the fall of the Bastille; we could not believe it. The troop I was leading hurried forward to reach the spot in time, and accused me of delays which might prevent it from sharing in the glory of the Bastille's capture; but soon the frantic excitement and the shouts of the crowd returning from the Bastille, which blocked our way when we came level with the Jesuits' house in the rue Saint-Antoine, left us in no doubt about this great event.

I should try in vain to describe the effect of this popular triumph, the mingled joy and fury displayed by the crowd, armed with such motley weapons, that soon filled the rue Saint-Antoine from side to side. The spectacle of this turbulent multitude was rendered even more terrifying by the shouts which we heard in the distance and which were repeated by the inconceivable number of women, children and old men who seemed ready to leap out of the windows of the houses, crying: 'Here they are, the wretches! we've got them!'

I tried to break through this crowd so as to take a few steps forward away from my troop, but I was soon swept away by the torrent and practically carried as far as the Saint-Jean arcade. Here I struggled free, with the help of a few soldiers of the town who were guarding the door of the little stair which connects this archway with the Hôtel de Ville, and extricated myself from the crowd which was rushing on towards the place de Grève. With renewed difficulty I succeeded in making my way through the multitude that obstructed the passages leading to the main hall; I was swept forward and knocked down, and if I was not crushed underfoot, this was due to three vigorous men who picked me up, saying that I was an elector. I subsequently had the good fortune to be of some service to one of those who saved my life at this moment. I forced my way up to the desk, saying that I had come from the Bastille, which was not true, and by confirming the news of its fall, which had already reached the Hôtel de Ville but of which the crowd, the majority of the Electors and, in particular, the *Prévôt des marchands* still stood in doubt.

M. de Flesselles seemed almost calm as he went on unsealing the letters that had been laid on his desk, when the cries that arose in the square outside, repeated by the multitude that thronged the stairs and passages of the Hôtel de Ville, announced the arrival of the Conquerors of the Bastille. I must observe that at this moment, the memory of which will never fade from my memory, when the universal cry '*The Bastille has fallen!*' echoed through the great hall, I saw the *Prévôt des marchands* turn pale and almost tremble; the suspicions which I was unable to repress had made me observe him closely. I am by no means anxious to accuse him or to hold him guilty on this account, but I can still picture the sort of stupefaction that possessed him when the fall of the Bastille was confirmed by the triumphant shouts of the crowd and, soon, by the presence of its conquerors.

It was amidst these cries of victory, or rather amidst the confused noise of a hundred thousand voices surrounding or filling the Hôtel de Ville, that we saw the Conquerors of the Bastille enter, or rather rush into, the great hall. This horde of men of all conditions, armed in such diverse manners, all breathing vengeance and carnage, were dragging with them thirty or forty pensioners or Swiss guards and shouting: '*Hang them! death! no quarter!*' These men, whose faces and eyes blazing with anger were as terrifying as their cries, were followed by a crowd of citizens mingled with *gardes-françaises*, bearing brave Elie aloft in their arms. What a sight was there! This man, wearing the uniform of the Queen's regiment, on which the stains of blood could be clearly seen, hatless, his hair standing up wildly on his brow, holding in his left hand a sword which was warped in several places and almost buckled, striving vainly to free himself from the arms of those who, forcing their way through the eager throng, sought to carry him, and indeed, succeeded in carrying him, up to the desk. Ah, how splendid brave Elie looked, as the marquis de la Salle walked before him, holding out for the crowd to see the keys of the Bastille and the form of surrender which Elie had handed over to him! I saw him carried up to the desk and borne aloft for a long time in men's arms, looking the very image of the god of war. They raised him on to a table which was soon surrounded by prisoners and loaded with the trophies brought from the Bastille. On the dais stood M. de la Salle, showing the people the keys of the Bastille, which he held up for some time above the head of M. de Flesselles, who sat there as though beneath a thunderbolt which was about to strike him. Motionless during this scene, which was watched by an excited crowd whose movements I should try in vain to represent, the unfortunate Flesselles seemed a dead man already. Soon a new crowd brought into the hall, and led to the feet of Elie, a youth who had seized the banner of the Bastille, and another man bearing at the end of his gun a thick record-book which was said to be the register of the Bastille; they were followed by a considerable number of citizens who filed in carrying a quantity of old armour they had seized in the arsenal of the Bastille, and the Governor's silver plate. Elie was surrounded by all these trophies, which were offered him by the people, and which I repeatedly saw him refuse.

But soon arose a terrible cry, the memory of which still freezes my blood: '*Here he is, here he is!*' heralded the arrival of the Governor of the Bastille. I dreaded seeing him appear in the great hall, because his inevitable death would have been the signal for the public slaughter of the prisoners, when an even more terrible cry, echoing like thunder, told us that some dreadful event was taking place on the square outside. We learned before long that the people, in spite of the efforts that had been made, as I shall shortly describe, to bring M. de Launey to the Hôtel de Ville, had massacred the unfortunate Governor on the lowest steps of the perron.

APPENDIX 4

A Newspaper Report: *Les Révolutions de Paris,* no. 1, July 17th, 1789

A Detailed Account of Tuesday July 14th

The night of Monday the 13th passed very quietly, except that the *garde bourgeoise* arrested some thirty-four vagrants guilty of robbing and damaging the monastic house of Saint-Lazare; they were taken to jail.

This morning an order of the Electors, assembled at the Hôtel de Ville, determined the insignia of the citizens' militia: yesterday, the green and white cockade was being worn; today it is cast underfoot, and replaced by the blue and red, colours in keeping with the arms of the city.

The troops encamped on the Champs-Elysées moved away last night; it is not yet known whither they have withdrawn.

While the perfidious *Prévôt des marchands* was closing his meeting, a citizen came to testify that a convoy of powder and shot had just been stolen from us by the soldiers encamped around Paris; in vain this citizen repeated his evidence, confirming it with authentic proofs, de Flesselles would not listen to him; finding himself at last obliged to reply, he said with a careless smile: '*Well, we'll have to make a note of all that.*' What an excess of patriotism!

Since he kept promising to deliver arms, and failing to deliver them, the decision was made to march to the Invalides: the gentlemen of the legal profession, accompanied by a crowd of people, made their way thither; already they were scrambling over ditches and up walls, when the gunners and pensioners, seeing that resistance was useless, opened the gates; they rushed to the armouries and discovered vast quantities of arms; cannon were seized; the good curé of Saint-Etienne-du-Mont brought along his militia; citizens hurried there in throngs, and from ten o'clock in the morning until nightfall were busily collecting weapons; indeed it is impossible to reckon the vast number of arms removed; some people say twenty-six thousand guns, not to mention pistols, swords and bayonets.

To avoid any risk of a surprise attack, it was thought prudent to search all carriages and all couriers coming in and out of the capital; this precaution revealed more than one case of treachery; the military police summarily hanged several individuals who were convicted of disloyalty or accused of heinous intentions towards the citizens and the fatherland. Convoys were discovered, one intended for the King, consisting of several cartloads of grain: quantities of equipment: two waggons bearing the arms of the Queen, loaded with clothes for use as disguise: a number of aristocrats intending to take refuge on their estates, carrying with them their treasures and their weapons. The seizure of these various effects finally made patent the treachery of the *Prévôt des marchands*; he had kept up a secret correspondence with our bitterest foe; several letters prove this, notably that which he wrote to the Governor of the Bastille; it was then that, despite the protests and entreaties of certain members of the Committee who wanted to find him innocent, he was definitively declared guilty; he was then forced to leave the eminent place he occupied and go down on to the place de Grève, to appear before a crowd inspired by hatred and perhaps by a sense of justice; its murmurs now gave way to a horrifying calm; one man seized a dagger, another a pistol, a third a cutlass, blows fell thick and fast, his life was quickly over and his head went rolling afar in mud and filth, while his body fell a prey to all the fury of a populace transported with rage and revenge.

But a signal and illustrious victory, which will still amaze our grandsons, was the capture of the Bastille in the space of about four hours.

The citizens gathered at the Hôtel de Ville, aware of the urgent need to capture so redoubtable a fortress, had already sent, that morning, a deputation consisting of four electors and twenty-four other deputies to demand arms from the Governor and summon him to surrender the citadel. He duly promised to hand over weapons and not to fire on the citizens; he even wrote to the curés of Saint-Paul and Sainte-Marguerite, urging them to reassure the people with words of peace; but orders from a superior authority made him change his mind. This is confirmed by a letter from the baron de Besenval, that odious foreigner, urging him to '*hold out against the people ; he'd soon manage to get rid of them*'.

The people first took the rue Saint-Antoine in an attempt to enter this citadel, into which no man ever went except by leave of the monster Despotism, who still reigned there. The treacherous Governor hung out the white flag of peace. Then the citizens advanced fearlessly. A detachment of *gardes-françaises*, with some five or six hundred armed townsfolk, made their way into the courtyards of the fortress; but as soon as a number of people had crossed over by the first drawbridge, it was promptly raised again: a volley of artillery fire laid low several *gardes-françaises* and some soldiers; the cannon was fired on the city, and the people were seized with panic; a great many persons were killed or wounded; but they rallied, they took shelter from the gunfire; they rushed off to get cannon; those belonging to the Invalides had just been seized; an urgent summons was sent to all districts to send help promptly; the arms from the Invalides were put at the citizens' disposal; a great crowd of people arrived from the faubourg Saint-Antoine; they placed guns on the edge of the moat, so as to attack the Bastille by way of its gardens; while some fresh detachments of *gardes-françaises* and of people from the districts hurried up along the Port au bled [the grain wharf] with pieces of ordnance. They made their way through the Cour des Célestins, and tried to attack through the Arsenal gardens; but this attempt was unsuccessful; they advanced into the Cour des Salpètres; they soon crossed this, and arrived in front of the drawbridge, where they took possession of the guardroom and the pensioners' lodgings. It was proposed to make a ladder with bayonets thrust into the wall, so as to climb up and saw off the posts to which the chains of the drawbridge were fastened; but the danger was too imminent; it was decided to smash them by gunfire. Meanwhile the enemy's fire and our own was intensifying every moment; an ingenious device served us admirably. Two cartloads of dung and straw were unloaded and set on fire; the thick smoke formed an impenetrable cloud which concealed our manoeuvres from the garrison. The chains of the first drawbridge were soon broken; it fell, the people rushed across and entered the first courtyard; here they found the first victims of the battle, the sight of whom inspired them with fresh courage; the attackers laid formal siege, amidst incessant fire from either side; the Governor's lodging was set on fire, while the officer in charge of powder and saltpetre was arrested. Because of his uniform, he was mistaken for the traitor de Launey; he was roughly handled and taken off to the Hôtel de Ville, where at last he was recognized and set free. But to return to the Bastille: our people were in front of the second drawbridge; they sought to penetrate the fortress, for the first court stands outside its precincts. The fighting became more and more violent; the citizens had become inured to fire; on all sides they were climbing up on to roofs, into rooms, and as soon as a pensioner appeared between the battlements on the tower he became a target for a hundred marksmen, who shot him down instantly, while gunfire and a hail of cannon balls pierced the second drawbridge and broke its chains; the cannon on the towers roared in vain, our men, whose fury was at its height, were safe from it, or rather they braved death and danger; women did their utmost to back us up; even children, after every volley from the fortress, ran here and there picking up bullets and shot, then dodged back joyfully to take shelter and give these missiles to our soldiers, who then sent them back to carry death through the air to the despicable garrison. In vain these traitors feigned surrender, no one believed in their signals; at last, soon afterwards, the enemy produced a document which they thrust through the opening of the drawbridge, but distance made this impossible to read. The citizens ran to fetch planks to lay across the moat; the first who ventured across was an unfortunate civilian who fell into the moat, a victim of his zeal. A second stepped forward and brought back the letter; it contained the words: *We have twenty thousand pounds of powder; we will blow up the garrison and the whole neighbourhood, unless you accept our capitulation.* Meanwhile the firing went on; the cannon balls hurled against the drawbridge finally broke one of its chains; the enemy saw that the bridge was about to fall, and realizing that there was no hope, lowered the small drawbridge of the passage-gate. Three men, Elie, Hullin and Maillard, then leapt on to the bridge and fearlessly demanded that the last gate should be opened; the enemy obeyed; our men sought to force an entrance; the garrison defended itself; we slaughtered all who opposed our progress; every gunner that stepped forward bit the dust; the people rushed on, breathing vengeance; the staircase was reached, the prisoners seized, the people forced their way in everywhere; some took possession of the guardrooms, others rushed on to the towers; they hoisted the sacred flag of the nation, amid the applause and raptures of a vast crowd.

And now the great drawbridge was lowered; the hunt was on for the Governor; an intrepid Grenadier, brave Arné, caught sight of him; he dashed forward and arrested de Launey, who tried to stab himself; Arné disarmed him, handed him over to Hullin and Elie, and then rushed off to face fresh dangers. Meanwhile the treacherous Governor was in the hands of his conquerors, who tore his insignia from him, indicting him as an infamous villain; as he was dragged forward amidst a vast crowd, he spoke to the youth who was leading him and trying to protect him from the insults of the populace: 'Ah,' he said, racked with remorse, 'I have betrayed my country!' and sobs choked his voice. Meanwhile the sub-governor, the major, the captain of artillery and all the prisoners of war had been arrested; the cells were thrown open to set free innocent victims and venerable old men, who were amazed to behold the light of day.[1] Holy, august Liberty, for the first time, was introduced into that region of horror, that fearful abode of despotism, of monsters and of crimes.

Meanwhile the attackers marched out amidst an enormous crowd; applause, excessive joy, insults and curses lavished against the captive traitors, all were intermingled; cries of vengeance and delight sounded on all sides; the victors, triumphant and loaded with honours, bearing the arms and trophies of the vanquished, the banners of victory, the militia mingling with the soldiers of the fatherland, the tributes offered them on every side, all this formed a terrible and a splendid spectacle. When they reached the place de Grève, the populace, impatient for revenge, did not allow de Launey nor the other officers to face the city's tribunal; wresting them from the hands of their captors, it crushed them underfoot, one after the other; de Launey was stabbed a thousand times, his head was cut off and carried, streaming with blood, on the end of a spear. Two other heads were being thus displayed when the

[1] A harmless old man had been imprisoned there for thirty years. It need not be said what an immense collection of documents, what a quantity of titles, registers of imprisonment, and all sorts of materials for the historian have been discovered in the Bastille; amidst a vast number of weapons and flags there were found, so it is said, instruments of death hitherto unknown to man. (*Note published by the newspaper.*)

325

pensioners from the Bastille were brought forward. The people demanded their death; but the generous *gardes-françaises* pleaded for mercy for them, and at their request a unanimous pardon was granted.

The events of this glorious day will astonish our enemies, and foretell at last the triumph of justice and liberty.

That night the city was illuminated.

APPENDIX 5

Memoirs of Bailly, Mayor of Paris, concerning the Events of July 17th, 1789

Extracts from the 'Collection of memoirs relating to the French Revolution'

Friday July 17th—I rose very early, intending to leave for Paris at seven o'clock, and before that to prepare what I was to say to the King on receiving him at the gates of Paris. I was sorry to leave Versailles; I had been happy there in an Assembly whose temper was excellent, and which was worthy of the great functions which it was called upon to fulfil. I had seen great things done, and had had some share in them. I was leaving all these memories behind: that day, my happiness was over. I have known splendid days since then and moments of satisfaction, but I have not been happy.

I had sent for a carriage. I was kept waiting to leave; I could not conceive why. When I went out, I was met by all the court coachmen, who offered me a tree loaded with flowers and ribbons. I was sorry to be leaving Versailles, and the people there were sorry to see me go. I had to allow them to fasten this tree to the front of my coach; all the coachmen accompanied me, letting off fireworks although it was broad daylight, right to the end of the avenue; I could not prevent this. Finally I left them at the end of the avenue, much touched by their friendly pageantry, and much relieved to be able to go on my way freely after being somewhat delayed. I incurred much praise in the newspapers for the simplicity with which, though chief official of the capital, I arrived in Paris in one of those carriages vulgarly known as 'chamber-pots'. Since then, satirists have censured me for ostentation. My own opinion was that the first official of the greatest city in the world ought to be simple in his person and in his way of living, as magistrate of the people, and at the same time should be surrounded by a certain grandeur, as representative of a great city and depositary of its dignity.

I had asked for a hired coach, which I found in the place Louis XV, where I left Madame Bailly, and which took me to the Hôtel de Ville, where I arrived at ten o'clock. I found everyone there busily preparing to receive the King. The aldermen (*échevins*) asked to be separated from the Electors and to appear in their municipal robes, which were of velvet. Such pretentiousness was utterly ridiculous. They were told: 'If you wish to distinguish yourselves from the Electors who have saved Paris, you are free to do so.' It is also said that the aldermen asked whether they should kneel down to speak; they were told 'that they were free, too, to perpetuate this servile attitude; but that in this case the Electors would wish to be separated from the aldermen.' I must add that the first request was made to me, as head of the municipal authorities, and that I know nothing about the second. It was not in the power of the aldermen to perpetuate this custom. It was my duty to speak, and no authority would have made me do so otherwise than standing upright. I had won this battle at Versailles, on behalf of the whole nation; I would not have consented to come to Paris to lose it on behalf of my fellow-townsfolk.

We left to meet the King, twenty-five chosen Electors, twenty-five members of the municipal body, the entire company of the City's guards; and I walked at the head, preceded by the Colonel of the guards and by MM. Buffault and Vergue, aldermen, carrying the city keys in a silver-gilt bowl, each in his turn. As I walked I asked a few questions about the ceremony of these keys; I asked what the King would do when I had handed them to him. 'He will give them back to you.' 'And what shall I do then?' 'You will keep them.' 'Do you think I am going to carry these great heavy keys all the way? I shall throw them down at the first opportunity.' 'On no account; these keys are precious; they're the ones that were presented to Henri IV.' This immediately gave me the idea for the opening words of my speech, which I hurriedly pencilled down.

In old days the city generally received the King at the place Louis XV, because the city boundaries were there, at the gate named 'de la Conférence', which has long since been demolished. We made our way beyond this, and went as far as Chaillot, opposite the fire-pump. We met some three hundred deputies who were on their way to Paris to make up the King's procession. I have said that Paris was not anxious for me to ask for the King's confirmation. M. de Clermont-Tonnerre had proposed to the Assembly, on the previous day, that his deputation should make this request to the King. Nothing had been decided about this suggestion. My own attitude was to remain calm and in readiness; the position was a new one; no forms were established, and it was not for me to lay down rules or make suggestions. My role was to wait. Presumably the matter had been attended to at Court; for the Prince de Poix, on his arrival, warned me that the King would say something to me about it. The King arrived. I presented the keys to him, saying:

'Sire,

'I bring your Majesty the keys of his good city of Paris: they are the very ones which were presented to Henri IV; he had reconquered his people, and here the people have reconquered their King.

'Your Majesty has come to enjoy the peace that you have restored to the capital; you have come to enjoy the love of your faithful subjects. It is for their happiness that Your Majesty has summoned to your side the representatives of the nation, in cooperation with whom you are about to lay the foundations of liberty and public prosperity. What a memorable day is this, when Your Majesty comes to sit as a father amidst this united family! having been escorted to your palace by the entire National Assembly! Protected by the representatives of the nation, surrounded by a vast and eager throng, your Majesty's august features expressed sensibility and happiness, while all around your people acclaimed you joyfully, and shed tears of emotion and love. Sire, neither your people nor yourself will ever forget this great day; it is the finest day of the monarchy; it marks the epoch of an eternal alliance between the monarch and the people. This event is unique in history; it confers immortality upon Your Majesty. I have witnessed this great day; and as though all happiness were bestowed upon me, my first function in the office to which my fellow-citizens have called me is to bring you the expression of their love.'

I spoke out of the fulness of my heart; I have always had personal affection for the King, but my devotion has been in keeping with circumstances and with reason, that is to say next to my country, and after having fulfilled all my duties towards the nation; all that I said here was true. My principles and my character have always made me averse to adulation; my greatest art and eloquence consisted in speaking nothing but the truth. This day of conciliation could have been the finest in the history of the monarchy and in the life of the King, if the first impulses had been constantly followed, above all by the King himself. The phrase: 'He had reconquered his people, and here the people have reconquered their King', won universal applause. Since then, the enemies of the state, who have used as one of their weapons the discrediting of respected men and of true and loyal citizens, have sought to blame me for it, claiming that I had dared tell the King that he was the people's captive. Such an interpretation would have found no listeners at the time; and indeed it was not put forward till a year later. The clear and only meaning of the phrase is: Henri IV had won back his people, here the people have won back their king. The word *reconquered* was used as being stronger and more vivid; but reconquered by means of affection, and the shunning of such counsels as had misled him.

M. de La Vigne spoke to the King after myself, as President, and in the name of the Electors.

The King replied that he was happy to receive the homage of the city of Paris and of the Electors.

The procession passed along the place Louis XV, the rue Saint-Honoré, the rue du Roule, and the embankment as far as the Hôtel de Ville; the way was lined on either side by rows of national guardsmen, three deep almost everywhere and even four deep, armed with muskets, swords, pikes, lances, scythes, cudgels, etc.; there were women to be seen, monks and friars with guns on their shoulders. The number of armed men has been reckoned at two hundred thousand. Although at a pinch Paris could provide so many, I think this figure is exaggerated, and since sixty thousand would be enough to line the road four deep, there were probably not above a hundred thousand armed men in Paris that day.

As the King passed through the place Louis XV, a rifle shot from somewhere near the Palais-Bourbon killed a woman in the vicinity of his coach. We have reason to suppose that this misfortune was a pure accident, but at the time it produced an extraordinary effect.

I preceded the whole procession, followed by the deputies to the National Assembly mingled with those of the Electors, and forming two very long files with the King's coach in the middle; four officers of the National Guard held the door handles; M. de La Fayette walked in front, surrounded by his aides de camp. It must be said in his praise and in that of the people of Paris that although the guard was a completely new one, the most perfect order was observed everywhere; nobody broke ranks or stepped out of line, although there was an immense crowd of spectators behind. After seeing this great concourse in all the streets it came as a surprise to behold on the place Louis XV and in front of the Hôtel de Ville a wide circle of guards surrounding a bare open space, which allowed the procession to spread out in stately fashion. 'The air rang with continuous acclamation: *Long live the nation! long live the King! long live MM. Bailly, La Fayette, the deputies, the Electors!*' and these cries were mingled with the sound of trumpets, of military music, and the noise of gunfire wherever cannon were placed.' (*Procès-verbal des électeurs*, vol. II, p. 92.) As I was walking in front, I was greeted with the first burst of general enthusiasm; cheers and applause were rapturously repeated throughout the whole of this long march; and this was for me one of those delightful moments which touched my heart deeply, but for which I was to pay very dear.

As I was the first to reach the Hôtel de Ville, I was invited to offer the King the three-coloured cockade which the Parisians had adopted since the Revolution, as a distinguishing badge. I did not know quite how the King would take this, and whether there was not something improper about such a suggestion; however, I felt that I was bound to present the cockade, and that the King was bound to accept it.

When the King stepped down from his carriage I went up to him and, walking a few steps in front of him, I presented it to him, saying: 'Sire, I have the honour to offer Your Majesty the distinctive emblem of the French people.' The King accepted it willingly and fastened it to his hat. He then went up the staircase of the Hôtel de Ville; he had no guard with him, but instead was surrounded by a number of citizens. They were all holding swords and forming an arch of interlacing blades above his head; the clash of these swords, the confused sound of voices and even the shouts of joy echoing in the vault overhead had a somewhat terrifying effect;

and I should not wonder if the King felt some stirring of dread at that moment. But the crowd thronged around him, he walked with confidence like a good king in the midst of his good people; it is said that when M. le Marechal de Beauvau tried to push aside those who were crowding round him, he said: 'Let them be, they are truly fond of me.' At his entry into the hall, applause and shouts of *vive le roi* broke out on all sides; all eyes, brimming with tears, were turned towards him; all the people held out their hands to him; and when he was placed on the throne which had been made ready for him, a voice from the back of the assembly uttered this heartfelt cry: *'Our king! our father!'* and at this cry the applause, the excitement, the shouts of *vive le roi!* redoubled.

Bibliography

General indications about the available sources, methods of research and the bibliography of the history of the Revolution between 1770 and 1799 will be found in my book *Les Révolutions*, Paris, Presses Universitaires de France, 1963, pp. 11–75 (revised edition, 1965; English translation, *France and the Atlantic Revolution of the Eighteenth Century, 1770–1799*, New York, 1965). References given here deal only with the particular problems treated in the present work.

I Manuscript Sources

The list and description of most of the sources relating to events in Paris will be found in the great compilation of Alexandre Tuétey, *Répertoire géneral des sources manuscrites de l'histoire de Paris pendant la Révolution française*, Paris, 1890–1914, 11 vols., 4to.

Tuétey, however, did not deal with the sources that enable us to analyse the social structure of the population. These consist chiefly of lawyers' records and the files of the registry office (called *insinuation* under the *ancien régime*), deposited, in Paris, in the Archives nationales, and in the provinces, in the departmental archives, with a few exceptions.

The following are of special interest:

In the Archives nationales, with reference to the Réveillon riots, files Y 10033, 12218, 13454, 13582, 15101; with reference to the events of July 14th, F 7 4609, 4650, 4667, KK 647.

In the Archives de la Guerre at Vincennes, the log-book of the Salis-Samade regiment, *Mémoires historiques*, vol. 619–626, and the marching orders given to the troops in June and July 1789, A 4 55.

Bibliography

In the Bibliothèque nationale, Department of MSS, *fonds français* 6680–6687, the journal of the bookseller Hardy, *Mes loisirs ou Journal d'événements tels qu'ils parviennent à ma connaissance.*

II Printed Sources

The printed sources referring to events in Paris have also been enumerated and described by Maurice Tourneux, *Bibliographie de l'histoire de Paris pendant la Révolution française,* Paris, 1890–1913, 5 vols., 4to. For a special study of the fall of the Bastille, see F. Funck-Brentano, *Bibliographie critique de la prise de la Bastille,* Société des études historiques, 1899, vol. I, pp. 284–291. The first part of Chapter IX of the present book contains a critical study of the documents about the fall of the Bastille. However, the following list enumerates the principal printed sources we have consulted classified in logical order.

1. *The Economic Crisis: the Problem of Supply and Subsistence*

Desbois de Rochefort, E.-M., *Mémoire sur les calamités de l'hiver 1788–89,* lu dans une assemblée tenue à l'Hôtel de Ville de Paris, le 9 janvier 1789, Paris, Saint-André des Arcs, n.d., 8vo.

Frier, R., *Observations relatives à la subsistance de Paris et aux moyens propres à détruire généralement la mendicité,* n.d., 8vo.

Piron, J., *Le Patriote sincère.* Moyens simples et d'une exécution facile pour faire venir à Paris abondamment des grains et des farines, Paris, Debray, 8vo.

Anonymous:

Mémoire sur le prix excessif des grains, par un citoyen des environs de Paris, Paris, 1789, Le Clerc, 8vo.

Essai d'un citoyen sur les causes de la famine de 1789 [Paris], Imprimerie de Cellot, 1789, 8vo.

Du pain ou Coup d'œil sur les moyens les plus sûrs et les plus prompts d'approvisionner Paris de grains et de farine, Paris, Blanchon, 8vo.

Lettre des boulangers de Paris au peuple, suivie d'un entretien de deux pères de famille sur la rareté de la farine, Paris, Grangé, 8vo sheet.

Young, Arthur, *Travels in France during the Years 1787, 1788, 1789*, Dublin, 1793; ed. C. Maxwell, Cambridge, 1929.

2. *Poverty and Fear of 'Brigands'*

Dufourny de Villiers, L.-P., *Cahiers du quatrième ordre, cahiers des pauvres journaliers, des infirmes, des indigents.* Correspondance philanthropique entre les infortunés, les hommes sensibles et les États généraux, no. 1, 25 April 1789, 8vo.

[Lambert, J. F.], *Au Roi et aux États généraux.* Supplique présentée d'abord à l'Assemblée du tiers état de Paris (le 13 mai) pour sauver le droit du pauvre et pour l'intérêt commun de tous les ordres, n.p., n.d., 8vo, 16pp.

Poulletier, *Mémoire sur les moyens d'occuper utilement les ouvriers et autres gens qui sont oisifs dans Paris* [August, 1789], Paris, Desprez, 8vo.

Suite de la Sûreté publique ou Moyens simples et indispensables pour réformer et prévenir les désordres occasionnés par les vagabonds et les gens sans aveu, n.p., n.d., 8vo sheet.

Lefebvre, G., 'Quelques documents sur le prolétariat parisien en 1789' (*Annales historiques de la Révolution française,* 1953, pp. 265–267).

3. *The Elections, the Cahiers and the Estates-General*

See A. Brette's great collection of documents on the elections to the Estates-General, *Recueil de documents relatifs à la convocation des États généraux de 1789*, Paris, 1894–1915, 4 vols., 8vo, together with an *Atlas des bailliages ou juridictions assimilées ayant formé une unité électorale en 1789*, Paris, 1890, folio.

The *cahiers de doléances* are still largely unpublished. The *cahiers généraux* have been published in the *Archives parlementaires*, vols. I–VI, and a certain number of parish *cahiers* have been published by the *Commission d'histoire économique de la Révolution*. On the elections and *cahiers* of Paris, see the collection by Chassin, Paris, 1889, 4 vols., 8vo. For more details, see Beatrice Hyslop, *A Guide to the General Cahiers of 1789*, New York, 1936; id., *Répertoire critique des cahiers de doléances pour les États généraux de 1789*, Paris, 1933, with a *Supplément*, Paris, 1952.

Bibliography

On the Estates-General, a great collection of documents is in course of publication: Georges Lefebvre, *Recueil de documents relatifs aux séances des États généraux, mai-juin 1789*, vol. I:1. *Les préliminaires, la séance du 5 mai*, Paris, Centre National de la Recherche Scientifique, 1953; 2. *La séance du 23 juin*, Paris, 1962.

4. The Nobles' Plot and the Attempt at Counter-revolution (*June–July 1789*)

La Thuillerie, C. de, *Le Ministre national ou Portrait de M. Necker*, Paris, Blanchon, 8vo.

[Lebois, R.-F.], *Lettre des Parisiens à M. Necker pour l'inviter à reprendre sa place*, Paris, rue de la Parcheminerie, 8vo.

[Saunier, P.-M.], *Les Sentiments de la Nation à M. Necker, l'appui des Français*, Paris, Delaguette, n.d., 8vo.

Lettre d'un citoyen de Paris à M. Necker en son château de Copet [sic], *en Suisse*, le 25 juillet 1789, Paris, Vidaillet, n.d., 8vo sheet.

[Louet], *Relation de ce qui s'est passé à Chaumont en Bassigny à l'arrivée de M. Necker dans cette ville* [26–27 July 1789], Paris, 8vo.

[Vidaillet], *Réjouissance nationale relative à l'arrivée de M. Necker à Versailles, le 1er août 1789*, Paris, Cailleau, 8vo.

Voeu national exaucé par l'arrivée du généreux ami des Français [2 août 1789], Paris, Cailleau, 8vo.

Le Sauveur de la France ou M. Necker à Versailles, Paris, Cressonnier, 8vo.

La Joie des Français ou l'arrivée de M. Necker, Paris, Momoro, 1789, 8vo.

Lettre des citoyens de Paris à M. Necker lors de son arrivée à Versailles, Paris, Lefèvre, 8vo.

Tribut d'un Parisien à M. Necker du jeudi 6 août 1789, Paris, Cailleau, 8vo sheet.

La Chasse aux bêtes puantes et féroces, suivie de la liste des proscrits de la Nation et de la notice des peines qui leur sont infligées par contumace, Paris, Imprimerie de la Liberté, 8vo.

Chasse nouvelle aux bêtes puantes et féroces qui continuent à dévaster le royaume, suivie d'une nouvelle liste des aristocrates inconnus jusqu'alors et des peines que la Nation leur inflige par contumace, en attendant l'heureux instant qui les mettra en sa puissance, Paris, La Lanterne, 8vo.

Les Crimes dévoilés, ordre de l'attaque de la Ville de Paris, projetée pour la nuit du 14 au 15 juillet 1789, n.p., 1789, 8vo, 7pp.

5. *First Stirrings of Popular Unrest*

Émeute du Palais-Royal, le 5 juillet 1789, n.p., n.d., 8vo.

Récit de ce qui s'est passé à Paris, le 12 juillet, n.p., n.d., 8vo.

Le Solitaire des Tuileries aux bons habitants des villes et des campagnes, n.p., n.d., 8vo (about the charge of the prince de Lambesc).

Le Sabreur des Tuileries dans l'embarras, nouvelle authentique et intéressante (26 juillet), Paris, Froullé, 8vo, 16 pp.

[Lamourette, abbé A.], *Désastre de la maison Saint-Lazare,* n.p., n.d., 8vo.

[Ducray-Duménil, F.-G.], *La Semaine mémorable* ou Tableau de la Révolution depuis le 12 jusqu'au 17 juillet, Nantes, Louis, 8vo.

Paris sauvé ou Récit détaillé des événements qui ont eu lieu à Paris depuis le dimanche 12 juillet 1789, une heure après-midi, jusqu'au vendredi suivant au soir, n.p., n.d., 8vo, 34 pp.

L'Ouvrage des six jours ou Lettres d'un membre du district des Feuillants à son ami, sur la révolution de Paris, Volland, 8vo, 7 pp.

[Courtive, de], *Révolutions de Paris* ou Récit exact de ce qui s'est passé dans la capitale . . . depuis le 11 juillet 1789 jusqu'au 23 du même mois, n.p., 8vo, 40 pp.

Ridet, P.-B., *Récit des événements remarquables qui ont opéré la liberté des Français,* 1er août 1789, Paris, Cailleau, n.p., 8vo.

Quinzaine mémorable (12–30 juillet), n.p., n.d., 8vo, 180 pp.

La Semaine mémorable, Nantes [October 1789], 8vo, 18 pp.

Il était temps ou La semaine des événements, n.p., n.d., 8vo, 15 pp.

Journées mémorables de la Révolution française, par demandes et par réponses, à l'usage de la jeunesse républicaine, par un citoyen de la section du Mont-Blanc, Paris, Barban, an III, 8vo.

'Le pillage de la maison de Réveillon au faubourg Saint-Antoine (27 et 28 octobre [*sic*] 1789)', *Revue de la Révolution,* 1887, A 9, pp. 73–75.

'Paris en 1789. Du 25 juin au 1er août 1789. Lettres et journal de

Gudin de la Ferlière', *Revue rétrospective,* 1889, vol. XI, pp. 1–17.

Brette, A., 'Relation des événements depuis le 6 mai jusqu'au 15 juillet 1789. Bulletins d'un agent secret', *La Révolution française,* 1892, vol. XXIII, pp. 348–368, 443–471, 520–547, and 1793, vol. XXIV, pp. 69–84, 162–178.

Veuclin, 'Les débuts de la Révolution de 1789, racontés par Adrien-Georges Buchey, citoyen de Bernay et député du tiers état à l'Assemblée nationale constituante, 1789–1791', *Bulletin historique et philologique,* 1900, pp. 274–277.

Pelissier, L. G., 'Les grandes dates de la Révolution d'après le conventionnel Picqué', *La Correspondance historique et archéologique,* 1901, vol. VIII, pp. 311–314.

Savina, J., 'Les mouvements populaires en juillet et en août 1789, d'après quelques lettres inédites de Ange Conen de Saint- Luc', *Bulletin de la Société archéologique du Finistère,* 1924, pp. 46–67.

Kastener, J., 'Un curieux pamphlet à propos d'une soi-disant aventure arrivée à Plombières en 1789 (sur l'état de l'opinion en juillet)', *La Révolution dans les Vosges,* 1927–1928, pp. 79–82.

Faurey, J., 'Relation inédite des journées de juillet', *Revue des études historiques,* 1930.

Marchand, J., 'Journal inédit de Creuzé-Latouche sur juin et juillet 1789', *Revue des questions historiques,* 1935.

Bouis, R., 'Grégoire et la crise de juillet 1789', *Annales historiques de la Révolution française,* 1948, pp. 179–180.

Palou, J., 'Un document sur les événements de juillet 1789', *Annales historiques de la Révolution française,* 1948, p. 358.

Rudé, G., 'Un témoignage oculaire sur les événements des 12 et 13 juillet 1789 à Paris', *Annales historiques de la Révolution française,* 1953, pp. 73–75.

Garmy, R., 'Encore une lettre sur les événements de juillet 1789', *Annales historiques de la Révolution française,* 1954, pp. 171–173.

Birembaut, A., 'L'affaire Réveillon vue par Hassenfratz', *Annales historiques de la Révolution française,* 1956, pp. 72–73.

Gandilhon, R., 'Cinq lettres sur les événements parisiens (30 août 1788–2 août 1789)', *Annales historiques de la Révolution française,* 1956, pp. 267–278.

Lokke, C., 'Sur la crise de juillet 1789', *Annales historiques de la Révolution française,* 1958, no. 1, pp. 65–66.

Bibliography

6. The Journée of July 14th, 1789

(a) OFFICIAL ACCOUNTS

Procès-verbal des séances et délibérations de l'Assemblée générale des électeurs de Paris, réunis à l'Hôtel de Ville de Paris le 14 juillet 1789, rédigé depuis le 26 avril jusqu'au 21 mai par M. Bailly, et depuis le 22 mai jusqu'au 30 juillet 1789 par M. Duveyrier, Paris, Baudoin, 1790, 3 vols., 8vo.

Relation exacte de ce qui s'est passé dans la députation parlementaire à la Bastille, et de tout ce qui l'a précédé, [n.p., n.d. (Paris)], rédigé le 15 juillet par un citoyen électeur et témoin oculaire.

Dusaulx, *De l'insurrection parisienne et de la prise de la Bastille*, Discours historique prononcé, par extraits, dans l'Assemblée nationale, Paris, Debure l'aîné, 1790, pp. xvi–269, 8vo.

(b) ACCOUNTS BY THE BESIEGERS

Précis exact de la prise de la Bastille, rédigé sous les yeux des principaux acteurs qui ont joué un rôle dans cette même expédition, et lu le même jour à l'Hôtel de Ville, n.p., 1789, 10 pp.

Supplément nécessaire au 'Précis exact de la prise de la Bastille', avec des anecdotes curieuses sur le même sujet, par le Cousin Jacques, n.p., n.d., 8 pp.

Histoire de France pendant six semaines ou Précis exact des faits relatifs à la Révolution du 20 juin au 30 juillet 1789 . . ., par le Cousin Jacques (Beffroy de Reigny), Paris, 1789.

[Beffroy de Reigny, or 'Cousin Jacques'], *Histoire de France pendant trois mois* ou Relation des événements qui ont eu lieu, à Paris, à Versailles et dans les provinces depuis le 15 mai, jusqu'au 15 août 1789, avec des anecdotes qui n'ont point encore été publiées et des réflexions sur l'état actuel de la France et suivie d'une épître en vers à Louis XVI, Paris, Belin, 1789, 8vo.

Humbert, J.-B., *Journée de Jean-Baptiste Humbert, horloger, qui le premier a monté sur les tours de la Bastille*, Paris, Volland, 1789, 8vo, 16 pp.

Boniface Culture, laboureur, ex-militaire, à Jérôme Moustache, son neveu, grenadier aux gardes-françaises et qui a coopéré à la prise de la Bastille, avec promesse aux Parisiens de leur envoyer du pain, Ballard, 8vo, 7 pp.

Détail intéressant et jusqu'à présent ignoré sur la prise de la Bastille et la suite des révolutions, fait par un assaillant de la Bastille, à un de ses amis, blessé au même siège, n.p., n.d., 4to, 32 pp. and 1 plan.

L'Achille français, le héros de la Bastille ou le Brave Elie récompensé, Imprimerie, Momoro, 1790, 8vo.

Cousin, J., 'La journée d'un vainqueur de la Bastille racontée par lui-même', *Bulletin de la Société de l'histoire de Paris et de l'Ile-de-France,* 1875, p. 50.

Fournel, V., 'Médaillons révolutionnaires. Le patriote Palloy et les vainqueurs de la Bastille, d'après des documents inédits', *Le Correspondant,* 1788, vol. CXII, pp. 5–29, 312–390, and 1879, pp. 144–170, 701–729, 1087–1108.

'Elie, sous-lieutenant au régiment de la Reine-Infanterie', account inserted in the *Mémoires* of Marmontel, ed. Tourneux, Paris, 1891, 3 vols.

'Lettre d'un officier aux gardes-françaises (14 juillet 1789)', *Revue rétrospective,* 1899, vol. II, pp. 26–28.

Civrays, M., 'Lettre d'un garde-française sur la prise de la Bastille', *Annales historiques de la Révolution française,* 1924, p. 464.

(c) ACCOUNTS OF THE FALL OF THE BASTILLE BY THE BESIEGED
La Bastille dévoilée, Paris, Desenne, 1789.

Letter from Lieutenant Deflue, published by Flammermont (*La journée du 14 juillet 1789,* Paris, 1892, pp. lxvii–lxviii and ccxxxiii–ccxxxv).

(d) ACCOUNTS BY EYE-WITNESSES
[Boucheron], *Récit de ce qui s'est passé, sous mes yeux, le mardi 14 juillet 1789,* en particulier à onze heures du matin, n.p., n.d., 8vo, 15 pp.

Soulès, *Événements de Paris* ou Procès-verbal de ce qui s'est passé en ma présence depuis le 12 juillet 1789 (17 juillet), Cailleau, 8vo, 18 pp.

Relation sur la prise de la Bastille. Réflexions d'un citoyen à ses frères d'armes, Hérault, 1790, 4to, 50 pp.

Récit fidèle, non publié jusqu'à ce jour, de la prise de la Bastille, le 14 juillet 1789, provoqué par la loi sur les récompenses à accorder aux vainqueurs de la Bastille votée le 23 janvier 1833, par un ancien officier des gardes françaises, Paris, Potey, 1833, 8vo, 38 pp.

Rambaud, A., 'Les premiers jours de la Révolution. Récit d'un témoin oculaire, le chevalier d'Aguila, d'après ses papiers inédits', *La Nouvelle Revue*, 1886, vol. XLIII, pp. 770–783.

Flammermont, J., *La Journée du 14 juillet 1789. Fragments des mémoires inédits de L.-G. Pitra, électeur de Paris en 1789*, Paris, 1892.

Pelissier, L.-G., 'Une nouvelle relation de la prise de la Bastille', *Bulletin de la Société de l'histoire de Paris et de l'Île-de-France*, 1899, pp. 107–112.

(e) ACCOUNTS BY FOREIGN AMBASSADORS AND TRAVELLERS

A Detail of the Wonderful Revolution at Paris or an Exact Narrative of all that passed in the Capital of France, from July 11th 1789 to the 23rd of the same Month, London, Ridgeway, 1789, 8vo.

Dr. Rigby's letters from France in 1789, London, 1880.

Flammermont, J., *Relations inédites de la prise de la Bastille par le duc de Dorset, ambassadeur d'Angleterre en France, et le comte de Mercy-Argenteau, ambassadeur de l'empereur d'Allemagne*, published with an introduction, Paris, Picard, 1885, 8vo, 32 pp.

De Grouchy, 'Le 14 juillet 1789, raconté par des diplomates étrangers', *Nouvelle Revue rétrospective*, 1898, IX, pp. 1–28.

Cart, L.-W., 'Trois semaines à Paris pendant la Révolution. Impressions du voyageur allemand Campe', *La Révolution française*, 1910, vol. LVIII, pp. 31–51, 97–116.

(f) OTHER ACCOUNTS BY CONTEMPORARIES

Historique de la grande journée du 14 juillet 1789, n.p., n.d., 8vo.

Observations patriotiques sur la prise de la Bastille du 14 juillet 1789 et sur la suite de cet événement, Paris, Debray, 8vo, 34 pp.

Extrait d'une lettre de Paris du 15 juillet 1789, n.p., n.d., 8vo, 7 pp.

Remarques historiques sur la Bastille, sa démolition et révolutions de Paris, en juillet 1789, Londres, 1789, 8vo, 137 pp.

Cholat, *Service fait à l'attaque et prise de la Bastille*, Paris, Brunet, 1789, 8vo, 16 pp.

Rouel, J., *Relation véritable de la prise de la Bastille, le 14 juillet 1789*, Paris, Imprimerie. Hérault, 1790, 8vo, 8 pp.

Desmoulins, C., Letter of 16 July in *Correspondance inédite*, 1836.

Guiffrey, J. J., 'Documents inédits sur le mouvement populaire du 14 juillet 1789 et le supplice de M. de Launey, gouverneur de la

Bibliography

Bastille, et M. Berthier de Sauvigni', *Revue historique*, 1876, vol. I, pp. 497–508.

La Journée du 14 juillet. Prise de la Bastille. Documents historiques, Paris, Dumoulin, 1882, 4to, 4 pp.

Destrem, J., 'Document sur le mouvement populaire du 14 juillet 1789 et sur le meurtre de Foulon et Berthier', *Revue critique d'histoire et de littérature,* 1883, vol. II, pp. 273–280.

Colonna Ceccaldi, 'Une lettre du 15 juillet 1789', *La Nouvelle Revue,* 1890, vol. LXV, pp. 96–108.

Pasquier (chancellor), Account in his *Mémoires*, vol. I, pp. 51–52, ed. Audiffret-Pasquier, Paris, Plon, 1893.

Barras, Account in his *Mémoires*, published by G. Duruy in *La Revue de Paris,* 1 May 1895, pp. 9–14.

'Notes de lecture. Une relation de la prise de la Bastille par Paré', *La Révolution française,* 1902, vol. XLIII, pp. 175–176.

'Lettres inédites de Barnave sur la prise de la Bastille et sur les journées des 5 et 6 octobre, publiées par J. de Beylié', *Bulletin de l'Académie Delphinale [Grenoble],* 1905, vol. XIX, pp. 279–305.

'Lettre d'un commerçant parisien sur la prise de la Bastille', *Intermédiare des chercheurs et des curieux,* 1923, p. 517.

'Détails sur la prise de la Bastille, d'après les *Mémoires* du prince de Montbarey', *Intermédiare des chercheurs et des curieux,* 1923, p. 575.

O. Clément, 'Les événements de 1789 vus par les horlogers suisses', *Annales historiques de la Révolution française,* 1962, pp. 77–85.

(g) POLITICAL JOURNALS

Courrier des planètes, par le Cousin Jacques (Beffroy de Reigny), paraît tous les jeudis (17 July 1788–December 1789), Paris, 8 vols., 12mo.

Gazette de France, à Paris, de l'Imprimeur de la Gazette de France, 4to (1762–1792).

Journal de Paris, Paris, rue du Four-Saint-Honoré, 4to (1777–1811).

Journal général de la France, Paris, 10 vols., 4to (1 January 1785–10 August 1792).

Journal général de l'Europe, politique, commercial et agricole, Paris (July 1785–December 1789).

Bibliography

Mercure de France, dédié au roi, 12ᵐᵒ (1778–December 1789).

Annales parisiennes, politiques et critiques, mais véritables, dédiées à tous ceux qui ont veillé à l'intérêt public dans la Révolution du 13 juillet 1789, no. 1, du 13 juillet au 13 août 1789, Paris, Knapen, 1789, 8ᵛᵒ.

Bulletin de l'Assemblée nationale (1 July–6 August 1789), Momoro, 31 numbers, 8ᵛᵒ.

Le Censeur patriote ou l'Esprit des feuilles politiques et nationales (no. 1:31 July 1789), Volland, 8ᵛᵒ, 8 pp.

Le Courrier de Paris ou Anecdotes intéressantes (23 July–20 August 1789), 19 numbers, 8ᵛᵒ.

Le Courrier de Versailles à Paris et de Paris à Versailles, par M. Gorsas, citoyen de Paris (5 July–17 October 1789), Paris, rue Tiquetonne, no. 31.

Courrier français, par Poncerlin, Paris, Gueffier jeune, 8ᵛᵒ.

Le Déclin du jour ou Résolutions de l'Assemblée nationale, Paris, 1789 (begins on 7 July).

Feuille politique de J. Le Scène-Desmaisons (2–30 July 1789), 22 numbers, 8ᵛᵒ.

Gazette nationale ou le Moniteur universel, commencé le 5 mai 1789. Précédé d'une introduction historique contenant un abrégé des anciens Etats généraux, des assemblées de notables et des principaux événements qui ont amené la Révolution, Paris, Panckoucke (5 May 1789–1810).

Journal de la Compagnie des citoyens arquebusiers royaux de la Ville de Paris sur la Révolution actuelle, par Ricart (3 July–3 September 1789), Paris.

Journal de Versailles ou Affiches, annonces et avis divers par Regnault de Saint-Jean-d'Angély (6 June 1789–31 December 1790), Versailles, Blaizot, 4ᵗᵒ.

Journal politique national (12 July–November 1789), Versailles, Blaizot, 23 numbers, 8ᵛᵒ.

Lettres à M. le comte de B . . . sur la Révolution arrivée en 1789, sous le règne de Louis XVI, avec des notes sur les ministres et autres gens en place, qui, depuis le règne de Louis XV, ont donné lieu à cette Révolution mémorable par des déprédations ou des abus d'autorité, par Duplain de Sainte-Albine (12 July 1789–28 March 1790), London and Paris, l'An de la Liberté 1789–1790, 7 vols., 8ᵛᵒ.

Nouvelles de Versailles, n.p., 1789, 8ᵛᵒ.

Bibliography

Le Point du jour ou Résultat de ce qui s'est passé la veille à l'Assemblée nationale, par Barère (19 June 1789–21 October 1791), Paris, 27 vols., 8ᵛᵒ.

Révolutions de Paris, dédiées à la Nation et au district des Petits-Augustins, publiées par le sieur Prudhomme à l'époque du 12 juillet 1789, 18 vols., 8ᵛᵒ.

Bulletin patriotique. Détail exact de ce qui s'est passé depuis le 12 jusqu'au 20 juillet 1789, par un officier de la milice bourgeoise de Paris (Grenoble), 1789, 8ᵛᵒ.

(h) FOREIGN JOURNALS PUBLISHED IN FRENCH

L'Avant-coureur, ouvrage périodique (January–30 September 1789), 2 vols., 12ᵐᵒ (Liège).

Mercure historique et politique de Bruxelles (1789–1792), 55 vols., 12ᵐᵒ.

Révolutions de Paris en 1789, avec des détails historiques et anecdotiques sur la Bastille, la prise de cette redoutable forteresse et les personnes et les papiers qui y ont été trouvés, auxquels des témoins oculaires ont ajouté un grand nombre d'anecdotes très peu connues, dédiées à la Nation, 4 vols., n.p.

Spectateur universel ou relation fidelle [*sic*] des principaux événements historiques et politiques du temps présent; extraits de la plupart des journaux et gazettes de l'Europe. July, August, September 1789, Louvain, 1789, 8ᵛᵒ.

La gazette de Leyde, etc.

See also Marat's article in *L'Ami du peuple,* no. 149, 30 June 1790.

(i) PAMPHLETS, ETC., ABOUT JULY 14TH

Aux Français, sur le 14 juillet,. n.p., n.d., 8ᵛᵒ, 6 pp.

[Gonchon, C.], *Projet d'une fête nationale pour être exécutée le 14 juillet 1790,* Paris, Hérissant, 8ᵛᵒ.

Porro (abbé), *Adresse à tous les citoyens de Paris,* du mercredi 15 juillet 1789, n.p., n.d., 8ᵛᵒ, 14 pp.

Lettre turque relative aux circonstances, Selim au pacha Nadeth, n.p., n.d., 8ᵛᵒ, 7 pp.

Figaro au roi, n.p., n.d., 8ᵛᵒ.

La Journée parisienne ou le Triomphe de la France, Volland, n.d., 8ᵛᵒ, 8 pp.

Le Triomphe des Parisiens, par l'auteur de 'Fanal', n.d., 8ᵛᵒ, 6 pp.

La Capitale délivrée par elle-même, n.p., n.d., 8ᵛᵒ, 15 pp.

La Victoire des Parisiens ou la Liberté française, Masson, 1789, 15 pp.

Harangue aux héros parisiens, Paris, n.d., 8ᵛᵒ, 8 pp.

Le Parisien fêté ou Tribut aux Parisiens sur la liberté qu'ils ont rendue à la France, Paris, 15 August 1789, Cailleau, n.d., 8ᵛᵒ, 8 pp.

Arx parisiensis expugnata et deleta (Liège), MDCCXC, 8ᵛᵒ, 31 pp.

Renommée de la nation française, dédiée au courage et à la valeur des bons citoyens de Paris (27 juillet), n.p., n.d., 8ᵛᵒ, 6 pp.

Les Lauriers du faubourg Saint-Antoine ou le Prix de la Bastille renversée, du lundi 20 juillet 1789, Gueffier jeune, n.d., 8ᵛᵒ, 8 pp.

A la Garde citoyenne (15 juillet), n.p., n.d., 8ᵛᵒ, 4 pp.

Remerciement des gardes-françaises au roi, 24 juillet 1789, Grangé, n.d., 8ᵛᵒ, 4 pp.

Réflexions et remerciements d'un citoyen adressés aux gardes-françaises, au sujet de la belle action qu'ils ont faite, n.p., n.d., 8ᵛᵒ, 7 pp.

Le grenadier patriote ou le Despotisme détruit en France, avec les détails les plus exacts sur la révolution présente, Paris, Garnery, 8ᵛᵒ, 48 pp.

Quelques anecdotes sur un grand événement, n.p., n.d., 8ᵛᵒ, 8pp.

Remarques et anecdotes sur le château de la Bastille, suivis d'un détail historique du siège, de la prise et de la démolition de cette forteresse, Paris, Goujon, 8ᵛᵒ.

Le Peur dissipée, lettre d'un Français à un Anglais qui quitte Paris par effroi, sur les affaires présentes, n.p., 1789, 8ᵛᵒ.

Patriae Salus et Gloria Regis. Devise sacrée de tous les bons Français sur laquelle un corps de bons citoyens, constitués volontaires de la Bastille, assurent à la mère patrie un milliard 119 millions de capital et 285 millions de revenu annuel (17 September 1789), n.p., n.d., 8ᵛᵒ.

(j) PAMPHLETS ABOUT EVENTS AFTER THE FALL OF THE BASTILLE

Testament de Charles de Launey, gouverneur de la Bastille, trouvé à la Bastille, le jour de l'assaut, n.p., n.d., 8ᵛᵒ.

La Mort tragique de l'intendant de Paris, n.p., n.d., 8ᵛᵒ.

Dialogue entre MM. de Launey, Flesselles, Foulon et Berthier aux enfers, Paris, n.d., 8ᵛᵒ.

Bibliography

Nouveaux dialogues des morts, Blanchon et Lecomte, n.d., 8ᵛᵒ, 16 pp.

Les Quatre Traîtres aux enfers, Paris, Volland, 1789.

Lettre du sieur de Flesselles à M. de Calonne sur l'arrivée de Foulon et de Bertier au pays des ombres ou les Secrets de l'enfer dévoilés, Paris, n.d., 8ᵛᵒ.

Adresse de remercîment de Mgr Belzébuth, prince souverain des enfers, au peuple parisien, sur l'envoi de cinq traitres exterminés les 14 et 22 juillet, n.p., n.d., 8ᵛᵒ.

(k) SONGS, POEMS, ILLUSTRATIONS, RELATING TO THE FALL OF THE BASTILLE

Chanson sur la prise des Invalides et de la Bastille, les lundi 13 et mardi 14 juillet 1789. A Paris, ce vendredi 17 où l'on attend le roi devant messieurs les trois cents électeurs et à l'Hôtel de Ville, et faite à l'hôtel de Tours, étant de patrouille à midi, Paris, Nyon, 1789, 8ᵛᵒ, 7 pp.

Desaugiers, *La Prise de la Bastille, hiérodrame tiré des livres saints,* suivi du cantique, en action de grâces, *Te Deum Laudamus,* Paris, Cailleau, 1789, 8ᵛᵒ.

Les Nouvelles Philippiques ou le *Te Deum* des Français après la destruction de la Bastille, ode dédiée aux amis de la Liberté, Paris, 1789, 8ᵛᵒ, 24 pp.

Ducray du Ménil, *Les Principaux Evénements de la Révolution de Paris* et notamment de la semaine mémorable, représentés par figures, avec un précis lapidaire, historique, suivi de la liste alphabétique des citoyens qui se sont distingués au siège de la Bastille, Paris, Maradan, 1789, 8ᵛᵒ, 177 pp.

Gravures historiques des principaux événements depuis l'ouverture des Etats généraux de 1789, Paris, Janinet, 1789–1790, 8ᵛᵒ.

Principaux événements de la Révolution, et notamment de la semaine mémorable, représentés par douze figures en taille-douce très bien exécutées, Paris, an II, 8ᵛᵒ, 187 pp.

Tourneux, M., 'Une estampe de Janinet', *La Révolution française,* 1888, vol. XV, pp. 5–8.

(l) MEMOIRS

Bailly, *Mémoires,* Paris, 1804.

Besenval, *Mémoires,* Paris, 1805.

Mathieu Dumas (general), *Souvenirs,* Paris, 1839.

346

Bibliography

Des Cars (Duc), *Mémoires*, Paris, 1890.
Pasquier (chancellor), *Mémoires*, vol. I, Paris, 1893.
Barras, *Mémoires*, vol. I, Paris, 1895.
Thiébault (General-Baron), *Mémoires*, Paris, 1895–1896, 5 vols.

III Books and Articles

(A list of general works on the Revolution will be found in my book
Les Révolutions, mentioned above.)

1. *Works on the Year 1789*

Gautier, H., *L'An 1789, événements, idées, œuvres et caractères*,
   Paris, n.d.
Kervan, A. de., *1789 et son histoire*, Paris, 1877.
Lefebvre, G., *Quatre-vingt-neuf*, Paris, 1939; *The Coming of the
   French Revolution*, trans. R. R. Palmer, London, 1947.
Soboul, A., *1789, L'An I de la liberté*, Paris, 1939.
Braesch, F., *1789, L'Année cruciale*, Paris, 1941.
Lefebvre, G., *La Révolution de 1789*, cours de Sorbonne, C.D.U.,
   Paris, 1942.
Michaud, J., *Les États généraux et le 14 juillet 1789*, Paris, 1960.
Ligou, D., 'A propos de la révolution municipale', *Revue d'Histoire
   économique et sociale*, 1960, pp. 146–177.

2. *The Hypothesis of a 'Masonic Plot' in 1789*

Barruel (abbé), *Mémoires pour servir à l'histoire du jacobinisme*,
   Hamburg, 1803.
Bord, G., 'La conspiration maçonnique de 1789', *Le Correspon-
   dant*, 1906, pp. 521–544 and 551–567.
Lannoy, (de), *La Révolution préparée par la franc-maçonnerie*,
   Paris, 1911.
Cardenal, L. de., 'L'origine des sociétés populaires et leurs
   rapports avec la franc-maçonnerie', *Annales historiques de la
   Révolution française*, 1924, p. 580.
Martin, G., *La franc-maçonnerie et la préparation de la Révolution*,
   Paris, 1926, 306 pp., 16mo.

Bibliography

Sée, H., 'La franc-maçonnerie et les origines de la Révolution française', *Grande Revue*, April 1927.

Poncins, L. de, *Les Forces secrètes de la Révolution française, maçonnerie et judaïsme,* Paris, 1929; *The Secret Powers behind Revolution: Freemasonry and Judaism,* London, 1929.

Cardenal, L. de, 'Le complot maçonnique de 1789', *La Révolution française*, 1933.

Delbecke (Baron), *La Franc-maçonnerie et la Révolution française et autres essais,* Anvers, 1938.

Faÿ, B., *La Grande Révolution,* Paris, 1959.

3. The Economic Crisis

(a) GENERALITIES

Mathiez, A., *La Vie chère et le mouvement social sous la Terreur,* Paris, 1927.

Sée, H., 'Les origines économiques et sociales de la Révolution française', *Revue d'histoire économique et sociale*, 1931.

Labrousse, C.-E., *Esquisse du mouvement des prix et des revenus en France aux XVIIIe siècle,* Paris, 1933, 2 vols.

Soreau, E., *Ouvriers et paysans de 1789 à 1792,* Paris, 1936.

Lefebvre, G., 'Le mouvement des prix et les origines de la Révolution française', *Annales d'histoire économique et sociale*, 1937, vol. IX, pp. 139–170.

Gueronik, P., *Le Mouvement ouvrier et paysan de juillet 1789 au 27 juillet 1794,* thesis, Paris, 1940.

Labrousse, C. E., *La Crise de l'économie française à la fin de l'Ancien Régime et au début de la Révolution,* Paris, 1943.

Sagnac, Ph., 'La crise de l'économie française à la fin de l'Ancien Régime et au début de la Révolution', *Revue d'histoire économique et sociale*, 1950, no. 3, pp. 226–242.

Leuilliot, P., 'Réflexions sur l'histoire économique et sociale à propos de la bourgeoisie en 1789', *Revue d'histoire moderne et contemporaine,* April, 1954.

(b) REGIONAL ASPECTS OF THE CRISIS IN FRANCE

Cahen, L., 'Le commerce et l'industrie à Paris à la fin du XVIIIe siècle', *Annales d'histoire économique et sociale*, 1931–1932,

p. 88; 'La question du pain à Paris au XVIIIᵉ siècle', *Cahiers de la Révolution*, 1934.

Bottinho, Ch., 'La population et la vie économique à Paris à la fin du XVIIIᵉ siècle', *Revue d'histoire du droit*, 1937, p. 475.

Vidalenc, J., 'Les revendications économiques et sociales de la population parisienne en 1789 d'après les cahiers de doléances', *Revue d'histoire économique et sociale*, 1948–1949, nos. 3 and 4, pp. 273–287.

4. Paris, 'Capital of the French Revolution'

Thureau-Dangin, P., *Paris, capitale de la Révolution française*, Paris, 1872.

Babeau, A., *Paris en 1789*, Paris, 1889.

Monin, H., *L'État de Paris en 1789*, Paris, 1889.

Lenotre, G., *Les Quartiers de Paris pendant la Révolution*, Paris, 1896.

Alger, J.-G., *Paris in 1789–1794*, London, 1902.

Descombes, L., *Recherches sur le faubourg Saint-Antoine*, Paris, 1905, 55 pp.

Cahen, L., *Paris au début de la Révolution (1789–1791)*, Melun, 1911.

Lenotre, G., *Paris révolutionnaire. Vieilles maisons, vieux papiers*, Paris, 1930.

Garrigues, G., *Les Districts parisiens pendant la Révolution*, Paris, 1932.

La Batut, G. de, *Les Pavés de Paris. Guide illustré de Paris révolutionnaire*, Paris, 1937, 2 vols.

5. The Crowd and the Revolutionary State of Mind

(a) THE RIOTERS

Gallier, A. de, 'Les émeutiers de 1789', *Revue des questions historiques*, 1883, A 34, pp. 115–147.

Rouff, M., 'Le personnel des premières émeutes de 1789 à Paris', *La Révolution française*, 1909, vol. LV, pp. 213–231.

Chuquet, A., 'Les républicains en 1789', *Feuilles d'histoire du XVIIᵉ au XXᵉ siècle*, 1910, vol. III, pp. 395–397.

Bibliography

Rudé, G., 'La composition sociale des insurrections parisiennes de
1789 à 1791', *Annales historiques de la Révolution française*, 1952,
pp. 256–288.

Lefebvre, G., 'A propos des récents articles de Georges Rudé',
Annales historiques de la Révolution française, 1953, pp. 289–
291.

Rudé, G., 'The motives of popular insurrection in Paris during the
French Revolution', *Bulletin of the Institute of historical Research*,
1953, vol. XXVI; 'Les ouvriers parisiens dans la Révolution
française', *La Pensée*, May 1953.

Soboul, A., 'Classes et luttes de classes sous la Révolution française', *La Pensée*, 1954.

Kan, S. B., 'Parizhskiye rabochiye v revolutsii 1789–1794 godov
(istorio-graficheskiy obzor) (The workers of Paris during the
Revolution of 1789–1794), *Voprosy istorii* (Problems of history),
Moscow, 1956, no. 1, pp. 131–145.

Chevalier, L., *Classes laborieuses et classes dangereuses à Paris
pendant la première moitié du XIXᵉ siècle*, Paris, 1958.

Rudé, G., *The Crowd in the French Revolution*, Oxford, 1959.

Schnerb, R., 'Sans-culottes et misérables parisiens', *L'Information
historique*, September–October 1959.

Rudé, G., 'Georges Lefebvre et l'étude des journées populaires
de la Révolution française', *Annales historiques de la Révolution
française*, 1960, pp. 154–162.

Daumard, A., and Furet, F., *Structures et relations sociales à Paris
au XVIIIᵉ siècle*, Paris, 1961.

(b) THE REVOLUTIONARY SPIRIT

Rocquain, F., *L'Esprit révolutionnaire avant la Révolution*, Paris,
1878.

Lebon, Dr G., *Psychologie des foules*, Paris, 1895.

Cabanés, Dr and Nass, Dr, *La Névrose révolutionnaire*, Poitiers,
1906.

Lebon, Dr G. *La Révolution française et la psychologie des révolutions*, Paris 1912; 'Le rôle du peuple pendant la révolution',
Revue hebdomadaire, 1912 pp. 289–306.

Aulard, A. 'La théorie de la violence et la Révolution française',
La Révolution française, 1923, p. 427.

Faÿ, B., *L'esprit révolutionnaire en France et aux États-Unis à la
fin du XVIIIᵉ siècle*, Paris, 1925.

Bibliography

Lefebvre, G., 'Foules révolutionnaires', *Annales historiques de la Révolution française*, 1934, pp. 1–26.

Brunot, F., 'Le mysticisme dans le langage de la Révolution', *Cahiers rationalistes*, 1935, no. 38.

Duhamel, J., 'Essai sur le rôle des éléments paranoïaques dans la genèse des idées révolutionnaires', *Annales historiques de la Révolution française*, 1935, p. 267.

Rogers, C. B., *The Spirit of Revolution in 1789. A Study of Public Opinion as Revealed in Political Songs and other Popular Literature at the Beginning of the French Revolution*, Princeton, 1949.

Cobb, R., 'Quelques aspects de la mentalité révolutionnaire (avril 1793-thermidor an II)', *Revue d'histoire moderne et contemporaine*, 1959, April–June.

Egret, J., *La Prérévolution*, Paris, 1962.

6. *Revolutionary* Journées

(a) GENERALITIES

Mathiez, A., *Les Grandes Journées de la Constituante (1789–1791)*, Paris, 1913.

Funck-Brentano, F., *Scènes et tableaux de la Révolution*, Paris, 1934.

(b) PARTICULAR ASPECTS OF THE *Journées*

Mathiez, A., 'Étude critique sur les journées des 5 et 6 octobre 1789', *Revue historique*, 1898, vol. LXVII, pp. 241–281, and 1899, vol. LXVIII, pp. 258–294 and vol. LXIX, pp. 41–66.

7. *Popular Unrest Before July 14th 1789*

(a) FEAR OF BRIGANDS, AND THE FIRST PEASANT RISINGS

Cortez, F., 'La révolte des paysans et la grand'peur de 1789 à Saint-Maximin (Var)', *Bulletin historique et philosophique*, 1897, pp. 530–547.

Conard, P., *La Peur en Dauphiné (juillet-août 1789)*, Paris, 1904.

Lefebvre, G., *Les Paysans du Nord et la Révolution française*, Lille, 1924; *La Grande Peur de 1789*, Paris, 1932.

Marion, M., *Le Brigandage sous la Révolution*, Paris, 1934.

Ado, A. V., 'Krest' yanskiye vosstaniye v nachale frantsuzskoy revo-
lutsii v 1789 g' (The peasant insurrection at the beginning of the
French revolution in 1789), *Iz istorii obshchestvennykh dvizheniy
(Tarlé Miscellanea)*, Moscow, 1957, pp. 148–169.
Duthuron, G., 'La Révolution française et la peur', *Miroir de
l'Histoire*, 1957, no 91, pp. 62–72.

(b) THE 'NOBLES' PLOT'
Sepet, M., 'Le serment du Jeu de Paume et la déclaration du 23
juin', *Revue des questions historiques*, 1891, vol. XLIX, pp. 491–
546.
'La première rencontre de l'Ancien Régime et de la Révolution:
La Revellière-Lépeaux et le marquis de Dreux-Brézé', *La
Révolution française*, 1883, vol. V, pp. 408–411.
Caron, P., 'La tentative de contre-révolution, juin-juillet 1789',
Revue d'histoire moderne, vol. VIII, 1906, pp. 5–34 and 649–678.
Hocquart de Turtot, E., *La Conquête des communes (mai-juillet
1789). La préparation des États; les conférences; la réunion du
clergé; le Jeu de Paume; la séance royale; la réunion des ordres,
la rassemblement des troupes*, Paris, 1910.

(c) THE FIRST PARISIAN RIOTS
Baudon, A., 'L'affaire Réveillon', *La Révolution française*, 1885,
vol. IX, pp. 307–312.
Flammermont, J., 'Les gardes-françaises en juillet 1789', *La
Révolution française*, 1899, vol. XXXVI, pp. 12–24.
Chuquet, A., 'Camille Desmoulins en juillet 1789', *Feuilles
d'Histoire du XVIIe au XXe siècle*, 1910, vol. IV, pp. 17–35.
Farge, R., 'Camille Desmoulins au jardin du Palais-Royal',
Annales révolutionnaires, 1914, vol. VII, pp. 446–474.
Collot, J., 'L'affaire Réveillon', *Revue des questions historiques*,
1934, vol. CXXI, pp. 35–55; 1935, vol. CXXII, pp. 239–254.
Clercq, V. de, 'L'incendie des barrières de Paris en 1789', *Bulletin
de la Société d'histoire de Paris et de l'Ile-de-France*, 1938.

8. *The 'Parisian Revolution' (July 14th 1789)*

(a) GENERAL STUDIES OF THE ORIGINS, EVENTS AND CONSE-
QUENCES OF JULY 14TH, 1789

Fournel, V., *Les Hommes du 14 juillet. Gardes-françaises et vainqueurs de la Bastille,* Paris, 1890.

Sepet, M., 'La Révolution de juillet 1789', *Revue des questions historiques,* 1891, pp. 499–558.

Flammermont, J., *La Journée du 14 juillet 1789,* Paris, 1892; 'Une nouvelle histoire de la Bastille et de la journée du 14 juillet 1789', *La Révolution française,* 1894, vol. XXVII, pp. 385–405.

Roman, J., 'La prise de la Bastille', *Revue Bleue, politique et littéraire,* 1902, vol. XVIII, pp. 62–64.

Monin, H., 'La prise de la Bastille. Histoire et légende (critique d'un article de H. Spont dans *Le Petit Journal,* 14 juillet 1910)', *Revue historique de la Révolution française,* 1910, vol. I, pp. 547–549.

Durieux, J., *Les Vainqueurs de la Bastille,* Paris, 1911.

Aulard, A., 'La prise de la Bastille et le prolétariat', *Floréal,* 1920, pp. 353 et seq.

Durieux, J., *La Capitulation de la Bastille,* Paris, 1925.

Béraud, H., *Le 14-Juillet,* Paris, 1929.

Soreau, E., *La Chute de l'Ancien Régime. La Révolution du 14 juillet : ses origines,* Paris, 1937.

Martin, G., *14 juillet 1789,* Paris, 1939.

Chauvet, P., *L'Insurrection parisienne et la prise de la Bastille,* Paris, 1946.

Mistler, J., *Le 14-juillet,* Paris, 1963.

(b) SPECIAL STUDIES ON THE EVENTS OF JULY 14TH

Delteil, E., 'Fusils prêtés par le Mont-de-Piété pour la prise de la Bastille', *Bulletin de la Société de l'histoire de Paris et de l'Île-de-France,* 1881, pp. 118–120.

'Fournier l'Américain. Son rôle en juillet 1789', *Revue rétrospective,* 1889, vol. II, pp. 17–26.

Hagues, P. d', 'Les derniers vainqueurs de la Bastille', *Revue hebdomadaire,* 1911, pp. 381–408.

Chuquet, A., *Historiens et marchands d'histoire,* Paris, 1914, pp. 30–43.

Vauthier, G., 'Les vainqueurs de la Bastille après 1830', *Annales révolutionnaires,* 1919, pp. 257–261.

Durieux, J., 'Les victimes du siège de la Bastille', *La Nouvelle Revue,* 1920, vol. XLVIII, pp. 129–148.

Gottschalk, L.-R., 'Marat dans la journée du 14 juillet 1789', *La Révolution française,* 1923, vol. LXXVI, pp. 13–18.

Bibliography

'Un Vicquois, J.-B. Desca, à la prise de la Bastille', *Revue des Hautes-Pyrénées,* 1924, vol. XIX, pp. 7–10.

Durieux, J., *Quelques vainqueurs de la Bastille,* Paris, 1925.

Pollio, E., 'Deux Hulin confondus par M. Gautherot', *La Révolution française,* 1931, pp. 349–351.

Barrucand, V., *La Vie véritable du citoyen Jean Rossignol, vainqueur de la Bastille et général en chef des armées de la République dans la guerre de Vendée,* Paris, 1933.

Gasterbois, V., 'Un Argentanais à la prise de la Bastille', *La Révolution française,* 1934.

Rami, 'La méprise de la Bastille', *Le Nouveau Candide,* no. 167, 8–15 July 1964.

(c) WORKS ON THE BASTILLE

The *Mémoires* of Linguet on the Bastille, Paris, 1821.

Dufey de l'Yonne, *La Bastille,* Mémoires pour servir à l'histoire secrète du gouvernement français depuis le XIVe siècle jusqu'en 1789, Paris, 1833.

Fougeret, *Histoire générale de la Bastille depuis sa fondation (1369) jusqu'à sa destruction (1789),* Paris, 1834.

Joigneux, P., *Histoire générale de la Bastille,* Paris, 1838, 3 vols.

Arnould and Alboize du Pujol, *Histoire de la Bastille depuis sa fondation (1374) jusqu'à sa destruction,* Paris, 1844, 8 vols.

'La Bastille et les faïenciers', *La Révolution française,* 1881, vol. I, pp. 115–122.

Bingham, D., *The Bastille,* London, 1888, 2 vols.

Remy, G., *Histoire de la Bastille et de la rue Saint-Antoine avant 1789,* Paris, 1888.

Couret, A., *La Bastille depuis ses origines jusqu'à sa chute (1369–1789),* Orléans, 1889, 40 pp.

La Bastille devant l'Histoire, accompagné d'un plan de la Bastille, Paris, 1890.

Cœuret, A., *La Bastille, 1370–1789. Histoire, description, attaque et prise,* Paris, 1890.

Biré, E., 'La Bastille sous Louis XVI', *Le Correspondant,* 1892, vol. CLXVIII, pp. 3–39.

Bournon, F., *Histoire générale de Paris. La Bastille, histoire et description des bâtiments, administration, régime de la prison, événements historiques,* Paris, 1893.

Bibliography

Funck-Brentano, F., *Légende et archives de la Bastille*, Paris, 1898; *La Bastille, ses dernières années*, Paris, 1898.

Kircheisen, F. M., *Die Bastille*, Berlin, 1927.

(d) THE SYMBOLIC DESTRUCTION OF THE BASTILLE

André, F., 'Un souvenir de la Bastille', *Bulletin de la Société d'Agriculture, Industrie, Sciences et Arts du départment de la Lozère*, 1872, vol. XXII, p. 7.

Bord, G., 'Réception d'une pierre de la Bastille à Angers', *Revue de la Révolution*, 1883, vol. II, pp. 176–179.

Sorel, A., 'Envoi d'une pierre de la Bastille à la Ville de Compiègne', *Bulletin de la société de Compiègne*, 1884, vol. VI, p. 64.

Bonnemère, E., 'La dernière pierre de la Bastille'. *Revue illustrée de Bretagne et d'Anjou*, 1886, vol. I, pp. 117–119 and 134–137.

Jaloustre, 'Une pierre mémorable, souvenir de la Bastille (Clermont)', *Revue d'Auvergne*, 1897, vol. XIV, pp. 221–240.

Dubois-Desaulle, G., 'L'entreprise de démolition de la Bastille (1789–1792)', *Revue Blanche*, 1902, vol. XXVIII, pp. 401–412.

Van Geluwe, L., 'Une épave de la Bastille', *La Cité*, 1902, pp. 228–234.

Lemoine, H., 'Les comptes de démolition de la Bastille', *Bulletin de la Société de l'histoire de Paris et de l'Ile-de-France*, 1929, pp. 77–83; *Le Démolisseur de la Bastille, la place de la Bastille, son histoire de 1789 à nos jours*, Paris, 1930.

Guichonnet, P., 'Deux pierres de la Bastille', *Revue de Savoie*, 1954, 3rd quarter, pp. 216–226.

(e) CONSEQUENCES AND SIGNIFICANCE OF THE FOURTEENTH OF JULY, 1789

Bord, G., *La Prise de la Bastille et les conséquences de cet événement dans les provinces jusqu'aux journées des 5 et 6 octobre 1789*, Paris, 1882.

Charavay, E., 'Le lendemain de la prise de la Bastille', *La Révolution française*, 1885, vol. IX, p. 354.

Fournel, V., *Le Patriote Palloy et l'exploitation de la Bastille, l'orateur du peuple Gonchon*, Paris, 1892.

Bourne, H. E., 'Improvising a government in Paris in July 1789', *The American Historical Review*, 1904–1905, vol. X, pp. 280–

308; 'Municipal politics in Paris in 1789', *The American Historical Review,* 1905–1906, vol. XI, pp. 263–286.

Mathiez, A., 'Les capitalistes et la prise de la Bastille', *Annales historiques de la Révolution française,* 1926, vol. III, pp. 578–582.

Lefebvre, G., *La Grande Peur de 1789,* Paris, 1932.

Lhéritier, M., 'La Révolution municipale, point de départ de la Révolution française', *La Révolution française,* 1939, pp. 121–135.

Stewart, J. H., 'The fall of the Bastille on the Dublin stage', *The Journal of Royal Society of Antiquaries of Ireland,* vol. LXXXIV, 1954, pp. 78–91 [review by J. Godechot, in *Annales historiques de la Révolution française,* 1956, pp. 222–223].

Durand, M.-J., 'Premières répercussions de la prise de la Bastille à Romans et à Bourg-de-Péage', *Bulletin de la Société d'archéologie et de statisque de la Drôme,* 1956, vol. LXXIII, pp. 97–99.

Vellay, E., 'Les agents de change et la prise de la Bastille', *Chercheurs et curieux,* 1956, vol. VI, no. 58, pp. 26–30.

Author's Books on Related Subjects

Les Commissaires aux armées sous le Directoire: Contribution à l'étude des rapports autre les pouvoirs civils et militaires, Paris, 1937.

Les Institutions de la France sous la Révolution et l'Empire, Paris, 1951.

La Grande Nation: L'expansion révolutionnaire de la France dans le monde de 1789 à 1799, Paris, 1956.

La Contre-révolution: Doctrine et action 1789–1804, Paris, 1961.

Les Révolutions, 1770–1799, Paris, 1963 (new ed. 1965); *France and the Atlantic Revolution of the Eighteenth Century, 1770–1799*, trans. Herbert H. Rowen, New York, 1965.

La Pensée révolutionnaire en France et en Europe, 1780–1799 (editor), Paris, 1964.

Index

359

Index

Besançon, 109, 129, 132
Besenval, baron de: Réveillon riots, 141, 144; bread riots, 169; commands army in Paris, 180, 189–92, 195, 198, 214–16, 247, 248, 251, 252, 254, 269
Besse, 130
Beuvron, duc de, 173
Bezier, 242
Bicêtre, 86, 97, 176, 195
Biron, duc de, 15, 85, 112
Bohemia, revolt in (1619), 3
Bonnemère, 229
Bons Ragoûts, 32
Bordeaux, 4, 37
Boscary, 201
Boston rising, 10–11
Boucheron, 208, 234, 235
Bouclans, president, 129
Bouillon-Infanterie, 179, 180
Bourg-en-Bresse, 172, 202
bourgeoisie, status and aspirations of, 41, 50, 52, 55, 271
Bray-sur-Seine, 131
Brazey-en-Plaine, 125
bread, price of, 12–17, 65, 111, 120–23, 130–31, 137, 167–9, 172–3, 182, 187, 192, 193. *see also* Paris, provisioning of, price of bread in, Brest, 225
Breteuil, baron de, 91, 184–7, 249, 254, 256
Breton club, 158
Brie, 12
Brienne, Loménie de, 101–4, 106, 111–14
brigands, fear of, 171, 172, 199
Brignolles, 130
Brisset, 111
Broglie, duc de: commanding army of Paris, 178, 180, 186, 214, 253, 257–8; as War Minister, 189, 248–50, 269
Bruguières, 83
Burke, Edmund, 20, 24

cabinet noir, 81
Caen, 132, 174
cahiers de doléances, 54, 118, 124–8, 135, 138, 154, 164, 165, 172, 178
cahiers généraux, 118, 126
Calas, 25

Calonne, C.-A., de, 54, 99–102, 104, 105, 186
Cambrai, 128, 167
camisards, 4
Campe, 212
Camus, 158
Capellen, Van der, 34
capitation, 40
Cappello, Antonio, 211, 268
Carré, Henri, 16
Carré (miller of Dijon), 12
Castela regiment, 180
Castelnau, 31
Castries, duc de, 186
Catholic League, 2, 3
Catholic Relief Act, 19–21, 23, 24, 27
cercle de l'égalité, 32
Châlons-sur-Marne, 173
champarts, 39, 124
Champion de Cicé, 156
Chantilly, 131
Chappe, 14
Charenton, 86, 97, 179, 180, 263
Charles I of England, 3
Charles V of France, 54, 87
Charleville, 258
Châtelet, 86, 195, 196
Châtelet, duc de, 141
Château-Gontier, 202
Châteaulin, 167
Châteauvieux regiment, 190
Chaunu, Pierre, 3
Chauny, 15
Chauvet, 30, 270
Chavigné, Davy de, 98
Chénon, 104
Choisy-le-Roi, 180
Chol, 201–2
Cholat, 208
Circello, marquis de, 210
Civil War in England, 3
Clavière, 30, 32
clergy: estates of, 39, 41; exempt from *taille*, 40; in elections to Estates-General, 117; in Estates-General, 156–7, 159–60, 162, 166, 178; 'plot' by, 150. *see also* tithes.
Clermont-Tonnerre, comte de, 166, 256
Club Olympique, 58
Coindre, Nicolas, 201
Colbert, 61, 122
common land, 43

Index

Index

Faure, Edgar, 16
Fäy, Bernard, 16
Ferrand, 105, 239
Ferrières, marquis de, 249
Fersen, Axel de, 257
feudal regime: attacks on, 6, 9–10, 126–7; system in France, 38–44, 52; beourgeois resistance to, 51; end of, 99. *see also* seignorial dues, serfs, *corvée, mainmorte, champart,* tithes.
fiefs, 38
Fieffé, E., 210
Fisher, Lord, 25
Flammermont, J., 205, 208, 229
Flesselles, de, 198, 233, 244, 251, 253
'Flour War'. *see Guerre des Farines*
Flournoy, 30
Folitot, 225
Fort l'Evêque, 86
Fougères, 168
Foulon, 186, 244
Founitillat, 225
Fournier, 236
Fourqueux, Bouvard de, 102
France: alliance with United States, 11, 35; intervention in Geneva revolt, 30–32, 35
François I, 100
Frankenhausen, 2
Frankfurt, 2
Frederick II, 31
free trade, 12, 15, 16, 71, 103, 129, 168
freemasons, 267–9
Freiburg-im-Breisgau, 2
Frénilly, 56, 57
Fréron, Stanislas, 226
Fréteau, 110
Fronde, 3, 87
Furet, F., 47

Gage, General, 11
Gaillac, 132, 174, 272
garde de Paris, 145, 151
gardes-françaises, 84, 104–5, 141–6, 150–51, 175–7, 183, 185, 189–95, 198, 204, 206, 207, 228, 235–9, 243, 248, 249, 268
garde nationale, 83, 256
Gautier de Biauzat, 212
Gazette de Leyde, 78, 213
Geneva, revolt in (1782), 29–33, 225, 270
Geoffrin, Mme, 95

George III, 18
Givet, 258
Glasgow, rioting in, 19
Goltz, count von der, 211
Gordon, Lord George, 18–20, 23, 25, 28, 29
Gordon riots, 17–29, 68
Gorsas, 213
Gravelines, 36
Grégoire, 159, 250
Grenier brothers, 25
Grenoble, 110–11, 272
Grenus, 30, 32
Gudin de la Ferlière, 212
Guerre des Farines, 12–17, 67, 99, 149
Guiard, corporal, 240
Guilhermy, 268
Guillotin, Dr., 161
Guingamp, 128

Hainault, 175
Hancock, John, 11
Hardy (bookseller), 14, 16, 17, 24, 59, 104, 112, 140, 146, 149, 170–71, 176, 183, 214
harvests, importance to public of, 5, 6, 12, 16, 65, 108, 111, 119, 120, 167, 174–5, 196
Hazebrouck, 128, 167
Helvétius, 77
Hémery, d', 75
Henri II, 100
Henri III, 2
Henri IV, 2, 3
Henriot, 136, 139–42, 148
Holland, disturbances in, 33–36
Hondschoote, 128
Honfleur, 202
Honnecourt, 167
Houdon, 98
Huber, 212
Huguet, 212
Hulin, 236–8, 242, 243
Humbert, 208, 217, 225, 230–31, 238, 242
Hyde, Judge, 21, 22
Hyères, 130

Ile-de-France, 12, 15
Invalides, Les, 198, 215–18, 228, 235, 247, 248, 250, 251
invalides of Bastille, 209, 218, 220, 227, 228, 230, 231, 235, 240, 241, 248

Index

Index

Senlis, 180
Sens, 169, 174
serfdom, 39
Servan, 98, 110
Sèvres, 177, 252–3
Sézanne, price of grain in, 120–21
Sieyès, 115, 124, 128, 156, 158, 159
  160, 165, 181
Sillery, marquis de, 146–7, 211
Simolin, 210, 261
social structure, analysis of, 44–50,
  135. *see also* crowds
Soissons, 15, 179, 180, 182
Solages, comte de, 92, 263
Soleilhas, 130
Solliés, 130
Sombreuil, 198, 215, 216, 230, 248
sources of information on Bastille,
  205–15
Souza Continuo, Don Vicente, 211
Staël, baron de, 185, 211
Staël, Mme. de, 186, 236
stage, censorship of, 78
stamp duty, 103, 104
Steffens, Heinrich, 262
strikes, 63
Swiss guards, 84–5, 141, 145, 146, 258.
  see also Salis-Samade

Tailhardat de la Maisonneuve, 268
taille, 40, 100, 102, 106
Taine, 149
Talbert, 129
Talleyrand, 128
Target, 110, 115, 157, 158
Tavernier, 92, 263
taxes: rise in prices due to, 124;
  discussion of in Estates-General,
  153–4, 160, 163, 164; suspended,
  186. *see also* land tax, *taille, capitation, vingtième*
Terray, abbé, 100
Test Bill, 18
textile industry, 6
Thélusson, 65
Thiard, comte de, 108
Thiaucourt, 174
Third Estate: double representation
  of, 101, 110, 114–16, 164; election
  by 117, 133; deputies of, 128;
  difficulties in Estates-General, 152–
  57; becomes National Assembly,
  158–62, 165–6

Thirty Years War, 3
Thodure, 168
Thuriot de la Rozière, 207, 226–9, 233
tithes, 39–41, 124, 164, 168
Titon, 137
Toul, 179, 258
Toul-Artillerie, 180
Toulon, 130
Toulouse, 45–8, 108
Tournay, 229
Tremblay, Leclerc du, 91
Trier, 2
troops: police forces in Paris, 82–6;
  used in demonstrations of 1788, 112;
  concentration round Paris, 179–87,
  204, 246, 249–52, 255, 258, 269;
  disaffection of, 132, 175–7, 183–4,
  216, 217, 247–53, 257, 268, 272.
  see also regiments of Armagnac-
  Infanterie, Bercheny, Bouillon-In-
  fanterie, Castela, Châteauvieux,
  Dauphin-Dragons, Diesbach, Ester-
  hazy, *gardes-françaises, garde de
  Paris*, Lauzun's hussars, Maistre de
  Camp Général de Cavalerie, Nassau-Infanterie, Provence-Infanterie,
  La Reine-Infanterie, Reinach,
  Royal-Allemand, Royal-Cravate,
  Royal-Dragons, Ruffevielle's com-
  pany, Salis-Samade, Swiss guards,
  Toul-Artillerie.
Troyes, 132, 174
Turgot, 12, 15, 16, 67, 71, 99, 100,
  186

Ulm, 2
unemployment, 6, 42–4, 63, 108, 123,
  137, 138, 149
United Provinces, alliance with
  United States, 11
Utrecht, demonstration at, 34, 35
Uzès, 168

Vainqueurs de la Bastille, 221–6
Vannes, 108, 128
Valenciennes, 128, 167, 179
Valserres, 129
Vanves, 253
Vauban, marquis de, 31
Vaucelles, 167
Vaugirard, 177, 253
Verdun, 180, 258

Index